THE MUSLIM WORLD

GLOBAL ISSUES

THE MUSLIM WORLD

Jamie Stokes

Foreword by Jeffrey T. Kenney
DePauw University

Facts On File
An imprint of Infobase Publishing

GLOBAL ISSUES: THE MUSLIM WORLD

Facts On File, Inc.
An imprint of Infobase Publishing
132 West 31st Street
New York NY 10001

Library of Congress Cataloging-in-Publication Data
Stokes, Jamie.
  The Muslim world / Jamie Stokes ; foreword by Jeffrey T. Kenney.
    p. cm. — (Global issues)
  Includes bibliographical references and index.
  ISBN 978-0-8160-8086-1
  1. Islamic countries—History—Juvenile literature. 2. Islamic civilization—Juvenile literature. 3. Islam—History—Juvenile literature. I. Title.
  DS35.6.S76 2011
  909'.09767—dc22   2010020267

Facts On File books are available at special discounts when purchased in bulk quantities for businesses, associations, institutions, or sales promotions. Please call our Special Sales Department in New York at (212) 967-8800 or (800) 322-8755.

You can find Facts On File on the World Wide Web at http://www.factsonfile.com

Text design by Erika K. Arroyo
Composition by Mary Susan Ryan Flynn
Cover printed by Art Print, Taylor, Pa.
Book printed and bound by Maple Press, York, Pa.
Date printed: November 2010
Printed in the United States of America

10 9 8 7 6 5 4 3 2 1

This book is printed on acid-free paper.

CONTENTS

List of Maps, Graphs, and Tables

Foreword

Globalization has made the world a smaller place. We now perceive and experience more immediately and more intensely than at any other time in history events that occur in countries far removed from our own. Indeed, events that an earlier generation would have come to know about first in a book, long after they took place, are now watched live on television and the Internet. Globalization has, at the level of our experience of other peoples and places, foreshortened time and distance, transforming the world into what the communications theorist Marshall McLuhan once called a "global village." In such a global village, contact with others, both directly and virtually, is unavoidable, and contact always carries with it the potential for conflict, cooperation, or both. Key to avoiding conflict and facilitating cooperation in a globalized world is knowledge and understanding, both of which one finds in abundance in the Global Issues series.

The importance of understanding the Muslim world has been slow to dawn on most Westerners. It has historically been an area of knowledge dominated by policy experts and academics. This may not seem unusual, but knowledge of the West has long been of importance in Muslim societies. I observed this difference firsthand several years ago when I visited Morocco with a group of American students. Moroccans with whom we spoke showed a keen awareness of American history and politics, and many were eager to point out to us that Morocco was the first world power to officially recognize the independence of the United States. None of the American students on the trip knew this fact, and none could remember ever having read about it in school.

For far too many Americans and Westerners in general, it took the dramatic terrorist attacks of September 11, 2001, to realize that the Muslim world matters. The immediate reaction to the attacks was anger and calls for revenge. During the months following the attacks, however, the United States also witnessed a sharp increase in sales of the Quran, the sacred text of Islam, as Americans tried to understand the mindset of the terrorists and the culture that shaped them.

Of course, the causes of modern militant Islam are not to be found in a seventh-century text, sacred or not. But for Americans searching for answers in the aftermath of the attacks, Islamic culture seemed a logical place to start. After all, the suicide attackers and their spiritual leader, Osama bin Laden, came from Muslim societies quite foreign to most Westerners; and they had legitimized violence against the West by quoting verses of the Quran and other Islamic literary sources. Moreover, in the decade prior to September 11 a much-publicized debate took place in Western intellectual circles and beyond about the so-called clash of civilizations that divided the Christian West and the Muslim East. Thus culture or, more accurately, cultural difference seemed to matter a great deal. Or did it?

The tendency to reduce complex events and problems to differences in culture—what has been termed *cultural essentialism*—is one of the biggest obstacles for non-Muslims to overcome when they study the Muslim world, for it prevents a clear understanding of the challenges facing Muslim societies as they modernize. It may also prevent people from seeing the potential of shared cultural values to bring them together to resolve common problems. Culture, then, can be both a barrier and bridge.

The need to build a cultural bridge between the Muslim world and the West was a major theme of President Barack Obama's famous speech in Cairo, Egypt, delivered in June 2009, just a few months after he took office. Speaking before a select audience of academics, students, religious leaders, politicians, businesspeople, and journalists at Cairo University, the president called for a "new beginning between the United States and Muslims around the world, one based on mutual interest and mutual respect, and one based upon the truth that America and Islam are not exclusive and need not be in competition. Instead, they overlap, and share common principles—principles of justice and progress; toleration and the dignity of all human beings."

By emphasizing a new beginning, Obama hoped to ease the tensions that divided the West and the Muslim world, tensions rooted in the recent colonial past and in the ongoing presence of Western military forces in two Muslim-majority countries: Iraq and Afghanistan. And by emphasizing shared principles, he hoped to show that the cultural divide between Muslims and the United States was not as great as many assumed it to be and that progress on practical issues of mutual concern—issues that often create tensions—was possible. The specific issues Obama cited were violent extremism, the Palestinian-Israeli conflict, nuclear weapons, democracy promotion, religious freedom, women's rights, and economic development.

For many in the West, this list reflects issues that the Muslim world either has too much of—violent extremism, conflict between Palestinians and Israelis, and nuclear weapons—or too little of—democracy, religious freedom, women's rights, and economic development. As a result, the West wants the Muslim world to change, and to change in a direction that brings the Muslim world more in line with Western social norms and foreign policies. This call for change is clearly rooted in a sense of Western achievement and superiority. It assumes that the Muslim world is lagging behind the West and that as soon as it catches up—socially, politically, and economically—these tension-causing issues will disappear.

Muslims, not surprisingly, see these issues quite differently, and they resent the Western assumption that it is only the Muslim world that must change. In fact, according to the popular view on the Muslim street, the West and its interventionist policies deserve much of the blame for the current problems facing their societies. Take the promotion of democracy as an example. Two of America's most important allies in the Middle East, Egypt and Saudi Arabia, have never held free and fair elections, limit free speech, and use repressive tactics to eliminate challenges to state power and authority. The U.S. government, under both Republican and Democratic leadership, has ignored these democratic failings and built strong relations with Egypt and Saudi Arabia to further foreign-policy goals. In the case of Egypt, peace with Israel, the suppression of radical Islamists, and a friendly voice in the Arab world have proven more important goals for the United States than promotion of democracy; in the case of Saudi Arabia, the free flow of oil, permission to establish military bases, and security of the Gulf region have proven more important.

To many observers, Muslim and non-Muslim, such policies have come at the expense of local Muslim populations and the stated political values of the United States. The United States no doubt regards its relations with Egypt and Saudi Arabia as necessary compromises, a kind of realpolitik. But compromising on promoting democracy in Muslim societies has lent support to authoritarian rule, increased popular resentment of the United States, and tarnished the image of democracy. Moreover, it has also provided militant organizations such as al-Qaeda rhetorical evidence of the West's duplicitous dealings with and indifference toward the Muslim world, and perceptions of mistreatment, historic and ongoing, are what fuel anti-Western sentiment and give rise to radical actions.

American foreign policies have practical consequences on how Muslims live and how they see the world around them. The point here is neither to criticize U.S. foreign policy nor to suggest that the Muslim world does not have real problems for which it must take responsibility. Rather, it is to show how complex these problems are, how interconnected they are to larger global events.

Whether the United States and the Muslim world manage to create a new beginning, as Obama stated they must, depends in part on steps taken by governments—steps that often appear far removed from the everyday lives of citizens. It is important to remember, however, that governments rely on the understanding and support of citizens to shift policy direction or implement new ones. Thus, any new beginning between the United States and the Muslim world must include individuals, in the Muslim world and the West, who are willing to look beyond their cultural stereotypes and learn about the other.

This volume is a good starting point for those seeking to explore the Muslim world and its global importance. It maps out, in a clear and concise manner, the challenges facing Muslim societies; it connects these challenges with the history, economy, and politics of other regions, in particular the United States. While intended for high school students, readers of all ages will appreciate its accessible style and insightful analysis, making it an excellent resource for global citizens of the 21st century.

—Jeffrey T. Kenney
DePauw University

PART I

At Issue

1

Introduction

WHAT IS THE MUSLIM WORLD?

The term *Muslim world* is not a simple one to define. Islam is the world's second-largest religion, after Christianity. There are approximately 1.5 billion Muslims living on every continent and in nearly every nation on Earth. In a cultural sense the Muslim world includes all Muslims wherever they live and, therefore, encompasses some 25 percent of the global population. Muslims often refer to the world community of Muslims as the *ummah*—an Arabic word meaning "community." In this sense several million U.S. citizens are also part of the Muslim world. It should be remembered, however, that there are numerous branches, sects, and schools of Islam within the *ummah* and that not all of them recognize one another as being true Muslims.

In a geopolitical sense the Muslim world can be more restrictively defined to include only those parts of the world where Muslims make up the majority of the population or hold political power. This is the sense most commonly used in this book. The Muslim-majority countries are concentrated in the Middle East, Southwest Asia, and the northern half of Africa with another outpost in Southeast Asia. The Middle East, which is itself a poorly defined term, is the historic heart of the Muslim world. Islam was founded on the Arabian Peninsula in the territory of present-day Saudi Arabia and spread rapidly to the rest of the Middle East and North Africa. All of Islam's holiest sites, such as Mecca, Medina, and Jerusalem are in the Middle East. This area remains the spiritual and political heart of the Muslim world to the present day. When discussing the Muslim world in a geopolitical sense, however, it must not be forgotten that there are many Muslim-majority states outside the traditional bounds of the Middle East. The three largest Muslim-majority countries, in terms of population, are well outside the Middle East. Indonesia is the most populous Muslim-majority state (about 240 million people, of whom 86 percent are Muslim), Pakistan is the second most populous (about

3

176 million people, of whom 95 percent are Muslim), and Nigeria the third (about 149 million people, of whom 50 percent are Muslim). The largest Muslim-majority nation in the traditional Muslim heartland of North Africa and the Middle East is Egypt (about 83 million people, of whom about 90 percent are Muslim).

PROBLEMS FACING THE MUSLIM WORLD

Today the Muslim world is in crisis. It is beset with intractable political and economic problems, wars, civil wars, revolutions, insurgencies, assassinations, and terrorist bombings. The Muslim world is the least democratic of the world's regions. Its republics are often little more than dictatorships. Its monarchies are near absolute monarchies. In many Muslim countries dissent is not tolerated; opposition leaders are jailed, as are ordinary citizens who express discontent, and draconian punishments are widely practiced. International human rights organizations give low grades to most countries in the Muslim world. Its peoples do not trust their legal systems, often with good reason.

The economies of many Muslim-majority countries are as dysfunctional as their politics. The only Muslim-majority states in the richest 25 percent of nations are those with large reserves of oil or natural gas, such as Saudi Arabia, Kuwait, and Qatar. Most Muslim-majority states are in the bottom 50 percent, and some of them, including Afghanistan and Bangladesh, are among the poorest states in the world. There are pockets of wealth and rapid growth in the Muslim world: Some of the smaller Persian Gulf States have used their oil revenues to modern'ze in interesting ways. Turkey, once the center of the Muslim Ottoman Empire, and the first Muslim country to remake itself into a modern, secular, democratic state, seems to have achieved these goals after a turbulent century, though it still lags far behind Europe economically. Turkish per capita GDP in 2009 was an estimated $11,200, only a third of Spain's $33,700.[1] Indonesia and Malaysia have shared in Asia's economic take off and now build the world's tallest skyscrapers to flaunt their success. Still, Indonesia's per capita GDP remains low at $4,000, and Malaysia's is little better than Turkey's at $14,800.[2] The citizens of Saudi Arabia and Iran benefit from a high standard of living thanks to oil revenues, and these countries boast a relatively well-educated population.

Estimates of unemployment in Muslim Arab countries range from 12.2 percent in 2007 (according to the World Bank) and 20 percent (according to the Arab League Economic Unity Council).[3] Unemployment is expected to grow in the coming years because young people are entering the workforce at more than twice the rate that jobs are being created.[4] Businesses that might create jobs are strangled by red tape from oversized bureaucracies.

Introduction

It is not that members of the Muslim world are denied education. Muslim governments invest heavily in education, and the Muslim world now supports a large secular education establishment. Most Muslims are literate, and many attend universities at home and abroad. In some Muslim-majority nations, however, the quality of this education does not appear to be very good by European and American standards—education in the Muslim world places a heavy emphasis on rules, memorization, and often on political indoctrination[5]—an approach that does not do a good job of developing its people's talents.

The Muslim middle class, the highly educated social stratum that would be expected to supply the Muslim world with its political leaders, retains many of its old, preindustrial characteristics, because capitalist development has continued to lag and the government remains the primary employer. Well-educated people tend to work for the government, and if they do not work for the government, they tend to be unemployed, because there are insufficient opportunities elsewhere. In the opinion of outsiders, such as the political analyst Kenneth M. Pollack, one of the most badly needed reforms in the Muslim world is the reduction of bloated bureaucracies staffed by college graduates who are ill-suited to their jobs but very attached to them. If this is true it is not hard to see why government employees oppose change since they owe their jobs to present conditions.

Muslim college graduates who do not work for the government are likely to feel cheated and frustrated. For decades during the early postcolonial period, Muslim, and particularly Middle Eastern, governments tacitly guaranteed a government job to every college graduate. With the pool of young graduates continuing to rise, governments in the Muslim world are no longer able to keep this promise. There is a growing class of well-educated young men who have been denied their expected place in the bureaucracy and who are also denied any influence on the decisions made by their leaders. In these circumstances radical reforming groups find a rich source of potential supporters.

Few people within the Muslim world or outside of it doubt that its problems are deep and regionwide. Influential voices within the Muslim world agree that the whole Muslim community suffers from a malaise. For example, in a speech given at the Tenth Islamic Summit Conference in 2003, soon after the U.S. invasion of Iraq, Mahathir Mohamad, prime minister of Malaysia, noted: "We are all Muslims. We are all oppressed. We are all being humiliated."[6]

Some would have us believe that, despite all these [problems], our life is better than that of our detractors. Some believe that poverty is Islamic, sufferings and being oppressed are Islamic. This world is not for us. Ours are the joys of heaven in the afterlife . . . Our weakness, our backwardness and our inability to help our brothers and sisters who are being oppressed are part of the Will of Allah . . .[7]

When it comes to the causes of the problems, however, observers disagree, and they disagree even more about the solutions.

TRADITION VERSUS MODERNIZATION

There is a tendency in the West to see the Muslim world's problems as the result of a failure to be more like the West. Seen through the eyes of a Westerner, the Muslim world's problems appear tantalizingly easy to solve: If only they had democratic governments, they would have order and freedom, or: If only they embraced free-market economics, they would be rich and secure. It is a view that ignores centuries of past interaction between the Muslim world and the West and generations of debate about the nature of progress within the Muslim world itself.

Modernization Theory

Modernization theory is the general term for a school of political and economic thought that believes in the benefits of encouraging underdeveloped states to follow the pattern set by developed nations. There are many forms of modernization theory, but in general they agree that developed nations, such as the United States and Western European countries, achieved their relatively high levels of wealth and political stability through a series of interrelated economic and social reforms. For example, a common thread in modernization theory holds that economic specialization in a society tends to foster the emergence of an urban middle class, which gradually supplants the traditional land-owning elite and leads to the establishment of formalized and democratic government. This is what happened in Europe, argue modernization theorists, and it would also happen in less developed parts of the world if they did the same thing. The roots of modernization theory are found in 18th-century ideas of progress, but it was in the 1950s and 1960s that modernization theory gained a powerful influence over the foreign policy of Western nations and the practices of institutions such as the International Monetary Fund and the World Bank through the work of Walt Rostow,[8] David Apter,[9] and other political theorists.

In the context of the West's view of the Muslim world, and especially of the Middle East, modernization theory suggested that Islam was a brake on development because it dominated political life in these states and tended to

Introduction

discourage innovation in favor of tradition. In his influential 1958 book, *The Passing of Traditional Society: Modernizing the Middle East,* academic Daniel Lerner wrote that the choice between "Mecca and mechanization" was the most important issue facing policy makers in the Middle East.[10] The view that the Muslim world clings blindly to tradition at the cost of embracing Western ideas and their potential benefits remains a powerful one to the present day. It is, however, misleading; political and religious thinkers in the Muslim world have been grappling with the problem of how to incorporate material advances developed in the West into Muslim-majority cultures, without surrendering their Muslim identity, for generations.

Modernization and the Ottoman Empire

In the 16th and 17th centuries the Ottoman Empire was not only the dominant power in the Middle East it was, arguably, the wealthiest and most powerful state in the world. By the early decades of the 19th century it had become economically stagnant and was rapidly being eclipsed by the growing industrial strength of Europe. The Ottoman political and intellectual elite were acutely aware of this problem and expended great effort in trying to reverse the trend. In 1839 the Ottoman sultan issued a series of radical political and economic reforms intended to modernize the empire and discourage the growth of nationalism among its constituent peoples. Among these reforms were the reorganization of public finances following the French model, the introduction of bank notes, wide-ranging reforms of civil and criminal law along European lines, and the establishment of railways, factories, universities, a stock exchange, and a prototype parliament. The decades that followed, up until 1876, and the establishment of the first Ottoman constitution are known as the Tanzimat, or Reorganization, era in Ottoman history.

The Tanzimat reforms, and the reforms of the first constitution, failed to prevent the eventual breakup of the Ottoman Empire: Britain, France, and Italy occupied the North African Ottoman possessions of Egypt, Algeria, and Libya, respectively, and nationalist movements led to the independence of all Ottoman territories in Europe by 1914. However, the fact that these reforms took place at all is strong evidence against the view that the Muslim world has a history of resistance to modernization. On the contrary, the Ottomans saw modernization as the only effective way of resisting the encroachment of Western colonialism. After the Ottoman state was defeated in World War I, Turkish nationalists fought the Turkish War of Independence (1919–22) against British, French, Greek, and Italian occupation and established modern Turkey as a secular state governed through a European- or American-style parliamentary democracy. Turkish nationalists recognized the value of political and economic innovations developed in the West but were not willing to accept Western imperial domination along with them. In many ways, this is an attitude that still dominates the Muslim world today: a desire to modernize coupled with a distaste of Western imperialism.

Muslim Reformers

Reforms imposed by the political authorities of the Ottoman Empire in the 19th and early 20th centuries were accompanied by a reforming movement in Islam that attempted to reconcile Islam with concepts such as industrialization and scientific progress. Muslim thinkers such as Jamal ad-Din al-Afghani (1838–97) and his student Muhammad Abduh (1849–1905) were at the forefront of this movement.

Al-Afghani is regarded as one of the founders of pan-Islamism. He spent much of his career as a journalist and political and spiritual activist fiercely opposing the encroachment of British imperial power into the Muslim world and urging the political unification as the best means of resisting it. His early ideas on pan-Islamism went hand-in-hand with a strong belief in the desirability of adopting Western concepts and institutions that he believed would strengthen the Muslim world. Al-Afghani's legacy was complex and controversial. He was called a liberal reformer by contemporary European admirers but never advocated democracy and was involved in politically motivated violence against Muslim leaders on more than one occasion. He believed himself a devout Muslim but was exiled from Egypt and Iran as an apostate. He is regarded as a hero today both by some who seek to oppose Western influence with a rifle and some who seek peace. Perhaps his least ambiguous influence on ideas about modernization in the Muslim world was his belief that Islam was not only wholly compatible with rational inquiry but required of Muslims. Muhammad Abduh was to become the chief inheritor of this idea.

Abduh, like his one-time teacher and mentor al-Afghani, was opposed to Western political influence in his native Egypt but admired those elements of Western culture that he saw as having brought great freedom and power to European civilization. He firmly believed in education as a means of developing what he saw as the God-given faculty of reason, so that it could be used to understand the revelation of the Quran. Abduh rejected blind obedience to established commentaries on Islam's sacred texts and urged the application of rational, logical thought to the examination of the texts themselves. Regarded as a potentially dangerous radical as a young man—he was exiled from Egypt for six years for supporting the Urabi Revolt (1879–82) against British influence—he later became a highly respected jurist and was

8

appointed mufti, or leading Muslim scholar, of Egypt in 1899. Abduh revolutionized Egypt's education system by introducing modern sciences into its universities and placing the emphasis on practical, rational instruction over rote learning for younger students.

The Impact of Colonialism and the Rise of Arab Nationalism

The period of European colonial domination in the Middle East was short-lived, compared to that in much of Africa and South Asia, but it had a profound impact on the Muslim world. The defeat of the Ottoman Empire brought the territories of the present-day states of Iraq, Palestine, Jordan, Syria, and Lebanon under direct British or French rule through League of Nations mandates. Egypt, Libya, and Algeria had already come under what amounted to direct European control in the 19th century, and Iran was fighting a losing battle against British and Russian influence that would end with an Anglo-Soviet invasion and occupation in 1941.

The near-total subjugation of the Muslim world by European powers was a severe blow to the pan-Islamist movement. The project had failed. The Muslim world was fragmented and in the grip of foreign infidels. Arab nationalist movements and pan-Arabism took over as the leading drivers of opposition to colonial rule. The religious ideals of al-Afghani and Abduh seemed less compelling now that European domination, feared for so long in the Muslim world, had become a reality. The restoration of sovereignty was the first priority. Ideologically, Arab nationalism and pan-Arabism placed Islam, along with Arabic, at the center of their vision of a future Arab superstate, but in reality it was the yearning for political independence rather than for a reinvigorated form of Islam that drove the majority of Arab nationalists. Islam became a powerful standard behind which the masses could be rallied for the fight against the European occupiers. Arab nationalist propagandists glorified Islam as the force that had allowed the Arab peoples to build a spectacular empire in the seventh and eighth centuries. They painted a picture of restored Arab glory that included Islam as a pervasive background but took little trouble to define exactly which form of Islam this would be or how it would fit with the political structures they envisaged.

In the first half of the 20th century two diverging ideological strands developed in the Muslim world, both of them owing something to the modernizing ideas of the second half of the 19th century. One strand focused on the idea of stripping away centuries of interpretation and returning to a "pure" understanding of Islam as a way of strengthening the Muslim world; the other concentrated on political and economic reform and pushed Islam into the background. The Muslim Brotherhood was an example of the former, while the political philosophy of Egypt's Gamal Abdel Nasser and the Arab Socialist Baath Party were examples of the latter.

The Muslim Brotherhood was founded by Egyptian schoolteacher Hassan al-Banna in 1928 and remains an influential movement in the Middle East to the present day. Its fundamental aim is the establishment of a single state encompassing all Muslim-majority lands governed according to the principles of the Quran and sunna—the words and practices of Muhammad and his companions (those who accepted his leadership), as set forth in other writings. The Muslim Brotherhood is regarded as the first Islamist organization—the term *Islamist* referring to a broad school of thought that emphasizes the political role of Islam. It is not a political party, but its members are active in political parties across the Muslim world.

The Baath Party is a secular Arab Nationalist political party founded in Syria in 1940 with the aim of uniting the Arab world into a single state governed according to the principles of Arab socialism—a distinctive form of socialism adapted to the social history of the region. The Muslim Brotherhood and the Baath Party both emerged under colonial rule and shared the urgent goal of eliminating Western influence in the Middle East. Both groups were "modernizers" in the sense that they saw radical change as the only hope of shaking off European domination and bringing about a renaissance in the Muslim world; for the Muslim Brotherhood and similar groups, this radical change was to be the elevation of Islam to the center of political and social policy, for the Baathists the solution lay in economic and industrial development and the expulsion of Islam from political life. Part of the Baathists' motivation for downplaying Islam was a desire to escape from the influence of sectarian conflict—both among different branches of Islam and between Muslim and non-Muslim Arabs.

The two branches of modernization and reform represented by the Muslim Brotherhood and Arab socialism vied for ideological supremacy in the Muslim world through the middle decades of the 20th century. Up until the end of the 1960s it was Arab nationalism and Arab socialism as expressed by the Baath Party and Nasser that had the upper hand. Nasser and the Baath Party were political rivals, but their fundamental beliefs and vision for the Arab world were similar. Israel's swift and comprehensive defeat of an Arab alliance led by Egypt, Syria, and Jordan in the 1967 Arab-Israeli War (also known as the Six-Day War) was a devastating blow to Arab nationalism. Nasser had been a hugely influential figure in the Muslim world since he had nationalized the Suez Canal, taking it out of the hands of its French and British owners, and emerged victorious from the subsequent British, French, and Israeli invasion during the 1956 Suez crisis. Egypt's defeat in 1967 represented the failure of Nasserism to many Muslims—it had resulted

Introduction

in a humiliating defeat at the hands of Israelis, who were widely regarded as puppets of Western colonialists.

The perceived failure of Arab nationalism had two related consequences. The political and social models it had espoused had been discredited, but the longing for a return to a mythical golden age of Muslim supremacy that had been engendered by its propaganda remained. The Islamist agenda, as represented by the Muslim Brotherhood, was still very much alive and seemed to offer an alternative route to a renaissance in Muslim culture and fortunes. The Muslim Brotherhood and other, similar, organizations that had emerged in the intervening decades had not been idle. Through the networks of grassroots charity and educational programs set up by the Muslim Brotherhood and others, many ordinary Muslims had become familiar, at least in passing, with the Islamist agenda.

Two events in the last decades of the 20th century brought this other strand of reformist thought to the fore: the Iranian Revolution of 1979 and the victory of the Afghan mujahideen over the Soviet occupation of their country in 1989. In the first case the Muslim world witnessed a devout non-Arab Muslim called Ruhollah Khomeini overthrow a corrupt secular regime that had been closely tied to the United States and in power for decades; in the second fighters styling themselves holy warriors achieved a victory in the name of Islam over the world's most powerful atheist state. The effect on the Muslim world was electrifying. The boost to the fortunes of those who looked to the Quran rather than technological or socialist ideologies for the salvation of the Muslim world was considerable. A new term, *Islamic extremism*, was introduced to an apprehensive world.

Political Islam and Islamic Extremism

From the point of view of a Western observer living in a largely secular society the idea that Islam should become a more dominant rather than a less dominant element in the politics of the Muslim world is counterintuitive and disturbing. The things that worry the Western world about the Muslim world—state-sponsored terrorism and regional conflict—seem to be associated with the growing influence of Islam in the political arena. In fact, this is the result of a confusion between Islamic extremism and political Islam or Islamism.

Unsurprisingly, there is no clear and universally agreed definition of *Islamic extremism*. It is a Western coinage that is often applied indiscriminately to distinct elements in the Muslim world with widely differing beliefs and aims. For consumers of the Western media the term is more or less synonymous with Muslim terrorism and is associated with a belief that there is a school of thought in the Muslim world that advocates the establishment

11

of a worldwide caliphate through any means necessary. Osama bin Laden is the archetype for this view of Islamic extremism. It is certainly true that there are Muslims who support violent action against the West and other Muslims who want to impose universal sharia (religious law), but they inhabit the fringes of an influential movement in the Muslim world that is more properly called *Islamism* or *political Islam.*

Islamism and political Islam encompass a wide range of views and are not subject to easy definition. Broadly, Islamism can be described as the belief that Islam is inherently political—that its teachings apply to every aspect of human life, including the political arena. Consequently, Islamists believe that Muslims should be subject to sharia rather than any form of law arrived at by human decisions. Islamists also usually reject Western influence and advocate the political unity of all Muslims in a single state. Some Muslim thinkers and non-Muslim observers reject the terms *Islamism* and *political Islam* altogether as representing artificial distinctions. They argue that it is not possible to be a Muslim without recognizing the political role of Islam and, therefore, that a Muslim and an Islamist are the same thing. Many other Muslims disagree and see a distinction between mainstream Islam and a minority with a reforming agenda that can be described as Islamist. The Muslim-owned and -operated media network Al Jazeera, for example, refers to groups such as the Islamic Salvation Front in Algeria or Jamaa Islamiya in Egypt as Islamist.

The Islamist movement includes a very large range of groups with varying tactics and goals. The Turkish Justice and Development Party, for example, has a broadly Islamist agenda and works within the democratic system of Turkey to achieve its aims. Hamas, another Islamist-inspired party, has taken part in democratic elections in the Palestinian Territories but also has a paramilitary wing that has engaged in conflict with rival Palestinian party Fatah. At the most extreme limits of this continuum are organizations such as the Armed Islamic Group of Algeria that completely reject democratic methods and embrace terrorist tactics.

The idea that the Muslim world should be more religious rather than less appears to be gaining ground among Muslims. Surveys, such as those included in the 2005 Pew Global Attitudes report "Islamic Extremism: Common Concern for Muslim and Western Publics," indicate that many Muslims welcome a growth in the influence of Islam in their countries as a means of combating political corruption and immorality. Pluralities in Jordan, Morocco, Turkey, and Indonesia supported the growing influence of Islam in their national politics and agreed with the statement that Islam was playing a greater role in politics because of "growing immorality in our society." Large minorities in Lebanon, Jordan, and Indonesia also agreed with the statement that Islam was playing a greater role in national politics because of: "concerns about Western influence in our country."[11] What the report also makes very clear, however, is the low level of support among Muslims for violent action to end Western influence or to impose strict Islamic law. As the title implies, Muslim publics are just as concerned about Islamic extremists gaining control over their governments as Western publics.

Islamism has been described as the most influential political ideology in the Muslim world today. It remains an underground movement in the sense that few Islamists hold political office in Muslim states, but its ideas have had a powerful influence on Muslim public opinion and contributed to a feeling among Muslims that Islam is the answer to a raft of problems rather than a cause. Modern Islamism, in so far as it can be described as a single movement, is the direct descendant of the Muslim Brotherhood, Jamaat-i-Islami, and similar organizations that emerged in the Muslim world during the period of Western colonial domination. In this sense it represents the continuation of a strand of reforming thought that began in the middle of the 19th century with Jamal ad-Din al-Afghani. Many of the factors that made these organizations attractive 60 years ago are, if anything, even more prominent today. As the results of the Pew survey make clear, many Muslims see their existing political elites as corrupt and the threat of Western domination as acute. With the collapse of Arab nationalism and the failure of Arab socialism, Islamism represents the only homegrown ideology that has not demonstrably failed the Muslim world.

PETROPOLITICS AND THE RESOURCE CURSE

Much of the analysis of the Muslim world's problems concentrates on political and religious issues, but there are alternative avenues of inquiry. Some economists, for example, believe the true roots of the Muslim world's malaise may lie in its spectacular resource wealth. The Muslim world has a treasure. It contains enormous reserves of oil and natural gas. Modern industrialized economies depend on these resources, the values of which have therefore risen and are expected to keep rising. Yet much of the Muslim world is poor, and for decades its economic growth has stagnated. Some observers see this as an example of the "resource curse" or "paradox of plenty" phenomenon, identified in 1993 by British academic Richard Auty.[12]

According to the resource curse thesis an abundance of nonrenewable natural resources such as minerals and fuels can slow down a country's or region's economic growth. Thus, between 1964 and 1998, the per capita GDP of citizens in the Organization of Petroleum Exporting Countries (OPEC) declined by an average of 1.3 percent. During those same years per capita gross national product in the rest of the developing world grew at an average 2.2 percent. The resource curse also has negative effects on the politics of a region. It is said to warp political systems and economies in several ways:

Territorial Conflicts: It provokes conflicts as factions compete for the resource. In Iraq, for example, when Shia, Sunni, and Kurdish factions contend over territory they are often fighting over the places where the oil reserves are located.

Static Economy: Natural resource exports stall growth in other sectors of the economy. Profits from mineral exports raise wages. They strengthen the local currency against foreign currencies and bring increased government spending on health and welfare. All these factors benefit citizens in the short term, but they make labor so expensive that the country's other potential exports—in manufacturing and agriculture—cannot compete on the world market. As a result, the economy fails to grow. The standard of living suffers ultimately.

Wasted Talent: Talented, well-educated people capable of building other parts of the economy are drawn instead to the high wages available in the extraction industries.

Accrued Debt: Since world prices for natural resources go up and down (witness the sharp rise and fall of oil prices in 2008) it is dangerous to depend on them. Governments that rely on revenues from mineral wealth tend to overspend during booms. When prices fall, they borrow money to keep paying for the services to which their citizens have become accustomed. This borrowing burdens the economy with debt and interest payments. The leaders may know it, but they are trapped because, if they fail to borrow, they face political unrest.

Political Corruption: Resource riches lead to political corruption. Among governments that have little transparency or accountability leaders take the wealth for themselves. They retain power by distributing wealth or concessions to their supporters. It is sometimes said by political commentators that the Muslim world's political culture centers around patronage—people are loyal to individuals who offer them protection and assistance rather than to the state or its institutions. If it is true that the Muslim world has a patronage culture, it is a pattern that the resource curse tends to perpetuate.

Journalist Thomas L. Friedman expounded one side of the resource curse thesis in a 2006 article, "The First Law of Petropolitics," published in the May/

June 2006 issue of *Foreign Policy,* in which he suggests a link between wealth gained through oil export and poor political leadership. "When I heard the president of Iran, Mahmoud Ahmadinejad, declare that the Holocaust was a 'myth' I couldn't help asking myself: 'I wonder if the president of Iran would be talking this way if the price of oil were $20 a barrel today rather than $60 a barrel . . .'" Friedman also says: "I noticed that the first Arab Gulf state to hold a free and fair election, in which women could run and vote, and the first Arab Gulf state to undertake a total overhaul of its labor laws to make its own people more employable and less dependent on imported labor, was Bahrain. Bahrain happened to be the first Arab Gulf state expected to run out of oil."[13]

Not all analysts believe in the resource curse thesis. In a study published in *Science* magazine in 2008 C. N. Brunnschweiler and E. H. Bulte argue to the contrary that it is poor government and conflict that tend to force a state to become dependent on the export of resources, not that states with great mineral wealth are more prone to poor government or conflict.[14] Some of the problems attributed to it might be the result of adoption by some among the developing world's nations of Soviet-style planned economies, especially from the 1950s to the 1970s. Many resource-poor countries have dictators and a record of human rights abuses; and it remains true that countries that do have oil tend to have a better standard of living than those without it. During its own period of early development, the United States obviously benefited from its abundance of coal, oil, and metals. However, the United States also started with a relatively diverse economy, a large and expanding home market, a strong agriculture, a well-organized government, and a free press, and in the 1800s two oceans offered it protection from more powerful enemies. Countries in the Muslim world do not enjoy these blessings.

A SHORT HISTORY OF ISLAM

Islam gives a remarkable consistency to the culture and attitudes of hundreds of millions of people who are ethnically, geographically, and historically very diverse. An examination of the religion and its history is a good place to start for any attempt to see the Muslim world as Muslims see it.

The Muslim world, like other communities, has always been prey to sharp division. Some of its members have always experienced injustice. The era that Islamists often look back to as their utopia was, in fact, a time of conquest, pillage, and civil war.

Doctrines and Practices of Islam

Islam is a religion based on the revelations that, Muslims believe, God gave to the prophet Muhammad in the seventh century. Like Christianity and

Judaism, to which it is historically related, Islam asserts that there is one God who created and rules the universe. Islam is intended as a religion for all mankind; it is, like Christianity, a proselytizing faith. Islam shares with other great world religions the conception of each individual's life as a moral journey. In Islam God is just and wants people to be just.

Muslims believe Islam to be part of a monotheistic tradition of prophecy beginning with Adam and continuing with Noah, Abraham, Moses, and Jesus. Muhammad is regarded as the final and greatest in this tradition of lawgivers and prophets. The essence of Islam is submission to the will of God. One can become a Muslim by affirming, in front of two witnesses, that "there is no god but God *(La ilaha illa'Llah)* and that "Muhammad is the Messenger of God" *(Muhammadun rasul Allah).*[15]

Submission to God's will includes obedience to rules of behavior prescribed by the Quran and in the sunna—the words and practices of Muhammad and his companions (those who accepted his leadership), as set forth in other writings. The sunna has been elaborated by Islamic scholars into a body of holy law called sharia. In theory the religious leaders of Islam are merely experts in holy law; they do not have to be ordained, and none of the rituals of Islam require the assistance of a clergyman. In practice Islam's religious leaders have a great deal of influence and prestige. Still, in Islam no essential difference exists between lay and clergy. In this respect it resembles Judaism. It also resembles orthodox Judaism in being a complete guide to life, providing rules for family relations, politics, and business. Because obedience is a religious duty, Islam gives a religious character to activities a Christian might regard as morally neutral, such as abstaining from eating pork. In addition, religious duties include the obligation to declare one's faith in Allah and the prophet; to pray five times a day in the direction of Mecca; to fast all day until sundown during the month of Ramadan; to make, at least once in a lifetime, a pilgrimage to Mecca; and to give alms to the poor.

These key observances—the declaration of faith, prayer, fasting, pilgrimage, and almsgiving—are called the "five pillars" of Islam. Some Islamic jurists and theologians impose a sixth duty on Muslims: jihad—an Arabic word literally meaning "struggle." In the history of Islam some scholars have emphasised the implication that the struggle Muslims are expected to engage in is the personal struggle to lead a life in accordance with the will of God; others have interpreted it as a duty to take up arms against Islam's enemies.

In the Christian scriptures, Jesus makes a remark that has been interpreted as recommending a separation between religion and politics: "Render unto Caesar that which is Caesar's, and unto God that which is God's." Islam does not acknowledge this division. As Seyyed Hossein Nasr emphasizes: "According to Islam, religion is not only a matter of private conscience . . . it is also concerned with the public domain, with the social and economic, and even political lives of human beings."[16] Many observers note that Muslims tend to be uncomfortable with the idea that government should not interfere in the religious lives of its citizens.

The Quran

According to tradition the Quran is a collection of Muhammad's recitations, every word of it inspired by God. Its original exists in heaven, eternal and uncreated, but it was brought together in one earthly book after Muhammad's death. The Quran occupies a central place in Muslim worship and in the lives of devout Muslims. When Muslims pray, they recite verses from the Quran accompanied by a series of prescribed physical movements. It is considered meritorious to memorize the Quran, and better to recite from memory than to read from it. The Quran is usually chanted, more or less musically, and always in Arabic, a language that the vast majority of the world's Muslims do not speak. Muslims recite the Quran at times of private family crisis, and phrases found in the Quran are a feature of everyday conversation.[17]

Since the Quran is a guide to life, it is at the center of modern controversies over Islamic attitudes toward war, the equality of the sexes, and religious toleration. The Quran has a great deal to say about these matters. The abundance of scriptural advice does not end debate, however, since the Quran can be quoted selectively to support differing viewpoints. As a further difficulty, tradition holds that some verses of the Quran, recited in the city of Medina later in Muhammad's career, overrule verses revealed earlier in Mecca.

In any case, as might be expected in a text from the seventh century, the Quran contains views that are difficult to accept for many Westerners: It promises paradise to those who die fighting the infidel, advocates the killing of idolators, permits slavery, and insists on the superiority of men over women. It recommends punishments, such as the cutting off of thieves' hands (Sura 5:38) and the flogging of fornicators (Sura 24:2–4) that have shocked outsiders—as well as many Muslims—when put into practice by modern Islamic governments.

The Bible, too, contains much to offend a modern humanist—it recommends that people be put to death for adultery (Leviticus 20:10), homosexuality (Leviticus 20:13), and bestiality (Exodus 20:19); that if any town is judged to be a nest of idolators, every human being and animal in it should be killed; and that women should be subordinate to men (1 Corinthians 11:3, 5–9; Ephesians 5:22–24; Colossians 3:19). The difference is that, today, the Bible is not used as the law in any country, while holy law based on the Quran—and oftentimes harsher than the Quran—is considered to be the law of the land in

Iran and Saudi Arabia, and a majority of Muslims say they want Islamic holy law to be more widely implemented in the Muslim world.

Hadith and Schools of Jurisprudence

In the early days of Islam a vast library of writings grew up around the Quran to help believers apply it to daily life. The most important of these are the Hadith—accounts of the sayings and deeds of Muhammad and his companions, based on oral traditions that are said to preserve original eyewitness testimony. Muslims believe Muhammad's words, actions, and practices to be a crucial guide to God's will; collectively they are known as the sunna. The importance of the Hadith is that they are a record of the sunna, albeit an imperfect one. In the Middle Ages, Muslim scholars concluded that many of the accounts in the Hadith were not authentic. Numerous commentators made lists and collections of trustworthy Hadith. Shia Muslims recognize a substantially different collection of Hadith than do Sunni Muslims.[18]

Islamic jurists have codified sharia, the Islamic law, based on their interpretations of the Hadith, the Quran, and oral traditions. There are four main schools of Sunni sharia in wide use today, each associated with the name of a particular scholar. Adherence to different schools is a source of regional variation among the world's Muslims, with the Muslims of West Africa following one school, the Muslims of Egypt another, and so on.

Most non-Muslims have heard of the two other Islamic institutions the mosque, which is the Muslim house of worship, and the madrassa, which is a religious school attached to a mosque. After the attacks of September 11, 2001, the word *madrassa* acquired sinister connotations for many Americans, who learned that the Islamic fundamentalist leaders of the Taliban had been trained in madrassas and that some madrassas taught their students to be fiercely antimodern and anti-American. In fact the madrassa is a traditional feature of life in the Muslim world and madrassas are associated with a variety of Muslim creeds and political views. Financial support provided by Saudi Arabia has led to the proliferation of madrassas in which the highly conservative Saudi creed of Wahhabism (or Muwahhidism) is taught. Many Muslims and non-Muslims who agree that most madrassas do not promote terrorism nevertheless question whether their teaching—which centers on the memorization of the Quran—is an adequate preparation for modern life.

Varieties of Islam

Fourteen hundred years of history and geographical expansion among different cultures has given rise to a great deal of variety in Islam. The deepest divisions are those between Sunni Muslims (who represent roughly 85 percent of Muslims) and the several Shia sects (about 15 percent).[19] The division derives from an ancient dispute over the leadership of the Islamic community. The dispute was never merely political, since Islam was a community founded on religion, and over centuries it has taken on a more deeply religious character.

Islam also has a mystical, ecstatic tradition, known as Sufism. A form of worship rather than a set of doctrines, Sufism has been enormously popular for most of the history of Islam. It crosses class and sectarian lines—Sufis are found among the Shia and among the Sunni as well—and Sufism is found across most of the Muslim world; however, some Muslims, such as the Wahhabis of Saudi Arabia, are hostile to it.

From time to time Islam has given rise to revivalist movements that have aimed to return Islam to its original form by wiping away the supposed encrustations of myth and error. Much like the Puritans of 17th-century England, Islamic revivalists advocate a strict morality and criticize the doctrines and ritual practices of other Muslims. The most important revival movement in the present Muslim world is Wahhabism, which arose in Arabia in the 1700s and that assisted the rise to power of the monarchy that rules Saudi Arabia today. Wahhabism is the creed of Osama bin Laden and also of the Taliban.[20] Thanks in part to the missionary efforts of the oil-rich Saudis, Wahhabism has been spreading rapidly to other parts of the Muslim world, and it is popular among some young people who want to be more Islamic and more militant than their parents.[21]

The Origin and Spread of Islam
THE LIFE OF MUHAMMAD

Tradition traces the origin of Islam to the prophet Muhammad, born in 570 C.E. on the Arabian Peninsula in the small oasis town of Mecca close to the Red Sea coast. Mecca was a destination for pagan religious pilgrimages, thanks to the Kaaba, a shrine there containing 360 stone idols.[22] At that time the majority of Arabs were polytheists, though some Arabs were Jewish or Christian and others had embraced a nonsectarian form of monotheism.[23] Most Arabs were nomads, organized into tribes that sometimes acted as mercenaries for the empires and kingdoms that surrounded Arabia. Muslims use the term *jayliyyah* (the age of ignorance) to describe the time before the prophethood of Muhammad as one of superstition and lawlessness.

Muhammad's medieval biographers depicted him as an exemplary seventh-century Arab, a successful merchant, and a devoted husband and father who sometimes retired to pray and fast in a cave near the summit of Mount

Hira, just outside Mecca.[24] According to Muslim belief it was in that cave on the 17th night of the month of Ramadan in the year 610 that Muhammad heard a voice say: "Muhammad, you are God's messenger." Muhammad fell to his knees, and the voice, which he later decided was the voice of the angel Gabriel, commanded: "Recite." "What shall I recite?" Muhammad asked, and immediately he found himself saying the words that became the oldest of the suras (chapters) of the Quran.[25]

Convinced that his recitations were the word of God, Muhammad began reciting to others in Mecca, and he soon attracted a devoted following. Mecca's tribal leaders saw Muhammed's growing power as a threat. In 622, in danger of their lives, Muhammad and his followers made a 220-mile journey to the community of Yathrib (later renamed Medina), where news of his preaching had spread and he had been invited to settle a dispute between two tribal federations. This journey is called the Hijra, and marks the beginning of the Islamic calendar.[26]

With Medina as his base, Muhammad led a series of military campaigns against the city of Mecca. In the end his forces were victorious, and in 629, at his order, the 360 pagan idols were destroyed and the Kaaba rededicated as a shrine to Allah, which is simply the Arabic word for God. By this time, Muhammad was the most powerful man in Arabia. Nomadic chiefs pledged their fealty to him. The Arabs had found unity in Islam.

THE FOUR "RIGHTLY GUIDED" CALIPHS AND ORIGINS OF THE SHIA-SUNNI SCHISM

After Muhammad's death in 632 his followers had to choose a successor. This man would not be a prophet—God had declared Muhammad the last of the prophets—but he would be the military, political, and spiritual leader of all Muslims. He would be called the *caliph*, a word that means "successor" and that has generally been taken to mean successor of the prophet.[27] Disagreements over the succession gave rise to the division between the majority Sunni sect and the several Shia sects of Islam.

Some of Muhammad's companions maintained that he had intended Ali, his cousin and son-in-law, to be the caliph; others said that he had chosen no successor and community leaders were free to elect one. This second group prevailed, choosing Abu Bakr, one of Muhammad's fathers-in-law. (Muhammad had married several times.) During his two-year reign Abu Bakr suppressed dissent among the Arabian tribes and led several spectacularly successful military campaigns against the Roman (Byzantine) Empire's possessions in Syria. On his deathbed he named Umar, another of Muhammad's fathers-in-law, the second caliph.[28] Under Umar the Arabs wrested vast territories from the Byzantine Empire and Persian (Sassanid) Empire. In 644 Umar was assassinated by a Persian slave. Some factions wanted Ali to become the new caliph, but once again another man, this time Uthman, was chosen.[29]

Uthman standardized the text of the Quran and had all variants destroyed to end disputes over its accuracy—a solution many found impious. Uthman seems to have been a divisive leader. He was accused of advancing the narrow interests of his family, his tribe, and his native city of Mecca. In 656 his own army assassinated him in his palace in Medina and hailed, as their new caliph, Ali—the man who, many believed, ought to have been the first caliph 24 years earlier. The choice led to a civil war between the faction favoring and the faction opposing Ali.

In 657 Uthman's cousin Muawiyah, then the governor of Syria, met Ali in battle. The outcome was indecisive, but Muawiyah persuaded Ali to agree to a truce and to put the issue of the succession to a committee of arbitration. Ali's decision outraged a group of his followers, subsequently called the Khariji (the "succeeders") who cursed his name and formed a long-lived, extremely violent sect fiercely opposed to the Shia (the "partisans" of Ali).

The arbitrators ruled against Ali, but he refused to abide by the decision. In 661 Ali was assassinated by a Khariji. At that point Ali's followers looked to his son Hasan to take up their cause, but Hasan disappointed them by conceding his rights to Muawiyah, who went on to found the Umayyad dynasty, which ruled by hereditary succession until 749 when they were overthrown and replaced by the Abbasid dynasty.

One episode in dispute over the early leadership of the Muslim community still resounds in the Muslim world. When Ali's son Hasan died, his followers placed their hopes in Husayn, Hasan's brother. Husayn led a revolt against the second Umayyad ruler, Yasid I. In 680 Husayn and his followers, whom tradition calls the Shia i-Ali (partisans of Ali), were ambushed near the city of Karbala, in present-day Iraq, and Husayn was killed. This event is still commemorated and mourned each year by the modern-day Shia community. Future Shia revolts would engender an elaborate body of legend and religious doctrine in the centuries to come.

As Shia Muslims see it, the Islamic community took a wrong turn when Mohammed died and Ali was passed over in favor of Abu Bakr. They believe that only during the brief reign of Ali was a legitimate leader in power. Sunnis consider the succession legitimate, though curiously they classify Ali, despite his short and disputed reign, among the four "rightly guided" caliphs who led the Islamic community during a time of moral perfection and obedience to Allah's will. Despite the bloodshed and infighting that surrounded the reigns of the first four caliphs, Sunni Muslim scholars concluded ultimately that all four were rightly guided because they were all companions of the prophet and, therefore, that it is impious for Muslims of a later generation to question their actions and decisions.

EXPANSION OF THE MUSLIM WORLD

Under the first two Muslim empires, those of the Umayyads and the Abbasids, Islam became the heir to the Roman Empire and the Persian Empire. The inhabitants of these lands were first subjected to a bloody conquest. Like other wars of the time, the wars of jihad were wars of booty and plunder. The inhabitants of entire cities were slain or enslaved, and survivors were made to pay tribute. Taxes that had been paid to previous governments were now paid to the new Arab rulers, who lived in fine style and sometimes fought among each other over the spoils of war.

Once conquest was achieved and the new order established, the Islamic empire brought many benefits. The imposition of one rule over vast territories encouraged trade and the spread of learning. Muslim scholars translated ancient Latin and Greek texts into Arabic and built on this heritage, making major contributions to world literature, philosophy, architecture, astronomy, mathematics, optics, medicine, and physics. In the words of Bernard Lewis, Islam was for centuries "at the forefront of human civilization and achievement."[30] The Islamic dynasties ruled a multiethnic society that absorbed and built on cultural elements of all the peoples it had subjugated, among them, the Egyptians, Persians, and Byzantines.

It was also a multireligious society, despite the fact that Islam served as the central lore of the empire. For a long time more Jews, Christians, and Zoroastrians inhabited the Muslim world than did Muslims. However, it was no egalitarian utopia. Peoples conquered by the early Arab expansion became second-class citizens in their own countries, subject to special taxes, ritual humiliation, and sporadic episodes of persecution, mob violence, and forced conversion. Still, some non-Muslims occupied important administrative posts in the various Islamic empires in the centuries to come. Their numbers dwindled as people converted to Islam, encouraged by the prospect of full equality enjoyed by free male Muslims.[31]

By the 11th century Islamic civilization had fragmented into kingdoms and empires whose leaders made war upon each other—often accusing the enemy of apostasy (the abandonment or rejection of religion) to get around the Islamic rule against Muslim fighting Muslim. The Muslim world was never again united under a single ruler. Yet Islam, the sharia, and the Arabic language, which replaced most of the languages of the Middle East and North Africa, continued to provide unity to Muslim civilization. Islam continued to spread, though it was no longer spread primarily by the Arabs. Long before the official end of the Abbasid Dynasty, Arabs had lost control of this vast collection of Islamic polities.

Ibn Khaldun (1332–1406), a widely traveled Muslim scholar, historian, and administrator, proposed a novel theory of history in a work called the *Muquaddima* (Introduction). Ibn Khaldun's theory may be summarized as follows: A warlike, nomadic people—tough, simple folk bound by fierce ties of loyalty—conquers a settled state and develops a dynamic new community. Within a few generations the former nomads grow soft, corrupted by the civilization they have conquered. It is then their turn to be conquered by another group of hardy, warlike nomads from the outlands.[32] With many exceptions and complications, Ibn Khaldun's scheme can serve as a summary of several hundred years of the Muslim world's history. First, the Arabs conquered the Persian Empire and much of the Byzantine Empire. Combining their own institutions with the culture of the societies they had conquered, they created a new civilization under the Umayyads and then the Abbasids. The Abbasids ruled in name only by the early 900s; by then their power had passed to the Seljuk Turks from Central Asia and Berber tribesmen from North Africa (who helped spread Islam by conquest north to Spain and south deep into Africa). In the 13th century the Seljuk Turks in turn were overthrown by the Mongols, who were so wedded to their nomadic way of life that they systematically turned crop-growing lands into pasture, re-creating the economy of their Central Asian homeland. But even the Mongols eventually became Muslims and helped to spread Islam in Central Asia. Rule of the Islamic heartlands in the Middle East then fell to another Turkic people, the Ottomans.

MODERNITY AND WESTERN IMPERIALISM

Today Muslims often point to the Crusades as proof of the imperialist nature of the West. In the broad sweep of Islamic history, however, the Crusades were a relatively minor episode, and Muslims themselves were unapologetic imperialists in the same era. Until 1683—the date of the last unsuccessful Ottoman attempt to capture the city of Vienna, in present-day Austria—the Christian West was usually on the defensive against Islamic expansion. Constantinople, the last bastion of the Byzantine Empire, fell to the Ottomans in 1453. The Ottomans conquered much of the Balkan Peninsula and for hundreds of years used it as a region from which to recruit Christian boys, who were converted to Islam and trained as soldiers in the service of the Ottoman ruler, the sultan.

By the 18th century the Muslim world lagged behind the West, and the *Dar al-Islam* fell victim steadily to Western imperialism. Muslim decline had many causes. Bernard Lewis cites the Mongol invasions, the neglect of agriculture, an uneven balance of trade with the Far East, and a decentralization of government. But the rest of the world also fell behind the West. The West had undergone an economic, social, and scientific revolution that gave it a powerful edge over other societies. Karen Armstrong, author of *Islam: A Short History*, emphasizes how new and comprehensive these changes were:

> *Instead of relying on a surplus of agricultural produce [the new society] was founded on a technology and an investment of capital that enabled the West to reproduce its resources indefinitely, so that Western society was no longer subject to the same constraints as an agrarian culture. This major revolution in reality . . . demanded a revolution of the established mores on several fronts at a time: political, social and intellectual. It had not been planned or thought out in advance, but had been the result of a complex process which had led to the creation of democratic secular social structures.*[33]

One word for this new social order is "modernity." Eventually leaders in many non-European societies decided to modernize—in effect, to Europeanize—themselves, making an effort to acquire not only factories and armies but also newspapers, written constitutions, parliaments, banks, and political parties. However, as Armstrong points out, it was impossible to achieve in one or two generations the changes that had taken Europe 300 years to achieve.

Nearly every Muslim on Earth came under European domination or influence. The political conquest of the Muslim world was accompanied by an economic conquest, as a flood of cheap European manufactured goods overwhelmed local industries and Muslims were forced into a dual role as consumers of European products and suppliers of raw materials to European industry. Like other colonized peoples, however, Muslims also adopted Western ideas, sometimes enthusiastically.

For more than a century prior to its breakup the Ottoman Empire struggled to reform itself using Europe as a model. The effort created a debate about the costs and benefits of modernity that continues in the Muslim world today. Along with administrative reforms and Western-style military drills, the Ottoman sultans hired Western architects to build their palaces, and they introduced Western dress. The adoption of trousers and fitted shirts testify, as Bernard Lewis points out, "to the authority and attraction of Western culture, even among those who explicitly and vehemently reject it."[34]

The Ottoman attempt to achieve modernity by imitation of the West was associated with a painful, wrenching abandonment of Muslim traditions, a policy epitomized by the decision in the 1920s by Kemal Atatürk, the first leader of modern Turkey (the Ottoman Empire's much smaller successor state), to abolish the office of the caliph. Caliphs had not possessed any real political power since the 10th century, and it was not the first time the office had disappeared, but the caliphate had symbolized Muslim aspirations to unity as a sacred Islamic polity dedicated to God and the Prophet.

While Atatürk aggressively sought to Westernize Turkey, making it officially a secular state and declaring his intention to make Turkey a part of Europe, the British and the French continued to Westernize the areas they controlled. Since Western governments were not inclined to use religious motives to justify their domination, as Muslims once had when they conquered Persia, Byzantium, and India, they employed arguments citing their ability to introduce democratic governing principles and economic modernization. Defending Great Britain's de facto rule of Egypt, British statesman Arthur Balfour told Parliament: "You may look through the whole history of the Orientals in what is called, broadly speaking, the East, and you never find traces of self-government. All their great centuries—and they have been very great—have been passed under despotism, under absolute government . . ."[35] Balfour suggested that an Eastern philosopher might consider good government "dirty work," but in any event it was the work the British were well equipped to do and the Egyptians would be better off for it.

Rule by foreigners from the lands of the crusaders was never popular among Muslims, and it is remembered today with profound shame and anger. Yet the benefits that Balfour claimed for Western imperialism were not entirely illusory. Population and lifespan increased in the Muslim world. Europeans built roads and laid telegraph wire, encouraged trade, and even, as Bernard Lewis points out, gave the Middle East "an interlude of liberal economy and political freedom. That freedom was always limited and sometimes suspended, but in spite of these limitations and suspensions, it was on the whole more extensive than anything they experienced before or after."[36] Many Muslims learned to speak English or French, increasing the influence of Western culture and ideas.

During the 1930s and in the two decades following World War II (1939–45), most of the Muslim world achieved independence in terms shaped by its period of Western domination. In some cases, as in Egypt and Iraq, the Europeans left willingly; they had lost the economic strength and lacked the political will to hold onto their colonies. In other cases, as in Indonesia and Algeria, Europeans were forced out by war. Muslims in Central Asia remained citizens of the USSR until its breakup in 1991.

Most of the nations that emerged, though they might be the site of ancient civilizations, had no history as nations-states. For thousands of years they had been parts of shifting empires—Greek, Roman, Persian, Arab, Turkish, Mongol, Mughul, Russian, and European. Often their borders had been drawn for the convenience of Europeans, and their leaderships chosen by Europeans. As educated Muslims, many of them educated in the West, debated the future of their societies, they weighed the contrasting benefits of nationalism, democracy, equality, capitalism, socialism, and secularism. All of these terms and the concepts they defined had been borrowed from the West.

THE POLITICAL CLASS OF THE MUSLIM WORLD: BRIBED OR ALIENATED?

Who were these Muslims debating the future of their society and shaping political life in the newly independent states of the Muslim world? In the early 20th century it was a comparatively small group. There was little capitalist development. Therefore investors, bankers, industrialists, factory workers, and trade unionists, all important shapers of the political scene in Europe and the United States, hardly existed there. Rather, the Muslim world constituted a society made up of peasants, artisans, merchants (often members of non-Islamic national and religious minorities, such as Jews, Greeks, and Armenians), landowners, military officers, government officials, teachers, dentists, doctors, newspaper editors, and the *ulama* (the clergy, some holding official government posts). In many places, the tribal structures of the early days of Islam had survived into modern times, and tribal leaders were a political factor. The tribes that tradition associates with the leadership of Islam enjoyed some of the prestige they had in the time of Muhammad. For example, Hashemites became kings of Arabia, Transjordan, and Iraq.[37] The Hashemites derived their authority from their ancestral links to Muhammad (their patriarch Hashim ibn Abd al-Manaf was Muhammad's grandfather) and their traditional role as tribal leaders in the Hejaz region of the Arabian Peninsula.

Intellectual debate among Muslims in the mid-20th century was conducted by a relatively small but expanding group of educated people, often members of learned professions. It is common when reading of a seminal thinker and activist, the founder of a party, a pressure group, or a liberation front to learn that he is a physician, a dentist, or a schoolteacher. The most modern institution in many Muslim countries has often been the military, and military officers often took the lead, not only to grab power for their own benefit, but also to reform society and create the basis for a stable state. In the later 20th century the proportion of Muslims who participated in political life expanded, until it embraced virtually the whole population.

The political and economic elite of the Muslim world that emerged from the period of colonial domination was culturally distant from the mass of the people they ruled. Ahmed Ben Bella, for example, one of the leaders of Algeria's struggle for independence and the country's third president, served in the French army, spent much of his early life in France, and did not speak Arabic. An alternative vision of the Muslim world's future that fiercely rejected Western influence also existed. It was a vision that placed Islam, rather than economics or Western-style modernization, at its center. Among the agricultural and urban poor of the Muslim world, the ideas of Islamist groups such as the Muslim Brotherhood gradually gained ground as the political elites who had secured independence became ever more distant and corrupt. In the last decades of the 20th century these ideas began to make themselves felt in the political arena, and in the first decade of the 21st century they became globally significant.

[1] Central Intelligence Agency. *The World Factbook.* "Turkey" and "Spain." Available online. URL: https://www.cia.gov/library/publications/the-world-factbook/geos/tu.html. Accessed May 11, 2010.

[2] ———. *The World Factbook.* "Indonesia." Available online. URL: https://www.cia.gov/library/publications/the-world-factbook/geos/tu.html. Accessed May 11, 2010.

[3] Kenneth M. Pollack. *A Path out of the Desert: A Grand Strategy for America in the Middle East.* New York: Random House, 2008, p. 75.

[4] ———. *A Path out of the Desert,* p. 75.

[5] ———. *A Path out of the Desert,* pp. 85–96.

[6] Anti-Defamation League. "Speech by Prime Minister Mahathir Mohamad of Malaysia to the Tenth Islamic Summit Conference in Putrajaya, Malaysia, October 16, 2003." Available online. URL: http://www.adl.org/Anti_semitism/malaysian.asp. Accessed August 30, 2009.

[7] Speech by Prime Minister Mahathir Mohamad of Malaysia, op. cit.

[8] W. W. Rostow. *The Stages of Economic Growth: A Non-Communist Manifesto.* Cambridge: Cambridge University Press, 1960.

[9] David E. Apter. *The Politics of Modernization.* Chicago: University of Chicago Press, 1965.

[10] Daniel Lerner. *The Passing of Traditional Society: Modernizing the Middle East.* Cambridge, Mass.: MIT Press, 1958.

[11] Pew Research Center. "Islamic Extremism: Common Concern for Muslim and Western Publics." July 7, 2005. Available online. URL: http://pewglobal.org/reports/display.php?ReportID=248. Accessed May 1, 2010.

[12] R. M. Auty. *Sustaining Development in Mineral Economies: The Resource Curse Thesis.* London: Routledge, 1993.

[13] Thomas L. Friedman. "The First Law of Petropolitics." *Foreign Policy,* May/June 2006. Available online. URL: http://www.foreignpolicy.com/story/cms.php?story_id=3426. Accessed August 30, 2009.

[14] John Tierney. "Rethinking the Oil Curse." *New York Times,* May 5, 2008. Available online. URL: http://tierneylab.blogs.nytimes.com/2008/05/05/rethinking-the-oil-curse/?hp. Accessed May 6, 2010.

[15] Seyyed Hossein Nasr. *Islam: Religion, History and Civilization.* San Francisco: HarperSanFrancisco, 2003, p. 3.

[16] ———. *Islam: Religion, History and Civilization*, p. 32.

[17] Michael Cook. *The Quran: A Very Short Introduction*. Oxford: Oxford University Press, 2000, pp. 77–84.

[18] Seyyed Hossein Nasr. *Islam: Religion, History and Civilization*, p. 56.

[19] Muslims scholars such as Nasr quarrel with the word *sect*, but the variations in doctrine and practice among Shia Muslims are as great as between groups conventionally called *sects* in Christianity; it is unusual in any religion for people to identify themselves as members of a sect since, of course, members believe they are merely living according to the dictates of the one true faith.

[20] P. M. Holt, Ann K. S. Lambton, and Bernard Lewis. *The Cambridge History of Islam*, Vol. I. New York: Cambridge University Press, 1970, pp. 80–81; Seyyed Hossein Nasr. *Islam: Religion, History and Civilization. Islam*, pp. 180–181.

[21] Micheal Slackman. "Stifled, Egypt's Young Turn to Islamic Fervor." *New York Times*, February 17, 2008. Available online. URL: http://www.nytimes.com/2008/02/17/world/middleeast/17youth.html. Accessed August 30, 2009.

[22] Dilip Hiro. *War without End: The Rise of Islamist Terrorism and the Global Response*. London and New York: Routledge, 2005, p. 6.

[23] Bernard Lewis. *The Middle East: A Brief History of the Last 2000 Years*. New York: Simon & Schuster, 1995.

[24] Karen Armstrong. *Islam: A Short History*. New York: Modern Library, p. 3.

[25] Solomon A. Nigosian. *Islam: Its History, Teaching, and Practices*. Bloomington: Indiana University Press, 2004, p. 8.

[26] ———. *Islam: Its History, Teaching, and Practices*, p. 10.

[27] Some early caliphs, with ambitions to absolute power, may have taken the word to mean "God's deputy." Patricia Crone and Martin Hinds. *God's Caliph: Religious Authority in the First Centuries of Islam*. Cambridge: Cambridge University Press, pp. 4–23.

[28] Dilip Hiro. *War without End*, p. 10.

[29] ———. *War without End*, pp. 10–11.

[30] Bernard Lewis. *What Went Wrong: Western Impact and Middle Eastern Response*. New York: Oxford University Press, 2002, p. 3.

[31] Bernard Lewis. *The Middle East*, pp. 55, 211.

[32] Vernon O. Eggar. *A History of the Muslim World since 1260: The Making of a Global Community*. Upper Saddle River, N.J.: Prentice Hall, 2008, pp. 40–41.

[33] Karen Armstrong. *Islam: A Short History*, p. 142.

[34] Bernard Lewis. *The Middle East*, p. 5.

[35] Arthur James Balfour, quoted in: Edward Said. *Orientalism*. New York: Vintage, 1979, pp. 32–33.

[36] Bernard Lewis. *The Middle East*, p. 355.

[37] Muhammad was a member of the Hashemite clan of the Quarash tribe. The kings that the British put in charge of constitutional monarchies in Arabia, Iraq, and Transjordan were also Hashemites, a fact that the British hoped would make them acceptable to the people.

2

Focus on the United States

Many Muslims have a negative view of the United States, and their opinions have become more negative in recent years. In a 2007 poll most non-American Muslims were found to hold negative views of the influence of the United States. For example, 93 percent of Egyptians said they had an "unfavorable" view of the U.S. government, and 86 percent had a "very unfavorable" view. In Morocco 76 percent had an unfavorable view, and 49 percent a very unfavorable view.[1] What is particularly worrying for the United States is that Morocco and Egypt have relatively good relations with the United States at the government level, compared to Iran, for example, and yet the overwhelming majority of their citizens disapprove of America. Such high levels of disapproval of the United States among the general public of Muslim-majority nations is a cause for concern among U.S. policy makers, but it should be seen in the context of widespread disapproval of U.S. foreign policy among the citizens of many nations. In a 2007 poll conducted in 25 countries around the world, both Muslim and non-Muslim, more than 70 percent of respondents disapproved of the way the United States had handled Iraq, more than 65 percent believed the U.S. presence in the Middle East caused more problems than it solved, and 65 percent disagreed with the United States's policy toward the Palestinian-Israeli conflict.[2] In other words, global public opinion of the United States, not just Muslim public opinion, was low.

There are several reasons for these negative views among the general public of Muslim-majority countries. Many non-American Muslims believe the United States wants to weaken the Muslim world as part of a strategy to control the Middle East's oil reserves and to spread Christianity. In a 2007 poll conducted in Egypt, Morocco, Pakistan, and Indonesia, on average almost 80 percent of Muslims believed the United States wanted to "weaken and divide the Muslim World." About the same percentage believed the United States wanted to gain "control over the oil resources of the Middle East," and 64 percent believed it to be a U.S. goal to "spread Christianity" in the Middle

East. For many Muslims the U.S. "war on terror" is in fact a war on Islam by another name. When asked what they believed the principal motivation for the U.S. war on terror was, only 16 percent said it was to protect the United States against terrorist attacks. The majority believed it was either to control Middle East oil or to undermine Islam.[3]

These very negative opinions about U.S. motives have a powerful effect on Muslim public opinion about U.S. involvement in the Muslim world. The U.S.-led invasions of Afghanistan in 2001 and Iraq in 2003 and the presence of U.S. and allied troops in other parts of the Middle East are strongly disliked by the great majority of Muslims. A majority of all Muslims are against the presence of U.S. and other non-Muslim forces in the Middle East and support the goal of removing them as soon as possible. The proportion of Muslims who support violence to achieve this end varies from region to region. A majority of Muslims in the Middle East support attacks on U.S. troops in Afghanistan and Iraq, but Indonesian Muslims do not, and Pakistani Muslims are divided. On the other hand, the great majority of Muslims worldwide disapprove of attacks on civilians.[4]

A number of non-Muslim critics of the invasions of Afghanistan and Iraq and the war on terror have claimed that these military interventions are counterproductive. They suggest that using military force against Muslim-majority countries or Muslim groups is likely to increase anti-American feeling among Muslims and inspire more of them to support or join terrorist groups such as al-Qaeda. Public opinion polls certainly suggest that U.S. military interventions in the Middle East increase anti-American feeling but not that they increase support for terrorists. The majority of Muslims have some sympathy with al-Qaeda's goals, but they disapprove of its methods. In the 2007 Program on International Policy Attitudes poll, Muslims in four countries were asked for their views on several al-Qaeda goals, including stopping U.S. support for Israel in its conflict with Palestinians, keeping Western values out of Muslim countries, removing U.S. forces from all Muslim countries, bringing strict sharia law to all Muslim countries, and unifying all Islamic countries into a single Islamic state. An average of at least 70 percent of Muslims polled approved of all of these goals apart from the goal of unifying all Islamic countries into a single Islamic state, which was supported by 65 percent.[5] As stated above, however, only about 5 percent of Muslims supported the use of violence against civilians, which is one of the principal strategies of al-Qaeda and other terrorist groups.

Beyond specific objections to U.S. foreign policy, many non-American Muslims have negative views of Americans and Westerners in general. A 2006 public opinion poll conducted in Indonesia, Jordan, Turkey, Egypt, and

Pakistan as well as among Muslims living in Nigeria, the United Kingdom, Germany, France, and Spain found large majorities who associated a number of negative characteristics with Westerners. In Muslim-majority countries some 60 percent of respondents described Westerners as arrogant, violent, and selfish. A large proportion of Muslims living in European countries also held these views, though they were less common than among Muslims in Muslim-majority countries. In the same survey non-Muslims were found to have similar negative views of Muslims. Large proportions of non-Muslims described Muslims as fanatical, violent, and arrogant. These figures were lower in the United States than in many other Western countries. For example, only 43 percent of non-Muslim Americans described Muslims as "fanatical" whereas the figure in Spain was 83 percent. Only 45 percent of non-Muslim Americans described Muslims as "violent" as opposed to 73 percent of non-Muslim Nigerians and 59 percent of non-Muslim Russians.[6]

The United States not only has an image problem in the Muslim world, it also has an image problem in the world in general. Mistrust of the United States among Muslims has a long history because of perceived U.S. support for Israel. Since the start of the Persian Gulf War against Iraq in 1991, however, Muslim distrust has had a new focus—the direct intervention of the United States in the Middle East. The U.S.-led invasions of Afghanistan and Iraq have brought these concerns into sharp focus in the first decade of the 21st century. Muslims are suspicious of U.S. motives, especially in the Middle East. According to the findings of opinion polls, the fear that the U.S. war on terror drives Muslims to support terrorism is unfounded—the vast majority of Muslims remain firmly against violent attacks on civilians, believing them contrary to the precepts of Islam. The war on terror does, however, provoke strong feelings against U.S. troops in Muslim countries. President Barack Obama took steps early in his administration to reassure Muslims of U.S. intentions and to open a cultural dialogue with the Muslim world. In a speech delivered in Cairo, Egypt, in 2009 Obama called for a "new beginning" in the relationship between the United States and the Muslim world and a break in the "cycle of suspicion and discord" that had marred this relationship in the past.[7] The United States faces an uphill struggle to overcome decades of mistrust in the Muslim world especially as long as it continues to try to balance its vital strategic interests in the Middle East with the sensitivities of the world's Muslims over interventions in Islam's historical heartland. Just hours before the president's landmark speech in Cairo Ayatollah Ali Khamenei, Iran's supreme leader, delivered his own speech in which he said that the United States remained "deeply hated" and that "beautiful and sweet" words would not change that.[8]

MUSLIMS IN THE UNITED STATES

The history of Muslims in North America is as long as the history of Christians in North America. The first known Muslims on the continent arrived along with European explorers in the 16th century. Throughout the colonial period and the early history of the United States small groups of Muslims, most of them enslaved, lived in America. The immigration of Muslims to the United States began slowly in the first half of the 20th century, accelerated in the second half, and has grown rapidly in the past three decades. In addition to the immigrant Muslim community a large group of non-immigrant Muslims that is predominantly African American live in the United States.

The Muslim Population of the United States

Nobody knows exactly how many Muslims live in the United States today; the U.S. Census Bureau does not collect data on religious affiliation. The City University of New York conducted a survey of religious identity in 2001 and concluded there were about 1.1 million Muslims in the country.[9] The Encyclopedia Britannica Book of the Year for 2006 gives a figure of 4.7 million.[10] The Council on American-Islamic Relations estimated a figure of between 6 and 7 million Muslims in 2001.[11] If the lowest of these estimates is true Muslims make up about 0.4 percent of the population of the United States. If the highest is true they make up about 2.3 percent.

The wide variation in these figures, between just more than 1 million and up to 7 million, is due to several factors. Some sources claim that figures have been exaggerated or underestimated for political purposes, others report that some Muslims are afraid to identify themselves because they fear discrimination. Another complication is the fact that some descendents of Muslim immigrants may describe themselves as Muslims even though they no longer observe many Islamic practices. Between one-third and one-quarter of Muslims in the United States today are native-born Americans who have converted to Islam. Of these the majority are African Americans, but there are also significant groups of Anglo- and Latino-Americans.

In 2009 there were about 1,200 known mosques in the United States. The largest of these was in Dearborn, Michigan, a city that has had a Muslim population since the middle of the 19th century and has perhaps the largest Muslim population in the United States today. It is estimated that more than 80 percent of mosques in the United States have been built since 1980, reflecting the large growth of Muslim immigration to the United States that has occurred in the last three decades.

Focus on the United States

The First Muslims in America

Some historians believe that Muslims from the Iberian Peninsula (present-day Spain and Portugal) may have sailed to the Caribbean as early as the 12th century. The earliest Muslim known to have visited North America was Estevánico of Azamor, a Berber from North Africa who traveled to the American Southwest in 1527 with the Spanish explorer Álvar Núñez Cabeza de Vaca. Estevánico was enslaved, as were the great majority of Muslims who arrived in America over the next 250 years. Not all arrived as slaves, however. In 1790 South Carolina officially recognized a community of Muslims from Morocco. This was 12 years after Morocco became one of the first states to recognize the newly independent United States and six years before U.S. president John Adams signed a treaty of friendship with Morocco including a phrase stating that the United States has no "character of enmity against the laws, religion, or tranquillity, of Mussulmen."

It is difficult to say exactly how many of the slaves brought to North America were Muslims. Slave traders rarely kept records of the ethnic origins or religion of the people they traded. It is certain that some slaves were Muslims or had knowledge of Islam because many of them came from parts of Africa where Islam had been established for centuries and because historical records exist of slave communities practicing Islam. Of the approximately half a million African slaves imported into North America between the 1520s and the 1800s,[12] up to 50 percent may have come from areas in Africa where Islam was an established faith among at least a part of the population. Tens of thousands of slaves were probably either Muslims or well acquainted with Islam.[13] Most Muslim slaves were prevented from openly practicing their religion, but not all. Records exist of practicing Muslim communities on some plantations, and some individuals have left religious texts written while they were enslaved.

Early Muslim Immigration

The earliest Muslim immigrants to the United States came from parts of the Ottoman Empire in the mid-19th century. Immigrants from areas now in Yemen and Turkey formed the first Muslim communities in the United States in Michigan, Massachusetts, and North Dakota.[14] The town of Ross, North Dakota, was the site of the first known mosque and Muslim cemetery in the United States.[15] Some of the earliest Muslim immigrant communities came from Europe rather than the Middle East. Tartars from Poland, Russia, and Lithuania founded the first Muslim organization in New York City in 1907, and Bosnian Muslims started a Muslim social organization in Chicago in 1906. The first purpose-built mosque in the United States was erected in 1934 in Cedar Rapids, Iowa. These groups founded the first Muslim communities in North America, but their numbers were small compared to the number of migrants from other parts of the world.

Modern Muslim Immigration

The number of Muslims who have emigrated to the United States in recent decades is difficult to determine. Neither the U.S. Census Bureau nor the Department of Homeland Security keep statistics relating to the religion of immigrants, but they do track the national origin of immigrants, and from these it is possible to estimate the number of Muslims entering the United States by looking at immigration from Muslim-majority countries. A change in U.S. immigration policy in 1965 removed restrictions that had been in place since 1924 that effectively banned immigration from most Muslim-majority countries. Since 1965 the number of Muslims immigrating to the United States has grown at an increasing rate.

In 2002 the Center for Immigration Studies issued a report showing that immigration from the Middle East had grown twice as fast as overall immigration from the rest of the world over the previous 30 years.[16] Although immigration from the Middle East grew more quickly than from other regions in this period, the number of immigrants was still smaller than from regions such as Latin America and East and Southeast Asia. In 1970 approximately 200,000 Middle Eastern immigrants lived in the United States, and in 2001 approximately 1.5 million. The report also states that the proportion of Middle Eastern immigrants who were Muslim grew in the same period from only 15 percent in 1970 to about 73 percent in 2001.

A 2007 analysis of immigration, also by the Center for Immigration Studies,[17] shows growth in the number of immigrants originating from the Middle East dropping off after 2001 but steady growth in the numbers coming from South Asia, which includes the Muslim-majority nations of Pakistan and Bangladesh. The number of immigrants originating in South Asia grew from 249,000 prior to 1980 to 727,000 in the period 2000–07. Immigrants from the Middle East numbered 398,000 in the period 1980–89, 324,000 in the period 1990–99, and 244,000 in the period 2000–07. Total immigration from South Asia and the Middle East in the period 2000–07 was just 9.5 percent of overall immigration. By comparison, immigration from Latin America made up more than 58 percent of overall immigration in the same period.

The Diversity of American Muslims

The Muslim population of the United States is the most ethnically diverse Muslim population living in a single country anywhere in the world. About

30 percent of Muslims in the United States are nonimmigrants. A large proportion of these are African Americans (it is estimated that between 25 and 35 percent of all Muslims in the United States are African Americans), but by no means all of them. There are also nonimmigrant Latino-American, Anglo-American, and Asian-American Muslims. The remaining 70 percent are immigrants from more than 80 countries. Almost every creed, branch, and school of Islamic thought is represented. South Asians are the largest single ethnic group in the total Muslim community of the United States, making up about 32 percent. About 26 percent are Arabs, and about 17 percent are from African nations. Pakistani-Americans make up the single largest nationality grouping at around 17 percent.[18]

A survey conducted by Gallup in 2008 and published in 2009[19] confirmed the ethnic diversity of American Muslims. Of all respondents who identified themselves as Muslim, 28 percent described themselves as white, 35 percent as African-American, 1 percent as Hispanic, and 18 percent as belonging to another race. In a similar survey carried out in 2007 by the Pew Research Center,[20] 37 percent of Muslims described themselves as white, 24 percent as black, 20 percent as Asian, 4 percent as Latino, and 15 percent as other or mixed race. The four other major religious groupings—Protestants, Catholics, Mormons, and Jews—were all found by comparison to be predominantly white (88, 76, 91, and 93 percent, respectively).

These surveys also revealed interesting data about the education, economic status, and political views of American Muslims. In both surveys the majority of Muslims were more likely to be employed and were earning more than the national average wage. In the Gallup survey Muslim women registered as one of the most highly educated groups of women in the country, second only to Jewish women. Gallup also found less disparity between the amounts earned by Muslim women and Muslim men than in any other religious grouping. When asked if religion played an important part in their daily lives, 80 percent of Muslims confirmed that it did. This figure was slightly higher than that for Protestants, 76 percent of whom responded affirmatively, and significantly higher than for Catholics (68 percent) and Jews (39 percent). Only among Mormons was the figure higher, at 85 percent. Muslims appeared toward the bottom of the rankings in surveys on voter registration among the young and positive expectations of the future.

Fewer young Muslims (aged 18 to 29) were registered voters than were the young among any other religious grouping—only 51 percent of young Muslims reported being registered voters compared to 78 percent of Protestant, 56 percent of Catholics, 69 percent of Mormons, and 73 percent of Jews in the same age bracket. When asked whether they would describe themselves as "thriving" (doing well and expecting things to improve), only

41 percent of Muslims agreed. Asked the same question, 48 percent of Protestants, 45 percent of Catholics, 51 percent of Mormons, and 56 percent of Jews described themselves as "thriving."

Islam and African Americans

Islam began to become a significant force in the African-American community in the first decades of the 20th century. Since then Islam has become one of the fastest growing faiths in the United States, and the majority of its new converts are thought to be African Americans. As with other aspects of Islam in the United States, it is difficult to be sure how fast Islam is growing or exactly how many new converts are African American since no clear central source of statistics exists. The question is also confused because some African Americans who describe themselves as Muslims are not recognized as such by the wider Muslim community.

Several groups in the United States describe themselves as Muslim but hold beliefs that contradict mainstream Islam. The best known of these is the Nation of Islam, a group that became highly influential during the Black Nationalism movements of the 1950s and 1960s. The Nation of Islam was founded by Wallace Fard Muhammad in Detroit, Michigan, in 1930. From 1935 to 1975 the organization was led by Elijah Muhammad, who was the organization's most influential and controversial leader. After Elijah Muhammad's death in 1974, his son, Warith Deen Mohammed, became the group's leader. Warith Deen Mohammed changed the organization's name to the World Community of Al-Islam in the West, and rejected many of his father's beliefs. In 1978 Louis Farrakhan split from the reformed World Community of Al-Islam in the West and established a second organization called the Nation of Islam, which returned to Elijah Muhammad's teachings. The World Community of Al-Islam in the West was renamed the American Society of Muslims in 1985.

Under Elijah Muhammad's leadership the Nation of Islam held several beliefs in opposition to traditional Islamic teaching. They included the belief that the group's founder, Wallace Fard Muhammad, was an incarnation of God and that Elijah Muhammad was a prophet sent by God.[21] Orthodox Islamic teaching holds that Muhammad was the final prophet and that it is blasphemous to claim that God would appear in human form. The Nation of Islam was also criticized for its attitude toward race relations. In speeches and writings Nation of Islam leaders claimed that "Black people" were the original human beings and were superior to all other races.[22] This teaching of the Nation of Islam proved attractive to some African Americans at a time when they felt discriminated against and oppressed in a society controlled by a white elite. Others were attracted to the Nation of Islam's interpretation of history, which claimed that African Americans were the descendents of African peoples who had been part of an ancient and advanced civilization.

The Nation of Islam became closely associated with Black Nationalism (a movement that rejects multiculturalism and aims to create an independent "Black" nation) through Malcolm X. Born Malcolm Little in 1925, he renamed himself Malcolm X in 1952 after joining the Nation of Islam. As Malcolm X he became a highly controversial and influential spokesperson for the Nation of Islam. Through his speeches and interviews Malcolm X brought the Nation of Islam's beliefs to a wide audience. He supported the idea of a separate state for black people[23] and rejected the nonviolence of the Civil Rights movement claiming instead that African Americans were justified in using any means to protect themselves.[24] Malcolm X left the Nation of Islam in 1964 and began adopting more orthodox Muslim beliefs. He completed a pilgrimage to Mecca the same year and, in his autobiography, he wrote that, after witnessing Muslims of different races interacting as equals during the pilgrimage, he came to believe that Islam could be the solution to racial strife.[25] Before his assassination in 1965 Malcolm X had begun to form closer relationships with Civil Rights leaders, but he continued to believe that the separation of the races was the best solution for African Americans and that nonviolence was a mistake.

The American Society of Muslims, the successor to the original Nation of Islam, also aligned itself more closely with traditional Muslim beliefs, specifically the tenets of Sunni Islam. Under the leadership of Warith Deen Mohammed, the American Society of Muslims rejected the idea that Wallace Fard Muhammad was an incarnation of God and that Elijah Muhammad was a prophet. The organization also distanced itself from the racist rhetoric of the past and allowed Anglo Americans to join for the first time.[26] Warith Deen Mohammed became a respected figure both in the United States and in the wider Muslim world. He met political and religious leaders from many faiths all over the world to promote interfaith understanding and was honored with awards from many governments. Today the American Society of Muslims is thought to be the largest nonimmigrant Muslim grouping in the United States with more than 2 million members.[27] The majority of its members are African American. The reformed Nation of Islam founded by Louis Farrakhan is also dominated by African Americans, but it is a much smaller organization, with a membership of between 30,000 and 70,000.[28]

Conflict between African-American Muslims and Immigrant Muslims

Until the late 1960s the overwhelming majority of Muslims in the United States were African Americans who had been born in the United States. A change in U.S. immigration policy in 1965 caused this balance to alter. From 1924 until 1965 the National Origins Act was in force. This act restricted the number of immigrants who could be admitted from any country to 2 percent of the number of people from that country who were already living in the United States in 1890. It effectively banned immigration from every Muslim country. In 1965 the Immigration and Nationality Act was passed, which lifted these restrictions and replaced them with quotas for every nation. A rapid rise in immigration from Asia and Africa resulted, which brought a new population of Muslims to the United States. From 1970 to the present the balance has shifted—African Americans, once the majority of U.S. Muslims, are now in a minority.

In many ways the interaction between U.S.-born African-American Muslims and immigrant Muslims was a positive one. The immigrants came from countries where Islam originated or had been established for centuries and brought a wealth of literature and tradition that enriched understanding of the faith among African Americans. They also provided cultural links between the historical centers of Islam and the previously isolated African-American community. But interaction also caused problems. New immigrants to the United States had little understanding of the economic and social difficulties faced by African Americans in the 1960s and 1970s, and some African-American Muslims found the newcomers' interpretations of Islam to be naïve and unhelpful in the context of life in urban America.

While most African-American Muslim groups have come to appreciate links with the Islamic traditions of the Middle East, some have not. For many African Americans who embraced Islam in the 1950s and 1960s, being a Muslim was, in part, a way of distancing themselves from the Christian traditions, which they saw as part of an oppressive society dominated by whites. Being Muslim was seen by these people as a way of reconnecting with a society that existed before the slave trade and of rejecting a society that carried out the slave trade. In some ways conversion to Islam was more a political act than an act of faith. The fact that the beliefs of organizations such as the Nation of Islam included very specific references to the political destiny of African Americans is evidence of this. The arrival of immigrants from the wider Muslim community, who brought with them their own prejudices and perspectives, led some African-American Muslims to question whether Muslims from these older cultures deserved to be seen as representing a deeper and better form of Islam. Some African-American Muslim scholars produced books that pointed out the prominent role played by Arab Muslims in the slave trade and that identified racist statements in the writings of historical Arab-Muslim religious figures.[29, 30]

The two groups are not completely reconciled, and a strand of criticism of the Islam of Asia and the Middle East continues to the present day. In general, however, relations between African-American Muslim groups and immigrant Muslims have become closer over time and, through this relationship, African-American Muslims have become tied to the wider Muslim community.

Muslim Women in the United States

Many Muslim immigrants to the United States come from strongly patriarchal societies. In some Muslim-majority states, such as Iran, Oman, Pakistan, Saudi Arabia, and Yemen, women are subject to legal systems that are based on sharia (Islamic law). Western commentators have fiercely criticized these Muslim-majority countries for their poor treatment of women. Some critics have even described Muslim-majority nations as practicing "gender apartheid."[31] Islamic feminist groups in some of these countries are also critical of what they regard as oppressive policies, often at great risk to themselves. In the United States these women and their female children have faced the challenge of reconciling their desire to take advantage of freedoms and rights guaranteed under U.S. law with their desire to retain traditional Islamic values.

The most common subject for public debate about the role of Muslim women in the United States is the wearing of *hijab*—the traditional "modest dress" worn by Muslim women that covers every part of the body except the face and hands—and face veils such as the *niqab* and burka (note that *hijab* is sometimes used to refer only to a head scarf). Some non-Muslim Americans are uncomfortable with women wearing face-covering veils in situations in which they work face-to-face with members of the public. Some Western feminists regard *hijab* as a symbol of female oppression in Muslim societies.[32] On the other hand a growing trend among young Muslim Americans exists to adopt *hijab* as a feminist statement. From the point of view of these women, the modesty of *hijab* is a reaction to what they see as an excessive fascination with the female body in American culture and a defense against being judged according to their weight or body shape.[33, 34]

Some young Muslim-American women are turning to the teachings of Islam itself as a way of challenging the traditions of their immigrant parents. When Islam was founded in the seventh century, it offered many improvements to the lives of women in Arab society. Islamic precepts stipulated women's rights in marriage, divorce, and inheritance, and Islamic principles called for education and political involvement for women that had not previously existed in these societies and that preceded similar rights for women in Western societies by hundreds of years.[35] Some historians argue that these reforms have conflicted with pre-Islamic patriarchal traditions in Arab countries ever since and that it is these traditions, and not Islam, that have resulted in the modern oppression of women in these societies.

Young Muslim-American women are turning to the rights provided by early versions of Islam and using these to challenge the patriarchal traditions of their parents. An example is arranged marriage. Arranged marriages, in which parents or other family elders decide who their children are to marry, have been traditional in many Muslim-majority countries since before the advent of Islam, and they continue to the present day. According to sharia a marriage contract can be entered into only with the full consent of the woman, but many women in Muslim-majority societies are unaware of this proviso or are prevented from voicing their preferences. Muslim women in America tend to be more aware of their rights under Islam and more willing and able to insist on them. By abiding by the precepts of Islam, such as wearing *hijab* and observing prayers, they can show their acceptance of the faith while rejecting traditions that restrict their ability to live the lives of modern American women. This does not mean, however, that all Muslim-American women accept or adopt *hijab*.

Islam has also become attractive to nonimmigrant American women for similar reasons. Increasing numbers of African-American, Latino-American, and Anglo-American women are drawn to Islam because of its principles of female modesty and the framework of rights it seems to offer. While Muslim women face the challenge of being accepted as "normal" Americans by the majority, they also have the advantage of living in a society where the law protects their human rights in a way that might not be true in the societies from which they or their parents originated. Many immigrant Muslim women and their daughters have abandoned *hijab* and other traditional practices while continuing to regard themselves as Muslims. Other immigrant Muslim women came from Muslim-majority countries with secular governments, such as Turkey, where the wearing of *hijab* is not common and where women hold more rights than in more conservative states.

Muslim-American Identity

The immigrant Muslim population of the United States is a relatively recent addition compared to other large immigrant populations. Immigrant American Muslims and their children are in the process of figuring out how, and how much, to integrate into mainstream U.S. society. Mainstream U.S. society is also going through a process of coming to terms with the Muslim community, a process that has been made more difficult by the confrontation between the United States and radical Muslim terrorism.

The issues facing the immigrant Muslim community in multicultural America can be examined in three parts: ethnic identity, religious identity, and national identity. The idea of examining identity issues in this way was popularized, though not originated, as "the three circles of identity" by Egyptian president and leading voice in the Arab Nationalist movement Gamal Abdel Nasser.[36] All of these areas tend to conflict with each other. For example, it may be difficult to retain all of one's ethnic traditions, such as polygamy, when they conflict with the legal norms of a host society. This would constitute a conflict between ethnic identity and national identity. In a highly ethnically diverse group such as the Muslim-American community, conflicts exist also within different ethnic and religious groupings. For example, the ethnic traditions of African-American Muslims are different from the traditions of Pakistani-American Muslims, which are in turn different from the traditions of Turkish-American Muslims. In religious identity many differences also are found between the multiple creeds and branches of Islam represented in the Muslim community in America.

Against the background of this complex set of identity questions, American Muslims face a series of difficult questions about the place of Islam in U.S. society and about Islam itself. Perhaps the largest of these questions concerns the relationship between Islam and democracy. Many, though not all, Muslim immigrants come from nations where democracy is held in low regard or where democratic processes are considered by many commentators to be corrupt and ineffective. In these cultures the tenets of Islam are often regarded as a better and more justifiable source of political authority. In the United States these Muslims find themselves living in a culture in which democracy is one of the central pillars of political belief. The issue is particularly contentious because of the stated ambition of the United States to bring democracy to Muslim majority nations such as Afghanistan and Iraq.

Other issues facing the Muslim community include gender equality, religious and racial tolerance, and social justice. The gender equality movement in the United States is more established and has had more success than in the majority of Muslim-majority countries. Immigrant Muslim Americans face the challenge of answering criticism from the wider U.S. society about the position of women in Islam as well as questions from Muslim women, and especially younger Muslim women, within their own community. Religious and racial tolerance are enshrined in U.S. law in a way that is not the case in the legal systems of some nations from which immigrant Muslims originated. Some American Muslims are compelled to come to terms with the need to insist on their rights to religious and racial equality in a nation where they now are a minority and maintenance of former attitudes hostile to religious and racial equality in their nations of origin where they were part of the majority. For example, in Saudi Arabia there is no legal protection for freedom of religious expression, and Christians in the country have faced persecution.

Muslim Americans are adopting a variety of approaches to these questions. Muslim Americans who question the legitimacy of a democratic political system as opposed to a political system based on Islam are divided about the best approach to political involvement in the United States. A minority believes that becoming involved in the American political system would be to condone an illegitimate system. The majority argues that engagement is the only way to produce reform. For most American Muslims, however, the question is largely irrelevant since they accept the legitimacy of the democratic system. American Muslims are also divided over questions of gender equality, religious tolerance, and social justice. Some American Muslims are eager to adopt the precepts of Western gender- and racial-equality movements, often because they consider these principles to be in line with basic Islamic teachings. Other American Muslims are less keen to embrace these movements because they see them as conflicting with Islam or with their ethnic traditions. Debate is ongoing in the American-Muslim community about which, if any, aspects of Western culture should be adopted to strengthen and improve Islam. A minority of American Muslims prefer to remain as isolated from the wider U.S. culture as possible, but many argue that engagement and dialogue with that wider culture are the only possible avenues to follow if their community is to grow and prosper on American soil.

American Muslims after September 11, 2001

Since the attacks of September 11, 2001—when American Airlines Flights 11 and 175 flew into the World Trade Center in New York City, American Airlines Flight 77 crashed into the Pentagon in Arlington, Virginia, and United Airlines Flight 93 crashed into a field near Shanksville, Pennsylvania—were carried out by Arab Muslims, American Muslims have faced new difficulties in being accepted into U.S. society. Although no U.S. citizens, Muslim or otherwise, were involved in the attacks, some Americans feared that U.S. Muslims might be harboring or helping future terrorists. In the weeks and months immediately following September 11 numerous attacks against American Muslims occurred across the United States, including some murders.

The stereotype of the Arab-Muslim terrorist predates the events of September 11, 2001, by decades. Muslim terrorists threatening the United

Focus on the United States

States have been appearing in American television programs and popular Hollywood movies since the 1970s. The 1977 movie *Black Sunday* featured Palestinian Muslims involved in a plot to bomb the Super Bowl. The popular 1985 family movie *Back to the Future* features "Libyan terrorists" wielding AK-47s bent on obtaining plutonium to build weapons of mass destruction. Although the 1993 bombing of the World Trade Center was the first known terrorist attack carried out by Muslims within the United States, several earlier terror attacks had been carried out by Muslims against U.S. targets in other parts of the world. Notable examples include the 1973 attack on Rome airport in which a Pan American aircraft was destroyed and 14 Americans killed; the 1983 bombings of the U.S. embassy and marine barracks in Beirut, Lebanon; the 1986 bombing of a nightclub in Berlin, Germany, frequented by U.S. service personnel; and the 1988 bombing of Pan American Flight 103 over Scotland. These events and others that occurred between 1993 and 2001 created suspicion of Islam and Muslims even though they were carried out by a tiny minority of the world's approximately 1.5 billion Muslims.

Before September 11, 2001, non-Muslim Americans held a variety of attitudes to Muslim Americans. The most common attitude was indifference. The majority of Americans did not regularly encounter Muslim Americas or were not aware that they did, and the majority of Muslim Americans kept their faith private. Awareness of the size of the Muslim community in the United States was not widespread, and few people were concerned about it. The second attitude, held by a much smaller number of Americans, was awareness and acceptance. Some non-Muslim religious groups actively sought out better understanding and dialogue with the growing Muslim community. Some political parties and groups also made efforts to connect with, and appeal to, American Muslims as voters. In a speech made by Jesse Jackson at the 1984 Democratic Party convention he said: "We are bound by Moses and Jesus, but also connected with Islam and Mohammed."

Negative attitudes toward Muslim Americans were less common but sometimes voiced vociferously. Some commentators argued that Islam represented a real and growing danger to the safety of the United States and urged the government to watch Muslim communities for potential plots. Some religious leaders, such as Pat Robertson, also described Islam as inherently evil and promoted programs to convert American Muslims to Christianity.[37]

In the aftermath of September 11 indifference to the presence of the Muslim community in the United States evaporated rapidly. Suspicions that American Muslims may have been involved in the attacks and fear that further attacks might originate from the American-Muslim community were widespread in the emotionally charged atmosphere following September 11. Negative attitudes toward American Muslims have grown stronger since 2001, but are a minority view. Many more Americans came to believe that the Muslim community in the United States should be subjected to closer scrutiny by law-enforcement agencies, even if this meant restricting liberties. In a 2004 poll conducted by Cornell University, 44 percent of respondents agreed that the U.S. government should curtail the civil liberties of American Muslims in an effort to improve national security. A total of 27 percent favored requiring all Muslim Americans to register their place of residence with federal authorities, and 26 percent approved using law-enforcement agencies to monitor mosques. In the same poll, 47 percent of respondents believed that Islam was more likely to encourage violence than other faiths—among "highly religious" non-Muslim Americans this figure was 65 percent.[38] In a 2006 poll conducted by the *Washington Post* and ABC News,[39] 46 percent of respondents reported a negative view of Islam, and 33 percent believed that Islam encouraged violence against non-Muslims. A 2008 Gallup poll found that 23 percent of Americans had a negative view of Islam.[40] These figures indicate that public opinion in the United States has become less negative with regard to Islam in general since 2001 but that a significant proportion of Americans remain suspicious of Islam and, therefore, suspicious of the American-Muslim community. Bad feelings toward American Muslims have remained strong within public opinion since 2001 for two reasons.

MILITARY CAMPAIGNS IN IRAQ AND AFGHANISTAN

The first is a negative view of Islam that has come from the involvement of the United States in military campaigns in Afghanistan and Iraq. The U.S. invasions of both these countries were presented to the American public partly as wars of liberation. Afghanistan was framed as a campaign to liberate oppressed Afghans from a harshly oppressive Taliban regime and Iraq as one of liberation from a despotic dictator. The strong insurgent movements against U.S. and coalition troops that followed the initial victories in both these countries have led some Americans to believe that all Muslims are unappreciative of democracy and U.S. attempts to improve their lives. These negative reactions to events in Afghanistan and Iraq tend to influence views by some Americans of Muslims in the United States. Many more Americans, however, regard these insurgencies as a predicable reaction to long-term occupation by foreign troops and insensitive efforts to impose a foreign political system.

CONVICTED MUSLIM AMERICANS

The second factor has been the arrest and conviction of a number of Muslim-American citizens on terrorism charges. Notable cases include the 2002 arrest and subsequent conviction of a group of Yemeni Americans known as the Buffalo Six on charges of providing material support to al-Qaeda, the 2003 conviction of Iyman Faris for conspiracy and for providing material support and resources to al-Qaeda, the 2005 conviction of Ahmed Omar Abu Ali for providing material support and resources to al-Qaeda and conspiring to assassinate the president, and the 2005 conviction of Ali al-Tamimi for recruiting American Muslims to fight against the United States in Afghanistan.[41]

It should be noted, however, that the number of American Muslims convicted on terrorism charges is extremely small, considering the size of the American-Muslim community. It is also true that every important Muslim organization in America has condemned the September 11 attacks and all forms of terrorist violence and that the majority of American Muslims are opposed to terror tactics. A 2007 poll conducted by the Pew Research Center questioned American Muslims on their attitudes toward "Islamic extremism" and "terrorists and their tactics."[42] In this survey 51 percent of American Muslims described themselves as "very concerned" and 25 percent as "somewhat concerned" about "the rise of Islamic extremism around the world." When asked if they were concerned about the "rise of Islamic extremism in the United States," 36 percent reported being "very concerned" and 25 percent "somewhat concerned." When asked if the suicide bombing of civilian targets is ever a justified tactic in the defense of Islam, 78 percent of American Muslims replied that it was "never justified" and only 8 percent replied that it was often or sometimes justified. The percentage of American Muslims claiming that suicide bombings are often or sometimes justified was half that of Muslims polled in France, Spain, and Great Britain for a 2006 Pew Global Attitudes Project survey. American-Muslim attitudes toward al-Qaeda were also generally negative. In the 2007 Pew survey 68 percent described themselves as having a "very unfavorable" or "somewhat unfavorable" view of al-Qaeda and only 5 percent reported a "favorable" view.

Given the lack of support among American Muslims for terror tactics, Islamic extremism, and al-Qaeda, and the very small number of American Muslims who have been found guilty of terrorist activities, some critics have described the suspicion of non-Muslim Americans toward Islam as "Islamophobia"—an irrational fear and hatred of Muslims and Islam.[43] Conversely some commentators have argued that the suspicions of the American public toward Islam are justified given the evidence that Muslim terrorists are willing to commit acts of extreme violence and the fact that a number of plots against U.S. targets have been uncovered within the Muslim community in America.

U.S. INTEREST IN THE MIDDLE EAST
Energy Needs

The United States consumes more energy than any other nation. According to the U.S. Energy Information Administration, the United States consumes about 20 percent of the world's total energy production each year. Around 80 percent of this energy is produced by burning fossil fuels, including oil.

Two important shifts in the relationship of the United States to oil have occurred over the past 100 years. The first came in the 1950s when oil replaced coal as the most important source of the nation's energy. The second came in the early 1990s when, for the first time, the United States began to import more oil than it produced.

It is often assumed that the United States gets most of its oil imports from the Middle East, but this is not a true picture; its sources of oil are much more diverse. In 2007 the United States imported 3,642 thousand barrels of oil a day from states around the Persian Gulf (including Saudi Arabia), but in the same year it also imported 3,520 thousand barrels of oil a day from its two closest neighbors, Canada and Mexico. The five biggest sources of oil imported into the United States are Canada (18.2 percent), Mexico (11.4 percent), Saudi Arabia (11 percent), Venezuela (10.1 percent), and Nigeria (8.4 percent). Taken together these countries supply 59.2 percent of U.S. oil imports, and only one of them is a Muslim-majority Middle Eastern state.

It is true that not all of the oil the United States imports comes from the Muslim world, but it is also true that a large proportion of it does. This has been a powerful factor in U.S. foreign policy toward the Muslim world and especially the oil-rich Muslim-majority countries of the Middle East. The historical and cultural heart of the Muslim world coincides geographically with the world's largest reserves of oil. It is unlikely the United States would have become so closely involved in the Middle East over the past 50 years if it did not rely on oil imports and if the Middle East was not the world's largest source of that vital commodity. It is also unlikely that commentators and politicians would be talking about the dangers of a so-called clash of civilizations between Islam and the West if that source did not lie in the Middle East. This is not a one-way street though. Many of the Middle East's oil-rich nations depend heavily on revenue from oil exports as the backbone of their economies. Without the flow of income from customers such as the United States they would have few if any means of supporting their ambitions for development.

This interdependence can be seen in the history of the relationships between the United States and these countries. In many cases the earliest diplomatic contacts between Middle Eastern nations and the United States came about as Western oil companies arrived to negotiate the search for oil there in the 1930s. World War II emphasized the strategic importance of the region for the United States and, during the cold war, Washington expended a great deal of energy and expense trying to prevent the region from coming under Soviet influence. Since the end of the cold war in the late 1980s the United States has become even more embroiled in the Middle East as it has faced the strategic threat of so-called rogue states and Islamic or nationalist movements opposed to U.S. influence.

For their part, the oil-rich states of the Middle East have had to walk the difficult path of pursuing their own interests and desires while maintaining a trading relationship with a world superpower and its allies. The United States is the world's single largest customer for oil, but its close traditional allies in western Europe and Japan are, taken together, an even larger customer. With the collapse of the Soviet Union, the United States remains the only super-power, and negotiating this path has become arguably more, rather than less, difficult. In theory the oil states of the Persian Gulf have a powerful bargaining tool in the threat to withhold oil, which they can use to oppose the will of the United States. In practice using this tool could have devastating consequences for their own economies. It has also been extremely difficult for these states to act together given the animosities and rivalries that exist between them. Saudi Arabia, the world's largest single producer and exporter of oil, is a good example of this dichotomy. It has often vehemently opposed U.S. foreign policy, particularly over Israel, but it has also gone to great lengths to maintain a close relationship with the United States, which it finds beneficial.

It is clear that, in the long term, the Middle East's oil will be gone. Some oil states in the Persian Gulf have already begun to plan for that day by investing trillions of oil-revenue dollars to restructure and diversify their economies. In the United States and other industrialized countries many groups are arguing that reducing dependency on oil is essential for long-term economic and environmental health. For the time being though, oil consumption continues to rise year after year, and as long as this is the case, it seems unlikely that the charged and sometimes violent relationship between the United States and the oil states will end. The continuation of this relationship also means a continuation of U.S. engagement with the wider Muslim world.

Economic Interdependence

The trade in oil forms the basis for the economic relationship between the United States and several nations in the Middle East, but it is not the only factor. At the most simple level, the United States is the world's largest consumer of oil, and states such as Saudi Arabia and Kuwait are the world's largest suppliers of oil. The economic relationship is more complex, however, than these facts might suggest. Persian Gulf States use the money they earn from the sale of oil to invest in their own countries and abroad. These countries have so much money that their decisions about where to invest and where not to invest can have a significant impact on the global economy. For decades much of this oil money has been invested in the United States in one form or another. It has become a major factor in the U.S. economy. Conversely, the performance of the U.S. economy is of great interest to Persian Gulf States that have invested in it. The United States and certain Gulf States are tied together by hundreds of billions of dollars of investment. The most important form of investment in this context is foreign direct investment (FDI). When an individual, company, or government buys part or all of a company in another country, they make a foreign direct investment. This individual, company, or government then receives a return on its investment—usually a share of any profits. For example, a Saudi Arabian company might buy or pay for a factory to be built in the United States. The money paid for the factory goes into the U.S. economy, and the Saudi Arabian company receives part or all of the profits made by the factory as long as it continues to own it. Officially an investment is said to be FDI when a 10 percent or greater controlling interest is purchased.

Sovereign Wealth Funds

Sovereign wealth funds are among the wealthiest and most active foreign direct investors. A sovereign wealth fund is a state-owned investment company. An example is the Abu Dhabi Investment Authority—a sovereign wealth fund owned by the government of the United Arab Emirates. The Abu Dhabi Investment Authority is believed to own between U.S. $600 and $900 billion worth of assets, much of it through FDI. Sovereign wealth funds such as the Abu Dhabi Investment Authority were set up by national governments as a way of managing state income from exports such as oil. By investing this money abroad these governments can use the profits to develop their own countries over decades. Several of the other most important sovereign wealth funds belong to oil-rich Persian Gulf States, including the Kuwait Investment Authority and the Qatar Investment Authority.

FDI into the United States contributes to the economy by adding to the gross domestic product. Since World War II the United States has been one of the most attractive places for foreign investors to invest their money. This is because the U.S. economy has grown consistently throughout this period. Investors such as sovereign wealth funds are interested in long-term steady growth, and the U.S. economy has provided this. In the 1980s levels of FDI into the United States grew rapidly as the U.S. stock market soared and the government reduced taxes to make investment more attractive. Persian Gulf States and their sovereign wealth funds were some of the biggest investors in the United States during this period.

Some commentators claim that the effects of FDI on the U.S. economy might be negative in the long term. They worry that allowing foreigners to buy up hundreds of billions of dollars worth of U.S. capital stock puts the security of the United States at risk. Critics imagine a scenario in which the United States becomes involved in a war or dispute with a country that owns large parts of the equipment, buildings, intellectual property, or other assets that make the U.S. economy work. A foreign power could theoretically use its ownership of assets in the United States to damage the U.S. economy. In practice this is unlikely ever to happen. First, all the assets owned by all non-U.S. organizations in the United States amount to fewer than 5 percent of the U.S. total capital stock. Second, the U.S. government has the power to seize assets if it is thought such assets might be used against U.S. interests.

Still, individual cases of FDI have been controversial. In 2006 an outcry was raised when it was revealed that a state-owned United Arab Emirates's company, Dubai Ports World, was buying eight U.S. seaports. Critics argued that selling ports to a company owned by a foreign power compromised the security of the United States. That the foreign power in question was an Arab-Muslim country added to some people's fears, given the threat of Muslim terrorism. In the wider context of FDI coming into the United States from Persian Gulf States and other countries, the controversy made little sense. A British company had owned the seaports in question for many years before the proposed deal with Dubai Ports World, and many other ports and airports in the United States are wholly are partly owned by non-U.S. companies. In addition, the U.S. Coast Guard and U.S. Customs and Border Protection would have remained in control of security at all ports as they always have, regardless of who owns them. That the story caused public concern at all is an indication of how little the American public in general understands about the role of FDI in the U.S. economy. For supporters of the deal, including President George W. Bush, attempts by Congress to block the sale were seen as potentially disastrous for foreign investment in the United States, particularly from the Muslim world. The controversy was resolved when Dubai Ports World decided to sell its interests in U.S. ports to an American company, but the issue had a continuing impact on FDI from Muslim countries. Investors got the message that they might be blocked from doing business in the United States simply because they were Muslims. With the global economic crisis that began in 2008, the United States has made efforts to reassure the Muslim world that America still welcomes its investments. In 2009 Secretary of the Treasury Timothy Geithner visited Saudi Arabia to reassure Arab investors that the United States had "put into place a series of reforms designed to safeguard national security, while providing more clarity, predictability and transparency to investors."[44]

TREASURY SECURITIES

Investors from the Muslim world are also an important part of the structure that underpins the value of the U.S. dollar. To introduce new money into the economy the U.S. Department of the Treasury issues U.S. treasury securities. These securities, or bonds, are sold to investors with the promise that the U.S. government will pay these investors their money back with interest at a later date. If the government decides to add a billion dollars to the economy, for example, it sells a billion dollars worth of treasury securities promising to pay this billion dollars back, plus interest, after a period of between one and 30 years. The U.S. government essentially borrows the billion dollars from investors—treasury securities are government debts. Individuals, companies, and foreign governments can buy treasury securities, and oil-rich Arab states are some of the largest buyers. As long as the U.S. government can continue selling treasury securities it can introduce new money into the economy. Investors are attracted to securities because there is much less risk of losing money with them than with most other investments—the U.S. government can always raise taxes to pay them back. On the other hand, the attractiveness of treasury securities can decline if the value of the dollar against other currencies falls. Other countries also sell securities, and these can become more attractive to investors. The value of the dollar against other currencies is decided, in part, by the attractiveness of treasury securities.

The largest holder of U.S. treasury securities is China with about $800 billion worth (about 35 percent of the total). Japan is second with about $680 billion worth (about 21 percent). The oil-exporting countries, a category that includes the Persian Gulf States as well as Ecuador, Venezuela, Indonesia, and Nigeria, hold about $193 billion worth (about 6 percent). From these figures it is clear that the oil-exporting states of the Muslim world are important, but not critical, holders of U.S. debt. FDI from these states is a more important factor in the U.S. economy. In 2009 it was estimated that Saudi Arabia alone held $400 billion worth of foreign assets, much of it in dollars.

CONFLICTS BETWEEN THE UNITED STATES AND THE MIDDLE EAST

Iran

The story of the relationship between the United States and Iran is a story of dramatic change. Fifty years ago Iran was one of the closest allies of the

United States in the Middle East. Today the two countries are the bitterest of enemies. The confrontation between Iran and the United States, centered on the oil-rich states of the Persian Gulf, is perhaps the most important strategic problem facing the United States today. The resolution of this conflict will have a powerful long-term effect on the region and the world.

Relations between the United States and Iran began as early as 1856 when the shah (the title of Iran's kings) dispatched Iran's first ambassador to Washington, D.C. For the next 100 years most of the interaction between the two countries was commercial and philanthropic. Toward the end of the 19th century, a growing reform movement in Iran sought to end the poor government and corruption of the Qajar dynasty, which had ruled the country since 1781. These Iranian reformers saw modernization and industrialization as the best way to improve their country and looked to the example of the United States. Although the Iranian shah technically ruled the country, Great Britain and Russia had both gained great influence and fought each other for control of Iran's resources. Some Iranians saw a close relationship with the United States as a way of ending this humiliating situation and building a new nation. Many American businesses were happy to establish links with Iran, and Americans also established new schools and colleges to help train a new generation of Iranians in modern industrial, economic, and medical methods.

THE IRANIAN COUP OF 1953

Until the 1950s and the start of the cold war the United States had no firm policy toward Iran.[45] Between World War I and World War II the United States was content for Britain to maintain its long-standing influence over the country, an arrangement that benefited Britain through its ownership of the Anglo-Iranian Oil Company. As tensions between the Soviet Union and the United States grew, however, the United States began to worry about the possibility of the Soviets moving into the Middle East and gaining control of its oil. Iran was an oil-rich country directly neighboring the Soviet Union, and Britain no longer possessed the military strength to resist a Soviet move into Iran on its own. For these reasons the United States began to take a great interest in closer ties with Iran.

In 1952 the reforming prime minister of Iran, Mohammed Mossadeq, began nationalizing the Anglo-Iranian Oil Company. Both Britain and the United States were concerned that this might be the first step that would lead Iran to cut ties with the West and invite Soviet friendship instead. In 1953 the U.S. Central Intelligence Agency and Britain's MI6 conducted a secret operation inside Iran to remove Mossadeq's government. The plan was to discredit the democratically elected government and strengthen the position of the shah, Mohammad Reza Pahlavi, who was known to be pro-Western. The operation proved successful and returned the shah to power. The United States continued to support the shah's regime over the next 25 years, and the shah became a loyal ally of the United States in the region.

THE IRANIAN REVOLUTION OF 1979

The shah proved a good ally of the United States in the cold war, but his regime became oppressive and was hated by many Iranians. The shah's policies angered diverse sections of Iranian society. He transformed the country's elected parliament into a powerless institution packed with landlords, businessmen, and officials loyal to himself, and he banned all antiroyalist parties. Dissent was ruthlessly stamped out by his pervasive internal security service SAVAK (National Intelligence and Security Organization), which routinely tortured and executed political opponents of the shah.

Beginning in 1963 the shah attempted to modernize Iran using Western industrialized states as a model. Known as the White Revolution, the program was funded by Iranian oil revenues and investment from Western companies and the Soviet Union. Giant construction projects, such as the building of dams, new ports, petrochemical plants, and oil pipelines, were implemented, and the shah passed laws to change the structure of Iranian society, including measures to redistribute land to peasants and to launch a massive rural literacy campaign. A package of reforms to improve the lives of women included the right to divorce and a ban on marriage before the age of 15.

The reforms of the White Revolution were welcomed by the United States and other Western states, but they did nothing to change the fact that ordinary Iranians had virtually no political power. The economic and industrial reforms were also badly coordinated and often resulted in huge waste. Expensive equipment was bought for which there were too few qualified Iranian operators, and new plants and facilities could not be used because there was insufficient infrastructure to support them. The shah's attempts to remodel Iranian society on a Western model also enraged the country's conservative Muslim clerics.

By 1978 internal opposition to the shah was reaching a critical level. Riots broke out in the streets of Tehran, and mass strikes paralyzed the country's economy. In January 1979 the shah left Iran in fear for his safety, and by mid-February his regime had been overthrown. The sudden collapse of the shah's regime caught the United States by surprise. While the riots and strikes of 1978 were going on, the CIA issued a report that stated: "Persia is not in a revolutionary or even a 'prerevolutionary' situation."[46] The administration of President Jimmy Carter, which took office in 1977, was critical of the shah's regime but did not foresee its imminent collapse. Unlike earlier U.S. presidents, Jimmy Carter spoke out against Iran's human rights record and banned the sale of antiriot equipment to Iran. At the same time the United States privately assured the shah that it would support him in the event of an uprising against his rule. U.S. National Security Advisor Zbigniew Brzezinski reportedly told the shah that the United States would "back him to the hilt,"[47] and as events became more serious the Carter administration urged the Iranian army to stage a "last-resort coup d'etat."[48] In the event, the Iranian army declared its neutrality and allowed the revolution to happen.

The United States was unsure in the immediate aftermath of the Iranian revolution what kind of regime would replace that of the shah and what its policy toward the United States might be. When the shah left the country, an interim government under Shapour Bakhtiar held power. Bakhtiar dismantled SAVAK, lifted media censorship, freed political prisoners, and planned elections for a new government. For a short time it seemed to the United States that a pro-Western democratically elected government might emerge, but it was not to be. Bakhtiar made the decision to allow a popular Muslim cleric called Ruhollah Musavi Khomeini to return to Iran from exile in France. Khomeini had been a leading voice in the movement against the shah for years and was widely admired by ordinary Iranians.

Khomeini took control of the revolution within days of his return to Iran. In a March 1979 referendum it was announced that more than 98 percent of the population had voted to replace the monarchy with an "Islamic Republic." A second referendum in December of the same year approved a new constitution, which created the post of Supreme Leader with ultimate religious and political authority over the nation. Ruhollah Khomeini became Iran's first Supreme Leader on December 3, 1979.

THE HOSTAGE CRISIS

As Iranians found themselves embroiled in the emotional, difficult process of redefining their nation, a crisis in relations with the United States suddenly arose. In October 1979 the United States agreed to allow the exiled shah to enter the United States to receive medical treatment. U.S. embassy staff in Tehran had strongly advised against this decision[49] because they recognized that it would strengthen anti-American feeling. Khomeini responded by describing the United States as "the Great Satan," and he issued a warning that America was plotting against the revolution.[50] Many Iranians, especially Khomeini's supporters, were outraged at the U.S. decision. Fear was widespread that the United States might be planning a coup, as it had in 1953, which would return the shah to power.

On November 4, 1979, a large group of students calling themselves the Muslim Student Followers of the Imam's Line broke into and occupied the

U.S. embassy in Tehran. The students later said that they planned to occupy the embassy and hold the embassy staff "for a few days, maybe one week, but no more."[51] In fact, 52 of the embassy staff were held captive for 444 days. Khomeini approved the occupation in a statement in which he called the embassy an "American spy den in Tehran,"[52] and large crowds gathered outside the building to register their support. An American hostage reported that one of his captives said: "You have no right to complain, because you took our whole country hostage in 1953."[53] The main demand of the hostage takers was for the shah to be extradited to Iran to face trial. They also wanted the United States to apologize for its role in the 1953 coup and to release Iranian funds that had been frozen in the United States.

The Iranian hostage crisis, as it came to be known, marked the first serious encounter by the United States with radical Islam. It shocked the American public, who had never seen images of such fervent hatred of their country before, and it damaged U.S.-Iranian relations so seriously that they have not yet been repaired 30 years later. The inability of President Carter to negotiate the release of the hostages and the failure of a rescue mission in which eight U.S. military personnel died damaged his presidency and contributed to his defeat by Ronald Reagan in the 1980 presidential election. The hostages were released minutes after Ronald Reagan's inauguration in January 1981. The negotiations that led to their release were carried out through the offices of an Algerian diplomat and required the United States to promise: "It is and from now on will be the policy of the United States not to intervene, directly or indirectly, politically or militarily, in Iran's internal affairs."

The crisis eliminated the possibility of close U.S. relations with Iran and caused the United States to turn instead toward Iraq. From the Iranian point of view, the crisis greatly strengthened Khomeini's popular support particularly after the failure of the U.S. rescue mission, which some Iranians interpreted as an intervention by God to defend the revolution. Anti-American feeling in Iran, which was already strong, became almost a national obsession.

THE IRAN-IRAQ WAR

Iraqi forces invaded Iran in September 1980, starting a war that was to continue for eight years and that would lead to the deaths of more than a million people. Iraq and Iran had been rivals for centuries, and relations between the two countries had been poor since the overthrow of the Iraqi monarchy in 1958. Saddam Hussein's decision to invade at this time was probably inspired by two factors: the chaotic situation in Iran due to the revolution and the fact that the United States was no longer Iran's ally. Evidence exists also that the United States secretly agreed to help Iraq before the war began[54] or at least that Washington knew that Iraq planned to invade and gave its tacit approval by not opposing the plan.

The U.S. decision to help Iraq in its war against Iran stemmed directly from the sudden ending of the U.S. relationship with Iran. The Islamic revolution in Iran unbalanced the entire system of U.S. strategic alliances against Soviet influence in the Middle East.[55] Diplomatic links between Washington and Baghdad had been severed after the 1967 Arab-Israeli War and had not been restored in the intervening decade. Aware that the United States needed a new ally in the region, President Carter undertook a review of U.S.-Iraqi relations as the Iranian hostage crisis was unfolding.

In the early stages of the war the United States did not directly aid Iraq. Rather, it undertook to negotiate with neighboring states to ensure they stayed out of the conflict. Throughout 1980 the hostage crisis dominated U.S. foreign policy, and the Carter administration continued efforts to negotiate with Iran. When the Iraqi advance into Iran stalled and then turned into a retreat in 1982, the new U.S. administration of Ronald Reagan began to consider aiding Iraq more directly. When Iran invaded Iraq later in 1982 with the stated aim of overthrowing Saddam Hussein's regime and bringing an Islamic revolution to Iraq, the United States feared that Iraq might lose the war. Over the next five years the United States aided Iraq in its war effort in a number of ways.

Dual-Use Technology: Exports of so-called dual-use technology from the United States to Iraq became possible when Ronald Reagan removed Iraq from the list of state sponsors of terrorism in 1982. Dual-use technology consists of equipment that may have military applications as well as nonmilitary applications, including advanced computers, radar and communications equipment, and transport vehicles.

Financial Funding: Billions of dollars of credit were made available to Saddam Hussein's regime.[56]

Shared Intelligence: More direct help came in sharing U.S.-gathered intelligence about Iranian troop movements and strategic targets with the Iraqi air force[57] and ensuring that Iraq could find replacements for its Soviet-made hardware and ammunition via private arms dealers.[58]

In the closing stages of the Iran-Iraq War the United States military became involved in direct attacks on Iranian targets. In 1984, with the ground war in a stalemate, both Iran and Iraq began targeting each other's oil production and transport facilities. Iran adopted a policy of attacking any oil tanker in the Persian Gulf that was carrying Iraqi oil or that was owned by a state supporting Iraq. Iraq also attacked shipping in the Persian Gulf. In 1987 the United States offered naval protection to any vessel flying the U.S. flag after Kuwait appealed for outside help to protect its tankers. Several Kuwaiti-owned oil tankers began operating under the U.S. flag and with U.S. crews, and when one of these tankers was hit by an Iranian missile, the U.S. Navy destroyed Iranian oil platforms that were reportedly being used to direct Iranian attacks. In the same period, U.S. special forces carried out operations against Iranian vessels laying mines in the region. In 1988 a U.S. warship was damaged by an Iranian mine, prompting the United States to launch an attack on more Iranian oil platforms. In the ensuing battle U.S. forces destroyed several small Iranian gunboats, sunk an Iranian frigate, and shot down an Iranian military aircraft.

The presence of U.S. naval ships in the Persian Gulf escorting oil tankers and the high tensions created by engagements between U.S. and Iranian forces led to a tragedy that further damaged U.S.-Iranian relations. In July 1988 the USS *Vincennes,* a U.S. Navy cruiser in the Persian Gulf on escort duties, shot down an Iranian civilian passenger airline, killing all 290 passengers and crew onboard. Iran described the incident as an intentional and unlawful act that amounted to an international crime.[59] The United States maintained that the incident was an accident, affirming that the crew of the USS *Vincennes* believed the airliner was a military aircraft intending to attack them.[60]

When the Iran-Iraq War ended in August 1988, relations between Iran and the United States had plummeted further beyond the strained relations during the hostage crisis almost a decade earlier. The United States continued to support Iran's principal enemy in the region, Iraq, and little chance of reconciliation seemed possible between the U.S. and Iranian governments.

THE HEZBOLLAH-IRAN CONNECTION

Hezbollah is a Shia political and paramilitary organization that emerged in Lebanon during the early 1980s. At that time Lebanon was in the middle of a devastating civil war that lasted from 1975 until 1990. In 1982 Israeli forces invaded neighboring Lebanon to combat Palestine Liberation Organization (PLO) groups that were launching attacks across the border into Israel. Hezbollah is believed to have been formed partly as a response to this invasion. The United States regards Hezbollah as a terrorist organization and believes it is partly funded and equipped by Iran and Syria.[61]

Iranian officials have never admitted to involvement in the foundation of Hezbollah or in funding the organization, but evidence exists that links occurred between Hezbollah in the 1980s and the Iranian military. A force of Iranian Revolutionary Guard Corps were present in Lebanon in the early 1980s, and the United States believes they helped to train Hezbollah. The stated aims of Hezbollah at that time also imply close links with Iran. In a 1985 statement known as the Hezbollah Program the group declared: "We obey the orders of one leader, wise and just, that of our tutor and *faqih* (jurist) who fulfills all the necessary conditions: Ruhollah Musawi Khomeini." Ruhollah Musawi Khomeini was the Supreme Leader of Iran at the time. The statement also defined Hezbollah as "the party of God (Hizb Allah) the vanguard of which was made victorious by God in Iran."[62]

Between 1982 and 1986 a series of suicide-bomb attacks were launched against U.S., French, and Israeli forces in Lebanon. They included the April 1983 attack on the U.S. embassy in Beirut, Lebanon, that killed 63 people and the October 1983 attack on the U.S. Marine and French paratrooper barracks, also in Beirut, which killed 241 U.S. servicemen and 58 French troops. An organization calling itself Islamic Jihad claimed responsibility for the bombings,[63] but the United States believed that "Islamic Jihad" was a front for Hezbollah or a group closely affiliated with it. The United States laid part of the responsibility for the attacks on Iran. Hezbollah has always denied involvement.

Since the end of Lebanon's civil war Hezbollah has become a powerful force in Lebanese politics and a provider of social services such as schools, hospitals, and agricultural services to Lebanese Shias. Hezbollah has also been involved in a series of conflicts with Israel, which have ensured that it remains an enemy of the United States. Partly because of its continuing alleged support for Hezbollah, Iran has remained on the U.S. list of state sponsors of terrorism to the present day.

THE IRAN-CONTRA AFFAIR

At the height of the Iran-Iraq War a political scandal emerged in Washington over allegations that the administration of Ronald Reagan had sold weapons to Iran in exchange for the release of U.S. hostages held by Hezbollah in Beirut, Lebanon. The U.S. government publicly described Iran at the time as a sponsor of terrorism and had imposed a strict embargo on the sale of weapons to the country.

The aim of the U.S. plan was to facilitate the sale of weapons to a group of Iranians believed to be opposed to the regime of Ayatollah Khomeini on the understanding that this group would attempt to secure the release of U.S. hostages held by Hezbollah.[64] The sale of weapons was conducted via Israel. The plan was changed later so that the weapons were to be supplied to moderate Iranian army officers. The plan became more complicated when some of the profits from the weapon's sales were used to fund anticommunist rebels in Nicaragua known as contras. Providing military aid to the contras was prohibited under U.S. law at the time.

Investigations into the Iran-contra affair resulted in the conviction of 11 U.S. government officials, including then secretary of defense Caspar Weinberger. The scandal damaged the reputation of President Ronald Reagan, although official investigations found no evidence that he knew of or condoned any illegal actions.[65] The Iranian government viewed the affair as an indication that the United States was engaged in secret plans to undermine the regime.

THE "AXIS OF EVIL" AND THE IRANIAN NUCLEAR PROGRAM

Following the death of Iran's first Supreme Leader, Ayatollah Khomeini, a period of change and political reform took place in Iran. For a time it seemed that relations between the United States and Iran would improve, but continuing suspicions about the involvement of Iran in funding terrorism and aggressive anti-American rhetoric from Iranian leaders made the United States hesitate. In the first decade of the 21st century a new set of issues have caused tensions between the two nations. These include U.S. allegations of Iranian support for elements of the anti-American insurgency in Iraq and support for Hezbollah attacks against Israel, Iran's nuclear program, and Iranian rhetoric against Israel and other Middle Eastern states.

In January 2002 President George W. Bush made a speech in which he referred to an "axis of evil" made up of states that he described as supporting international terrorism and with ambitions to build weapons of mass destruction. President Bush included Iraq, Iran, and North Korea in the "axis of evil." Referring to so-called weapons of mass destruction, President Bush said: "Iran aggressively pursues these weapons and exports terror."[66] In the case of Iran, the weapons of mass destruction the president was referring to were primarily nuclear weapons. A Central Intelligence Agency report issued in 2003 stated: "The United States remains convinced that Tehran has been pursuing a clandestine nuclear weapons program, in violation of its obligations as a party to the Nuclear Nonproliferation Treaty (NPT)."[67] The controversy over Iran's alleged nuclear weapons program and attempts to acquire missile technology with which such weapons could be delivered dominated U.S.-Iranian relations for much of the decade. Throughout this period Iran has consistently said that its nuclear program is intended solely for the purpose of building nuclear power plants and not for weapons.

Iran began a program to build nuclear power stations in cooperation with the United States in 1957. Under President Dwight D. Eisenhower's Atoms for Peace program the United States provided enriched uranium and advanced equipment over a 10-year period to Iran. In 1968 Iran became a signatory to the Nuclear Nonproliferation Treaty, an international treaty intended to limit the spread of nuclear weapons and encourage the peaceful use of nuclear technology. France and Germany also offered help to Iran, and by the mid-1970s Iran had contracts with French and German companies to build nuclear power plants and supply fuel. The Iranian Revolution of 1979 that brought the anti-American regime of Ruhollah Khomeini to power prompted an urgent rethink by U.S. policymakers of attitudes toward Iran obtaining nuclear technology. Nuclear reactors being built by a German company were left uncompleted, and France withdrew from a contract to supply fuel. Iranian research into nuclear technology was severely hampered by these developments.

In the mid-1980s Iran began developing the means to mine and refine nuclear fuel from uranium deposits within its borders. The refining of uranium so that it can be used in nuclear reactors and weapons is known as enrichment. Uranium enrichment requires advanced technologies that are an essential part of any nuclear fuel or nuclear weapons program. The degree of enrichment needed to produce nuclear fuel is less than that needed to produce material for nuclear weapons, but the processes and technologies are similar. Uranium that has been enriched sufficiently for use as a nuclear fuel is known as low-enriched uranium (LEU), uranium that has been enriched sufficiently for use in nuclear weapons is known as highly enriched uranium (HEU). By developing the means to mine and enrich uranium Iran was developing technology that could, theoretically, be used to produce material for nuclear weapons (HEU) as well as nuclear fuel (LEU). Iran has maintained that its only aim has been to produce nuclear fuel (LEU), but the United States and other nations believe it has wanted to produce material for nuclear weapons (HEU) and has been secretly doing so.

Iran has announced some of its programs to produce LEU. It is permitted to do so under the terms of the Nuclear Nonproliferation Treaty as long as the facilities are open to inspection by the International Atomic Energy Agency (IAEA)—an autonomous organization dedicated to promoting the peaceful use of nuclear energy and stopping the spread of nuclear weapons. The IAEA has inspected Iran's uranium-enrichment facilities on several occasions and maintained that they are not capable of producing HEU. However, Iran has not always been open about its enrichment programs, particularly those that began in the 1980s. In 2003 the IAEA declared that Iran had failed to meet some of its obligations to report enrichment programs,[68] but after receiving further information from the Iranian government, it declared later the same year that Iran had submitted a "comprehensive" declaration of its nuclear program and that no evidence existed that Iran was pursuing a program to build a nuclear weapon.

The United States and other nations, including France, Germany, and the United Kingdom, remained unconvinced and called for Iran to close down all of its uranium-enrichment facilities. Iran attempted initially to reassure the United States and its allies by suspending enrichment and agreeing to additional and more extensive IAEA inspections at the end of 2003. However, in 2004 Iran reacted angrily to continued allegations that it was keeping HEU enrichment secret and restarted its suspended LEU program. The principal Iranian objection to demands that it stop enriching uranium has been to assert that it has the right, as any sovereign nation does, to pursue nuclear technology for peaceful means.

The IAEA's response to Iran restarting its enrichment program was negative but guarded. It did not, at first, support the imposition of sanctions. In 2006, with U.S. allegations of the continuing existence of an Iranian nuclear weapons program and Iran's announcement that it had successfully enriched uranium, the IAEA voted to report Iran to the United Nations Security Council for breach of the Nuclear Nonproliferation Treaty. Later the same year the United Nations Security Council issued Resolution 1696 calling on Iran to suspend all uranium enrichment or face sanctions. Iran rejected the resolution as unjustifiably restricting its right to pursue peaceful nuclear technology. In December 2006 the United Nations Security Council issued Resolution 1737 banning the export of nuclear fuel and technologies to Iran and freezing the assets of companies involved in Iran's enrichment program.[69] Two further resolutions in 2007 (Resolution 1747) and 2008 (Resolution 1803) have tightened and enlarged these restrictions. A 2009 IAEA report stated that Iran continued to enrich uranium and was allowing some, but not unlimited, inspections of its facilities. The IAEA continued to declare that it had no evidence Iran was working on producing nuclear weapons.

The U.S. invasion of Iraq in 2003 stood in the background to this intense international debate. One of the stated reasons for the invasion was to prevent Saddam Hussein acquiring and using weapons of mass destruction.[70] The fact that the United States had attacked Iraq partly because it believed Iraq had weapons of mass destruction combined with President George W. Bush's 2002 speech in which he claimed Iran was also developing weapons of mass destruction, led some Iranians to fear that the United States was planning to attack Iran after Iraq. U.S. officials have repeatedly denied any intention to attack Iran, but they have not ruled out the possibility of responding to any Iranian aggression against itself or others. Israel has also become embroiled in the crisis. It fears the possibility of Iran acquiring nuclear weapons both because Iranian leaders have frequently given speeches claiming Israel has no right to exist and because Israel, along with the United States, believes Iran is responsible for funding anti-Israeli groups such as Hezbollah and Hamas. In

Focus on the United States

1981 Israeli planes destroyed a French-built nuclear reactor in Iraq because they suspected it might be used to produce material for a nuclear weapon. In 2009 Israeli prime minister Benjamin Netanyahu stated that he would give time for U.S. negotiations with Iran over the nuclear issue to take effect, but that he would leave open the possibility of using military force to prevent Iran from obtaining nuclear weapons that could threaten Israel.[71]

A "NEW BEGINNING"?

U.S. president Barack Obama took office in 2008, and, in his inaugural speech he suggested that his administration would make greater efforts to achieve close ties with the Muslim world. In a March 2009 speech addressed to the Iranian people, Obama referred to a "new beginning" in the relationship between the United States and Iran. He also stated: "My administration is now committed to diplomacy that addresses the full range of issues before us."[72] These issues include Iran's continuing commitment to its uranium-enrichment program and U.S. and United Nations sanctions imposed because of this commitment. Other issues include Iran's support for Hezbollah and Hamas and its anti-Israeli rhetoric.

The Iranian presidential elections of June 2009 put a hold on further developments in a potential dialogue between Iran and the United States. Violent confrontations took place between supporters of opposing candidates and state security forces when it was announced that incumbent president Mahmoud Ahmadinejad had won the election by a large majority. Some sources described protests against the election results as the largest Iran has seen since the revolution of 1979.[73] Dozens of people are thought to have died in clashes with police.[74]

Iraq

The history of relations between the United States and Iraq is a history of dramatic reversals. Over the past 70 years diplomatic relations between the two countries have been severed and reestablished twice. The United States has aided Iraq in one war and fought two wars against it. Public consciousness by Americans of the U.S. relationship with Iraq came to the fore in 1990 with the buildup to the Persian Gulf War and again with the U.S.-led invasion of Iraq in 2003. The continuing occupation of Iraq by U.S. forces in the face of a violent and deadly insurgency has been the most controversial aspect of U.S. foreign policy in recent years.

The first diplomatic contact between the United States and the people of Iraq came with the appointment of the first U.S. diplomat to the Ottoman Empire, which Iraq was then part of, in 1831. The first U.S. consul in Baghdad was appointed in 1888. After the defeat and dissolution of the Ottoman

Empire at the end of World War I, the United States supported Britain's administration of Iraq as a mandate of the League of Nations on the understanding that it would eventually become independent. The United States recognized Iraq's independence in 1930 and established diplomatic relations in 1931. The U.S. legation in Iraq was upgraded to that of an embassy in 1946, reflecting the increased awareness by the United States of the strategic importance of Iraq in the post–World War II period. In 1958 the United States recognized the formation of the Arab Union—a union between Iraq and Jordan. The Arab Union was dissolved later the same year.

REVOLUTIONS IN IRAQ, 1958–1968

When Iraq became fully independent from British administration in 1932 it was ruled by Hashemite kings. During World War II Britain invaded Iraq and restored the monarchy after the government led by Rashid Ali al-Qailani seemed likely to establish links with the Axis powers. The Hashemite Dynasty remained in power until 1958 when it was overthrown in a military coup that brought Abdul Karim Qassim to power.

In 1955 the United States engineered the formation of the Central Treaty Organization (CENTO), also known as the Baghdad Pact. CENTO was a mutual defense organization intended to prevent the spread of Soviet influence in the Middle East. Iraq became a founding member in 1955 along with Iran, Pakistan, Turkey, and the United Kingdom. Following the 1958 coup in Iraq, Abdul Karim Qassim withdrew from CENTO and formed close ties with the Soviet Union. A contributing factor behind the coup was dislike among elements of Iraqi society of the monarchy's pro-Western stance. Iraq's withdrawal from CENTO constituted a major blow to Washington's Middle East strategy. The United States maintained relations with Iraq but began to develop much closer links with Iran and Saudi Arabia to compensate for increased Soviet influence in Iraq.

In 1963 a second military coup carried out by army officers affiliated with the Baath Party overthrew the government of Abdul Karim Qassim and brought Abdul Salam Arif to power. The Baath Party was a pan-Arab organization founded in Syria in the 1940s with branches in several Arab states. Speculation has since been raised that the United States helped the coup leaders topple Abdul Karim Qassim's anti-American government.[75] Abdul Salam Arif soon fell out with Baathist members of his cabinet and sacked them. In 1968 a third coup brought the Baath Party to power under Ahmed Hasan Al-Bakr. Saddam Hussein, who was a young Baath Party member involved in the 1963 coup, became Iraq's president in 1979. According to some reports, Saddam Hussein had been employed by the U.S. Central Intelligence Agency since 1963 because he was seen as a useful tool against communism in Iraq.[76]

Diplomatic relations between Iraq and the United States were broken off in 1967 over U.S. support for Israel in the 1967 Arab-Israeli War, but they were partially reestablished in 1972.

THE IRAN-IRAQ WAR

As Saddam Hussein came to power in Iraq the long relationship the United States enjoyed with neighboring Iran was coming to an end. Iran's 1979 Islamic revolution brought the fanatically anti-American regime of Ruhollah Musavi Khomeini to power. The same year also saw the start of the Iranian hostage crisis, in which Iranian revolutionaries held more than 50 U.S. embassy staff for 444 days, further souring U.S.-Iranian relations.

When Saddam Hussein invaded Iran in 1980 the United States remained neutral. The crisis in relations between Iran and the United States emboldened Saddam Hussein to attack Iran, safe in the knowledge that the United States would not leap to its defense. From the point of view of the United States Iraq's invasion was convenient—it had the potential to topple Khomeini's regime or at least to keep the regime too occupied to export its revolution beyond Iran's borders.

Though at first successful, Iraq's invasion soon lost momentum and ground to a halt. By 1982 Iran had gone on the offensive and began pushing Iraqi forces back. When Iranian forces crossed into Iraq in pursuit of the retreating Iraqi army, the United States began to fear the possibility of an Iranian victory. If an Iranian triumph had led to the collapse of Saddam Hussein's government and the establishment of an Iranian-backed regime in Baghdad, it would have been disastrous for U.S. strategic policy in the Middle East. Iran's chief-of-staff said the country should "continue the war until Saddam Hussein is overthrown so that we can pray at Karbala and Jerusalem."[77] Rather than risk such an outcome, the United States made rapid moves to aid Iraq's war effort.[78]

Although U.S. support for Iraq's war effort was open, little public comment was heard outside the Senate and House of Representatives. In 1982 the administration of President Ronald Reagan removed Iraq from the U.S. list of state sponsors of terrorism. Although an embargo on U.S. companies supplying arms to either side in the conflict was in place, this move enabled the sale of so-called dual-use technology to Iraq. Dual-use technology includes equipment that can be used for both military and nonmilitary purposes, such as computers, radar and communications equipment, and transport vehicles. Ronald Reagan sent a special envoy to the Middle East, Donald Rumsfeld, to Baghdad in 1983 and 1984 to discuss closer relations between Iraq and the United States. Full diplomatic relations between the two countries were restored in 1984 following Rumsfeld's second visit. The United States began sharing military intelligence with Iraq early in the conflict, and Washington extended billions of dollars of credit to Saddam Hussein, ostensibly for agricultural development, that was used to buy arms via private arms suppliers.[79]

In retrospect, one of the most controversial questions surrounding U.S. support for Iraq during the Iran-Iraq War is the degree to which the United States was aware of Iraq's use of chemical weapons against Iran and against Kurdish Iraqis. Some sources claim that the United States was not only aware of their use but also aided in their deployment against Iranian forces.[80] In 1994 it was revealed that the United States had also sold Iraq biological materials that could be used to develop biological weapons.[81] In the runup to the 2003 invasion of Iraq, the administration of George W. Bush claimed that Iraq possessed weapons of mass destruction, including chemical and biological weapons. Critics pointed out that Iraq had probably first obtained the materials to build such weapons from the United States during the Iran-Iraq War.

THE PERSIAN GULF WAR

Just two years after the end of the Iran-Iraq War a new crisis erupted in U.S.-Iraqi relations. In August 1990 Iraqi forces invaded and quickly occupied neighboring Kuwait. The Kingdom of Kuwait is one of the world's leading producers of oil, and animosity had existed between the kingdom and its much larger Iraqi neighbor for decades. Using the powerful forces it had built up with the help of U.S. funding, Iraq had precipitated exactly the kind of crisis in the oil-rich Persian Gulf States that the United States had been trying to avoid by aiding Iraq against Iran. The United States broke off diplomatic relation with Iraq in February 1991 as it prepared to lead a coalition of forces to liberate Kuwait. Starting from bases in Saudi Arabia, U.S. and British forces swiftly overwhelmed Iraqi forces and pursued them deep into Iraq. Within a few days coalition forces drove to within 150 miles of Baghdad and had thoroughly destroyed the Iraqi army. President George H. W. Bush declared a cease-fire and withdrew U.S. forces from Iraq. The decision not to continue the advance and force Saddam Hussein out of power was criticized later when the United States faced a second war with Iraq in 2003. Immediately after the 1991 war the United States encouraged opposition groups in Iraq to overthrow Saddam Hussein.[82] Revolts by Kurds in the north and Shia groups in the south were brutally put down by Iraqi forces, and the United States faced criticism for not supporting them.

Iraq's invasion of Kuwait created profound difficulties in relations between the United States and other Arab-Muslim countries. Saudi Arabia agreed to host the large buildup of U.S. and other Western military personnel and equipment on its territory even though Saudi Arabians and other Arab Muslims were uncomfortable having an army of foreign, non-Muslim troops on the Arabian Peninsula—a region that is particularly sensitive to Muslims because it is the location of the two holiest sites in Islam. Saudi Arabia agreed to host the forces partly because it feared Iraqi forces might push on from Kuwait into its own territory, despite criticism of its decision among voices in the wider Muslim world. During assemblage of the U.S.-led coalition, Saddam Hussein offered to withdraw from Kuwait on the condition that Israel withdrew from the West Bank, Golan Heights, and Gaza Strip. The offer constituted an attempt to drive a wedge between the United States and Muslim nations that were supporting the buildup in Saudi Arabia. Perceived support for Israel by the United States serves as a source of anger and resentment for many in Muslim nations. By reminding them of this issue Saddam Hussein hoped to make these states think twice about supporting America in a war against another Muslim country. The strategy failed, but it served as a reminder of the degree of delicacy required of U.S. diplomacy in dealing with the Muslim world.

THE IRAQ LIBERATION ACT

In 1998 the administration of President Bill Clinton signed the Iraq Liberation Act into law. The act made it U.S. policy to support efforts to remove the regime of Saddam Hussein and encourage the establishment of a democratic system of government in Iraq. The justifications for the act included statements that Iraq had violated international law, failed to keep agreements made with the United States at the end of the Persian Gulf War, and failed to comply with United Nations Security Council resolutions. Specifically these points referred to claims that Iraq was stockpiling biological and chemical weapons and pursuing the development of nuclear weapons. Between 1991 and 1998 the United Nations Special Commission on Iraq (UNSCOM) sent weapons inspectors into Iraq to find and destroy Iraq's large stockpiles of biological and chemical weapons. Although the inspectors were able to locate and order the destruction of many of these stores, Iraqi officials became increasing uncooperative as the years passed. By 1998 UNSCOM inspectors were still unsatisfied that Iraq was free of chemical and biological weapons, and they were withdrawn. The Iraq Liberation Act was a direct response to continuing suspicions that Iraq had secretly retained some of its biological and chemical weapon capabilities and was hiding them from UNSCOM inspectors.

In December 1998 the United States and Britain carried out four days of intensive bombing of Iraqi military and government targets in an attempt to disrupt Iraqi rearmament. Throughout 1999 American and British planes conducted regular raids against targets in the northern no-fly zone—a demilitarized zone in northern Iraq mandated after the Persian Gulf War to help protect Iraqi Kurds from government attacks.

THE 2003 INVASION OF IRAQ

The commitment to regime change in Iraq, which had been introduced into U.S. policy by the Iraq Liberation Act, became firmer under the new administration of George W. Bush. The United States wanted to invade Iraq for two main reasons. The first reason was a continuing suspicion that Iraq had weapons of mass destruction that could be used to threaten its neighbors. The second reason was the belief that Iraq was supporting terrorist groups. In the aftermath of the September 11 attacks on the United States President George W. Bush linked action against Iraq with the wider war on terror. In a speech to the United Nations Security Council U.S. secretary of state Colin Powell alleged ties existed between the Iraqi government and a Jordanian named Abu Musab al-Zarqawi, whom he linked to al-Qaeda.[83]

The United States was the driving force behind the United Nations Security Council's decision to pass Resolution 1441, which gave Iraq a final chance to comply with the disarmament agreements it had signed after the Persian Gulf War. President George W. Bush began pressing the United Nations Security Council to support military action against Iraq in September 2002.[84] Staff of the United Nations Monitoring, Verification and Inspection Commission (UNMOVIC) and International Atomic Energy Agency inspectors were sent to Iraq to verify Iraqi compliance. Both groups failed to find any evidence that Iraq had undeclared weapons.[85, 86] In October 2002 Congress passed the Authorization for Use of Military Force Against Iraq Resolution (also known as the Iraq Resolution), which authorized the president to use U.S. forces against Iraq. The United States and its allies continued trying to persuade the United Nations Security Council that military action against Iraq was justified, but these efforts failed. Some Security Council members remained unconvinced that Iraq had weapons of mass destruction or supported continuation of diplomatic efforts rather than approve a war. The U.S.-led coalition launched its invasion of Iraq in March 2003 without United Nations Security Council (UNSC) support. The United States and its allies maintained that the invasion was justified because Iraq was already in breach of earlier UNSC resolutions.

Hundreds of thousands of U.S. troops, tens of thousands of British troops, and smaller contingents from Australia, Spain, Denmark, and Poland advanced swiftly into Iraq. Coalition forces were inside Baghdad about three weeks from the start of the invasion, effectively ending Saddam Hussein's regime. Many Iraqi government officials and military units surrendered or disbanded without opposing the invasion. In May 2003 the United States and its allies established the Coalition Provisional Authority (CPA) as a transitional government in Iraq. In June the CPA set up the Iraqi Governing Council consisting of Iraqi politicians, religious figures, and tribal leaders as an advisory body under CPA authority. The CPA remained the government of Iraq until the establishment of the Iraqi Interim Government in 2004, which was superceded by the Iraqi Transitional Government in 2005. The Iraqi Interim Government was appointed by the elected Iraqi National Assembly. Elections to the National Assembly marked the first general election held in Iraq since the invasion of 2003. A permanent government took power in 2006 following a second general election. The United States reestablished diplomatic relations with Iraq in 2004 following the official transfer of sovereignty from the CPA to the Iraqi Interim Government.

THE IRAQI INSURGENCY

The U.S.-led campaign to overthrow Saddam Hussein's regime was a quick and comprehensive success. Saddam Hussein was effectively out of power within a few weeks of the invasion in 2003, and he was later captured by U.S. forces. Unfortunately the victory over Saddam Hussein did not lead quickly to the establishment of a democratic and peaceful Iraq. After the successful overthrow of Saddam Hussein, the United States and its allies became embroiled in violent civil unrest. Dozens of Iraqi factions fought each other and the occupying forces for years after the invasion. The combination of an insurgency against U.S. troops in Iraq and bitter political and religious infighting between elements of Iraqi society made U.S. efforts to reshape Iraq into the democratic society it had envisioned before the war extremely difficult.

After the fall of Saddam Hussein a complex political situation emerged as differing factions tried to gain power and eject the occupying forces. The main groups were Shia militias, Sunni militias, former Baath Party members, Iraqi nationalists opposed to the former Baath regime, Muslim fighters from other Middle Eastern countries (such as Egypt, Syria, and Saudi Arabia), secular political groups, and nonviolent activists. Alliances and enmities between these groups shifted frequently making the situation even more complex. In addition, many Iraqis were willing to work with the Coalition Provisional Authority and the series of governments that succeeded it.

U.S. policy in Iraq had four main pillars throughout the insurgency. The first was a commitment to building democratic institutions in Iraq that could eventually produce a consensus government; the second was the continued presence of a large military force to support the new democratic institutions; the third was the formation and training of a new Iraqi army and police force that could eventually replace coalition troops; and the fourth was massive investment in rebuilding Iraq's industrial infrastructure. The insurgency and political infighting in Iraq made all of these policies difficult to implement. The formation of a consensus government proved extremely difficult in a climate in which some groups were prepared to use violence to support their aims. The continued presence of a large number of coalition troops drew violent attacks on those troops and involved the United States in military counterinsurgency operations that were highly controversial in the international community. Forming a new Iraqi army and police force was also difficult in an environment in which insurgents targeted Iraqis seen as cooperating with the occupiers. U.S. investment in Iraq was also controversial since many Iraqis were frustrated by the slow progress of efforts to restore public services such as water and electricity, and many critics accused the U.S. government of allowing private U.S. corporations to profit excessively from reconstruction contracts.

The continued U.S. involvement in Iraq became a major political difficulty for the administration of George W. Bush. Those Americans who had opposed the war before it began became more angry as the occupation continued year after year. Public opinion was also adversely affected by the steady stream of casualties suffered by U.S. forces in a conflict that seemed to have no clear end in sight. Reports of abuses committed by U.S. forces against Iraqi civilians also made many Americans uneasy. In 2008 the United States and Iraq signed an agreement that called for the complete withdrawal of U.S. forces from Iraq by the end of 2011. In 2009 President Barack Obama announced that most U.S. troops would be out of Iraq by mid-2010 and all of them by the end of 2011.

THE POST-INSURGENCY ERA

The United States is likely to remain closely involved with Iraq for decades to come. U.S. companies have invested billions of dollars in the country, and the new U.S. embassy in Baghdad is one of the largest and most expensive ever built. In the immediate aftermath of the 2003 invasion the U.S. government spent approximately $20 billion on reconstruction projects, much of which went to U.S. contractors and was concentrated on Iraqi oil and gas infrastructure.[87] Foreign investment (including U.S. investment) in Iraq plummeted during the period from 2005 until 2007 when the violence of the insurgency was at its height. Since 2007, however, investment has grown rapidly. In 2007 foreign investment in Iraq was about $2.7 billion, and in 2008 it leaped to $43 billion.[88] A great deal of this investment came from countries other than the United States. The United Arab Emirates was the largest investor in 2008, the United States second, and the United Kingdom third. Other large and growing sources of investment include China, Turkey, and western Europe.[89] Some U.S. economic commentators warned that U.S. companies were in danger of losing the opportunity to make profitable investments in an Iraq where greater political stability had been won at the cost of U.S. lives. From a broader perspective the U.S. government is keen to promote trade and investment. It is hoped that by tying Iraq more closely to world trade, Iraq's wealth and stability will improve, both of which are likely to produce an Iraq with a greater interest in friendship with the United States. Given the ongoing tensions between the United States and Iraq's neighbor, Iran, a stable and friendly Iraq is desirable for the United States.

Saudi Arabia

The relationship between the United States and Saudi Arabia is one of the closest that the United States has developed with any Middle Eastern nation other than Israel. Like the association of the United States with Israel, historians, journalists, and public officials have often described it as a "special relationship." Also like the U.S.-Israel relationship, that with Saudi Arabia has never been without its tensions and is often misunderstood. Many Americans believe that the unwritten contract between the United States and Saudi Arabia constitutes a mutual exchange—a guarantee of protection on the part of the United States met with a guarantee of access to Saudi Arabia's oil. The truth is more complex and has changed over time.

Modern Saudi Arabia was founded as a kingdom by Abdul Aziz al-Saud (better known as Ibn Saud) in 1928. At that time it was known as the Kingdom of Hejaz and Nejd, only becoming formally unified as the Kingdom of Saudi Arabia in 1932. The United States recognized Saudi Arabia in 1931 and established diplomatic relations; but, at first, it had little interest in close ties. Following the discovery of oil in neighboring Bahrain in 1932, Saudi Arabia granted permission for the California Arabian Standard Oil Company (Casoc) to prospect for oil reserves in its territory. Casoc was a wholly owned subsidiary of Standard Oil of California (known as Chevron today). The Texas Oil Company (known as Texaco today) bought a 50 percent share of Casoc in 1936, and in 1938 Casoc discovered the first commercially viable oil field in Saudi Arabia. Casoc was renamed the Arabian American Oil Company (Aramco) in 1944.

The steady growth of its oil exporting industry brought welcome economic benefits to Saudi Arabia, which had few other natural resources, and proof of its oil reserves increased U.S. awareness of the strategic importance of the country.

WORLD WAR II AND THE FOUNDATION OF ISRAEL

The oil production facilities at Dhahran on Saudi Arabia's Persian Gulf coast were strategically important to the U.S. war effort and were bombed by the

Italian air force early in the conflict. Fearing further attacks might destroy their nascent oil industry and dissuade Muslim pilgrims from visiting Mecca, Saudi Arabia gave permission for the United States to establish a military airfield on Saudi territory. This base was used to protect Saudi Arabia and to facilitate U.S. operations in Iran and the Soviet Union.

The first tensions in the relationship between the United States and Saudi Arabia arose over proposals to create a Jewish state in Palestine. Saudi Arabia was highly respected in the Muslim world both because it was the site of Mecca and Medina, the two holiest sites in Islam, and because the Arabian Peninsula was regarded as the historical homeland of the Arabs. The Saudi royal family was one of the leading voices opposed to the idea of a Jewish homeland in the region. This brought them into conflict with successive U.S. administrations, which favored the concept. The United States took the position with Saudi Arabia that, though Washington supported a Jewish state, it would not help to create one. Combined with U.S. military assistance during World War II, this position allowed the relationship between the two countries to survive the establishment of Israel in 1948.

THE COLD WAR AND SAUDI-EGYPTIAN RELATIONS

In the decades immediately following World War II the top priority of the United States in its relations with Muslim countries was to prevent the Soviet Union from securing an influence over them. For the United States, Saudi Arabia was one of the most important of these states both because of its oil reserves and because of the influence of the Saudi royal family in the region. In 1947 President Harry S. Truman assured Saudi Arabia that the kingdom's independence constituted a cornerstone of U.S. foreign policy, and in 1951 the United States and Saudi Arabia signed the Mutual Defense Assistance Agreement. Under this agreement the United States gave military training and equipment to Saudi forces and established a permanent United States Military Training Mission, which continues to operate to the present day.

When Abdul Aziz Al Saud died in 1953 his eldest son became King Saud. His reign was to be a difficult period in the "special relationship." At that time the voice of Egypt's Gamal Abdel Nasser grew increasingly influential in the Arab-Muslim world. Nasser was a leading figure of Arab Nationalism, a political movement that wanted to reduce the influence of Western powers over Arab nations. In 1952 Nasser led a revolution in Egypt that overthrew the pro-Western government of King Farouk and abolished the monarchy. After becoming president of Egypt in 1956, Nasser encouraged Arab nationalists in other countries, including Saudi Arabia, to overthrow regimes that he believed were too strongly influenced by the West. King Saud, who came to the throne in Saudi Arabia the year after the Egyptian revolution, was frequently criticized by Arab nationalists for his extravagant personal spending and for allowing a continued U.S. military presence in his country. Saudi Arabia in turn sponsored antirevolutionary propaganda in Egypt.

In 1962 a revolution inspired by Arab nationalists overthrew the Yemeni royal family and established the Yemen Arab Republic. Saudi Arabia grew alarmed at this development in its neighbor and became even more worried when Egypt began providing troops and equipment to the Yemeni nationalist government in its continuing conflict with royalist forces. Saudi Arabia supported the royalists and gave them money to purchase weapons. During the war Egypt stationed as many as 70,000 troops in Yemen as well as fighter aircraft and bombers. Egypt had close links with the Soviet Union at this time, and the United States grew concerned about the conflict spreading into Saudi Arabia, which would give the Soviets a foothold on the peninsula. In 1963 U.S. president John F. Kennedy responded to a Saudi request for help by deploying warplanes to Saudi Arabia and setting up a training program for Saudi forces.[90, 91] The Yemen conflict dragged on until 1970 and ended with victory for the nationalists, who quickly established relations with the Soviet Union. The presence of a Soviet stronghold on Saudi Arabia's southern border strengthened U.S. determination to protect the kingdom.

THE 1973 ARAB-ISRAELI CONFLICT AND OIL CRISIS

U.S.-Saudi relations reached their lowest point during the 1973 Arab-Israeli War (also known as the Yom Kippur War). The war began when Egyptian and Syrian forces attacked across cease-fire lines that had been drawn after the 1967 Arab Israeli War (or Six Day War). Saudi Arabia knew about the planned invasion and gave Egypt money and weapons to help Cairo defeat Israel.[92] They also promised to cut off oil supplies to any country that helped Israel, including the United States. By this time the Saudi oil industry was so large that it effectively controlled the world's spare capacity for supplying oil. Saudi Arabia was angry with the United States because it had not changed its policy of giving aid to Israel after Egypt had expelled Soviet forces from its territory in 1970. The Saudis felt that this move by Egypt reduced the Soviet threat in the Middle East and that the United States therefore did not need to continue protecting Israel. In a television interview in May of 1973, King Faisal said: "America's complete support for Zionism and against the Arabs makes it extremely difficult for us to continue to supply the United States with oil, or even to remain friends with the United States."[93] At the same time, Washington officials were publicly warning that the United States might use force to seize oil wells in Saudi Arabia or other Arab countries if an embargo were put in place.[94]

In the first days of the 1973 war the United States expected Israel's armed forces to easily defeat Egypt and Syria, as they had done in 1967. When it became obvious that this was not going to happen, the United States decided to quickly supply Israel with the weapons and ammunition it would need to survive. It did so partly out of fear that Israel might use nuclear weapons, which might then cause the Soviet Union to intervene. Days after the decision to help Israel was announced, Saudi Arabia and other oil-producing Arab nations stopped all oil supplies to the United States. The effect on the economy of the United States was quick and disastrous. The United States was still able to supply oil to meet its domestic needs from its own oil reserves, but there were shortages, and the sudden rise in the price of oil caused by reduced supply produced an economic crisis. Oil prices continued to rise throughout the 1970s even though the oil embargo ended after only a few months. The embargo was one factor that caused the United States and other industrialized nations to begin looking for other sources of oil and energy.

Israel won the 1973 war without using nuclear weapons. The oil embargo continued until March 1974 after which relations between the United States and Saudi Arabia slowly improved. Saudi Arabia had shown that it had the power to hurt the U.S. economy, but it never used the oil weapon again. From the point of view of the Saudis the embargo did not work, and they feared using it again might damage the future market for their oil.

THE PERSIAN GULF WAR AND OSAMA BIN LADEN

When Iraq invaded Kuwait in August 1990 the United States grew alarmed that Iraqi forces might continue into neighboring Saudi Arabia and gain control of its oil fields. A small contingent of U.S. military personnel was stationed in Saudi Arabia at the time, as there had been since the 1951 Mutual Defense Assistance Agreement, but the United States recognized that it needed to deploy a very large force in the kingdom if it was to deter Iraq from invading Saudi Arabia and go on to liberate Kuwait. The presence of U.S. forces had always been unpopular with most Saudi citizens because they found it offensive to have non-Muslim soldiers on their soil. Since the 1950s the problem had been relatively minor since the number of troops was small, but the sudden arrival of hundreds of thousands of U.S. troops in the kingdom was always going to be controversial.

Three days after the invasion of Kuwait, U.S. secretary of defense Dick Cheney visited Kind Fahd to discuss the deployment and told the king: "After the danger is over, our forces will go home."[95] After the war was won and Kuwait liberated, however, they did not go home. Strong U.S. and coalition forces remained in Saudi Arabia for more than a decade until the Second Gulf War in 2003. Their continued presence in the kingdom was justified by the argument that Iraq had to be contained or it would threaten invasion again. The Saudi government reluctantly agreed, but some elements

72

of Saudi society became increasingly angry. Public opinion in Saudi Arabia stood strongly against U.S. forces staying in the kingdom, and demonstrations broke out and written attacks launched against the Saudi royal family, especially among younger Saudi citizens. In 1995 terrorists bombed a military training facility in Riyadh killing seven people, five of whom were U.S. soldiers. The following year, 19 U.S. military personnel were killed by another terrorist bomb in Dhahran. The bombings in Riyadh and Dhahran signified a growing dissatisfaction among some groups in Saudi Arabia. These groups had strongly traditionalist views of Islam and regarded the Saudi royal family as corrupt and too much under the influence of the United States.

During the 1990s the United States began pursuing suspected terrorists in the Middle East, including Osama bin Laden, the leader of the so-called al-Qaeda organization, who was born in Saudi Arabia into a wealthy family. Osama bin Laden had frequently spoken against the Saudi royal family and the presence of U.S. forces in Saudi Arabia. The United States suspected him of involvement in the bombing of a hotel in Aden, Yemen, which was intended to kill U.S. troops on their way to Somalia. Although both the United States and Saudi Arabia were keen to end Osama bin Laden's activities, their efforts were not well coordinated, which led to frustration on the part of the Americans. By 1992 Osama bin Laden was living in Sudan, where he continued his attacks on the Saudi royal family. Saudi Arabia stripped Osama bin Laden of his Saudi citizenship in 1992, and the United States put pressure on the government of Sudan to expel him from the country. Saudi Arabia refused to request the extradition of Osama bin Laden from Sudan, making it possible for him to travel to Afghanistan in 1996. At the same time the Saudi government was giving financial aid to the Taliban regime in Afghanistan, which welcomed Osama bin Laden and gave him safe refuge.

Relations between the United States and Saudi Arabia during this period were characterized by a lack of coordination and trust that had serious consequences for the United States in 2001. These difficulties can be seen as stemming from the tensions created by the continued presence of American troops in Saudi Arabia. On one hand the Saudi government recognized the wisdom of hosting strong U.S. forces against possible Iraqi aggression, while on the other it wanted to show the rest of the Muslim world that Saudi Arabia was not willing to do whatever the United States wanted. At the same time the efforts of President Bill Clinton's administration to solve the Palestinian issue and put in place a Middle East peace deal helped to keep Saudi Arabia friendly.

THE SEPTEMBER 11, 2001, ATTACKS

Fifteen of the 19 hijackers who killed more than 3,000 people in the September 11, 2001, attacks were Saudi Arabian. Although the terrorists appeared to be loyal to Osama bin Laden, who had been stripped of his Saudi citizenship nine years earlier, and the Saudi government was in no way involved in the plot, the attacks were a great shock to U.S.-Saudi relations. The September 11 incidents took place at a time when relations between the United States and Saudi Arabia were already at a low point. The Clinton administration's Middle East peace plan failed to bring Israeli prime minister Ehud Barak and Palestinian leader Yasser Arafat together in agreement at the Camp David Summit in July 2000. Attempts to revive the plan were undermined by the Second Intifada (or Al-Aqsa Intifada), which began in September 2000. The Second Intifada was a violent uprising by Palestinians living in the territories of the Palestinian Authority and Arab citizens living in Israel against what they regarded as occupation and oppression by Israel. Palestinians staged strikes and mass demonstrations as well as launching armed attacks on Israeli forces and civilians. Israel responded by restricting the movement of Palestinians through checkpoints and imposing economic sanctions on the Palestinian Authority. Israeli forces killed more than 300 Palestinians in the first months of the Intifada, and a much smaller number of Israelis were killed by Palestinian actions.

The breakdown of the peace process and the deaths of many Palestinians at the hands of Israeli forces caused public anger in Saudi Arabia and frustration in the Saudi government. The long-standing issue of perceived U.S. support for Israel once again became a hot issue. At the same time Saudi expectations that the new U.S. administration of George W. Bush would mark a return to the closeness they had enjoyed under the administration of his father, George H. W. Bush, during the Persian Gulf War proved not to be forthcoming. When U.S. and British warplanes based in Saudi Arabia launched a major attack on Iraqi installations in January 2001 without first informing the Saudi government, it brought the delicate issue of the continuing presence of U.S. forces in the kingdom to the fore once again. A senior Saudi prince said at the time that the "reputation of the United States in the Arab region has dropped to zero."[96] The United States was shocked by public celebrations of the September 11 attacks in Saudi Arabia and other Arab countries[97] even though the governments of these countries officially condemned the attacks. These factors combined to cool U.S.-Saudi relations to the point where they were polite but shallow.

WAR IN AFGHANISTAN TO THE PRESENT

In the immediate aftermath of the September 11 attacks the United States laid plans to overthrow the Taliban regime in Afghanistan that had sheltered Osama bin Laden and his organization. Saudi Arabia was the obvious place from which to launch air attacks against the Taliban in preparation for an invasion, but the Saudi government made it clear that it would refuse permission to do so. The Saudi royal family worried that public opinion would turn against them, as it had done after the Persian Gulf War, if they were seen to be helping the United States to attack another Muslim nation. However, the Saudi government did cut financial and diplomatic links with the Taliban.

Public actions in Saudi Arabia and the United States added to difficulties in the relations between the two countries. In Saudi Arabia some sources repeatedly expressed doubts that Saudi citizens had been involved in the September 11 attacks,[98] and a charity telethon was held to raise money for the families of Palestinians killed in the Intifada, including those of suicide bombers,[99] angering the United States, which regarded such actions as support for terrorism. The arrest and detention of several Saudi citizens at the Guantánamo Bay Naval Station in Cuba also caused resentment in the kingdom. Tourism to the United States from Saudi Arabia dropped dramatically, popular boycotts of U.S.-made products were staged, and Saudi companies withdrew large investments from the United States.[100] Journalists in the United States published articles in the aftermath of September 11 accusing the Saudi government of encouraging anti-American feeling in order to dampen dissent against the regime, and U.S. commentators criticized the Saudis for failing to deal with dangerous radicals such as Osama bin Laden.[101] U.S. public attitudes toward Saudi Arabia fell even further in the wake of reports describing the Saudi regime as undemocratic and oppressive toward women and minorities.[102]

Direct military intervention by the United States in Afghanistan in 2001 and in Iraq in 2003 has prevented the rebuilding of close relations with Saudi Arabia. Saudi public opinion is strongly against U.S. involvement in Muslim countries whatever the motivation. An opinion poll taken in Saudi Arabia in early 2002 found that 64 percent of Saudis had a negative view of the United States.[103] Continuing violence between Palestinians and Israelis has also had a negative effect in Saudi Arabia, where most people think the United States does too much to support and defend Israel and too little to help the Palestinians. Another opinion poll in 2002 found that 87 percent of Saudis disliked U.S. policy toward the Palestinians.[104] Many Saudis also expressed vociferous opposition to the U.S.-led invasion of Iraq in 2003. Opinion polls from 2003 showed that 81 percent of Saudis were against U.S. policy in Iraq and 94 percent had a negative view of U.S. policy toward the Palestinians.[105] In 2003 and 2004 a series of terrorist attacks against U.S. citizens and installations in Saudi Arabia shocked the kingdom and strengthened attitudes that it would be better if U.S. forces left. Many of the victims of these attacks were Saudi bystanders.

In the U.S. action against Iraq, the Saudi government at first opposed use of the American air base in the kingdom to attack Iraq. Just one month before

U.S. bombings began in March 2003 the Saudis agreed to allow attacks to be launched from Saudi Arabia. In return, the United States agreed to withdraw almost all of its forces from the kingdom once the air war was over. In April the United States Combined Air Operations Center (CAOC) was relocated from Prince Sultan Air Base in Saudi Arabia to Al Udeid Air Base in Qatar. By the end of the year just 500 U.S. service personnel were left in Saudi Arabia. The U.S. government was criticized at home for this move because it was seen by some as giving in to one of the demands made by Osama bin Laden—that foreign forces should leave Saudi soil. For the Saudi government, however, the move has lessened criticism from political opponents and made relations with other Arab states easier.

Since the end of the war to remove Saddam Hussein from power, U.S.-Saudi relations have improved slowly but they remain tense. The continued occupation of Iraq by U.S. forces and the ongoing U.S. military operation in Afghanistan engender anti-American feelings in Saudi Arabia. Israeli actions in the Palestinian territories and Lebanon have also kept tensions high. On the other hand the administration of George W. Bush made great efforts to reassure the Saudis that America remained a firm ally. George W. Bush visited Saudi Arabia twice in 2008, and Saudi king Abdullah visited the United States in 2005 and 2008. King Abdullah has also reinstated programs to pay for thousands of Saudi students to study in the United States.

The issues that have dominated U.S.-Saudi relations for much of the past 80 years remain much the same at the end of the first decade of the 21st century. The Saudis now own their oil-producing and oil-exporting facilities, and the United States today exploits other sources of oil, but the sheer size of Saudi Arabia's oil resources make it impossible for the United States to ignore the country's strategic importance. Thanks to its oil wealth Saudi Arabia now has a large and well-equipped military of its own, but it still faces threats against which only the United States can protect it. Unfriendly regimes in Iran are one. The vulnerability of ships carrying Saudi oil through the Persian Gulf is another. As long as Saudi Arabia remains the world's largest oil producer and the United States the world's largest oil consumer and military superpower, both countries will endeavor to find ways to make their relationship work.

---

[1] Worldpublicopinion.org. Dr. Steven Kull. "Negative Attitudes toward the United States in the Muslim World: Do They Matter?" Testimony of Dr. Steven Kull Director, Program on International Policy Attitudes, May 17, 2007.

[2] BBC.co.uk. "World View of US's Role 'Worse." January 23, 2007. Available online. URL: http://news.bbc.co.uk/2/hi/americas/6286755.stm. Accessed August 28, 2009.

[3] "Muslim Public Opinion on US Policy, Attacks on Civilians and al Qaeda." *The Program on International Policy Attitudes at the University of Maryland*, Sections 1 and 2, April 24, 2007.

Focus on the United States

[4] "Muslim Public Opinion on US Policy, Attacks on Civilians and al Qaeda." *The Program on International Policy Attitudes at the University of Maryland,* Sections 3 and 6, April 24, 2007.

[5] "Muslim Public Opinion on US Policy, Attacks on Civilians and al Qaeda." *The Program on International Policy Attitudes at the University of Maryland,* Section 8, April 24, 2007.

[6] "The Great Divide: How Westerners and Muslims View Each Other." *Pew Global Attitudes Project,* June 22, 2006.

[7] BBC.co.uk. "Obama Reaches Out to Muslim World." June 4, 2009. Available online. URL: http://news.bbc.co.uk/2/hi/middle_east/8082676.stm. Accessed August 28, 2009.

[8] ———. "Iran Marks Ayatollah Khomeini Anniversary." June 4, 2009. Available online. URL: http://news.bbc.co.uk/2/hi/middle_east/8082386.stm. Accessed August 28, 2009.

[9] City University of New York. "Religious Identification Survey." December 19, 2001.

[10] Karen Jacobs Sparks. *Encyclopedia Britannica 2006.* "The 2005 Annual Megacensus of Religions." Chicago: Encyclopedia Britannica, 2006.

[11] Ihsan Bagby, Paul M. Perl, and Bryan T. Froehle. "The Mosque in America: A National Portrait." Council on American-Islamic Relations, Washington, D.C., April 26, 2001.

[12] Hugh Thomas. *The Slave Trade.* New York: Simon & Schuster, 1997.

[13] Michael A. Gomez. "Muslims in Early America." *Journal of Southern History,* 60, no. 4, November 1994.

[14] Michael Koszegi and J. Gordon Melton. *Islam in North America: A Sourcebook.* New York: Garland Publishing, 1992, pp. 26–27.

[15] Amadou Mahtar M Bow and M. Ali Kettani. *Islam and Muslims In the American Continent. Dialogue of Cultures and Religions.* Beirut: Center of Historical, Economical and Social Studies, 2001, p. 109.

[16] Steven A. Camarota. "The Muslim Wave—Dealing with Immigration from the Middle East." *National Review,* 54, no. 17: 24, 2002.

[17] ———. *Immigrants in the United States, 2007: A Profile of America's Foreign-Born Population.* Washington, D.C.: Center for Immigration Studies, 2007.

[18] Philippa Strum and Danielle Tarantolo. *Muslims in the United States: Demography, Beliefs, Institutions.* Washington, D.C.: Woodrow Wilson International Center for Scholars, 2003.

[19] Gallup and the Muslim West Facts Project. "Muslim Americans: A National Portrait." Available online. URL: http://www.muslimwestfacts.com/mwf/116074/Muslim-Americans-National-Portrait.aspx. Accessed August 27, 2009.

[20] PewResearchCenter Publications. "Muslim Americans: Middle Class and Mostly Mainstream." Available online. URL: http://pewresearch.org/pubs/483/muslim-americans. Accessed August 27, 2009.

[21] Elijah Muhammad. *Message to the Blackman in America.* Chicago: Muhammad Mosque of Islam No. 2, 1965.

[22] Dorothy Blake Fardan. *Yakub and the Origins of White Supremacy: Message to the Whiteman & Woman in America.* Chicago: Lushena Books, 2001.

[23] Malcolm Little and Benjamin Goodman. *The End of White World Supremacy: Four Speeches.* New York: Merlin House, 1971, p. 78.

77

[24] Louis E. Lomax. *When the Word Is Given; A Report on Elijah Muhammad, Malcolm X, and the Black Muslim World.* Cleveland: World Publishing, 1963, pp. 173–174.

[25] Malcolm X and Alex Haley. *The Autobiography of Malcolm X.* New York: One World/Ballantine Books, 1992, pp. 388–393.

[26] "Religion: White Muslims?" *Time Magazine,* June 30, 1975. Available online. URL: http://www.time.com/time/magazine/article/0,9171,917589,00.html. Accessed August 27, 2009.

[27] Rosemary Skinner Keller, Rosemary Radford Ruether, and Marie Cantlon. *Encyclopedia of Women and Religion in North America.* Bloomington: Indiana University Press, 2006, p. 752.

[28] Daniel B. Wood. "America's Black Muslims Close a Rift." *The Christian Monitor,* February 14, 2002. Available online. URL: http://www.csmonitor.com/2002/0214/p03s01-ussc.html. Accessed August 27, 2009.

[29] Chancellor Williams. *The Destruction of Black Civilization: Great Issues of a Race from 4500 b.c. to 2000 a.d.* Chicago: Third World Press, 1987.

[30] H. Madhubuti and Don L. Lee. *Enemies: The Clash of Races.* Chicago: Third World Press, 1978.

[31] Phyllis Chesler. *The Death of Feminism: What's Next in the Struggle for Women's Freedom.* New York: Palgrave Macmillan, 2006.

[32] K. Govier. "Shrouded in Black." *Toronto Star,* September 25, 1995.

[33] M. Farooqi. "Wearing Hijab Changed My Life." *Las Postias College Express,* October 29, 2002.

[34] K. Bullock. *Rethinking Muslim Women and the Veil: Challenging Historical & Modern Stereotypes.* Herndon, Va.: IIIT, 2002.

[35] Yvonne Haddad and John Esposito. *Islam, Gender, and Social Change.* Oxford: Oxford University Press, 1998.

[36] Philippa Strum and Danielle Tarantolo. *Muslims in the United States: Demography, Beliefs, Institutions.* Washington, D.C.: Woodrow Wilson International Center for Scholars, 2003.

[37] Mediamatters.org. "700 Club Website Scrubbed Robertson's Controversial Comments Calling Muslims 'Satanic.'" Available online. URL: http://mediamatters.org/research/200603140008. Accessed August 27, 2009.

[38] The Media & Society Research Group, Cornell University. "MSRG Special Report: Restrictions on Civil Liberties, Views of Islam, & Muslim Americans." December 2004.

[39] Claudia Deane and Darryl Fears. "Negative Perception of Islam Increasing." *Washington Post,* March 9, 2006.

[40] opednews.com. "American Muslims Seven Years after 9/11." September 11, 2008. Available online. URL: http://www.opednews.com/articles/American-Muslims-seven-yea-by-Abdus-Sattar-Ghaza-080 911-29.html. Accessed August 27, 2009.

[41] U.S. Department of Justice. "Fact Sheet: Department of Justice Anti-Terrorism Efforts since Sept. 11, 2001." September 5, 2006.

[42] Pew Research Center. "Muslim Americans: Middle Class and Mostly Mainstream." PewResearchCenter Publications, 2007.

43 Stephen Schwartz. "The 'Islamophobes' That Aren't." *FrontPage Magazine*, April 28, 2005. Available online. URL: http://www.frontpagemag.com/readArticle.aspx?ARTID=8781. Accessed August 27, 2009.

44 Aljazeera.net. "US Invites Gulf Arab Investment." July 14, 2009. Available online. URL: http://english.aljazeera.net/business/2009/07/2009714105532156288.html. Accessed August 28, 2009.

45 Stephen Kinzer. *All the Shah's Men: An American Coup and the Roots of Middle East Terror.* Hoboken, N.J.: John Wiley and Sons, 2003, p. 86.

46 U.S. House of Representatives Permanent Select Committee on Intelligence, Iran. *Evaluation of U.S. Intelligence Performance Prior to November 1978.* Staff Report, Washington, D.C., p. 7.

47 Richard Yann and Nikki R. Keddie. *Modern Iran: Roots and Results of Revolution.* New Haven, Conn.: Yale University Press, 2003, pp. 235–236.

48 Charles Kurzman. *The Unthinkable Revolution in Iran.* Cambridge, Mass.: Harvard University Press, 2004, p. 157.

49 Mark Bowden. *Guests of the Ayatollah: The First Battle in America's War with Militant Islam.* New York: Atlantic Monthly Press, 2006, p. 19.

50 Baqer Moin. *Khomeini: Life of the Ayatollah.* New York: Thomas Dunne Books, 2000, p. 220.

51 Afshin Molavi. *The Soul of Iran: A Nation's Journey to Freedom.* New York: W. W. Norton, 2005, p. 335.

52 Mark Bowden. *Guests of the Ayatollah: The First Battle in America's War with Militant Islam.* New York: Atlantic Monthly Press, 2006, p. 93.

53 DemocracyNow.org. "Stephen Kinzer on U.S.-Iranian Relations, the 1953 CIA Coup in Iran and the Roots of Middle East Terror." Available online. URL: http://www.democracynow.org/2008/3/3/stephen_kinzer_on_the_us_iranian. Accessed August 27, 2009.

54 Robert Parry. "Missing U.S.-Iraq History." *In These Times*, December 16, 2003.

55 Kenneth R. Timmerman. *The Death Lobby: How the West Armed Iraq.* New York: Houghton Mifflin, 1991.

56 Statement by former NSC official Howard Teicher to the U.S. District Court, Southern District of Florida, January 31, 1995. Available online. URL: http://www.webcitation.org/5flvP0UgC. Accessed August 27, 2009.

57 Alan Friedman. *Spider's Web: The Secret History of How the White House Illegally Armed Iraq.* New York: Bantam Books, 1993.

58 Ken Silverstein and Daniel Burton-Rose. *Private Warriors.* New York: Verso, 2000, pp. 60–61.

59 International Court of Justice. "Aerial Incident of 3 July 1988 (Islamic Republic of Iran v. United States of America)—Iranian submission: Part IV B, The Shooting Down of Flight IR 655," July 24, 1990.

60 U.S. Department of Defense. "Formal Investigation into the Circumstances Surrounding the Downing of Iran Air Flight 655 on 3 July 1988" July 28, 1988.

[61] U.S. Department of State Background Information on Foreign Terrorist Organizations. Available online. URL: http://www.state.gov/s/ct/rls/rpt/fto/2801.htm. Accessed August 27, 2009.

[62] "Nass al-Risala al-Maftuha allati wajahaha Hizballah ila-l-Mustad'afin fi Lubnan wa-l-Alam," published February 16, 1985 in *al-Safir* (Beirut).

[63] Robin Wright. *Sacred Rage.* New York: Simon & Schuster, 2001, pp. 73, 15–16.

[64] Ronald Reagan. *An American Life.* New York: Simon & Schuster, 1990.

[65] The Tower Commission's Report. Report of the President's Special Review Board, 1987. Report of the congressional committees investigating the Iran-Contra Affair, with supplemental, minority, and additional views, 1987.

[66] George W. Bush. 2002 State of the Union Address.

[67] Central Intelligence Agency. "Unclassified Report to Congress on the Acquisition of Technology Relating to Weapons of Mass Destruction and Advanced Conventional Munitions, 1 January through 30 June 2003."

[68] IAEA. "Implementation of the NPT Safeguards Agreement in the Islamic Republic of Iran." November 10, 2003.

[69] United Nations. "Security Council Imposes Sanctions on Iran for Failure to Halt Uranium Enrichment, Unanimously Adopting Resolution 1737," December 23, 2006.

[70] Sam Tannenhaus. "Deputy Secretary Wolfowitz Interview with Sam Tannenhaus." *Vanity Fair,* May 9, 2003.

[71] ABC News, July 5, 2009. "'This Week' Transcript: Exclusive: Vice President Joe Biden." Available online. URL: http://abcnews.go.com/ThisWeek/Politics/story?id=8002421&page=1 Accessed August 27, 2009.

[72] BBC News, March 20, 2009. "Obama Offers Iran 'New Beginning.'" Available online. URL: http://news.bbc.co.uk/2/hi/americas/7954211.stm. Accessed August 27, 2009.

[73] Al Jazeera English, 13 June, 2009. "Poll Results Prompt Iran Protests." Available online. URL: http://english.aljazeera.net/news/middleeast/2009/06/2009613172130303995.html. Accessed August 27, 2009.

[74] CNN, June 27, 2009. "Chaos Prevails as Protesters, Police Clash in Iranian Capital." Available online. URL: http://edition.cnn.com/2009/WORLD/meast/06/20/iran.election/index.html. Accessed August 27, 2009.

75 Roger Morris. "Remember: Saddam Was Our Man." *New York Times,* March 14, 2003.

[76] Richard Sale. "Saddam Key in Early CIA Plot." United Press International, April 10, 2003.

[77] Efraim Karsh. *The Iran-Iraq War, 1980–1988.* Oxford: Osprey Publishing, 2002, p. 22.

[78] Kenneth R. Timmerman. *The Death Lobby: How the West Armed Iraq.* New York: Houghton Mifflin, 1991.

[79] Alan Friedman. *Spider's Web: The Secret History of How the White House Illegally Armed Iraq.* New York: Bantam Books, 1993.

[80] Barry Lando. *Web of Deceit: The History of Western Complicity in Iraq, from Churchill to Kennedy to George W. Bush.* New York: Other Press, 2007.

Focus on the United States

81 U.S. Senate Banking Committee. "Second Staff Report on U.S. CBW-Related Dual-Use Exports to Iraq." May 25, 1994.

82 Robert Fisk. *The Great War for Civilisation: The Conquest of the Middle East.* New York: Alfred A. Knopf, 2005.

83 U.S. Secretary of State Colin Powell's address to the U.N. Security Council. February 5, 2003. Available online. URL: http://www.guardian.co.uk/world/2003/feb/05/iraq.usa. Accessed April 17, 2010.

84 George W. Bush. "President's Remarks at the United Nations General Assembly: Remarks by the President in Address to the United Nations General Assembly, New York, New York." The White House, September 12, 2002.

85 General Dr. Mohamed El Baradei. "The Status of Nuclear Inspections in Iraq: An Update, 7 March 2003." International Atomic Energy Agency, February 14, 2003. Available online. URL: http://www.iaea.org/NewsCenter/Statements/2003/ebsp2003n005.shtml. Accessed August 27, 2009.

86 guardian.co.uk. "Hans Blix's Briefing to the Security Council." February 14, 2003. Available online. URL: http://www.guardian.co.uk/world/2003/feb/14/iraq.unitednations1. Accessed August 27, 2009.

87 Jim Michaels. "Foreign Firms Investing in Iraq." *USA Today,* June 17, 2008.

88 AME Info. "Foreign Investment in Iraq, Study by Dunia." March 12, 2009. Available online. URL: http://www.ameinfo.com/188298.html. Accessed August 27, 2009.

89 AME Info. "Foreign investment in Iraq, study by Dunia."

90 Nadav Safran. *Saudi Arabia: the ceaseless quest for security.* Cambridge, Mass.: Belknap Press of Harvard University Press, 1985, pp. 96–97.

91 Parker T. Hart. *Saudi Arabia and the United States: Birth of a Security Partnership.* Bloomington: Indiana University Press, 1998, pp. 210–233.

92 Nadav Safran. *Saudi Arabia: The Ceaseless Quest for Security.* Cambridge, Mass.: Belknap Press of Harvard University, 1985, pp. 152–55.

93 Daniel Yergin. *The Prize: The Epic Quest for Oil, Money, and Power.* New York: Simon & Schuster, 1991, pp. 595–97.

94 Anthony Cave Brown. *Oil, God, and Gold: The Story of Aramco and the Saudi Kings.* Boston: Houghton Mifflin, 1999, pp. 299–301.

95 Bob Woodward. *The Commanders.* New York: Simon & Schuster, 1991, p. 270.

96 Susan Sachs. "Saudi Heir Urges Reform, and Turn from U.S." *New York Times,* December 4, 2000.

97 Cameron S. Brown. "The Shot Seen around the World: The Middle East Reacts to September 11th." *MERIA Journal,* 5, no. 4, December 2001.

98 Howard Schneider. "Man on Bin Laden Tape Now Said to Be Guerrilla." *Washington Post,* December 18, 2001.

99 Neil MacFarquhar. "No Jerry Lewis, but Saudi Telethon Reaches Goal." *New York Times,* November 9, 2001.

100 Roula Khalaf. "Saudi Investors Pull Out Billions of Dollars from U.S.: Move Signals Deep Alienation Following September 11." *Financial Times,* August 21, 2002.

[101] "Reconsidering Saudi Arabia." *New York Times,* editorial, October 14, 2001.

[102] "Saudi Arabia's Apartheid." *Washington Post,* December 22, 2001.

[103] F. Gregory Gause III. "Saudi Perceptions of the United States since 9/11." Tony Judt and Denis Lacorne, eds., *With US or Against US: Studies in Global Anti-Americanism.* New York: Palgrave Macmillan, 2005.

[104] Zogby.com. "Saudis Reject Bin Laden and Terrorism; Tragedies of 9/11 and in Riyadh Do Not Represent Saudi People or Islam, According to New Zogby International Poll Impressions of American Life and Culture Down from 2002 Study." Available online. URL: http://www.zogby.com/news/readnews.cfm?ID=725. Accessed August 28, 2009.

[105] Zogby.com. "Saudis Reject Bin Laden and Terrorism; Tragedies of 9/11 and in Riyadh Do Not Represent Saudi People or Islam, According to New Zogby International Poll Impressions of American Life and Culture Down from 2002 Study."

3

Global Perspectives

INDONESIA

The major centers of Islam in Southeast Asia are Indonesia, Malaysia, Brunei, and parts of the Philippines. A country comprised of some 17,000 islands, Indonesia has the largest Muslim population of any nation in the world. About 86 percent of Indonesia's 240 million people are Muslim.[1] By comparison, Egypt, the most populous Muslim-majority nation in the Middle East, has a population of 83 million, 90 percent of whom are Muslim.

Although Indonesia is the world's most populous Muslim-majority nation, unlike some states in the Middle East, it is not exclusively Muslim. About 14 percent of Indonesians are Christian or Hindus. Indonesia has a long history of religious tolerance, but that history has recently come under threat from extreme Muslim groups who have carried out terrorist attacks on religious minorities. After a long period of political repression under a dictatorial regime in the second half of the 20th century, Indonesia became a democratic state in 1999. Cultural analysts are paying close attention to the progress of what is one of the world's very few genuine democracies in a Muslim-majority state. The country's large population, its relatively prosperous economy, and the presence of significant numbers of non-Muslim minorities have made Indonesia something of a test case in examining the compatibility of democracy with Islam in a culturally diverse state.

The Doctrine of Pancasila

In 1945 Sukarno, the future first president of Indonesia, made a speech to the committee charged with establishing Indonesian independence in which he outlined the principles of a political and philosophical doctrine known as Pancasila. The word *pancasila* consists of two Sanskrit words meaning "five" and "pillar" or "principle," and it can be translated as "the five principles."

THE MUSLIM WORLD

The Pancasila doctrine sought to establish a set of principles that would allow the ethnically and religiously diverse peoples of the vast archipelago to live together in one nation. The five principles were as follows:

1. Belief in one supreme god
2. Humanitarianism (also expressed as justice and civilization for humanity)
3. Nationalism or the unity of Indonesia
4. Consultative democracy
5. Social justice

Sukarno and his supporters described the Pancasila doctrine as an attempt to apply the traditional values of Indonesian rural life to a nationwide level. At the time some Muslim groups pressed for Indonesia's proposed constitution to explicitly declare the new nation to be an Islamic state, but these efforts were resisted on the grounds that such a declaration would likely cause conflict between the Muslim majority and religious minorities. When Indonesia unilaterally declared its independence from the Dutch in August 1945, two days after the surrender of the Japanese who had been occupying the territory, the new constitution embodied the principles of Pancasila.

While the history of independent Indonesia in the 50 years after 1945 was not peaceful, Indonesia's conflicts during this period were not usually religiously motivated. Historians differ as to how much this absence of religious conflict was due to the Pancasila doctrine and how much to the powerful dictatorial grip on the nation exercised by Sukarno and his successor Suharto. Both Sukarno and Suharto were masters at balancing the opposing forces in Indonesian society against each other, and they ruled in an authoritative style that made it difficult for special interest groups to come to the fore. That the Indonesian political scene was divided into three blocks of roughly equal power, the Communist Party of Indonesia, the Indonesian armed forces, and the Indonesian National Party, facilitated the ability to maintain control. The Pancasila doctrine was admirably all-inclusive in its intentions but vague in its implementation. Attempts to draft meaningful legislation under the umbrella of Pancasila proved often unsuccessful because they caused resentment among one group or another. In other words, while Pancasila served as a guiding force in Indonesian politics, it was never enshrined in a rigorous and comprehensive set of specific laws that guaranteed the freedoms of individual groups and minorities. Religiously motivated conflict, though rare, was not unknown. In 1948 Indonesia agreed to cede part of the island of Java to the Dutch. Muslim groups in the ceded territory formed a rebel movement known as Darul Islam, which remained

84

active after the area returned to Indonesian control in 1949. Darul Islam fought a low-level guerrilla campaign against the Indonesian government until the early 1960s. Another Islamic extremist group known as Komando Jihad continued to operate in Java until the 1980s. It carried out the hijacking of a Indonesian Airways aircraft in 1981.

Pancasila under Threat

In 1998 a popular pro-democracy movement overthrew President Suharto. Open and free elections to the national and regional parliaments followed in 1999 and the country's first open election to the presidency since 1945 in 2004. Indonesia's sudden transition to open democracy has fulfilled the wishes of many, but it has also allowed long-suppressed antagonisms to bloom. Since the late 1990s a number of Muslim groups have begun campaigning for Indonesia to become an explicitly Islamic state under sharia law. Some of these groups have been willing to use violence to achieve their aim, and Indonesia has faced a serious terrorist threat. Radical Muslim groups in the country regard the Pancasila doctrine as tainted by its association with the dictators of the past as well as being fundamentally wrong in its assertion that Muslims are no more important than other religious groups. An economic downturn in Southeast Asia toward the end of the 1990s brought unemployment and hardship to many Indonesians just as the unraveling of the dictatorial regime of Suharto began to make possible free speech and public demonstrations of discontent. Muslim militants who had been exiled were able to take advantage of the government's weakness to return to Indonesia and reinvigorate their radical movements. Islamic preachers advocating a less tolerant form of Islam than that traditionally practiced in Indonesia also began to arrive in the country from Middle Eastern countries.[2]

Militant Violence

Since the transition to democracy in the late 1990s Indonesia has suffered a series of deadly terrorist attacks and insurgencies carried out by Islamic militants. In the province of Aceh on the northern tip of the island of Sumatra a separatist war that had been ongoing since the 1970s flared into deadly violence. The Laskar Jihad militia on the Moluccan Islands also began a violent anti-Christian campaign that took thousands of lives. Elsewhere in Indonesia Islamic militants carried out devastating bombing attacks aimed at foreign tourists and non-Muslim minorities.

THE ACEH INSURGENCY

The Free Aceh Movement emerged in the mid-1970s in response to the Indonesian government's policy of allowing foreign companies to prospect for oil and gas in the area. The movement was partly motivated by what some perceived as the government's unfair distribution of wealth resulting from the exploitation of the region's resources. However, Aceh has long been recognized as one of the most conservative Muslim-majority provinces of the country, and the conflict has always been motivated partly by a desire to introduce a more conservative interpretation of Islam than that in place across the rest of the nation. The northern tip of Sumatra is believed to have been the first part of the Indonesian islands where the inhabitants adopted Islam, and the region has one of the highest concentrations of Muslims anywhere in the country.

The first phase of the Aceh insurgency began when the province declared unilateral independence from Indonesia in 1976, a move that the government responded to with a military crackdown that eradicated the rebels as an effective force. A resurgence of the Free Aceh Movement beginning in 1989 was also met with a severe response from government troops and that resulted in the movement gaining greater local popular support. After the fall of President Suharto the movement once again attempted to secure independence for the province. Fighting between Free Aceh Movement rebels and government troops continued until 2004 when the tsunami of that year brought devastation to the region and put a stop to the conflict. In a subsequent peace deal the Indonesian government granted Aceh greater autonomy. Even as the fighting continued in 2003 Aceh had introduced its first sharia courts with the grudging acceptance of the central government.[3] Since that time Aceh's sharia courts have gained in power and scope. In 2009 Aceh's regional parliament passed a law making adultery punishable by stoning to death.[4] Laws of this kind allowing capital punishment for the infringement of religious duties, such as marital fidelity, rather than serious criminal offenses stand at odds with Indonesia's traditions, and Aceh is the only province in the country to have implemented any form of sharia law.

VIOLENCE ON THE MOLUCCAN ISLANDS

In 1999 violence broke out between Christian and Muslim communities on the Moluccan Islands, highlighting the danger of interreligious conflict across Indonesia. The Moluccan Islands are a group of islands within the larger Indonesian archipelago with a history of colonial domination stretching back to the 16th century. For hundreds of years they were the world's only source of nutmeg and mace, making them an attractive target for foreign control since these spices were, at one time, worth more than their weight in gold. The Portuguese brought Christianity to the islands early in the 16th century at a time when the population practiced Hinduism, Islam, and a range of indigenous faiths. The Christian community grew larger over the centuries as the islands were subjected to Spanish, Dutch, and English influences. The largest of the Moluccan Islands, Ambon became the center of Christianity in the archipelago, and the only large island in the entire Indonesian archipelago with a Christian majority.

Under Dutch rule the Christian community on the islands was given preferential treatment. Christians were recruited as soldiers in the pay of the Dutch and had access to better educational and job opportunities as a reward for their loyalty to the colonial overlords. During Indonesia's independence struggle some Moluccan Christians continued to support the Dutch, earning them the distrust of the non-Christian population. When it became clear the Dutch would withdraw, Ambon's Christian community fought to form their own independent state rather than be subsumed into a Muslim-majority Indonesia. When this effort failed, thousands of Ambonese Christians fled to the Netherlands. In the decades after independence many Moluccans felt that the Christians who remained on Ambon continued to receive preferential treatment under Suharto's regime. When Suharto's power collapsed at the end of the 1990s, long-term resentments on the part of Muslim Moluccans toward the Christians boiled over into a long and bitter interreligious conflict that left thousands dead.

Sporadic violence broke out in January of 1999 as Ambonese Muslims attacked and burned Christian churches and Ambonese Christians retaliated. Up until this time Ambon had been regarded as a model of religious tolerance under Indonesia's founding doctrine of Pancasila. Christian and Muslim villages and neighborhoods were intermingled across the islands and had cooperated with no apparent animosity for decades. As paranoia grew in both communities this close intermingling of Muslim and Christian areas brought a myriad of opportunities for casual violence that served to fuel the bad feeling on both sides. Though highly traumatic for both communities, the fighting was initially sporadic and disorganized. This changed when a new factor entered the equation in 2000 in the form of a radical Muslim militia calling itself the Laskar Jihad.

The precise origins of the Laskar Jihad are unclear. The original organization may have been formed by radicals from the northern Moluccan Islands, where Muslims are in a majority, but many sources have reported that the earliest fighters were later joined by thousands of recruits from other parts of Indonesia. Jafar Umar Thalib, the reputed leader of the Lasker Jihad, claimed to have fought alongside the mujahideen in Afghanistan and returned to Indonesia in the 1990s when he set up a network of schools teaching the Quran.[5] The Laskar Jihad was well equipped with modern weapons and communication equipment in contrast to the small local groups of Muslims and Christians that had been involved previously in the fighting. Some sources have claimed that Laskar Jihad elements traveled to the Moluccas with the help of the Indonesian armed forces, or at least that government troops did nothing to stop them from moving freely and transporting weapons.[6] The Laskar Jihad described the Christians of the Moluccas as "belligerent infidels," meaning they were legitimate targets of a "holy war." Laskar Jihad elements moved from village to village and town to town across the Moluccan Islands in a campaign aimed at killing or driving Christians out of the islands. The islands of Ambon, Seram, and Halmahera were hardest hit, and thousands were killed and tens of thousands were forced from their homes here. Christians began streaming out of the islands in search of shelter elsewhere in Indonesia, many of them ending up in refugee camps. As the crisis worsened, local police and Indonesian government troops sent to restore order were accused of taking sides. A military spokesman admitted that troops were becoming "emotionally involved" in the conflict as local units began fighting each other in defense of their own Muslim or Christian communities.[7]

The violence on the Moluccan Islands emerged as the most serious issue facing the Indonesian government as the nation made the difficult transition to democracy. The separatist conflict in Aceh, under way at the same time, threatened the unity of the country, but it centered on a disagreement between conservative and liberal Muslim elements. The Moluccan conflict, in contrast, constituted a religiously motivated war between two of Indonesia's oldest communities. The potential for similar conflicts to break out along Indonesia's many other religious and ethnic fault lines caused severe worries for the government and for the international community. The threat of such a scenario coming true grew when elements in Laskar Jihad became involved in the Aceh conflict and also arrived on the Indonesian island of Sulawesi, where they instigated months of deadly conflict between Muslims and Christians.

TERRORIST ATTACKS IN BALI AND JAVA

In October 2002 Muslim terrorists exploded three bombs on the Indonesian island of Bali, which killed 202 people and injured 240 others. Bali is a popular tourist destination, and the bombs were placed deliberately to target Western holidaymakers frequenting the island's bars and clubs. A total of 152 of those killed were foreign nationals. It was the most deadly terrorist attack in Indonesian history, and coming just a year after the September 2001 attacks in the United States, it served as a shocking reminder of the vulnerability of civilian targets to radical Muslim violence. The following year a car bomb detonated outside the Marriott Hotel in the Indonesian capital of Jakarta killed 12 and injured 150. Popular among foreign visitors, the hotel was often used by U.S.

embassy staff for official functions, though the majority of those killed and injured were Indonesians. In 2004 another car bomb was detonated outside the Australian embassy in Jakarta killing nine, injuring more than 100, and causing severe damage to the Australian and other nearby embassies. Terrorists struck tourist centers in Bali once again in 2005, killing 20 and injuring more than 100.

All of these attacks were blamed on a group calling itself Jemaah Islamiyah that was founded by two Muslim Indonesians, Abu Bakar Bashir and Abdullah Sungkar, in the early 1990s. Jemaah Islamiyah is dedicated to the establishment of an Islamic state in Southeast Asia that would encompass Indonesia, Malaysia, Singapore, Brunei, and part of the Philippines. At the time of the group's founding, both Abu Bakar Bashir and Abdullah Sungkar were living as exiles in Malaysia after fleeing arrest in Suharto's Indonesia. Both men returned to Indonesia after the fall of the Suharto regime, and Jemaah Islamiyah first came to public attention as one of dozens of Muslim and Christian militias involved in the fighting on the Moluccan Islands and Sulawesi in the early 2000s. The first major terrorist attack launched by Jemaah Islamiyah is believed to have been a series of bomb attacks on Christian churches across Indonesia on Christmas Eve in 2000. More than 20 bombs killed at least 14 people and injured more than 100. Following the U.S. invasion of Afghanistan in 2001, Jemaah Islamiyah turned its attention to attacking U.S. and other foreign targets in Indonesia and other parts of Southeast Asia. The 2002 Bali bombings and the attack on the Marriott Hotel in Jakarta were the clearest indicators of this new policy.

Against the backdrop of the war on terror, U.S. government agencies began searching for links between Jemaah Islamiyah and al-Qaeda or other Middle Eastern Muslim terrorist organizations. Some analysts have described Jemaah Islamiyah as an arm of al-Qaeda while others regard it, at most, as an affiliate or ally. According to Zachary Abuza, an expert in the funding of terrorism: "While Jemaah Islamiyah and Al Qaeda are linked, through some joint membership, financial support, and expertise, Jemaah Islamiyah has its own agenda and is not subordinate to Al Qaeda. Al Qaeda does not control JI [Jemaah Islamiyah] operations, although it has provided financial support and expertise to JI."[8] Abuza and others have argued that the Muslim community of Southeast Asia has been a source of funding and a useful place to conceal and transfer funds for Muslim militants worldwide since the 1980s and that militants in Southeast Asia share some of the broad aims of other militant movements in the Middle East and elsewhere. However, it is clear that Jemaah Islamiyah and other Indonesian-Muslim militant groups, such as the Laskar Jihad, owe their origins stemming from the particular socioeconomic conditions of the region and are not simply puppets of the Middle East–based global organization al-Qaeda. The United Nations officially listed Jemaah Islamiyah as a terrorist organization associated with al-Qaeda in 2002,[9] and the U.S. State Department also lists the group as a foreign terrorist organization.

Islam and Democracy in Indonesia

The Aceh insurgency, conflict between Muslims and Christians on the Moluccan Islands and Sulawesi, and the series of bomb attacks carried out by Jemaah Islamiyah and other groups all occurred within five years of Indonesia's transition from a secular dictatorship to democracy. On the face of it these incidents would seem to point to poor prospects for the success of democracy in a Muslim-majority nation. On the other hand, a decade after the end of Suharto's regime, much of this violence has been brought under control, and Indonesia's democracy is strengthening. Successive democratically elected Indonesian governments have faced the extremely delicate task of balancing the popular support enjoyed by some conservative Muslim elements with the need to protect the country's non-Muslim minorities as well as the wishes of the majority of Muslim Indonesians who do not support the conservative agenda. Writing about the spate of interreligious violence in Indonesia that followed the Southeast Asian economic crisis of 1997, Robert W. Hefner noted: "The crisis of 1997–99 did not prove the earlier claims of democratic Islam a fraud . . . but underscored the scale of the challenge faced by Indonesian democrats of all faiths."[10]

Hefner argues that the majority of Indonesia's Muslims support rather than oppose democracy due to their experiences under the dictatorial Suharto regime. Islam underwent a renaissance in Indonesia during the 1970s and 1980s. Construction of mosques, attendance at mosque, and pilgrimages to Mecca all grew. Hefner attributes this resurgence in part to Suharto's highly effective education program, which not only greatly improved literacy and high school graduation rates among the general population but also enforced mandatory religious instruction in all schools. A new generation of Indonesians emerged with a firm grounding in the teachings of Islam and sufficiently educated to engage in informed debate about their faith. As Suharto's regime became more repressive and official forums for discussion less open, Islam became the arena in which many Indonesians felt safe to openly discuss concerns. Many of them drew inspiration for how their country should be rebuilt from the egalitarian strands of the Quran. Pious young Muslims constituted one of the largest demographic groups involved in the anti-Suharto, pro-democracy campaign of the 1990s. As Hefner notes: "Equally important, as Muslim students in the anti-Soeharto movement showed, many pious youth find democratic and egalitarian values in their reading of Islam. Indeed, although conservative Islamists disapprove, the remarkable feature of the resurgence was that its central streams were democratic and pluralist . . ." To some extent the development of Islam in Indonesia between 1970 and the end of the 20th century is the story of the faith acting as an open door offering a way to escape a repressive state. From this perspective it is not surprising that the majority of Indonesian Muslims continue to prefer a tolerant and nonrigid form of Islam to a conservative form dictated by an elite.

Despite this history of the growth of democracy in a majority Islamic society, several sources of tension exist between Muslim elements and those supportive of pluralist democracy in Indonesia. In recent years an intense and sometimes violent debate has ensued over limits to freedom of religion centered on the Ahmadiyya sect. Ahmadiyya is a religious movement founded by Muslims in India at the end of the 19th century. Its followers believe themselves to be Muslim but their beliefs differ from those of most mainstream Muslims in that they regard the founder of their movement, Mirza Ghulam Ahmad, as the Mahdi (or messiah) prophesized by Muhammad. Many mainstream Muslims regard the Ahmadiyya sect as heretical and do not accept its followers as fellow Muslims. Ahmadis have often been persecuted for their beliefs in Muslim-majority countries but, until recently, Indonesia's 200,000-strong Ahmadi community has been left in peace. In 2008 conservative Indonesian-Muslim groups began calling for the sect to be banned and put pressure on the government to do so through a series of public demonstrations. When a government review concluded that the sect should be restricted, triumphant conservative Muslims attacked and burned an Ahmadi mosque and school. After weeks of national debate, during which liberal Muslim groups clashed violently with conservative Muslims, the government approved a decision to ban Ahmadi activities across the country, though it stopped short of declaring the sect illegal.[11]

The Indonesian government's decision to curtail the activities of Ahmadiyya has been sharply criticized by international human rights groups and by many Indonesians as a step toward the implementation of an Islamic state. Indonesian public opinion has been divided on the issue between those who seek an outright ban of the sect, those who believe the government has no right to interfere because of the freedom of religion guaranteed in Indonesia's constitution, and those who disagree with a ban but want Ahmadis to stop describing themselves as Muslims. Many liberal Indonesians were especially alarmed by the fact that a small group of extremists could apparently impose its will on the government without appealing to a democratic majority and in defiance of the spirit of the constitution.

Indonesian governments have also faced difficulties attempting to crack down on the activities of violent Muslim extremists. The majority of

Indonesians, Muslim or otherwise, abhorred the series of bombings carried out by Jemaah Islamiyah, but attempts to bring the group's alleged spiritual leader, Abu Bakar Bashir, to justice have been fraught with political difficulties. Dozens of Jemaah Islamiyah members have been arrested by Indonesian authorities and subsequently convicted of direct involvement in the bombings, but Abu Bakar Bashir has escaped relatively lightly. Although Abu Bakar Bashir was first arrested in 2003, after the Bali bombings, he was charged with offenses relating to the Christmas Eve bombings of 2000. He was convicted of relatively minor infractions of immigration law, but not of treason, and sentenced to three years in prison, of which he served just 20 months. Abu Bakar Bashir was arrested again in 2004 and charged with offenses relating to the 2003 Marriot Hotel bombing and, for the first time, the Bali bombings of 2002. He was found guilty of conspiracy in the 2002 attacks but not of involvement in the 2003 outrage. Sentenced to two years and six months in prison, he was released after 25 months, and in 2006 his conviction was overturned by Indonesia's supreme court. Some Indonesians have speculated that the court's failure to convict Abu Bakar Bashir of definitive involvement in Jemaah Islamiyah's bombing campaigns has more to do with his popularity among a vocal minority of the electorate than with concern for his guilt or innocence.

Jafar Umar Thalib, the self-professed leader of Laskar Jihad, has also escaped conviction on more than one occasion. In 2001 he was arrested for allegedly leading the stoning to death of a suspected rapist but was never prosecuted. In 2002 he was arrested again and charged with inciting religious violence in the Moluccas, where thousands had died after the intervention of Laskar Jihad, but he was cleared of any involvement. Given the widespread suspicions that Laskar Jihad was helped, and perhaps even equipped and funded by the Indonesian army and prominent political figures from the Suharto era, it is perhaps not surprising that Jafar Umar Thalib escaped punishment for his role in the violence.

A DECADE OF DEMOCRACY

Despite the ongoing challenges in Indonesia many commentators pronounce the country's decade-long experiment with democracy a resounding success. In July 2009 Indonesians went to the polls for the third time to elect a parliament. That the elections passed off largely peacefully and without dramatic irregularities testified to the faith of the majority of Indonesians, Muslim and non-Muslim, in the democratic ideal. Considerations of religious divisions aside, holding open and free elections in a nation of more than 240 million people divided into hundreds of ethnic groups spread across hundreds of islands is no mean feat. The 2009 polls resulted in the reelection of Susilo Bambang Yudhoyono as the country's president. Susilo Bambang Yudhoyono became Indonesia's first directly elected president in 2004, and with his 2009 victory he became the first Indonesian to be reelected to the office. Susilo Bambang Yudhoyono has been credited with stabilizing Indonesia's political scene during a first term that saw the arrest and conviction of dozens of individuals accused of involvement in earlier terrorist outrages. To become president in 2004 Yudhoyono's Democratic Party was obliged to form a coalition with Golkar, Suharto's former party. Reliance on the support of a coalition partner restricted Yudhoyono's ability to accomplish his objectives, but he nevertheless was able to implement free-market economic reforms that helped Indonesia weather the global economic crisis of 2008–09 more effectively than some of its neighbors, institute an independent court to tackle corruption, and oversee a successful campaign to find and prosecute members of terrorist organizations. Yudhoyono also finalized a peace deal with the Free Aceh Movement, ending decades of separatist violence in the province by granting a degree of self-rule. The 2009 election result was called: "as much . . . a vote of confidence for Indonesia's emerging democracy as a referendum on S.B.Y. [Susilo Bambang Yudhoyono]"[12] Susilo Bambang Yudhoyono's history as a prominent figure in Suharto's regime is a surprising, but revealing, fact about a man who became such a key figure in Indonesia's fledging democracy. He came to national prominence as a general during the Suharto era, but as the pro-democracy movement began to gain strength, he became a key figure in negotiations between the establishment that had ruled the country for three decades and prominent Muslim leaders. In 2000 he joined the government of Abdurrahman Wahid, Indonesia's first post-Suharto president, but he was forced to resign when, as chief minister for security and political affairs, he refused to declare a state of emergency during the impeachment crisis that brought down Wahid in 2001. In 2004 he also lost his job as senior political and security minister after a public disagreement with President Megawati Sukarnoputri. This apparent willingness to sacrifice his own interests rather than support unpopular but powerful politicians coupled with his close connections to Indonesia's politically powerful military and his history as a facilitator of the transition to democracy have made "the thinking general" a popular figure among many Indonesians.

Although seen as a triumph for democracy, Indonesia's 2009 elections coincided with a resurgence of terrorist violence that was clearly intended to undermine the process. Almost four years after the last bomb attacks thought to have been carried out by Jemaah Islamiyah and just a few days after the 2009 elections, suicide bombers attacked two U.S.-owned hotels in Jakarta.[13]

93

The explosions revealed that, though extremist groups have been weakened, they remain capable of hitting high-profile targets in the country's capital.

THE FUTURE

Indonesia is the world's most populous Muslim-majority state. Its transition from dictatorship to democracy has been watched closely by political commentators, many of whom see it as a critical test case for the compatibility of Islam with a democratic system. Ten years into the experiment the verdict is cautiously positive, but signs remain that the issue is far from settled. Islam in Indonesia has undergone a spiritual renaissance since the 1970s, and this renaissance has accelerated since the fall of Suharto in 1999. For the majority of Indonesian Muslims this has simply meant an increased awareness and respect for their own Muslim heritage as well as for Islam as it is practiced in the faith's Middle Eastern heartland. For a small but growing minority, however, it has led to a rejection of secular politics and non-Muslim cultural influences.

Conservative interpretations of Islam, such as the Salafi school of thought popular in some Middle Eastern states, have gained considerable ground in Indonesia at the expense of the country's own more liberal and inclusive tradition. Evidence of this exists in the growing trend for local governments to implement bylaws based on the principles of sharia law. These laws are allowed under 2000 legislation that sought to decentralize power in Indonesia, and they include prohibitions on the consumption of alcohol, requirements for men and women to wear conservative clothing in keeping with guidelines in the Quran, and bans on women out-of-doors alone after dark. In 2003 only a handful of Indonesian districts, known as regencies, had bylaws of this kind, but the number has multiplied in the last few years. In 2007 it was estimated that regencies in half of Indonesia's provinces had instituted sharia-inspired bylaws.[14] From a democratic point of view, these bylaws prove troublesome because they are imposed rather than adopted based on voter approval and they often apply to Muslims and non-Muslims alike. A law introduced in the city of Tangerang near Jakarta, for example, stipulated the arrest for prostitution of any woman found alone on the street after 10 P.M., while a law in Padang, West Sumatra, required Muslim and non-Muslim girls to wear head scarves at school. Liberal groups have criticized these laws as a contravention of the principles of freedom of religion and religious tolerance enshrined in Indonesia's constitution, but those in power have been reluctant to act against them for fear of alienating conservative Muslim voters.

While campaigns against sharia-based bylaws have met with little success, a national outcry erupted when the Prosperous Justice Party (PKS), which calls for the establishment of an Islamic caliphate in its founding manifesto, tried to pass a highly conservative national antipornography law. While many Indonesians supported the idea of reining in the country's pornography industry, a large number objected to sections of the bill that would have made public kissing illegal and banned some traditional Indonesian costumes as lewd. Had it been enacted in its proposed form the bill would have marked a major step toward forcing conservative Muslim mores on both Muslim and non-Muslim Indonesians. As it turned out the outcry against the bill was such that it had to be withdrawn and redrafted. A watered-down version was passed into law in 2008 but not before a fifth of parliamentarians walked out of the chamber, refusing to vote.

The democratic credentials of conservative Islam in Indonesia are often called into doubt by opponents who suspect some Islamist political parties of working within the democratic system simply so that they can gain enough power to change it. Conversely, conservative Muslims argue that the emergence of a stricter form of Islam in Indonesia is entirely democratic because it is what ordinary Indonesians want. Local leaders say they are simply implementing reforms that were desired but never possible under a centralized regime that ignored the wishes of the faithful. A Muslim cleric in West Java's Cianjur regency, where sharia-based bylaws were implemented in 2006 said: "People in Jakarta may not understand this, but Shari'a is the aspiration of the people, because it makes everyone, even government leaders, accountable."[15]

For Indonesia's estimated 30 million non-Muslims, no major politicians seem particularly interested in protecting their interests. While some mainstream parties go out of their way to court the conservative Muslim vote and every party is extremely wary of appearing anti-Islamic, no political mileage is gained in fighting for the rights of Indonesia's religious minorities. Over the course of a decade Indonesia has proved that democracy can flourish in a Muslim-majority state. What remains far from proven, though, is whether religious freedom can survive in a state where Muslims make up the overwhelming majority.

ALGERIA

Algeria is a large country on the Mediterranean coast of North Africa. It is the second-largest nation on the continent, after Sudan. The vast majority of Algeria's population live along the steeply sloping coastal region, the area that benefits from the greatest rainfall and the most fertile soils. South of an inland region of semiarid highlands, the Atlas Mountains separate the northern, densely populated part of the country from its vast desert interior. More than 80 percent of Algeria lies within the area of the Sahara, and this area is very sparsely populated. Although largely useless for agriculture, Algeria's desert regions do contain very large oil and natural gas reserves, which have been the principal source of the nation's wealth since it gained independence from France in 1962.

Historically, Algeria forms part of the Maghreb, a geopolitical term designating the northwest corner of Africa that also includes the modern states of Morocco and Tunisia. The Maghreb has been part of the Muslim world since the seventh century, and the term *Maghreb* is derived from the Arabic for "western" or "place of sunset." Ninety-nine percent of Algeria's population of 34 million are Sunni Muslim,[16] making Algeria one of the most religiously homogenous states in the Muslim world.

The Origins of Islam in Algeria

Islam arrived in this corner of North Africa with the Arab-Muslim armies that swept across the region in the seventh century. The Arab-Muslim conquest of the region that is now northern Algeria took place between about 670 and 710. The mountainous and desert parts of present-day Algeria remained largely outside the control of the Arabs. The indigenous population of the area, a people known as Berbers, adopted Islam in large numbers, but conversion was not complete. Although many modern Algerians describe themselves as "Arab" this is more of a cultural than an ethnic identifier in referring to their use of Arabic, their Muslim faith, and their other links with Arab culture. The great majority of modern Algerians are ethnically Berber with some Arab admixture, and some Algerians continue to identify themselves as culturally Berber rather than Arab. This minority still speaks Berber languages rather than Arabic and practices its own brand of Islam.

Lying thousands of miles from the center of the Arab world and isolated behind its mountain and desert barriers, the Maghreb developed its own distinctive form of Islam. In the 12th century the Almohad dynasty, a Berber Muslim clan, began to build an empire in the Maghreb that came to dominate much of North Africa as well as present-day Spain and Portugal by about 1200. Almohad rulers were notoriously zealous in their insistence on conformity to their own interpretation of Islam, and it is from their dynastic period that Algeria's present-day religious homogeneity dates. Pre-Muslim Berber traditions also had an influence on the development of Islam in the region. The uniquely North African tradition of marabouts is thought to be one example. Marabouts are religious scholars or traveling teachers who were associated with a specific school or tradition of Islam. They are sometimes called "Muslim saints." In the past in the Maghreb marabouts also traditionally made and sold amulets for good luck, predicted the future, and conducted ceremonies at births, marriages, and funerals. The tombs of famous marabouts were places of pilgrimage for many Maghreb Muslims until the 20th century, when the tradition was largely discredited by orthodox scholars.

Algeria became part of the Muslim Ottoman Empire in the 16th century and remained under nominal Ottoman authority until the 1830s when France invaded the coastal areas and began carving out a colonial territory. France was to rule the country for more than 130 years. Algerian resistance was fierce and often fought under the banner of Islam. Abd al-Qadir was a Sufi military and political leader who led a successful campaign against French incursions into the west of Algeria from 1830 until the early 1840s. He was to become an inspiration for generations of Algerian freedom fighters up to and including those who finally won independence from France in the 1960s. Mohamed el-Mokrani led another powerful, but ultimately unsuccessful, revolt against French rule in the 1870s. Under French rule Islam was tolerated but discouraged and underwent a slow degeneration as it was starved of contact with the mainstream Muslim world. Algerians were technically regarded as French subjects, but they were accorded full rights only if they renounced Islam. French culture had a deep and pervasive impact on Algeria but never eclipsed the indigenous Arab-Muslim culture.

Islam and Algeria's War of Independence

On November 1, 1954, Algerian insurgents began a campaign to win independence from French colonial rule with a series of attacks against civilian, military, and government targets across the country. The National Liberation Front (FLN), the organizers of the rebellion broadcast a message from Cairo, Egypt, calling on all Algerians to join the battle for the "restoration of the Algerian state—sovereign, democratic and social—within the framework of the principles of Islam."[17] It is revealing that Islam is the last, rather than the first, cause on this list.

Along with nationalism and socialism, Islam constituted one of the central pillars of the FLN's ideology. Islam was the cultural element by which the FLN distinguished the bulk of Algeria's indigenous population from the so-called *pied-noirs* (black feet)—the popular name for European colonists and Jews. As such it was one of the guiding principles of the campaign for Algerian independence and acted as a binding force to a popular movement that was otherwise fragmented by varying political views and ambitions. In the context of Islam, the "otherness" of the occupying power and foreign settlers, who were either Christian or Jewish, was undisputable. Like independence movements in many other parts of Africa, Algeria's struggle for self-determination was primarily a political rather than a religious movement. Also, like other independence movements, it was led primarily by intellectuals who envisaged a progressive socialist state that would replace what they saw as merciless economic exploitation by European rulers. Most FLN leaders regarded Islam as a tool that could be used to unite Algeria's masses behind their cause, but certainly not as a model for government. Ahmed Ben Bella, a leading figure in the FLN and future president of Algeria, is a good example of the kind of man who masterminded Algeria's independence. Ben Bella spoke French rather than Arabic as his first language, he served with great distinction in the French army during World War II, and his guiding philosophy was Arab Nationalism. As a friend and follower of Egypt's president Gamal Abdel Nasser, regarded by many as the father of Arab Nationalism, Ben Bella subscribed to the vision of a strong, independent Arab world that would create its own kind of society free of foreign influence. The Arab Nationalist ambition was secular, socialist, and looked to industrial and technological progress to provide social justice. Islam was recognized and respected as an element of Arab tradition, and one that was seen as having been suppressed under foreign rule, but Arab Nationalism was a very long way from the ideas of those who longed for the establishment of an Islamic state.

The roots of the strand of radical conservative Islam that has become such a controversial feature of the modern Muslim world were well established by the 1950s, but its time was yet to come. Reformers wishing to return to the imagined simplicity and purity of an older form of Islam had been active across the Muslim world for generations. As early as the 18th century the Muslim scholar Muhammad ibn Abd al-Wahhab had founded the ultraconservative Sunni school of thought known, disparagingly, as Wahhabism. Through its association with the House of Saud, Wahhabism became a powerful force on the Arabian Peninsula, eventually forming the dominant philosophy of the kingdom of Saudi Arabia from its foundation in 1922 to the present day. Islamic reformers were also at work in Algeria. Abd al-Hamid Ben Badis was a highly influential figure in the early-20th-century history of Islam in Algeria. During his religious education in Tunis, in present-day Tunisia, Ben Badis was exposed to, and became a firm supporter of, the principles of Wahhabism and the broader reforming philosophy of Salafism. Returning to Algeria in 1913, Ben Badis began teaching what he had learned to adults and children at mosques in the city of Constantine. As a popular teacher and journalist Ben Badis railed against the detrimental effects of French colonial influence on the faith of Algerians. He also worked tirelessly to eradicate what he saw as degenerate practices among Algerian Muslims, such as the long-standing tradition of honoring, and even worshiping, traveling Muslim marabouts.

In 1936 Ben Badis was instrumental in founding a national organization of religious scholars and leaders known as the Algerian Muslim Congress. When this organization was disbanded the following year, Ben Badis became the leader of a similar group calling itself the Association of Muslim Algerian Ulema. In this role he became the leading figure of peaceful Muslim opposition to French rule, and he served to inspire a small but growing section of Algerian society in which conservative Muslim ideals took firm hold. Ben Badis and his colleagues saw the influence of French norms and cultural customs as a direct and deadly threat to 1,500 years of Muslim tradition in Algeria. His eloquent writings and sermons persuaded many ordinary Algerians to a similar point of view and, therefore, had a profound influence on the ongoing development of Algerian society as it chaffed under foreign rule.[18]

It was against this background of passionate but largely peaceful opposition to French colonialism from Algeria's leading religious figures that the FLN launched its armed struggle for independence in 1954. The FLN leadership used the language of Islamic struggle, describing the war as a "jihad" and its victims as "martyrs," as a way of drawing on the support of this radicalized element of Algerian society and of establishing its religious credentials with the masses. The Algerian war of independence was to become one of the most infamous and devastating conflicts in modern African history. Algeria eventually won its independence, but victory was not delivered quickly or easily as France fought tenaciously to keep a grip on its valuable and long-held territory. By 1959 France had half a million troops in Algeria engaged in anti-insurgency operations. French forces tortured FLN suspects and ruthlessly bombed villages believed to be giving shelter to rebels. The FLN in turn became equally brutal in their tactics, switching its attacks from military to civilian targets. The embattled urban enclaves in which those French settlers who had not fled the fighting sheltered were repeatedly bombed by FLN guerrillas, causing widespread civilian deaths. By the time Algeria gained independence in 1962 up to 1 million people, the vast majority of them Algerian, had been killed in the fighting. Basking in glory as the liberators of Algeria, the FLN formed the country's first indigenous government, and Ahmed Ben Bella became the nation's first president. However, those elements of Algerian society who had been anticipating this moment as the opportunity to establish a new state based firmly on the principles of Islam were to be sorely disappointed.

Islam in the Post-Independence Period

The FLN had always constituted a front for a broad coalition of Algerian groups bound together by the overriding desire to win independence. It was at the forefront of the struggle because it was led by capable, educated men who understood, and could exploit, the nature of a war against a European military power like France. Many of its leaders had, like Ben Bella, served in the French forces and been educated under the French system. They were informed by the successes and failures of similar campaigns against European domination in Egypt and other parts of the Middle East. They understood the political dimensions of the battle, knowing how to impact French public opinion and the opinion of the world community. Indeed the war in Algeria had far-reaching effects in France resulting as it did in the fall of the Fourth French Republic and the establishment of the Fifth Republic under Charles de Gaulle (1890–1970). The FLN's authority was not unquestioned, however. For example, in Algeria and among the large Algerian expatriate community in France the FLN fought a second front against the Algerian National Movement throughout the war. Elements within the liberation movement who had ambitions for the establishment of an Islamic state in Algeria also sometimes came into conflict with the FLN, and some individuals were assassinated.

Describing the disappointment of conservative Muslims in the aftermath of the war, Abbas Madani, who was later to become a prominent voice in a new Algerian Islamist movement, said: "The Algerian state of 1962 had nothing to do with what had been projected on the first of November 1954, for which we had taken up arms: an independent state founded on Islamic principles. The state that has risen before our eyes was founded on secular, socialist principles. This was a serious deviation."[19] The FLN leadership seized and held on to power with ease after the war because the majority of Algerians saw them as the nation's liberators. This legitimization of the FLN's power continued for decades, making any form of resistance to their essentially secular and socialist program by conservative Muslim elements extremely difficult. Such resistance did exist, however, and grew in strength with every passing decade.

As early as 1964 a radical Muslim opposition calling itself Al Qiyam emerged in Algeria. Opposed to what it saw as the continuing dominance of Western ideas and practices in government and society, Al Qiyam called for a revolution in Algerian culture to match the revolution achieved with Algerian political independence. Al Qiyam had some success in pressuring the government of Ben Bella to introduce measures aimed at strengthening Islam in Algeria. For example, Islamic religious education was made compulsory in public schools, a policy that seemed at first glance to have little impact on the realization of Al Qiyam's goals but that, in the long term, was to form the basis for a powerful challenge to Algeria's ruling class.[20] A similar group calling itself Al-Irshad wa al-Islah was also active in the period soon after Algerian independence, calling for a purging of Western values from Algerian society. Both Al Qiyam and Al-Irshad wa al-Islah operated in the nonviolent tradition established by Abd al-Hamid Ben Badis in the last years of French rule. This reforming strand in Algerian society believed in gradual and incremental progress toward a modern state ever more in tune with the tenets of Islam.[21] Other groups advocated a more direct approach, but they were not tolerated by the increasingly dictatorial FLN.

ISLAM UNDERGROUND 1962–1988

Arab nationalists often pointed to post-independence Algeria as a prime example of a successful, secular Arab-Muslim state. However, serious flaws underlay the prosperous and peaceful face that the Algeria of the 1960s and 1970s presented to the outside world. Much of the nation's prosperity in this period was underpinned by oil and gas revenues. As the petrodollars rolled in, the chaos and inefficiency in Algeria's agricultural sector, where most of the nation's ordinary citizens worked, was masked. Corruption was also becoming a major drain on the economy though this, too, was hidden by ever-growing revenues from oil and gas exports. Algeria's political health was also failing.

The FLN declared a one-party state in 1963, and in 1965 a military coup removed Ben Bella from power and installed Houari Boumedienne, establishing the Algerian army as the dominant force in politics. Boumedienne ruled by decree until 1976 when a new constitution establishing a one-party socialist state allowed him to continue in power as an "elected" president. By the late 1970s the FLN and its direct descendent the Algerian army had effectively held absolute power for almost 20 years. During this period ordinary Algerians had virtually no political voice. When world economic conditions took a turn that hit Algeria's one-dimensional economy hard, the resentment of a generation of political oppression was coupled with increasingly desperate economic hardship to form an explosive mix. Throughout this period Algeria's reforming religious leaders had been increasingly marginalized by the ruling elite, but they had not remained inactive. A new and powerful grassroots movement, clustered around the decades-old dreams of Abd al-Hamid Ben Badis and energized by a new generation of radical homegrown and foreign preachers, was on the verge of sweeping aside Algeria's tired and corrupt system of government, or so they believed.

To the outside observer it is perhaps surprising to note the continuing strength of French cultural influence in Algeria after it achieved independence. The war for independence was so long and bitter that a complete rejection of every trace of the occupying power might have been expected.

This did not happened. Algeria's ruling elite continued to speak French, to study at French universities, and to maintain close political and economic links with the former colonial power. The sheer depth of French involvement in Algeria's history accounts, in part, for this development. Algeria was, in a sense, a French creation. Before France invaded and carved out the region from the borderless depths of the Sahara Desert, the area had never been a distinct polity under centralized rule. This fact is, of course, true of many other African states that owe their current borders and geographical identity to the whims of colonial mapmakers, but in Algeria's case the cultural influence of its conqueror was more deeply entrenched than in most former colonial territories. Early uprisings against French rule prompted France to adopt a policy of promoting settlement in its North African territories. By 1881 there were approximately 300,000 Europeans living in Algeria, making up more than 10 percent of the total population, and settlement continued into the 20th century. In urban areas, where many French settlers concentrated, their sheer numbers had a profound and lasting cultural impact on the indigenous society around them. Algerians who wished to make a better life for themselves could do so only by learning French and working for French businesses or for the government. It was from this Arab French-speaking middle class that the leaders of the independence movement emerged, and it was these leaders who formed the core Algeria's post-independence ruling class. Algerians living outside of the main population centers fought and suffered in the war for independence but, when it was over, found themselves ruled by a distant, urban French-speaking elite largely indistinguishable from the one that had gone before.

This profound schism in Algerian society between the Arabic-speaking majority and the French-speaking elite was startlingly visible in Algeria's universities. Thanks to the efforts of reforming groups such as Al Qiyam the Arabic language and religious education had become well established at all levels of Algeria's educational system, but they were restricted in scope. Law and the humanities were taught in Arabic, but scientific courses were taught in French. Since the Algerian economy was dominated by the petrochemical industry almost all the well-paid jobs went to French-speaking science graduates, while the ever-increasing number of Arabic-speaking graduates found few opportunities for work. The French speakers were, of course, largely the offspring of established French-speaking Algerian families who could afford to have their children educated abroad through their ties to the lucrative oil and gas industries or the government. A generation of radicalized opponents to the government steeped in Arabic culture and history and with a strong grounding in Islamic studies emerged from Algeria's universities in the 1970s and 1980s.[22] Early signs of the potential for radicalized students to destabilize the regime came in 1982 when bloody confrontations between students and police followed the publication of "A Charter for an Islamic State" at the University of Algiers. Muslim student groups were targeted by government security forces following the 1982 riots but continued to spread underground.

The ruling party never abandoned its Islamist rhetoric but, by the mid-1980s, it was starting to sound increasingly hollow in the ears of a growing Algerian underclass suffering in an economic downturn while the generals and politicians continued to grow fat on petrodollars. The state of Algerian law is a good example of the mismatch between rhetoric and action. Islam was established as Algeria's state religion in the first post-independence constitution, but few elements of traditional Islamic sharia law were present in statute. It was not until 1984, for example, when the threat of conservative Islam was becoming apparent to the government, that a sharia-inspired Algerian Family Code was passed into law. The code, which was fiercely opposed by secularists and women's groups, banned marriage between Muslim women and non-Muslim men, allowed men to take up to four wives, and made divorce more difficult for women. At the same time prohibitions that were in place in many other Muslim-majority states, such as on the sale of alcohol, were completely absent in Algeria. On the other hand, the FLN embarked on an ambitious program of mosque building after independence and encouraged religious scholars from Egypt and other parts of the Muslim world to visit and teach in Algeria. The voice of the Muslim establishment in the country was kept under firm government control, however. The Ministry of Religious Affairs oversaw all religious education and training, administered religious charity funds, and issued standardized Friday sermons to be delivered across the country.

THE RISE OF THE ISLAMIC SALVATION FRONT

By 1988 pressures in Algerian society were reaching a critical level. The decline in oil prices that had been sapping Algeria's dangerously one-dimensional economy for much of the decade grew too serious for even the closeted political elite to ignore. The government launched a program of deregulation and liberalization that was intended to breathe new life into the failing petrochemical sector and sweep away some of the worst inefficiencies in other parts of the economy. The elimination of many social welfare provisions and subsidies made up one aspect of this program. Together with a loosening of state controls, these policies impacted the urban and rural working classes, plunging them even further into poverty. The already dramatic gap between rich and poor yawned wider still as the elite took advantage of economic liberalization to make even more money and ordinary Algerians lost the agricultural subsidies that had made their lives only just bearable. Galloping inflation and deepening corruption in the organs of the state added to the crisis.

The ruling FLN's mandate, based on its role as the liberator of Algeria, was already seriously strained. When the riots that erupted across Algeria's cities in the autumn of 1988 were repressed by government troops, who killed several hundred, it finally shattered completely. Then president Chadli Bendjedid, who had been in power since 1979, undertook a crash program of democratization and political liberalization, which was intended to restore public faith in the FLN. The constitution was amended the same year to allow, for the first time, the formation of political parties other than the FLN, and the role of the army in Algeria's government was severely curtailed. Dozens of political parties sprang up in the suddenly open political arena, the vast majority of them bitterly opposed to the FLN, and just as rapidly they began to gain mass support.

One of the many new political parties that emerged in the heady months after the liberalization of 1988 was known as the Front Islamique du Salut (Islamic Salvation Front, FIS). Like the FLN 30 years before the FIS was more of a loose amalgam of vaguely collaborating factions than a single movement with clear objectives. The one objective all elements of the FIS did share, however, was their determination to replace the FLN as the font of national political power. The FIS never published a definitive set of policies, and its leaders often contradicted each other. In fact the party did not even have agreed-upon rules for the discussion and adoption of policies. The party's modus operandi was to promise all things to all men with the bland assurance that it was everything the FLN was not. Even its choice of leaders was contradictory. Established Muslim moderates such as Abbas Madani made speeches lauding pluralism and democracy while known radicals such as Ali Belhaj promised the establishment of a strict Islamic republic based on sharia law. Madani, who had the upper hand in the FIS's leadership as long as the national process of democratization was moving forward, said: "Pluralism is a guarantee of the cultural wealth and diversity needed for development. Democracy, as we understand it, means pluralism, choice and freedom."[23] At the other end of the spectrum Belhaj was quoted as saying "When we are in power there will be no more elections because God will be ruling."[24] In a more stable and settled democratic atmosphere than that which existed in Algeria at the time, the contradictions evident in the FIS's political platform might have made it a laughing stock, but the mass of Algerians were unused to open political debate and lapped up the FIS's bland assurances of peace and prosperity for all. Individual strands of FIS rhetoric appealed to a wide range of elements in Algerian society. The young heard the message of freedom and a national cleansing of the old guard and their corrupt ways, and the old heard the message of reinstated social welfare provisions and a return to traditional values; reforming firebrands latched onto the call for the establishment of sharia law, and moderates were reassured by talk of pluralism and democracy.

The depth of Bendjedid's folly became clear in the summer of 1990 when the FIS made an astonishing showing in local government elections. Gaining approximately 35 percent of the total national vote, the FIS took power in almost half of all local assemblies across the country and in more than 90 percent of local assemblies in urban areas. If this achievement made waves among the political old guard and army leadership it was nothing compared to the shock when the FIS won 188 out of 231 parliamentary seats in the first round of legislative elections in December 1991.[25] If the FIS could garner a similar level of support in the second round of elections for the remaining 199 seats it would sweep to power on an unassailable mandate. This was too much for the increasingly unsettled old guard to take, and in January 1992 the army stepped in, canceling the electoral process and forcing Bendjedid to resign. It was a decision that was to have devastating consequences for Algeria.

THE ALGERIAN CIVIL WAR

As part of the de facto military coup of 1992 that ended Algeria's brief experiment with democracy the army moved to suppress the FIS as a priority. The party was declared illegal, and its leaders were arrested and sentenced to long prison terms. Many radical opponents of the government who had, until this point, been held in check by the runaway democratic success of the FIS decided they had no alternative but to take up arms. Disparate groups took to the hills of Algeria's sparsely populated interior and began launching attacks on government troops. At first many of these guerrilla bands were small and led by individuals who had taken part in the great jihad against Soviet forces in Afghanistan a decade earlier. The coup discredited the notion of winning power through the ballot box for radical elements of the FIS and reinforced their belief that it could be obtained only at the end of an assault rifle. One prominent guerrilla group that emerged from the remnants of the FIS called itself the Armed Islamic Group (GIA). It declared that: "Power is within the range of our Kalashnikovs."[26] The extremists believed they had failed to win power because of insufficient religious piety. By participating in what they saw as the Western-imported, anti-Islamic process of democratic elections, they had forgotten the lessons of Afghanistan, where armed jihad had succeeded in defeating a seemingly invincible enemy. Consequently, groups such as the GIA were as fanatically opposed to the FIS as they were to the government.

Algeria's civil war was essentially a conflict between an entrenched secular government and an Islamist opposition. This opposition was, however, deeply divided. Rebels loyal to the, now illegal, FIS fought to force the government to concede open elections in which they expected to complete the democratic victory they had so nearly won in 1992. Fighting both the government and groups loyal to the FIS guerrilla armies, the GIA had no interest in elections and simply wanted to force the establishment of their vision of a pure Islamic state. FIS loyalists eventually coalesced to form the Islamic Salvation Army (AIS), while the GIA became the leading practitioners of the jihad model of opposition. Although the GIA started out by targeting government and military targets, it quickly turned to terrorizing ordinary Algerians suspected of supporting the FIS or AIS. Throughout the conflict, but particularly in its later stages, the GIA carried out massacres of civilian populations across the country. Targeting villages or urban neighborhoods, GIA fighters systematically murdered men, women, and children whom they considered guilty of betraying Islam. While the AIS was content to boycott elections held by the government in this period, the GIA adopted the slogan "one vote, one bullet" in an attempt to terrorize the population out of voting. These massacres horrified both the FIS and AIS, although some sources claim both groups also took part in massacres, to the point where they began to consider a cease-fire with the government. The political leaders of the FIS and AIS were worried that Algerians would come to associate all Islamic parties and groups with the horrors perpetrated by the GIA. In October 1997, after five years of fighting, the AIS declared a unilateral cease-fire in the hope that this would "unveil the enemy that hides behind these abominable massacres." The AIS formally disbanded and handed in its weapons in 1999. With the withdrawal of the AIS from the conflict, Algeria's civil war became a two-way fight between government forces and the increasingly embattled GIA. As internal divisions sapped the GIA's cohesiveness the army was able to mop up its operations. Having declared all Algerians who did not support them as apostates and, therefore, legitimate targets, the rapidly shrinking GIA withdrew further into Algeria's interior, where it was systematically hunted down and eliminated. By 2005 the GIA was destroyed. The civil war came to an end after more than a decade of fighting that had produced more than 100,000 deaths. But very little had changed. The army-dominated government remained more firmly in power than ever—it had never come close to being deposed. Infighting among the guerrillas had weakened the entire opposition front. Because Algeria's main source of funding, the oil and gas fields of the Sahara, had remained undisturbed throughout the war, the government's old ruling elite remained as firmly entrenched in 2005 as they had been in 1992.

If anything the war proved a major setback to the Islamist cause in Algeria. The excesses of the GIA appalled most Algerians—despite their best efforts, the FIS and AIS were tarred by the same brush in the popular imagination. The September 11, 2001, attacks in the United States and the subsequent U.S. war on terror added to the poor perception among foreign observers of Algerian Islamist groups—groups that had, in fact, been fighting to restore democracy. Few people remembered the groundbreaking events of 1995 when the FIS and many other Islamist opposition groups had signed the Rome Accords promising to renounce "the use of violence to gain or maintain power" and demanding the reestablishment of democracy in Algeria. The Algerian government rejected the accords out of hand, and the AIS declared a cease-fire the following year.

POLITICAL ISLAM AFTER THE CIVIL WAR

During the later stages of the civil war, and in the years since its end, overtly Islamist political parties have suffered a serious decline in support among Algeria's electorate. Even as the war was under way Islamist political parties—those that were highly moderate—continued to take part in national politics. The Movement for the Society of Peace (MPS), for example, was formed in the early 1990s and continued to contest elections throughout the war. As an affiliate of the international Muslim Brotherhood movement the MPS distanced itself from the populist FIS, a fact that allowed it to survive the military crackdown of 1992, and it opposed the Islamist insurgency that started the civil war. In 1995 the MPS's presidential candidate polled 25 percent of the popular vote, placing him second behind the military-backed victor Liamine Zeroual. In 1997 the party gained just 15 percent of the vote in national parliamentary elections, and this figure fell even further to 7 percent in the elections of 2002. The MPS first declared its support for the winning presidential candidate Abdelaziz Bouteflika in 1999, and it has remained part of a coalition supporting Bouteflika ever since, essentially abandoning any ambitions to form a government of its own. Other Islamist parties have suffered a similar drop-off in popular support, and those that remain in parliament do so as distinctly minority voices. The Movement for National Reform, another moderate Islamist party that formed from a breakaway group of the MPS after the MPS decided to support Bouteflika, is probably the strongest of the independent Islamist parties in Algeria, but it managed to win only three seats in parliament in the 2007 elections, and its presidential candidate, Djahid Younsi, polled only 1.4 percent of the national vote in 2009.

The FLN has pulled off the remarkable feat of repositioning itself as the party most trusted by the electorate to reconstruct Algeria's economy and ensure peace while the Islamist movement has been largely discredited by its involvement in the long and devastating civil war. A majority of Algerians might have been prepared to endorse an Islamist party promising economic and political reform in 1991, but 20 years later very few are prepared to support utopian idealists who have shed so much blood. The cause of moderate Islamist groups in Algeria today is further hindered by a hard core of radicals who continue to perpetrate terrorist outrages. In 2002 a group calling itself the Salafist Group for Preaching and Combat split from the GIA and has continued to fight for the cause of an Islamic state. Later renaming itself the al-Qaeda Organization in the Islamic Maghreb, this small group has attacked police and military targets as well as murdering and kidnapping foreign workers and tourists in the country. As long as such groups continue to exist in Algeria, they serve to remind the traumatized electorate of the indiscriminate killings carried out by the GIA and other radical Islamist insurgents during the civil war, and calls for an Islamic state that these groups advocate are unlikely to appeal to voters.

ALGERIA GOING FORWARD

Algeria is an overwhelmingly Muslim-majority state, and many Algerians are devout Muslims. In the decades since Algerian independence Islam has undergone a renaissance in the country, as it has in many other parts of the Muslim world. The Arabization and religious education programs introduced by the ruling FLN have produced a generation of Algerians who are more conscious of, and better informed about, their Islamic heritage. The eclipse of Islam in Algeria by Western cultural norms that was so feared by religious leaders such as Abd al-Hamid Ben Badis in the first decades of the 20th century has not happened. In fact, the reverse is true. More mosques are being built, many Algerian women have voluntarily taken to wearing head scarves, and Algerians are generally more in touch with the mainstream currents and debates of the wider Muslim world. The government, too, although often described as secular, essentially reflects the strong faith of ordinary Algerians. Many members of the FLN are devout Muslims, Islam remains the constitutionally affirmed faith of the nation, and religious rhetoric is featured as an integral part of everyday political life.

Radical Islam of the kind that strives for the revolutionary establishment of an Islamic state is a largely discredited force in Algeria. It was never, in fact, a popular idea among the majority of Algerians. From a Western perspective Algeria's civil war can look like a "close call" in which the bogeyman of a repressive, violent, and antidemocratic Islamist state has been only narrowly averted, but the truth is far different. The overwhelming majority of those who took up arms against the government in 1992 did so because they were incensed at the suspension of the democratic process, not because they wanted to abolish democracy. The FIS, and its military wing the AIS, part of a long Algerian tradition of reforming Islam turned to violence only when provoked to the extreme by a ruling elite desperate to hold on to power. The extreme emotions and chaos of the conflict allowed ultraconservative Islamists to come to the fore in the form of the GIA, but this radical strand of Islamic thought never enjoyed widespread support among Algerians and quickly earned their intense hatred through its indiscriminate massacres and arrogant proclamations.

At the end of the first decade of the 21st century Algeria is a Muslim-majority nation in which Islam plays a central role in the daily lives of its citizens and the discourse of national politics. The likelihood of Algeria becoming an Islamic state has receded from a slim possibility in the mid-1990s to a distant unlikelihood in the 2000s. At the same time, prospects that Algeria will become a truly secular state with Islam retreating into the private sphere seem less likely today than they did in the immediate post-independence period. Algerians are weary of religiously motivated conflict, but at the same time they are more aware of and involved in their Muslim heritage. Algerian politicians who do not wear their Muslim faith on their sleeves are less likely to achieve power than are atheist candidates in a U.S. presidential election, but those who call for an Islamic revolution are given short shrift. Does this make Algeria a model for Muslim majority states in the modern world? At this point Algeria is enjoying a period of relative peace and stability in which the state is avowedly Muslim in its philosophy but merely regulates rather than directs religious affairs. It is unclear, however, how long this state of affairs will continue. The economic and social problems that precipitated the civil war remain largely unsolved a generation later. Although some progress has been made in modernizing and diversifying Algeria's economy, unemployment remains high, social inequalities wide, and corruption rife. The danger that Algeria's dispossessed, especially the young, could once again become the willing foot soldiers of a violent strand of Islamic thought cannot be discounted as long as these inequalities persist.

THE UNITED ARAB EMIRATES

The United Arab Emirates (UAE) is a highly unusual Muslim-majority state. Tiny in size but immensely wealthy thanks to its oil reserves, the federation has embarked on a program of economic reconstruction over the past 20 years that has revolutionized the nation. The UAE represents an intriguing attempt to marry a conservative Muslim society to the world of international finance, global tourism, and intercontinental real estate speculation. While many in the Muslim world have rejected Western influences as a threat to Islam, the government of the UAE has tried to find a way to engage with the West as a potential customer. The outcome of this bold experiment in economic restructuring, and the impact it will have on the UAE's social structure, is not yet clear, but many in the Muslim world are watching with interest.

The UAE in Context

The United Arab Emirates (UAE) is a federation of geographically contiguous states, known as emirates, on the Persian Gulf coast of the Arabian Peninsula. Its seven constituent states are Abu Dhabi, Ajman, Dubai, Fujairah, Ras al-Khaimah, Sharjah, and Umm al-Qaiwain. Abu Dhabi is by far the largest of the emirates, covering about 85 percent of the total territory of the UAE. Dubai is the second-largest emirates and Ajman is the smallest, with an area of just 100 square miles. Islam came to the area that would later become the UAE early—situated on the Arabian Peninsula, the birthplace of Islam, the Arab tribes of the region became Muslims in the seventh century.

Successive Muslim empires ruled the peninsula for almost 1,500 years, and the last of which, the Ottoman Empire, gained control over the emirates in the 16th century. The part of the Persian Gulf coast that would later become the UAE was notorious in the 18th and 19th centuries as the home of Muslim raiders, who habitually attacked European vessels sailing to and from India and Southeast Asia. The British launched a campaign to suppress what they referred to as the "pirate coast" in the first decades of the 19th century. In 1820 the rulers of several small states in the area signed peace treaties with Britain that put an end to piracy. A series of treaties agreed between Britain and local rulers throughout the 19th century led to these states becoming known as the Trucial States. The Trucial States became British protectorates in 1892, and they remained as such until Britain announced its intention to end all protection agreements with the Persian Gulf States in 1968. Six of the seven present-day emirates formed the UAE in 1971, with the seventh, Ras al-Khaimah, joining in 1972.

An Economic Miracle?

Until the late 1950s the economies of the seven emirates that would later form the UAE were dependent on fishing and a declining pearling industry. Their citizens were among the poorest in the world, infrastructure was primitive, and no social welfare system existed. Sixty years later the UAE is one of the most highly developed countries in the world according to socioeconomic indicators such as per capita gross domestic product (GDP), per capita energy consumption, and the Human Development index, which takes into account life expectancy, education, and standard of living. At the end of the first decade of the 21st century the UAE has one of the 40 largest economies in the world in terms of GDP—a startling achievement for a nation with a population of less than 5 million. This dramatic change has taken place because of two factors: an enormous influx of cash from the export of oil and natural gas and a decision by the emirates' rulers to use this money to greatly improve the lives of their subjects.

The UAE has the world's sixth-largest proven oil reserves.[27] However, more than 80 percent of these reserves are located in just one of the seven emirates, Abu Dhabi. The emirates of Dubai, Sharjah, and Ras al-Khaimah also have some oil and gas reserves, but far less than Abu Dhabi. Like other oil-rich Persian Gulf States, such as Saudi Arabia and Kuwait, the UAE's economy is dominated by its oil and gas industries. All of these states have long-term plans to diversify their economies, but for some the need is more urgent than for others. It is believed that Dubai will be able to maintain its current output of oil for only another 10 to 20 years. Dubai has been involved therefore in a spectacularly ambitious program to completely alter the structure of its economy before its oil revenues start to run out. By investing its own great wealth and offering generous tax and other incentives to foreign investors, Dubai's ruling family has transformed the economy such that oil and gas revenues make up only 6 percent of GDP. Abu Dhabi has followed a similar course but much more slowly and carefully. If the UAE is a potential model for the future development of oil-rich Muslim-majority states, Dubai is its showroom.

Dubai's restructuring program began in the mid-1990s when Mohammed bin Rashid al-Maktoum was named crown prince by his father, Emir Rashid bin Saeed al-Maktoum. Given the task of securing the emirate's economic future, the crown prince set up Dubai Holding, a holding company that directed the investment of government money through a range of subsidiary companies operating in real estate, tourism, finance, health care, technology, and media.[28] Mohammed bin Rashid al-Maktoum became emir of Dubai following the death of his father in 2006 and was also appointed prime minister and vice president of the UAE. As part of its development plan, Dubai created special economic zones intended to encourage foreign investment through very low or nonexistent taxation. Dozens of international corporations have taken advantage of these zones to set up regional centers in Dubai, adding to the emirate's rapid economic boom. One of the most visible results of Dubai's restructuring program has been an enormous construction and property boom. Driven by a number of government-sponsored mega-construction projects, Dubai city has been transformed in less than a decade. Impressive projects include the construction of artificial islands and peninsulas, adding hundreds of miles of coastline to the emirate; the Dubai Mall, one of the world's largest shopping centers; the Burj Dubai, the tallest building in the world; and Dubailand, an entertainment complex twice the size of Walt Disney World Resort in Florida.

For a decade Dubai's breakneck pace of development seemed unstoppable, but the global economic downturn of 2008 revealed weaknesses in the emirate's economic model that critics had been warning about for years. Rather than building an industrial base gradually over generations, Dubai opted to try to construct an entire economy based on service industries in one generation. The government spent its wealth on creating an infrastructure that would attract international corporations working in the service sector, such as banks, media companies, and information technology concerns, as well as tourists and wealthy individuals interested in acquiring luxury properties. The government changed the law to allow foreign individuals and companies to buy freeholds in the emirate, and it put in place a regulatory system that imitated the most attractive aspects of systems in other leading financial centers, such as London, New York, and Singapore. Dubai's economy boomed, but it was financed largely by foreign money. When the Western world plunged into recession in 2008 the money fueling Dubai's relentless growth dried up within months. Thousands of foreign entrepreneurs fled the country as property prices plunged by 50 percent or more, and they were soon followed by expatriates who had been made redundant. Reports appeared daily of expensive cars being abandoned at the airport by foreigners who preferred to cut their losses and leave rather than face the possibility of prison under Dubai's debt laws.[29] The building boom also ground to a halt as banks and foreign investors drew back from risky projects and work on scores of construction projects simply stopped. As one commentator noted: "[Dubai's] growth has been a direct result of it becoming an essentially tax-free zone for foreign nationals and companies. These companies, whilst providing jobs and income to people in the country, are not transferring any technical skills to the people."[30] It is a problem faced by many economies that have tried to take shortcuts to economic prosperity. Although Dubai, and the UAE as a whole, has invested a great deal on improving the nation's educational infrastructure, too little time has elapsed to produce a sufficiently large, technically educated Arab workforce.

Dubai's economic fortunes are almost certain to rebound; too much money has already been invested in infrastructure for it to be abandoned. At the height of the crisis Abu Dhabi stepped in with a multibillion dollar loan[31] to prevent Dubai from going bankrupt, but this money was essentially oil money and the rescue was, therefore, an admission of failure. If Dubai's plan to escape from an economy dominated by trading in oil has to be rescued with oil money when times are tough, the validity of the plan itself is in question.

Social Concerns

The UAE is a Muslim-majority state, but its indigenous Arab population lives as a minority in its own country. Only about 20 percent of the total population of 4.7 million are UAE citizens, the other 80 percent are immigrants. The great majority of these immigrants are from South Asia or other parts of the Middle East, and most are employed in the UAE as laborers or domestic servants. Westerners and East Asians, who are also in the UAE to work, make up about 8 percent of the total population.[32]

Since almost all UAE citizens are Muslim and the overwhelming majority of workers coming from Iran, Pakistan, India, and Bangladesh are also Muslim, the UAE remains a Muslim-majority state. About 96 percent of the total population, including immigrants, are Muslim.[33] Despite being a Muslim-dominated state the UAE is remarkably tolerant of other faiths and certainly more so than its conservative neighbor Saudi Arabia. Freedom of religion is guaranteed in the constitution, with a few restrictions, and generally upheld by the rulers of all the emirates. Non-Muslim groups are able to build places of worship on land granted for that purpose by the ruling emir of the emirate in which they live or to conduct religious activities in their own homes or rented spaces. There are several Christian churches in the UAE as well as places of worship for Hindus and Sikhs. The state maintains firm control over religious teaching in mosques. A government body, the General Authority for Islamic Affairs and Endowments, employs 95 percent of imams in Sunni mosques and issues weekly guidelines on the content of religious sermons, except in Dubai where the Department of Islamic Affairs and Endowments performs a similar role.[34] The UAE has a system of civil law for criminal offenses as well as a parallel set of sharia courts that deals with cases involving family law, inheritance, and some criminal offenses. Shia Muslims have their own courts.

TREATMENT OF IMMIGRANTS

The UAE has a generally good record on human rights, certainly better than many Middle Eastern Muslim-majority states, but serious concerns have been raised about the treatment of immigrant workers. Millions of South Asians have been attracted to the UAE over the past 30 years with promises of plentiful and well-paid work in the country's construction industry or as domestic servants. Many of them have found themselves trapped in the country by employers flouting employment laws or, in the worst cases, subjecting them to near slavery. Immigrants often pay large sums to employment agents in their home countries believing they will be able to pay these sums back from their wages in the UAE. Instead they find themselves working 12-hour shifts for much less than promised, crowded into labor camps, and without recourse to legal help in a country where trade unions and strikes are illegal.[35] UAE companies employing low-skilled workers have been accused of a catalog of abuses, including forcing workers to pay employment agency fees that should be paid by the employer, compelling workers to pay for visa renewals and other costs that should be covered by the employer, withholding wages for months or years at a time, confiscating passports to prevent workers from leaving the country, and failing to remedy dangerous working conditions.[36] In the economic downturn of 2008–09 conditions for these workers worsened. Many stopped receiving wages altogether but could not leave the country or find other jobs, forcing them into impossible debt. The already high suicide rate among immigrant workers rocketed. One Indian worker in the UAE who committed suicide left a note that read: "I have been made to work without any money for months. Now, for a month I've been suffering from a constant headache and wanted to visit a doctor to examine my condition. I asked my camp boss for 50 [$14] but he refused and told me to get back to work. After my death I want the company to pay all my salary dues to my family and repay the financial debt my family has incurred because of them."[37]

The UAE also faces a major problem with human trafficking for sexual exploitation. The U.S. Department of State claims that: "Women from Uzbekistan, Kyrgyzstan, Ukraine, Russia, Kazakhstan, Armenia, Azerbaijan, Ethiopia, Somalia, Uganda, India, Pakistan, the People's Republic of China, the Philippines, Iraq, Iran, and Morocco are reportedly trafficked to the U.A.E. for commercial sexual exploitation,"[38] and that many women from South Asia voluntarily traveling to the UAE to work as domestic servants "face conditions of involuntary servitude such as excessive work hours without pay; verbal, mental, physical, and sexual abuse; and restrictions on movement."[39] It is worth noting that all these abuses, against male and female workers, are strictly prohibited under UAE law and that the government has gone to some lengths to stamp them out.

POLITICAL STRUCTURE

Perhaps the most glaring anomaly for a Western observer is the almost complete lack of democratic accountability in a state that prides itself on its liberal interpretation of Islam and its progressive attitudes toward human rights. Each of the seven emirates are absolute monarchies ruled by male-dominated dynasties. These ruling families derive their authority from their traditional status as tribal leaders in a society where lineage and tribal loyalties remain as prominent political forces. On the federal level the president of the UAE is traditionally the emir of Abu Dhabi, the largest and wealthiest of the emirates, and the prime minister is the emir of Dubai, the second-largest and wealthiest emirate. These offices are, therefore, effectively hereditary. The country's parliament, known as the Federal National Council, does not have legislative power, acting only as an advisory body to the president and prime minister. Half of the Federal National Council's members are appointed by the government while the other half are elected to their posts by an electorate of just 7,000 residents of the emirates who are nominated by the emirs. In other words, less than 1 percent of the citizens of the emirates have an opportunity to vote for the members of their government, and in any case, those whom they elect have only an advisory role. Given the great prosperity enjoyed by the average UAE citizen it is perhaps unsurprising that no popular demands for democratic reform have been raised. In a 2005 survey of young people the BBC found little enthusiasm for democratic ideas. Comments such as "Everybody is happy, everything is going smoothly, and I don't think we should jeopardize that to be a democratic country," were the norm.[40] Migrant workers who make up 80 percent of the population in the UAE, some of whom suffer intolerable conditions, may feel otherwise, but prospects that they will gain a voice in government are minimal

Islam in the UAE

The government of the UAE is usually described as advocating a "liberal" form of Islam. The transformation of the nation from a homogenous, highly traditional Arab-Muslim society into a multicultural modern nation has presented challenges in the areas of human rights but has not resulted in the kind of conservative religious backlash that has been seen in other Muslim-majority states. Women are not required to wear traditional conservative dress, although many do so out of choice, and the constitution guarantees them equal employment opportunities and legal status. Alcohol consumption is tolerated among non-UAE citizens, and the media is relatively free, if inclined to self-censorship. As a result of its policies to encourage foreign investment the UAE has formed close links with many Western nations that some Muslim-majority states regard with suspicion.

The fact that the UAE has escaped the attentions of Muslim terrorists has surprised some commentators. The country's liberal laws, its large number of non-Muslim Western residents, its close ties to Western corporations, and the fact that the United States has frequently used its harbor facilities to support its military operations in other parts of the Muslim world would seem to make it a prime target for the anger of fundamentalists. However, no attacks, incidents, or outrages of the kind that have rocked many other Muslim-majority nations have occurred. In international relations the UAE has built close security and cooperation links with the United States and other Western nations to the extent that it concluded a deal with the United States to import nuclear technology, expertise, and fuel in 2009. A similar deal between the United States and most other parts of the Muslim world is almost inconceivable.

Several factors have been suggested to explain the UAE's good fortune in avoiding terrorist attacks. Its security forces are well trained and well equipped, and they benefit from close cooperation with the security forces of its allies. Its citizens are generally wealthy and want for little, and so little fertile ground exists for radicals to cultivate discontent. The UAE is also held in high regard in many parts of the Muslim world for its generous foreign aid to Muslim states and its role as an important trading partner. Still, two of the terrorists accused of attacking the United States in September 2001 were from the UAE, and wealthy emirates are known to have provided funding to al-Qaeda, the Taliban, and other extremist groups. Belief that the UAE might remain immune from extremist violence also suffered a blow in 2009 when government officials revealed that a terrorist cell associated with al-Qaeda had been broken up before it could carry out a series of planned attacks on high-profile targets in the country.[41]

THE TALIBAN

Afghanistan

The United Nations Human Development Index for 2009 ranks Afghanistan at number 181 out of 182 least developed countries. Average earnings, educational opportunities, life expectancy, and a host of other measures of standard of living in Afghanistan are among the lowest on earth. The reason for Afghanistan's appalling situation is not difficult to identify—40 years of war have devastated its economy and infrastructure.

A political and religious organization that ruled Afghanistan between 1996 and 2001, the Taliban has come to embody the strain of violent and radically conservative Islam that much of the international community regards as a deadly enemy. The Taliban was the prime target of the 2001 U.S.-led invasion of Afghanistan, and members have since become the leaders of an insurgency that has once again engulfed Afghanistan in war and brought terror and killing to neighboring Pakistan. The story of the Taliban's rise to power, its defeat, and its subsequent rebirth has been the most extreme and dramatic element of the Muslim world's troubles over the past 20 years.

History
THE SOVIET-AFGHAN WAR

Afghanistan sits at a geographical crossroads in the center of Asia. It has been a battleground, imperial frontier, and invasion route for centuries. The 1979 Soviet invasion of Afghanistan marked the beginning of four decades of conflict that continues to the present day, but it was neither the first nor the last invasion the Afghan people have had to endure. At the time of the Soviet invasion, the cold war, a period of heightened tension between the United States and the Soviet Union, was at its peak. Restrained from engaging in direct conflict with each other by the threat of mutual nuclear annihilation, the United States and the Soviet Union battled in a series of proxy wars to gain influence around the globe. The Soviet-Afghan War, which continued until 1989, was the last of these conflicts. The war began when the ruling Communist Party of Afghanistan requested military aid from the Soviet Union to put down anticommunist rebels known as mujahideen. It pitted the titanic might of the Soviet armed forces against disparate groups of Muslim-Afghan fighters, who were increasingly funded and armed by the United States and Pakistan.

Even before the Soviet invasion the United States was covertly supporting the anticommunist mujahideen in Afghanistan.[42, 43] Pakistan's intelligence services helped the United States train and supply the mujahideen from the beginning. With the election of Ronald Reagan to the U.S. presidency in 1981, U.S. aid to the mujahideen grew rapidly. The Soviet army occupied Afghanistan's major towns and cities, but the various mujahideen groups were able to operate in large parts of the rugged Afghan countryside. They conducted a guerrilla campaign against Soviet forces, harassing supply lines and patrols from hideouts in the hills. From the mid-1980s the United States began supplying advanced handheld missile systems to the mujahideen that allowed them to inflict heavy losses on Soviet aircraft.[44] Covert U.S. forces were directly involved in training, and sometimes they led mujahideen groups in Afghanistan throughout the conflict. The Pakistani secret service was also heavily involved in supporting the mujahideen in cooperation with the United States.

By the late 1980s the Soviet Union found itself in serious economic trouble, and the continuing occupation of Afghanistan in the face of a well-armed and determined insurgency by the mujahideen had become extremely unpopular among Soviet citizens. Soviet forces began preparing to withdraw from Afghanistan as early as 1985 by training and equipping an Afghan army. The Soviet withdrawal began in 1987 and was complete by 1989. They left behind a pro-Soviet government and Afghan army that had little control over the country outside of the major cities.

THE RISE OF THE TALIBAN AND AL-QAEDA

The United States was not the only country that supported the mujahideen against the Soviet army. Saudi Arabia and other Persian Gulf States also supported the mujahideen with large amounts of money. For many Muslims, the mujahideen's war against Soviet occupation was a religious war. As the name suggests the mujahideen were seen as Islamic warriors engaged in a holy war, or jihad, against a non-Muslim occupier. Young men from all over the Muslim world traveled to Afghanistan to take part in this jihad. Known as Arab mujahideen or Arab Afghans, these fighters made up only a small fraction of the overall mujahideen insurgency against Soviet occupation, but they were well funded by Middle Eastern governments and wealthy individuals, which gave them an influence among the native mujahideen that was disproportionate to their numbers. One of these Arab mujahideen, a Saudi Arabian named Osama bin Laden, was to become an infamous figure.

The son of a wealthy Saudi Arabian family, Osama bin Laden first traveled to Afghanistan soon after leaving college in 1979. By 1984 he had established an organization known as Maktab al-Khidamat (MAK) in Afghanistan along with Palestinian activist Abdullah Yusuf Azzam. MAK was created to raise funds for the Afghan mujahideen across the Muslim world and to recruit fighters for the cause. It is unclear how much money MAK raised or distributed between 1984 and the end of the Afghan-Soviet War in 1989 or how significant its activities were in the defeat of Soviet forces, but Osama bin Laden returned to Saudi Arabia in 1990 claiming to have played a major role in the victory. While Osama bin Laden was in Saudi Arabia, Iraq invaded and occupied neighboring Kuwait, thus starting the Persian Gulf War. Some sources claim that Osama bin Laden met with the crown prince of Saudi Arabia and offered the use of his Arab mujahideen organization to protect the kingdom from possible Iraqi aggression. When the Saudi government rejected this idea and allowed U.S. forces to be assembled on Saudi soil instead, Osama bin Laden criticized the Saudi government for allowing non-Muslim troops into the country. He left Saudi Arabia for Sudan in 1992, where he continued to vigorously criticize the Saudi regime.

While Osama bin Laden was in Saudi Arabia and Sudan, Afghanistan entered a new period of crisis. The pro-Soviet regime in Kabul surprised many observers by holding on to power after the Soviet army had left in the face of a continued mujahideen insurgency. The mujahideen, which was made up of many diverse Afghan groups, was not able to organize itself into an effective force capable of taking Kabul and establishing a government. As the fighting continued, a new group, calling itself the Taliban, emerged in Afghanistan and Pakistan. The Taliban was a fundamentalist Sunni Muslim political movement made up principally of Pashtuns, who are a large ethnic grouping in Afghanistan and one of the largest ethnic groups in neighboring western Pakistan. The precise origins of the Taliban are unclear, but they seem to have emerged as an armed force in the early 1990s. It is likely that the Pakistani government or elements of the Pakistani military were instrumental in turning the political movement into a trained and well-equipped fighting force that could battle the mujahideen. In the period immediately after the Soviet-Afghan War the mujahideen became increasingly fragmented, and many of its groups became little more than bandits preying on ordinary Afghans and on trade routes through the country. Millions of Afghan Pashtuns had fled to the Pashtun areas of Pakistan during the war. These exiles served as a ready source of recruits for a Pakistani-backed force that could be used to stabilize Afghanistan. Pakistan has always officially denied supporting the Taliban, but a number of sources associated with Pakistan's government at that time have since claimed Pakistan invested millions of dollars to help create and sustain the Taliban.[45]

The Taliban set out, first, to quell the lawlessness of the mujahideen and, second, to overthrow the government in Kabul and install a regime based on sharia law in its place. They began a military campaign in southern Afghanistan in 1994, and within two years this previously unknown group had captured large parts of the country and taken Kabul. At first the United States welcomed the advent of the Taliban as a potential cure for Afghanistan's years of division and violence. The international community began to have doubts about the Taliban regime, however, when reports emerged that it was banning girls from receiving education,[46] attacking non-Pashtun ethnic groups,[47] and engaging in other human rights violations.

As the Taliban rose swiftly to power in Afghanistan, Osama bin Laden came under increasing pressure in Sudan. The United States encouraged the Sudanese government to expel Osama bin Laden because Washington suspected him of involvement in a terrorist attack in Aden, Yemen. The Egyptian government wanted him dead for his involvement in an attempt to assassinate Egyptian president Hosni Mubarak in 1995, and the Saudi government had revoked his citizenship and persuaded his family to cut off his allowance. In 1996 Osama bin Laden traveled from Sudan to Afghanistan, where he formed a close relationship with the Taliban. Two years later terrorist bombs killed hundreds at the U.S. embassies in Dar es Salaam, Tanzania, and Nairobi,

Kenya. The U.S. government was convinced that Osama bin Laden and his al-Qaeda organization were involved in planning the attacks,[48] and U.S. forces launched missile strikes at suspected al-Qaeda bases in Sudan and Afghanistan. Washington also pressed the Taliban government in Afghanistan to extradite Osama bin Laden so that he could be tried in the United States, but all extradition requests were refused. U.S. relations with Afghanistan, already strained over the Taliban's human rights record, plunged to new depths.

THE SEPTEMBER 11 ATTACKS
AND THE INVASION OF AFGHANISTAN

Osama bin Laden's willingness to attack civilians had already been proven in U.S. eyes by the embassy bombings in Tanzania and Kenya in 1998. The attacks on New York City and Washington, D.C., on September 11, 2001, were immediately suspected to be the work of al-Qaeda and Osama bin Laden. Since the Taliban in Afghanistan had already made it clear that they were protecting Osama bin Laden, the regime became the prime target for American retaliation. Just nine days after the attacks on the United States, the U.S. government made a series of demands on the Taliban, including the immediate extradition of all al-Qaeda leaders in Afghanistan and the immediate closure of so-called terrorist training camps.[49] The Taliban rejected these demands, saying the United States had no evidence against al-Qaeda. U.S. and British forces began military operations against al-Qaeda and the Taliban in Afghanistan in October.

Operation Enduring Freedom, the U.S.-led assault on the Taliban regime and al-Qaeda in Afghanistan, successfully removed the Taliban from power and captured all Taliban-held cities within three months. Al-Qaeda's operations in Afghanistan were severely curtailed, but it is believed that many of its members and many Taliban members escaped the invading forces by crossing the border into Pakistan. The region of Pakistan bordering Afghanistan, known as the Federally Administered Tribal Areas (FATA), is a remote and mountainous area only tenuously controlled by the Pakistani government. The border between Afghanistan and the FATA is poorly policed, and many of the indigenous people of the FATA belong to the same Pashtun tribes that live in Afghanistan. Many al-Qaeda and Taliban fighters were able to easily slip across the border and find refuge among their fellow tribesmen.

THE TALIBAN RESURGENCE

During the winter of 2002–03 the Taliban regrouped in the mountainous regions along Afghanistan's border with Pakistan and in remote regions in the south of Afghanistan. Taliban fighters who had escaped the U.S. invasion by crossing into Pakistan were joined by new Afghan and Pakistani Pashtun recruits. In January 2003 a resurgent Taliban launched an insurgency against the U.S.-backed Afghan government that continues in 2010. In the latter half of the decade Taliban forces also became involved in an escalating conflict with Pakistani government forces in the Federally Administered Tribal Areas (FATA), which became known as the Waziristan War. In 2006 the NATO-led International Security Assistance Force (ISAF) in Afghanistan extended its area of operations to cover southern areas of the country as part of an effort to stamp out the Taliban insurgency. U.S. forces on operations against the Taliban in Afghanistan became part of this force, along with troops from 40 other nations. Other U.S. forces involved in training a new Afghan army remained under direct U.S. command.

The Waziristan War began when Pakistani forces entered the FATA searching for al-Qaeda and Taliban fugitives in an operation in cooperation with the U.S.-sponsored war on terror. What began as a series of small-scale engagements between Pakistani soldiers and al-Qaeda elements, Taliban forces, and other Pashtun rebels grew rapidly into a major conflict in which the Pakistani government has committed tens of thousands of troops. In 2009 the conflict began spreading as Taliban groups carried out a series of terror bomb attacks and shootings across Pakistan, striking at high-profile police and military targets. The conflict remains unresolved. Pakistani forces have declared their strategic aims as the elimination of Uzbek militants in the region, the capture or expulsion of "foreign fighters" from the Middle East and North Africa, and, finally, the disarming of local people supporting the Taliban. The Pakistani army has made progress in taking ground, but Taliban attacks continue in the FATA and across Pakistan.

[1] CIA World Factbook: Indonesia.

[2] BBC.co.uk. "Islam in Indonesia." October 25, 2002. Available online. URL: http://news.bbc.co.uk/2/low/asia-pacific/2357121.stm. Accessed November 2, 2009.

[3] ———. "Aceh's Sharia Court Opens." March 4, 2003. Available online. URL: http://news.bbc.co.uk/2/hi/asia-pacific/2816785.stm. Accessed November 2, 2009.

[4] ———. "Aceh Passes Adultery Stoning Law." September 14, 2009. Available online. URL: http://news.bbc.co.uk/2/hi/8254631.stm. Accessed November 2, 2009.

[5] ———. "Profile: Jafar Umar Thalib." January 30, 2003. Available online. URL: http://news.bbc.co.uk/2/hi/asia-pacific/1975345.stm. Accessed November 2, 2009.

[6] CDI.org. "In the Spotlight: Laskar Jihad." March 8, 2002. Available online. URL: http://www.cdi.org/terrorism/laskar.cfm. Accessed November 2, 2009.

[7] BBC.co.uk. "Analysis: Behind the Moluccan Violence." July 2, 2000. Available online. URL: http://news.bbc.co.uk/2/hi/asia-pacific/815610.stm. Accessed November 2, 2009.

[8] Zachary Abuza. "Funding Terrorism in Southeast Asia: The Financial Network of Al Qaeda and Jemaah Islamiyah." *NBR Analysis* 14, no. 5. The National Bureau of Asian Research. December 2003.

[9] United Nations Press Release SC/7548. Available online. URL: http://www.un.org/News/Press/docs/2002/SC7548.doc.htm. Accessed November 2, 2009.

10 Robert W. Hefner. *Civil Islam: Muslims and Democratization in Indonesia.* Princeton, N.J.: Princeton University Press, 2000.

[11] Asianews.it. "Indonesia to Ban Ahmadi Activities." September 6, 2008. Available online. URL: http://www.asianews.it/index.php?l=en&art=12466&size=A. Accessed November 2, 2009.

[12] Time.com. Hannah Beech. "Indonesia Elections: A Win for Democracy." July 8, 2009. Available online. URL: http://www.time.com/time/world/article/0,8599,1909198,00.html. Accessed November 2, 2009.

[13] Norimitsu Onishi. "Indonesia Bombings Signal Militants' Resilience." *New York Times,* July 17, 2009. Available online. URL: http://www.nytimes.com/2009/07/18/world/asia/18indo.html?_r=1. Accessed November 2, 2009.

[14] CBN.com. "Indonesia: Sharia-based Laws Creep into Half of Provinces." February 4, 2009. Available online. URL: http://www.cbn.com/cbnnews/shows/cwn/2009/February/Indonesia-Sharia-based-laws-Creep-i nto-Half-of-Provinces-/. Accessed November 2, 2009.

[15] Time.com. "A Call to Prayer." February 22, 2007. Available online. URL: http://www.time.com/time/magazine/article/0,9171,1592576-3,00.html. Accessed November 2, 2009.

[16] CIA World Factbook: Algeria.

[17] Proclamation of the Algerian National Front, Libertation Front (FLN), November 1954.

[18] John Ruedy, ed. *Islamism and Secularism in North Africa.* New York: St. Martin's Press, 1994. "Political Islam in Algeria: The Nonviolent Dimension." *Current History,* January 1995.

[19] Slimane Zeghidour. "Entretien avec Abbasi Madani." *Politique Étrangère,* no. 49, 1990, p. 180.

[20] Ricardo Rene Laremont. *Islam and the Politics of Resistance in Algeria, 1782–1992.* Trenton, N.J.: Africa World Press, 2000, pp. 10–103.

[21] John Entelis, ed. *Islam, Democracy and the State in North Africa.* Bloomington: Indiana University Press, 1997, p. 63.

[22] John Ruedy. *Modern Algeria: The Origins and Development of a Nation.* Bloomington: Indiana University Press, 1992, pp. 29–89.

[23] Ray Takeyh. "The Lineaments of Islamic Democracy." *World Policy Journal,* Winter 2001/2002.

[24] ———. "Islamism RIP." *The National Interest,* p. 30.

[25] Keith Sutton, Ahmed Aghrout, and Salah Zamiche. "Political Changes in Algeria: An Emerging Electoral Geography." *Maghreb Review,* 1992.

[26] Ray Takeyh. "Islamism RIP." p. 130.

[27] CIA World Factbook. Country Comparisons: Oil—Proved Reserves. Available online. URL: https://www.cia.gov/library/publications/the-world-factbook/rankorder/2178rank.html. Accessed November 6, 2009.

[28] Website of Dubai Holding: http://dubaiholding.com.

[29] Robert F. Worth. "Laid-Off Foreigners Flee as Dubai Spirals Down." *New York Times*, February 11, 2009. Available online. URL: http://www.nytimes.com/2009/02/12/world/middleeast/12dubai.html. Accessed November 6, 2009.

[30] Global Issues. "Dubai 'Miracle' Goes Bust." February 16, 2009. Available online. URL: http://adnan-globalissues.blogspot.com/2009/02/dubai-miracle-goes-bust.html. Accessed November 6, 2009.

[31] Chip Cummins. "Dubai Gets $10 Billion Bailout to Ease Debt." *Wall Street Journal*, February 23, 2009. Available online. URL: http://online.wsj.com/article/SB123532630416442781.html. Accessed November 6, 2009.

[32] CIA World Factbook: United Arab Emirates. Available online. URL: https://www.cia.gov/library/publications/the-world-factbook/geos/ae.html. Accessed November 6, 2009.

[33] CIA World Factbook: United Arab Emirates.

[34] Bureau of Democracy, Human Rights, and Labor: U.S. Department of State. "International Religious Freedom Report 2007." Available online. URL: http://www.state.gov/g/drl/rls/irf/2007/90223.htm. Accessed November 6, 2009.

[35] BBC.com. "Dark Side of the Dubai Dream." April 6, 2009. Available online. URL: http://news.bbc.co.uk/2/hi/uk_news/magazine/7985361.stm. Accessed November 6, 2009.

[36] Human Rights Watch. *Building Towers, Cheating Workers*. Section V. Exploitation of Migrant Construction Workers. November 11, 2006. Available online. URL: http://www.hrw.org/en/node/11123/section/6. Accessed November 6, 2009.

[37] "Worker Borrowed to Buy Stamp for Suicide Letter." *Construction Week*, no. 83, August 6–19, 2005.

[38] Under Secretary for Democracy and Global Affairs, U.S. Department of State. *Trafficking in Persons Report 2007. Country Narratives: United Arab Emirates*. Available online. URL: http://www.state.gov/g/tip/rls/tiprpt/2007/82807.htm. Accessed November 6, 2009.

[39] Under Secretary for Democracy and Global Affairs, U.S. Department of State. *Trafficking in Persons Report 2007*.

[40] BBC.com. "Few Want Vote in Booming Dubai." July 29, 2005. Available online. URL: http://news.bbc.co.uk/2/hi/middle_east/4724807.stm. Accessed November 6, 2009.

[41] Eli Lake and Sara Carter. "UAE Kept Tight Lid on Disrupted Terror Plot." *Washington Times*, September 17, 2009. Available online. URL: http://www.washingtontimes.com/news/2009/sep/17/uae-kept-tight-lid-on-disrupted-terror-plot/. Accessed November 6, 2009.

[42] Peter Bergen. *Holy War Inc.* New York: Free Press, 2001.

[43] Tim Weiner. *Blank Check: The Pentagon's Black Budget.* New York: Warner Books, 1990.

[44] Philip Heymann. *Living the Policy Process.* Oxford: Oxford University Press, 2008.

[45] Douglas Frantz. "A Nation Challenged: Supplying the Taliban." *New York Times*, December 8, 2001.

[46] Michael Griffin. *Reaping the Whirlwind: The Taliban Movement in Afghanistan.* London: Pluto Press, 2001.

[47] Richard C. Martin, ed. *Encyclopedia of Islam and the Muslim World.* New York: Macmillan Reference USA, 2004.

[48] "Osama bin Laden Tied to Other Fundamentalists." *National Intelligence Council Global Briefing,* 27, September 1998.

[49] "Transcript of President Bush's Address to a Joint Session of Congress." September 20, 2001.

PART II

Primary Sources

4

United States Documents

Mahommah Baquaqua (ca. 1803–?) was born in present-day Benin, West Africa, in about 1830. He was sold into slavery as a young man and shipped to Brazil, where he endured harsh treatment at the hands of several owners before being sold to a ship's captain. When his ship docked in New York, Baquaqua took the chance to escape, having heard that the United States was a "land of freedom." Baquaqua escaped slavery, made his way to Boston, and later traveled to Haiti. In 1850 he moved to McGrawville, New York, where he attended Central College. From there Baquaqua moved to Canada and then to Britain with the hope of returning home to Africa. Born and raised a Muslim, he converted to Catholicism while in Haiti. Baquaqua is known and celebrated today because of the biography he wrote while living in Canada in which he describes his experiences as a Muslim slave. The extract reproduced here gives Baquaqua's description of "the happiest moment of his life" when, still a slave traveling to the United States, he anticipates his escape.

We all had learned, that at New York there was no slavery; that it was a free country and that if we once got there we had nothing to dread from our cruel slave masters, and we were all most anxious to get there.

Previous to the time of the ship's sailing, we were informed that we were going to a land of freedom. I said then you will never see me any more after I once get there. I was overjoyed at the idea of going to a free country, and a ray of hope dawned upon me, that the day was not far distant when I should be a free man. Indeed I felt myself already free! How beautifully the sun shone on that eventful morning, the morning of our departure for that land of freedom we had heard so much about. The winds too were favorable, and soon the canvass spread before the exhilarating breeze, and our ship stood for that happy land. The duties of office, on that voyage, appeared light

127

to me indeed, in anticipation of seeing the goodly land, and nothing at all appeared a trouble to me. I obeyed all orders cheerfully and with alacrity.

That was that the happiest time in my life, even now my heart thrills with joyous delight when I think of that voyage, and believe that the God of all mercies ordered all for my good; how thankful was I. . . .

The first words of English that my two companions and myself ever learned was F-r-e-e; we were taught it by an Englishman on board, and oh! How many times did I repeat it, over and over again. This same man told me a great deal about New York City—he could speak Portuguese. He told me how the colored people in New York were all free, and it made me feel very happy, and I longed for the day to come when I should be there. The day at length came, but it was not an easy matter for two boys and a girl, who could only speak one word of English, to make their escape, having, as we supposed, no friends to aid us. But God was our friend, as it proved in the end, and raised up for us many friends in a strange land.

The pilot who came aboard of our vessel treated us very kindly—he appeared different to any person I had ever seen before, and we took courage from that little circumstance. The next day a great many colored persons came aboard the vessel, who inquired whether we were free. The captain had previously told us not to say that we were slaves, but we heeded not his wish, and he, seeing so many persons coming aboard, began to entertain fears that his property would take in their heads to lift their heels and run away, so he very prudently informed us that New York was no place for us to go about in—that it was a very bad place, and as sure as the people caught us they would kill us. But when we were alone we concluded that we would take the first opportunity and the chance, how we would fare in a free country.

One day when I had helped myself rather freely to wine, I was imprudent enough to say I would not stay aboard any longer; that I would be free. The captain hearing it, called me down below, and he and three others endeavored to confine me, but could not do so; but they ultimately succeeded in confining me in a room in the bow of the vessel. I was there in confinement several days. The man who brought my food would knock at the door, and if I told him to come in he would do so, otherwise he would pass along, and I got no food.

I told him on one occasion that I would not remain confined there another day with my life; that out I would get; and there being some pieces of iron in the room, towards night I took hold of one of them—it was a bar, about two feet long—with that I broke open the door, and walked out. The men were all busy at work, and the captain's wife was standing on the deck when I ascended from my prison. I heard them asking one another who had let me out; but no one could tell. I bowed to the captain's wife, and passed on to the side of the ship. There was a plank from the ship to the shore. I walked across it and ran as if for my life, of course not knowing whither I was going.

I was observed during my flight by a watchman who was rather lame, and he undertook to stop me, but I shook him off, and passed on until I got to a store, at the door of which I halted a moment to take breath. They inquired of me what was the matter, but I could not tell them, as I knew nothing of English but the word F-r-e-e. Soon after, the lame watchman and another came up to me. One of them drew a bright star from his pocket and showed it to me, but I could make nothing of it. I was then taken to the watch-house and locked up all night, when the captain called next morning, paid expenses, and took me back again to the ship along with him.

The officers told me I should be a free man, if I chose, but I did not know how to act; so after a little persuasion, the captain induced me to go back with him, as I need not be afraid. This was on a Saturday, and on the following Monday afternoon three carriages drove up and stopped near the vessel. Some gentlemen came aboard from them, and walked about the deck, talking to the captain, telling him that all on board were free, and requesting him to hoist the flag. He blushed a good deal, and said he would not do so; he put himself in a great rage and stormed somewhat considerably.

We were afterwards taken in their carriages, accompanied by the captain, to a very handsome building with a splendid portico in front, the entrance to which was ascended by a flight of marble steps, and was surrounded by a neat iron railing having gates at different points, the enclosure being ornamented with trees and shrubs of various kinds; it appeared to me a most beautiful place, as I had never seen anything like it before. I afterwards learned that this building was the City Hall of New York.

Source: Samuel Moore. *Biography of Mahommah G. Baquaqua.* Detroit, Mich.: Geo. E. Pomeroy and Company, 1854, 51–52, 54–56.

Mohammed Alexander Russell Webb, *Islam in America* (1893)

Mohammed Alexander Russell Webb (1846–1916) was an American journalist who became known as one of the first proselytizers of Islam in the United States. Raised a Presbyterian in Hudson, New York, Webb became a Muslim while serving as the U.S. consular representative to the Philippines in 1888. He later traveled to India to learn more about his faith and then returned to the United States, where he made many speeches extolling the virtues of Islam. Material from these speeches was later used in a series of publications, including his most famous, Islam in America. *As Webb notes in this extract, Islam was little understood and widely reviled in the United States at the time this was written. Webb's efforts did much to change this point of view, at least among the educated strata of U.S. society.*

I have been frequently asked why I, an American, born in a country which is nominally Christian, and reared, "under the drippings" of an orthodox Presbyterian pulpit, came to adopt the faith of Islam as my guide in life. A reply to this question may be of interest now to that large body of independent thinkers, who are manifesting a desire to know what the Islamic system really is. I am not vain enough to believe that I am the only American in this vast and progressive country capable of comprehending the system taught by the inspired Prophet of Arabia, and of appreciating its beauty and perfection. Nor do I believe that I am so deficient mentally as to accept, as truth, a religion which no one else in this country would be foolish enough to accept. But whether those who do accept it are wise or foolish in the estimation of their fellow men, I feel quite confident that at least a few may be benefited by my experience.

I was not born, as some boys seem to be, with a fervently religious strain in my character. I was emotional in later years, but not mawkishly sentimental, and always demanded a reason for everything. I will not even go so far as to assert that I was a good boy, such as fond and prejudiced mothers sometimes point out as shining examples for their own sons. I attended the Presbyterian Sunday school of my native town—when I couldn't avoid it—and listened with weariness and impatience to the long, abstruse discourses of the minister, while I longed to get out into the glad sunshine, and hear the more satisfying sermons preached by God Himself, through the murmuring brooks, the gorgeous flowers and the joyous birds. I listened incredulously to the story of the immaculate conception; and the dramatic tale of the vicarious atonement failed to arouse in me a thrill of tearful emotion, because I doubted the truth of both dogmas. Of course the narrow-minded church Christian will say at once, that the scriptural bogey-man, Satan, had me in his clutches as soon as I was born.

When I reached the age of twenty, and became, practically, my own master, I was so weary of the restraint and dullness of the church that I wandered away from it, and never returned to it. As a boy I found nothing in the system taught me in church and Sunday-school calculated to win me to it, nor did I find it any more attractive in later years, when I came to investigate it carefully and thoroughly. I found its moral ethics most commendable, but no different from those of every other system, while its superstitions, its grave errors, and its inefficiency as a means of securing salvation, or of elevating and purifying the human character, caused me to wonder why any thoughtful, honest and intelligent person could accept it seriously. Fortunately I was of an enquiring turn of mind—I wanted a reasonable foundation for everything—and I found that neither laymen nor clergy could give me any rational explanation of their faith; that when I asked them about God and the trinity, and life and death, they told me either that such things were mysteries, or were beyond the comprehension of ordinary mortals.

After trying in vain to find something in the Christian system to satisfy the longings of my soul and meet the demands of reason, I drifted into materialism; and, for several years, had no religion at all except the golden rule, which I followed about as closely as the average Christian follows it.

About eleven years ago I became interested in the study of the Oriental religions, beginning with Buddhism, as students of the Eastern systems usually do, and finding much to interest me in the Theosophical literature, which was not easy to be obtained in this country at that time. So intensely absorbed did I become in my studies and experiments, that I devoted four and five hours a day to them, often taking for that purpose time that I really needed for sleep. My mind was in a peculiarly receptive, yet exacting and analytical condition, absolutely free from the prejudices of all creeds, and ready to absorb the truth, no matter where it might be found. I was intensely in earnest in my efforts to solve the mysteries of life and death, and to know what relation the religious systems of the world bore to these mysteries. I reasoned that if there was no life beyond the grave, no religion was necessary to mankind; while if, as was claimed by many, there was a post-mortem life of far greater duration than the earthly existence, the nature and conditions of which were governed by our life on this globe, then it was of the greatest importance to know what course of life here would produce the most satisfying results in the next world.

Firmly materialistic, I looked at first to the advanced school of materialistic science, and found that it was just as completely immersed in the darkness of ignorance concerning spiritual things, as I was. It could tell me the name of every bone, muscle, nerve and organ of the human body, as well as its position, and (with one exception) its purpose of function; but it could not tell me the real difference between a living man and a dead one. It could tell me the name of every tree, plant and flower, and designate the species to which each belonged, as well as its apparent properties of attributes; but it could not tell me how and why the tree grew and flower bloomed. It was absolutely certain that man was born of woman, lived a brief period, and died; but whence he came, and whether he went were riddles which it confessed itself utterly unable to solve.

"Those matters belong to the church," said a scientist to me.

"But the church knows nothing of them," I replied.

"Nor do I, nor does science," was the helpless, hopeless way in which he dismissed the question from the conversation.

I saw Mill and Locke, and Kant and Hegel, and Fichte and Huxley, and many other more or less learned writers, discoursing, with a great show of wisdom, concerning protoplasm, and protogen, and monads, and yet not one of them could tell me what the soul was, or what becomes of it after death.

"But no one can tell you that," I fancy I hear someone say.

That is one of the greatest errors that poor, blind humanity ever made. There are people who have solved this mystery, but they are not the blind, credulous, materialistic followers of materialistic creeds.

I have spoken thus much of myself in order to show the reader that my adoption of Islam was not the result of misguided sentiment, blind credulity or sudden emotional impulse, but that it followed an earnest, honest, persistent, unprejudiced study and investigation, and an intense desire to know the truth.

After I had fully satisfied myself of the immortality of the soul, and that the conditions of the life beyond the grave were regulated by the thoughts, deeds and acts of the earth life; that man was, in a sense, his own savior and redeemer, and that the intercession of anyone between him and his God could be of no benefit to him, I began to compare the various religions, in order to ascertain which was the best and most efficacious as a means of securing happiness in the next life. To do this it was necessary to apply to each system, not only the tests of reason, but certain truths which I had learned during my long course of study and experiment outside the lines of orthodoxy, and in fields which priest and preacher usually avoid. . . .

There is no religious system known to humanity that is and has been, for centuries, so grossly misrepresented and thoroughly misunderstood by so-called Christians as that taught by the Prophet of Islam. The prejudice against it is so strong among the English-speaking people of the globe, that even the suggestion that it may possibly be the true faith and at least, worthy of a careful, unprejudiced investigation, is usually received with a contemptuous smile, as if such a thing was too palpably absurd to be considered seriously. It is this stubborn, unreasoning prejudice that prevents Europeans and Americans, who visit the East, from acquiring any accurate knowledge of Mohammedan social and religious life, or of the true doctrines of Islam. The air of superiority and self-sufficiency which they usually carry with them, repels the better and more enlightened classes of Mussulmans, and what is acquired from the lower classes cannot be taken as in any sense reliable. And yet it is this class of information that furnishes the inspiration for the magazine articles and books upon Mohammedan social life and beliefs which circulate in Europe and America. . . .

My study and observation among the Mussulmans [Muslims] of the East have led me to confidently believe that it is the most perfect system of soul-development ever given to man, and the only one applicable to all classes of humanity. It is founded upon that eternal truth, which has been handed down to man from age to age by the chosen prophets of God, from Moses to Mohammed. It is the only system known to man that is strictly in harmony with reason and science. It is free from degrading superstitions, and appeals directly to human rationality and intelligence. It makes every man individually responsible for every act he commits and every thought he thinks, and does not encourage him to sin by teaching him a vicarious atonement. It is elevating and refining in its tendencies, and develops the higher, nobler elements of humanity when it is faithfully, wisely and intelligently followed.

Source: Mohammed Alexander Russell Webb. *Islam in America: A Brief Statement of Mohammedanism and an Outline of the American Islamic Propaganda.* New York: Oriental Publishing Company, 1893, 11–14, 23–24.

Muhammad Sadiq's Missionary Work (1921–1923)

Muhammad Sadiq was one of the first known foreign Muslims to conduct missionary work in the United States. Sadiq belonged to the Ahmadiyya movement, a branch of Islam that arose in India at the end of the 19th century. Not all mainstream Muslims recognize Ahmadiyya as true Muslims. Sadiq's mission to America took place between 1920 and 1923, a period during which racial tensions were high in the United States. He became friends with Marcus Garvey, the founder of the Universal Negro Improvement Association (UNIA). He founded the magazine, Moslem Sunrise, *which was instrumental in introducing African Americans to the idea that many of their ancestors in Africa had been Muslims through his speeches and the journal.*

One Year's Moslem Missionary Work in America (1921)

It being the very first attempt to approach the Americans with the mission of Islam, I had to pass through all the difficulties that always confront a beginner of a work. I had no precedent before me to guide me and, therefore, much of my time has been spent in making experiences as regards the selection for my headquarters and the ways of approaching Americans. I cannot claim to have done any great work, but I do hope, in the grace of Allah, that in clearing the way for the future missionaries of Islam I have done some pioneer work and sown the seed of Truth throughout the land which will grow up in time and show in big, tall, strong trees to feed and shelter thousands, and send out healthy vibrations to millions.

The first difficulty I had to encounter was with the Immigration officers, who ordered me to return on the same steamer on which I had come, merely because I was a missionary of the Moslem faith, and on my refusal to return and asking permission to appeal to higher authorities in Washington I was placed in a detention house for about seven weeks. Those were the days of great trial, but I count them as the days of blessings, because I found the opportunity of offering prayers to God and meditation and planning the scheme for future work. Moreover, I began my work of preaching quietly among others detained like myself. The first of those who agreed with me there and joined our faith was Brother Hamid (Mr. R.J. Rochford), who was not allowed to land and was sent back with others. This good brother is now in England and keeps in touch with me by correspondence. He is my first convert to Islam after landing here. He is figuring to come over to Canada, and as he is zealous, I hope he will do great work in time to bring others to the blessed fold of Islam.

. . .

Brief Report of the Work in America (1921)

A learned Christian lady after reading the first number of "Moslem Sunrise" writes to me from Iowa: "It is so instructive and gives a person an insight into things which no matter how prejudiced they may be, can not but help to make them believe the facts produced by Divine power. But my dear Mufti, such is the way of the world, it is hard to convince us or to replace an image once deeply implanted in our bosom." How truly is reflected in these words the intensity of the hard task before a worker in faith. There is a proverb in India, "It is very difficult to drive away a literate demon." People like to remain stuck to their traditional thought and usages and have no mind to shake them off even if they find them wrong. This is the reason that the prophets and reformers are always abused by those very people for whom they are sincerely ready even to sacrifice their very lives. I am trying my best according to the means in my hands to convince the people of the truth of Islam but it will take some time to gain the desires of our hearts. Living being very high in this country it requires a big sum of money to start and continue all sorts of work to reach the people and give them our message. Hasbo-n-Allah wa-na-tawakkal aleihe—God is enough for us and in Him we put our trust.

Brother Mubarik and Sister Berket (Mr. and Mrs. Alberto), although new members themselves, have been zealous in spreading the truth and have secured two new converts in Florida.

Sheikh Abdullah Din Muhammad (Mr. J.L. Mott) is planning to build an Ahmadia Moslem Mosque in New Orleans. Some of his American friends have promised considerable help and he himself intends to put $500 into the funds out of his own pocket. May Allah assist him to accomplish this wonderful task.

Brother James Sodick—our young Russian Tartar Ahmade—is building a magnificent Ahmadi Moslem House in Chicago, Insha Allah [God willing].

In addition to the usual work at the centre I made a short tour through Toledo, Fort Wayne, Bremen, Chicago, and back via M.C. railroad, delivering lectures and giving interviews to the Press and the public. Thus I have made some new friends who have become interested in Islam and are studying your literature.

The correspondence work is growing very heavy. Mr. M. Yusuf Khan, the young Indian Ahmadi, has been helping me. The communications received for the quarter ending July, 1921, were 646 and those dispatched 2800, including that of the magazine. About 300 little leaflets and books also have been distributed.

Madame Rahatullah has been busy in New York making people interested in Islam and has already secured one American convert to Islam and one Moslem to the Ahmadia Order. Her enthusiastic little article on Islam appears in this magazine on page 39. Madam will start lecturing in New York assisted by Mrs. Emerson (Allahdin) of Oriental Shop there.

The Brethren in Chicago hold regular meetings every Sunday with Mr. L. Roman as their Secretary.

Brothers Muhammad Yaqoob (Mr. Andrew Jacob) and Ghulam Rasul (R. Elias Russell) have been working like missionaries in Chicago and have succeeded in bringing nine American souls to the fold of Islam.

. . .

**Crescent or Cross? A Negro May Aspire to
Any Position Under Islam without Discrimination (1923)**

The Teaching of the Prophet Is Being Profitably Imbibed—With Millions of Moslems the World Over Pressure Can Be Brought to Solve the Race Question.

Apart from a confederation of the African tribes or peoples of African origin, the possibility of which is an awful nightmare to the white man, he lives in fear and trembling that El Islam may become the religion of the Negro. And why should it not be? "El Islam" would be a wonderful spiritual force in the life of the colored races, uniting us in a bond of common sympathy and interest. We could then add to our motto of one God, one aim, one destiny, the words one language, and that language would be Arabic. It could easily be made the universal language of Negroes and would remove the barriers which now face us in the intercommunication of the different tribes in Africa. Arabic is already spoken by millions of Negroes.

Most white missionaries in order to keep up and encourage contributions to their foreign mission fund sometimes draw upon their imagination when they speak of the number of converts to Christianity, and would have us believe that the poor heathen is anxious to see more white men leading them to peace and happiness. The majority of the converts to Christianity in India and Africa are of the lower caste, people who have nothing to lose by changing their religious views and practices, but who expect in the new order of things to become the social equal of their superiors. They belong to that type which toadies to the white man and tamely submits to segregation and discrimination, believing that the white master is good, holy, just and meek.

In spite, however, of the desperate efforts being made by the "other fellow" to convert the African to Christianity in order to make his enslavement and exploitation easier and more secure, the African is slowly but surely realizing that under the Crescent he will be better able to reach the goal of his ambition than under the Cross. British administrators sometimes inadvertently admit that the Mohammedan natives are far superior in intelligence, morals and fighting spirit to the Christian native.

El Islam teaches its followers to be manly, self-respecting, charitable and ambitious, and, unlike his Christian brother, who waits for the good white man to restore him his rights, the follower of the prophet is always ready to draw his sword in defense of sacred right and honor.

Within recent years 53,000,000 natives have been converted to Mohammedanism in Africa. In Southern Nyasaland, where in 1900 you could not meet one native Mohammedan, there are mosques all over the country. In the region between Durba[n] and the Cape 1,000,000 natives were converted to Mohammed . . . last year. Under Islam a Negro may aspire to and attain any position in mosque or state, and Islam knows nothing of segregation and discrimination.

Yes, El Islam is spreading fast, and spreading not only in Africa but also in these United States. Within three months over 100 converts have been made to the cause of Mohammedanism in America. The spreading of El Islam cannot help but benefit the U.N.I.A. for they are desperately engaged in preparing for That Day—that day that we of the Universal are also preparing for.

Source: *Moslem Sunrise,* January 1921, 12; October 1921, 36; October 1923, 263.

WPA Interview with Mike Abdallah (1939)

The Works Progress Administration (WPA) was created in 1935 as one of the New Deal initiatives to provide work and income to millions of Americans during the Great Depression of the 1930s. As part of their work the WPA interviewed people seeking assistance to better understand the makeup of the United States's rural poor. Part of one of these interviews, with two Syrian-born Muslim Americans, is presented here. This is a rare record of the life and background of early Muslim immigrants to the United States. Like most Muslim immigrants at that time, Mike Abdallah and his wife came from the territories of the Ottoman Empire, which was in a period of terminal economic decline in the first decade of the 20th century.

I was born in Rufage, Rushia, Syria. I don't remember the date, nor the month but I believe that it was in 1886. (People in the Old Country did not keep track of their age or birth date because of the Turkish rule and they forced our boys into military service when they were of a certain age.) The village that I was born in had a population of about four hundred people. The land on the east of the village was level farm land and on the west at a short distance was mountains. My home was a one story six room stone building, about thirty by forty. The floor was made like all the other homes in the Old Country, poles about six inches in diameter were laid side by side on the ground. Then we mixed clay with water till it made a very thick mud, this was packed in between the poles and on top of the poles with a very heavy roller, then lime that we found was spread on the top of the clay while the clay was still wet and then the heavy roller was used some more until the lime was worked into the clay. When this became dry it would harden like cement. The floors for the second story of a two story house we made the same way.

I went to school one year. It wasn't a school like in this country. Father paid a man, living in our town to write and read our Bible [*Quran*]. That was my education.

Father was a farmer and until I was a full grown man, I worked at home for father. When I was old enough to work out for others, I received about twenty-five cents a day.

Taxes in the Old Country was much different from here. Taxes there were figured according to what your crop produced. For instance, for every ten bushels that the farmer got from the crop, the government took one bushel.

For seven years, I farmed for myself in the Old Country. I farmed about forty acres, with a team of oxen, wooden plow equipped with an iron lay, the rest of the farm work such as seeding, reaping and threshing, I had to do by hand. I had one cow and about a dozen chickens, but no goats or sheep as most people had.

We had church services every Friday. I belonged to the Moslem church in the Old Country the same as I do in this country. We didn't have any thing like confirmation. . . .

In the old country I only had forty acres to farm and only one cow so it was very hard to make a living. A man couldn't make a living by working out. Quite a few people from our town had already come to America and their letters told of lots of work for which they got big pay, free land to farm and live on, and much freedom. We didn't have any freedom in the Old Country as we were under the Turkish rule and we even had to be very careful what we said and the taxes we paid were taken by Turkey and we never got anything back for the taxes we paid. Our roads were terrible. Then the Turkish government made our men and boys serve in their army for sometimes many years.

When I left for America, I gave my land and things to my mother and sister, my father was dead. I borrowed seventy-five dollars besides the money I had saved, to make the trip. I brought only some clothes and enough food to last until I got to France. There were fifteen of us that left from our town at that time. H.A. Juma and Alley Farhart were in the group. I don't remember the names of the rest. We left from Beirut the spring of 1907 and sailed to Naples, Italy, on a cattle boat, from there we traveled through France by train and took a boat to Liverpool, England. I can't remember sailing from England to Montreal, Canada. It seems to me that I was only on a boat two times on the whole trip. (Field Worker's Note: Mrs. Abdallah tried to convince the informant that he must have crossed the ocean on a boat, but he could not recall it.)

I stayed in Montreal for one month and then came to Fargo, N.D., by train. I tried to peddle for about three months but I couldn't make a living at that, so I took the train to Ashley, N.D. There were other Syrians already there and I went to work on a farm; worked on farms there for three years, making from twenty-five to thirty dollars a month. In 1911, I came to Ross. I worked out for four years and during threshing I got $1.25 a day. When working by the month I got $30. In 1915, I filed on a homestead sec. 12-157-92. I lived on my homestead for two years and then lived with Frank Osman for a year. I got my Naturalization papers Oct. 2, 1916. In 1918, I moved to New Rockford, N.D. I stayed in New Rockford for five months and worked in the section crew. In 1919, I moved to Detroit, Michigan, and worked in the factories for two and a half years. In 1921, I moved back to Ross, N.D., as I got married in 1920 and had to settle down and make a home. I have lived around Ross ever since. I rented three farms and in 1927, I bought the farm we are now living on.

When I first came to America, I thought America was pretty funny. The way people done things seemed funny. The people were always in a hurry and when they got done there didn't seem to be any reason for the hurry. When they went someplace they were in a hurry; everything in the Old Country was much slower and people weren't in a hurry. I didn't like it for the first two years I was in America and many times I felt like I wanted to go back to the Old Country.

I couldn't talk or understand the American language when I came here and when I was peddling I had to talk to people by motions and when I wanted to tell anyone the price of a thing, I would take money from my pocket and show them the amount of the price. When I wanted to ask for a place to sleep, I had to lay down on the floor and play that I was asleep and then they knew what I wanted. Nearly everyone felt sorry for me because I couldn't talk their language. I remember one time when a bunch of people wanted to know what nationality I was so a man asked me if I was Jewish, and I nodded my head no. So he asked me if I was a sheeny [an archaic epithet for Jews]. It sounded enough like "Syrian" so I nodded my head meaning yes. Everyone laughed very hard. It took me about two years to learn enough English to get along good.

I was attracted to my first American residence by other Syrians living in that community and an opportunity to make a living. That was at Ashley, N.D. Hassyn Murray and Frank Osman live there in a Russian settlement. I guess my real first residence was on my homestead at Ross, N.D., as before that I only worked for others. I lived there to prove up my homestead. The Syrians living at Ashley came from the Old Country.

When I first started farming in this country I had a plow, harrow, and binder. I farmed 100 acres when I started and in 1924 I farmed 240 acres. Now I farm 160 acres. My best crop was in 1925, I had a real good crop that year. I believe, in fact my steadiest income has been from cattle and sheep. Until 1934 we depended mostly on the cattle, since it was so dry we have depended more on the sheep. I have 106 head of sheep, 9 cows, and 7 horses. I have more machinery now and do all my farming with horse. In 1934 I was forced to sell 39 head of cattle to the government because I didn't have feed for them.

I have not been able to make anything farming since 1929. I belong to the Agricultural Conservation Association. If it weren't for this there

139

wouldn't be any money in trying to raise a crop. I don't think we live any different now than we did before there was a depression. If we can't eat good there wouldn't be any use living. It was hard to have to sell my cattle to the government for so little money but they would have starved if had tried to keep them. I think the depression was because of the war.

My wife was born in Rufage, Rushia, Syria. We don't know the date of her birth but it was in the year 1886. (Field Worker's Note: Mrs. Abdallah told as a joke: there are several of the Syrians here that don't know their age, and they never get to be over 55 or 60 years old. I guess I am like the rest of them. Because of military reasons nobody in the old country kept track of their age and they still don't know. I am sure that some of them can't tell within 15 or 20 years of their correct age.) Mrs. Abdallah was married and had two children in the old country before coming to America. One of these was a girl and she remained in the old country and is married, the other also a girl born in 1910 in Rufage, Rushia, Syria. Her name is Nozema, now married. Sarah [was] born at Medina, N.D., born in 1914 (date of birth can be found in write-up on Allay Omar, as she is now Mrs. Omar). She completed the eighth grade in Ross Public School. Alley born July 4, 1915, at New Rockford, N.D. completed 6th grade. . . .

[*We don't have much recreation*] besides going to town, listening to the radio, the children try to play the mouth organ and the guitar. Sometimes we go to the neighbors to visit but most times we have work enough to keep us busy. The boys do a lot of trapping and hunting here in these hill and they like the sport of it and the cash they get out of it. My wife does a lot of sewing and the girls also do some of this. . . .

I suppose that the Old Country has changed a lot since I left there but at that time the work was very hard, as everything had to be done by hand, while in this country the work was really very easy as most of it was done by machinery even at that time. In the Old Country the climate is much better than here and it seemed to make old people feel young. You could work hard all day and go to bed real tired and when you wake up in the morning you feel as if you had never worked, while here a night's sleep doesn't make you feel that good. It sometimes snows a foot or more over there but still the people go bare-footed and the water under the snow feels as warm as though it had been warmed on the stove for about fifteen minutes. The water on the top of the ground is always too warm to drink and be good. I think that is the only way that the old country is better. In this country we get improvements for our tax money and we can think and say what we think while in the Old Country we could think what we wanted but we didn't dare say it.

In the Old Country we planted our winter wheat in August and planted our spring crop in April. Our harvest came in June.

If I had my life to live over again, I'd likely do about the same things only I'd come to America when I was younger and I settle down and stay there. I'd maybe settle in the state of Michigan or in No. Dak. I would get married younger and try to save for my old age. I wouldn't try to raise much crop if I was on a farm; I'd go into cattle and sheep. I can't really say that I am sorry that I lived the way I have because I have always enjoyed life.

Source: Works Progress Administration. North Dakota Writers' Project Ethnic Group Files, Series 30559, Roll 3, 1939.

Elijah Muhammad, "What Do the Muslims Want?" (1965)

Elijah Muhammad (1897–1975) was a pivotal figure in the history of Islam in the United States as the leader of the Nation of Islam from 1934 until his death. In his popular and controversial 1965 book Message to the Blackman in America *Elijah Muhammad laid out the definitive program of the Nation of Islam, which included one entitled "What Do the Muslims Want?" The beliefs and ambitions listed in these sections reveal both the Nation of Islam's strong agenda for racial separation and the theological elements that lead most mainstream Muslims to regard it as espousing a non-Muslim faith that has simply borrowed Islamic terminology, in particular the belief that Fard Muhammad was a messiah and that African Americans are God's chosen people.*

What Do the Muslims Want?

1. We want freedom. We want a full and complete freedom.
2. We want justice. Equal justice under the law. We want justice applied equally to all, regardless of creed, or class, or color.
3. We want equality of opportunity. We want equal membership in society with the best in civilized society.
4. We want our people in America whose parents or grandparents were descendants from slaves, to be allowed to establish a separate state or territory of their own . . . either on this continent or elsewhere. We believe that our former slave masters are obliged to provide such land and that the area must be fertile and minerally rich. We believe that our former slave masters are obligated to maintain and supply our needs in this separate territory for the next 20 to 25 years . . . until we are able to produce our own needs.

Since we cannot get along with them in peace and equality, after giving them 400 years of our sweat and blood, and receiving in return some of the worst treatment human beings have ever experienced, we believe our contributions to this land and the suffering forced upon us by white America, justifies our demand for complete separation in a state or territory of our own.

5. We want freedom for all Believers of Islam now held in federal prisons. We want freedom for all black men and women now under death sentence in innumerable prisons in the North, as well as the South.

We want every black man and woman to have the freedom to accept or reject being separated from the slave-masters' children and establish a land of their own.

We know that the above plan for the solution of the black and white conflict is the best and only answer to the problem between two people.

6. We want an immediate end to the police brutality and mob attacks against the so-called Negro throughout the United States.

We believe that the Federal government should intercede to see that black men and women tried in white courts receive justice in accordance with the laws of the land, or allow us to build a new nation for ourselves, dedicated to justice, freedom and liberty.

7 As long as we are not allowed to establish a state or territory of our own, we demand not only equal justice under the laws of the United States, but equal employment opportunities—NOW!

We do not believe that after 400 years of free or nearly free labor, sweat and blood, which has helped America become rich and powerful, that so many thousands of black people should have to subsist on relief or charity or live in poor houses.

8. We want the government of the United States to exempt our people from ALL taxation as long as we are deprived of equal justice under the laws of the land.

9. We want equal education—but separate schools up to 16 for boys and 18 for girls on the condition that the girls be sent to women's colleges and universities. We want all black children, educated, taught and trained by their own teachers.

Under such schooling systems we believe we will make a better nation of people. The United States government should provide, free, all necessary text books and equipment, schools, and college buildings. The Muslim teachers shall be left free to teach and train their people in the way of righteousness, decency and self respect.

10. We believe that intermarriage or race mixing should be prohibited. We want the religion of Islam taught without hindrance or suppression.

These are some of the things that we, the Muslims, want for our people in North America.

{What do Muslims Believe?}

1. We believe in the One God Whose proper Name is Allah.
2. We believe in the Holy Qur-an and in the Scriptures of all the Prophets of God.
3. We believe in the truth of the Bible, but we believe that it has been tampered with and must be reinterpreted so that mankind will not be snared by the falsehoods that have been added to it.
4. We believe in Allah's Prophets and the Scriptures they brought to the people.
5. We believe in the resurrection of the dead—not in the physical resurrection but in mental resurrection. We believe that the so-called Negroes are most in need of mental resurrection; therefore, they will be resurrected first.

Furthermore, we believe we are the people of God's choice, as it has been written that God would choose the rejected and the despised. We can find no other persons fitting this description in these last days more than the so-called Negroes in America. We believe in the resurrection of the righteous.
6. We believe in the judgment. We believe this first judgment will take place in America.
7. We believe this is the time in history for the separation of the so-called Negroes and so-called white Americans. We believe the black men should be freed in name as well as in fact. By this we mean that he should be freed from the names imposed upon him by his former slave-masters. Names which identified him as being the slave of a slave-master. We believe that if we are free indeed, we should go in our own people's names—the black people of the earth.
8. We believe in justice for all whether in God or not. We believe as others that we are due equal justice as human beings. We believe in equality—as a nation—of equals. We do not believe that we are equal with our slave master in the status of "Freed slaves."

We recognize and respect American citizens as independent people and we respect their laws which govern this nation.

9. We believe that the offer of integration is hypocritical and is made by those who are trying to deceive the black people into believing that their 400-year-old open enemies of freedom, justice and equality are, all of a sudden, their "friends." Furthermore, we believe that such deception is intended to prevent black people from realizing that the time in history has arrived for the separation from the whites of this nation.

If the white people are truthful about their professed friendship toward the so-called Negro, they can prove it by dividing up America with their slaves.

We do not believe that America will ever be able to furnish jobs for her own millions of unemployed, in addition to jobs for the 20,000,000 black people as well.

10. We believe that we who declared ourselves to be righteous Muslims should not participate in wars which take the lives of humans. We do not believe this nation should force us to take part in such wars, for we have nothing to gain from it unless America agrees to give us the necessary territory wherein we may have something to fight for.

11. We believe our women should be respected and protected as the women of their nationalities are respected and protected.

12. We believe that Allah (God) appeared in the Person of Master Fard Muhammad, July, 1930—the long-awaited "Messiah" of the Christians and the "Mahdi" of the Muslims.

We believe further and lastly that Allah is God and besides HIM there is no God and He will bring about a universal government of peace wherein we all can live in peace together.

Source: Elijah Muhammad. *Message to the Blackman in America*. Chicago: Muhammad's Temple, No. 2, 1965, 161–164.

George H. W. Bush, Address to Congress on the Persian Gulf Crisis (September 11, 1990)

Exactly 11 years before President George W. Bush spoke to the nation on the evening of September 11, 2001, his father, President George H. W. Bush, delivered a speech to Congress on the developing crisis in Kuwait, which was to lead to U.S. involvement in the Persian Gulf War against Iraq.

Mr. President and Mr. Speaker and Members of the United States Congress, distinguished guests, fellow Americans, thank you very much for that warm welcome. We gather tonight, witness to events in the Persian Gulf as significant as they are tragic. In the early morning hours of August 2nd, following negotiations and promises by Iraq's dictator Saddam Hussein not to use force, a powerful Iraqi army invaded its trusting and much weaker neighbor, Kuwait. Within 3 days, 120,000 Iraqi troops with 850 tanks had poured into Kuwait and moved south to threaten Saudi Arabia. It was then that I decided to act to check that aggression.

At this moment, our brave servicemen and women stand watch in that distant desert and on distant seas, side by side with the forces of more than 20 other nations. They are some of the finest men and women of the United States of America. And they're doing one terrific job. These valiant Americans were ready at a moment's notice to leave their spouses and their children, to serve on the front line halfway around the world. They remind us who keeps America strong: they do. In the trying circumstances of the Gulf, the morale of our service men and women is excellent. In the face of danger, they're brave, they're well-trained, and dedicated.

. . .

Our objectives in the Persian Gulf are clear, our goals defined and familiar: Iraq must withdraw from Kuwait completely, immediately, and without condition. Kuwait's legitimate government must be restored. The security and stability of the Persian Gulf must be assured. And American citizens abroad must be protected. These goals are not ours alone. They've been endorsed by the United Nations Security Council five times in as many weeks. Most countries share our concern for principle. And many have a stake in the stability of the Persian Gulf. This is not, as Saddam Hussein would have it, the United States against Iraq. It is Iraq against the world.

. . .

We stand today at a unique and extraordinary moment. The crisis in the Persian Gulf, as grave as it is, also offers a rare opportunity to move toward an historic period of cooperation. Out of these troubled times, our fifth objective—a new world order—can emerge: a new era—freer from the threat of terror, stronger in the pursuit of justice, and more secure in the quest for peace. An era in which the nations of the world, East and West, North and South, can prosper and live in harmony. A hundred generations have searched for this elusive path to peace, while a thousand wars raged across the span of human endeavor. Today that new world is struggling to be born, a world quite different from the one we've known. A world where the rule of law supplants the rule of the jungle. A world in which nations recognize the shared responsibility for freedom and justice. A world where the strong respect the rights of the weak. This is the vision that I shared with President Gorbachev in Helsinki. He and other leaders from Europe, the Gulf, and around the world understand that how we manage this crisis today could shape the future for generations to come.

The test we face is great, and so are the stakes. This is the first assault on the new world that we seek, the first test of our mettle. Had we not responded to this first provocation with clarity of purpose, if we do not continue to demonstrate our determination, it would be a signal to actual and potential despots around the world. America and the world must defend common vital interests—and we will. America and the world must support the rule of law—and we will. America and the world must stand up to aggression—and we will. And one thing more: In the pursuit of these goals America will not be intimidated.

Vital issues of principle are at stake. Saddam Hussein is literally trying to wipe a country off the face of the Earth. We do not exaggerate. Nor do we exaggerate when we say Saddam Hussein will fail. Vital economic interests are at risk as well. Iraq itself controls some 10 percent of the world's proven oil reserves. Iraq plus Kuwait controls twice that. An Iraq permitted to swallow Kuwait would have the economic and military power, as well as the arrogance, to intimidate and coerce its neighbors—neighbors who control the lion's share of the world's remaining oil reserves. We cannot permit a resource so vital to be dominated by one so ruthless. And we won't.

Recent events have surely proven that there is no substitute for American leadership. In the face of tyranny, let no one doubt American credibility and reliability. Let no one doubt our staying power. We will stand by our friends. One way or another, the leader of Iraq must learn this fundamental truth. From the outset, acting hand in hand with others, we've sought to fashion the broadest possible international response to Iraq's aggression. The level of world cooperation and condemnation of Iraq is unprecedented. Armed forces from countries spanning four continents are there at the request of King Fahd of Saudi Arabia to deter and, if need be, to defend against attack. Moslems and non-Moslems, Arabs and non-Arabs, soldiers from many nations stand shoulder to shoulder, resolute against Saddam Hussein's ambitions.

We can now point to five United Nations Security Council resolutions that condemn Iraq's aggression. They call for Iraq's immediate and unconditional withdrawal, the restoration of Kuwait's legitimate government, and categorically reject Iraq's cynical and self-serving attempt to annex Kuwait. Finally, the United Nations has demanded the release of all foreign nationals held hostage against their will and in contravention of international law. It is a mockery of human decency to call these people "guests." They are hostages, and the whole world knows it.

. . .

We're now in sight of a United Nations that performs as envisioned by its founders. We owe much to the outstanding leadership of Secretary-General Javier Perez de Cuellar. The United Nations is backing up its words with action. The Security Council has imposed mandatory economic sanctions on Iraq, designed to force Iraq to relinquish the spoils of its illegal conquest. The Security Council has also taken the decisive step of authorizing the use of all means necessary to ensure compliance with these sanctions. Together with our friends and allies, ships of the United States Navy are today patrolling Mideast waters. They've already intercepted more than 700 ships to enforce the sanctions. Three regional leaders I spoke with just yesterday told me that these sanctions are working. Iraq is feeling the heat. We continue to hope that Iraq's leaders will recalculate just what their aggression has cost them. They are cut off from world trade, unable to sell their oil. And only a tiny fraction of goods gets through.

. . .

The response of most of our friends and allies has been good. To help defray costs, the leaders of Saudi Arabia, Kuwait, and the UAE—the United Arab Emirates—have pledged to provide our deployed troops with all the food and fuel they need. Generous assistance will also be provided to stalwart front-line nations, such as Turkey and Egypt. I am also heartened to report that this international response extends to the neediest victims of this conflict—those refugees. For our part, we've contributed 28 million for relief efforts. This is but a portion of what is needed. I commend, in particular, Saudi Arabia, Japan, and several European nations who have joined us in this purely humanitarian effort.

. . .

I cannot predict just how long it will take to convince Iraq to withdraw from Kuwait. Sanctions will take time to have their full intended effect. We will continue to review all options with our allies, but let it be clear: we will not let this aggression stand.

Our interest, our involvement in the Gulf is not transitory. It predated Saddam Hussein's aggression and will survive it. Long after all our troops come home—and we all hope it's soon, very soon—there will be a lasting role for the United States in assisting the nations of the Persian Gulf. Our role then: to deter future aggression. Our role is to help our friends in their own self-defense. And something else: to curb the proliferation of chemical, biological, ballistic missile and, above all, nuclear technologies.

Let me also make clear that the United States has no quarrel with the Iraqi people. Our quarrel is with Iraq's dictator and with his aggression. Iraq will not be permitted to annex Kuwait. That's not a threat, that's not a boast, that's just the way it's going to be.

. . .

In the final analysis, our ability to meet our responsibilities abroad depends upon political will and consensus at home. This is never easy in democracies, for we govern only with the consent of the governed. And although free people in a free society are bound to have their differences, Americans traditionally come together in times of adversity and challenge.

Once again, Americans have stepped forward to share a tearful goodbye with their families before leaving for a strange and distant shore. At this very moment, they serve together with Arabs, Europeans, Asians, and Africans in defense of principle and the dream of a new world order. That's why they sweat and toil in the sand and the heat and the sun. If they can come together under such adversity, if old adversaries like the Soviet Union and the United States can work in common cause, then surely we who are so fortunate to be in this great Chamber—Democrats, Republicans, liberals, conservatives—can come together to fulfill our responsibilities here. Thank you. Good night. And God bless the United States of America.

Source: Milestonedocuments.com. "George H. W. Bush's Address to Congress on the Persian Gulf Crisis." Available online. URL: http://www.milestonedocuments.com/document_detail.php?id=87&more=fulltext. Accessed November 25, 2009.

United States Documents

Leila Ahmed, Muslim Women's Studies in America (2000)

Egyptian-born American academic Leila Ahmed is regarded as a leading figure in the modern study of women in Islam. Her 1992 book Women and Gender in Islam *was a radical new interpretation of the history of women in Islam in which she distinguished between what she saw as patriarchal interpretations of Islam deriving from the societies in which it developed and the teachings of Islam itself. In this extract she describes her experience of feminism in the United States, where she has taught for many years, and the challenges of overcoming Western prejudices against Islam.*

It was no easy transition, the transition to America and to women's studies.

First of all, live American feminism was not anything like what I had imagined. Reading its thoughtful texts in the quiet of the desert [of Abu Dhabi], I had, I suppose, formed a notion of feminism as tranquil, lucid, meditative—whereas, of course, the living feminism I encountered once on these shores was anything but a lucid, tranquil, meditative affair. Militant, vital, tempestuous, passionate, visionary, turbulent—any or all of these might be more apt. In the gatherings of feminists—at the various conferences, meetings, and public lectures that I now single-mindedly threw myself into attending—there was a kind of raw, exhilarating energy and a sense, intellectually, of freewheeling anarchy. Almost as if people felt themselves caught up in some holy purifying fire that was burning away the dross and obscurities from their minds, freeing them to dream dreams and see visions and to gather themselves up and prepare to unmake and remake the world, remake it as it had never been made before.

And all this *was* tremendously exhilarating and exciting. But along with exhilaration came shock. For I naturally made a point at these conferences of attending, and often participating in, sessions and panels on Muslim women. Not that these were common. The women's studies conferences I attended when I first came in 1980—I remember one at Barnard [College in New York City], and another in Bloomington, Indiana—focused primarily on white women and were overwhelmingly attended by white women. But such sessions on Muslim women as there were left me nearly speechless and certainly in shock at the combination of hostility and sheer ignorance that the Muslim panelists, myself included, almost invariably encountered. We could not pursue the investigation of our heritage, traditions, religion in the way that white women were investigating and rethinking theirs. Whatever aspect of our history or religion each of us had been trying to reflect on, we would be besieged, at the end of our presentations, with furious questions

149

and declarations openly dismissive of Islam. People quite commonly did not even seem to now that there was some connection between the patriarchal vision to be found in Islam and that in Judaism and Christianity. Regularly we would be asked belligerently, "Well what about the veil" or "What about clitoridectomy?" when none of us had mentioned either subject for the simple reason that it was completely irrelevant to the topics of our papers. The implication was that, in trying to examine and rethink our traditions rather than dismissing them out of hand, we were implicitly defending whatever our audience considered to be indefensible. And the further implication and presumption was that, whereas they—white women, Christian women, Jewish women—could rethink their heritage and religions and traditions, we had to abandon ours because they were just intrinsically, essentially, and irredeemably misogynist and patriarchal in a way that theirs (apparently) were not. In contrast to their situation, our salvation entailed not arguing with and working to change our traditions but giving up our cultures, religions, and traditions and adopting theirs.

And so the first thing I wrote after my arrival and within months of being in America was an article addressing the extraordinary barrage of hostility and ignorance with which I found myself besieged as I moved among this community of women. They were women who were engaged in radically rejecting, contesting, and rethinking their own traditions and heritage and the ingrained prejudices against women that formed part of that heritage but who turned on me a gaze completely structured and hidebound by that heritage; in their attitudes and beliefs about Islam and women in Islam, they plainly revealed their unquestioning faith in and acceptance of the prejudiced, hostile, and often ridiculous notions that their heritage had constructed about Islam and its women. I had come wanting to read and think and write about Muslim women, but it was this that commanded my attention as the subject that I desperately had to address. The first piece I wrote, "Western Ethnocentrism and Perceptions of the Harem," still rings for me with the shocked and furious tones of that initial encounter.

My first year in America, 1979, was also the year of the Iran hostage crisis, and I am sure now that the hostility toward Islam by which I felt myself besieged was more pronounced than usual because of that situation. But as I would learn soon enough, the task of addressing racism for feminists of color in the West is, and has to be, an ongoing and central part of the work and the thinking that we ordinarily do, no less so than the work of addressing male dominance. And so my first experience of American feminism was a kind of initiation and baptism by fire into what has indeed been an ongoing part of my thought and work ever since. Back then, though, it was still early in our understanding of the racist gaze the white feminist movement turned on women of other cultures and races. [African-American poet] Audre Lorde, at a conference in 1976 (in a presentation much-anthologized since), was among the first to identify, and speak out against, this strand in white feminist thought, and June Jordan, Bell Hooks, and others followed up with work on the subject.

Also making my initial experience of America a more arduous experience than it might otherwise have been was the fact that I took a job in women's studies. I had come intent on working in this field and had applied for an advertised position as a part-time lecturer at the University of Massachusetts at Amherst. Although the pay was low, I felt that a part-time job was the sensible way into the field, whose scholarly productions I'd been reading about in the desert but about which I had still an enormous amount to learn. A part-time job would give me the time, I thought, to do all the extra reading that I no doubt needed to do.

Of course I found that my part-time job, as is so often the case, was only technically part-time. In fact, preparing classes, teaching, and attending meetings took up every moment of my waking life. I have never worked so hard in my life as in my first couple of years in America. Of course, too, the fact that everything was new to me contributed to making those years so tough. Teaching in a new academic system in a new country must always entail demanding transitions, but I am sure that moment in the history of women's studies in America, rather than, say, taking a job in a more established department, created a whole set of unique hurdles and difficulties.

Women's studies programs in that era, including the program that I joined, had an embattled and precarious relationship with the university. There was sometimes open hostility from faculty members in other departments and, occasionally, condescension and a presumption that the women's studies faculty must be ignorant, undereducated fanatical women. For me, as someone coming from abroad who had not been part of the American feminist movement, there was one very particular difficulty that I had not anticipated when I imagined that, by working hard and reading widely, I could quickly master the ideas, theories, perspectives that I needed to be familiar with. I could not quickly master them through reading, for the simple reason that a lot of them had not yet found their way into print. The ideas that I heard passionately voiced and argued around me by faculty and also by students were part of a rich, vibrant, diverse, and internally contentious cargo of debates that had been generated by an intellectually vital social movement. This was what I had stepped into in joining women's studies—a living social movement of quite extraordinary but as yet mainly oral intellectual vitality, about to spill over and become a predominantly intellectual, academic, and theoretical force rather than, as it had in part

151

been in its beginnings, an activist social movement, and the continuing evolution of these ideas, that were providing the foundations of women's studies. I stepped, that is to say, too, into the stream of what was as yet a largely unwritten oral culture—the oral, living culture of the feminist movement, a culture to which there were as yet almost no guides, no maps, no books.

There were often passionate debates, both among my colleagues and in the feminist community more widely, between, say, Radical feminists and Marxist feminists, debates that could become quite furious. It was clear that there was a history here, a common, shared evolution, in the course of which particular positions, in relation to this or that issue, had been progressively defined and sometimes had become polarized. But to someone arriving from the Arab Gulf, what these positions and issues were and why they should generate such passion was, at first anyway, profoundly unfathomable. And there was nothing, or very little, in those days, that I could read that would enlighten me and make the issues, debates, and history accessible. Moreover, this culture and history that I had not been part of informed nearly everything in women's studies, not only intellectual issues but also ordinary routines and exchanges and conversations. It was this culture, for instance, that determined that all decisions were to be made by consensus and not by vote. It determined, too, the code of dress—as strict here, in its way, as in Abu Dhabi. For those were the days when whether you shaved your legs or wore a bra signaled where you stood on the internal feminist battle lines and/or your degree of feminist enlightenment. In Abu Dhabi it had been easy to ask about appropriate dress and the meaning of this or that style, but here not only were you supposed to just know, but supposedly there was no dress code and people here—as I was emphatically told when I ventured the question in my early innocent days—simply dressed exactly how they wished. And so there were many ways in which the women's studies culture in which I found myself was an unknown culture to me to which I had no key and maps. But, as with any other culture, after a period of intense immersion, my confusion naturally resolved into comprehension.

Source: Leila Ahmed. "From Abu Dhabi to America." In *A Border Passage: From Cairo to America—A Woman's Journey.* New York: Penguin, 2000, 291–295.

President George W. Bush, Address to a Joint Session of Congress and the American People (September 20, 2001)

This televised speech made by President George W. Bush nine days after the September 11, 2001, attacks on the United States is the first in which al-Qaeda is identified as the perpetrator of the attacks and Osama bin Laden as the organization's leader. In his speech, President Bush called on the Taliban, who were then in power in Afghanistan, to close all al-Qaeda facilities and turn its leaders over to the United States. There were strong indications throughout the speech that the president had decided on a military response. Bush draws a parallel between the September 11 attacks and the Japanese attack on Pearl Harbor in 1941 that brought the United States into World War II. He also promised to use "every necessary weapon of war" and in a message to U.S. armed forces said: "The hour is coming when America will act, and you will make us proud."

Mr. Speaker, Mr. President Pro Tempore, members of Congress, and fellow Americans:

In the normal course of events, Presidents come to this chamber to report on the state of the Union. Tonight, no such report is needed. It has already been delivered by the American people.

We have seen it in the courage of passengers, who rushed terrorists to save others on the ground—passengers like an exceptional man named Todd Beamer. And would you please help me to welcome his wife, Lisa Beamer, here tonight.

We have seen the state of our Union in the endurance of rescuers, working past exhaustion. We have seen the unfurling of flags, the lighting of candles, the giving of blood, the saying of prayers—in English, Hebrew, and Arabic. We have seen the decency of a loving and giving people who have made the grief of strangers their own.

My fellow citizens, for the last nine days, the entire world has seen for itself the state of our Union—and it is strong.

Tonight we are a country awakened to danger and called to defend freedom. Our grief has turned to anger, and anger to resolution. Whether we bring our enemies to justice, or bring justice to our enemies, justice will be done.

I thank the Congress for its leadership at such an important time. All of America was touched on the evening of the tragedy to see Republicans and Democrats joined together on the steps of this Capitol, singing "God Bless America." And you did more than sing; you acted, by delivering $40 billion to rebuild our communities and meet the needs of our military.

Speaker Hastert, Minority Leader Gephardt, Majority Leader Daschle and Senator Lott, I thank you for your friendship, for your leadership and for your service to our country.

And on behalf of the American people, I thank the world for its outpouring of support. America will never forget the sounds of our National Anthem playing at Buckingham Palace, on the streets of Paris, and at Berlin's Brandenburg Gate.

We will not forget South Korean children gathering to pray outside our embassy in Seoul, or the prayers of sympathy offered at a mosque in Cairo. We will not forget moments of silence and days of mourning in Australia and Africa and Latin America.

Nor will we forget the citizens of 80 other nations who died with our own: dozens of Pakistanis; more than 130 Israelis; more than 250 citizens of India; men and women from El Salvador, Iran, Mexico and Japan; and hundreds of British citizens. America has no truer friend than Great Britain. Once again, we are joined together in a great cause—so honored the British Prime Minister has crossed an ocean to show his unity of purpose with America. Thank you for coming, friend.

On September the 11th, enemies of freedom committed an act of war against our country. Americans have known wars—but for the past 136 years, they have been wars on foreign soil, except for one Sunday in 1941. Americans have known the casualties of war—but not at the center of a great city on a peaceful morning. Americans have known surprise attacks—but never before on thousands of civilians. All of this was brought upon us in a single day—and night fell on a different world, a world where freedom itself is under attack.

Americans have many questions tonight. Americans are asking: Who attacked our country? The evidence we have gathered all points to a collection of loosely affiliated terrorist organizations known as al Qaeda. They are the same murderers indicted for bombing American embassies in Tanzania and Kenya, and responsible for bombing the USS Cole.

Al Qaeda is to terror what the mafia is to crime. But its goal is not making money; its goal is remaking the world—and imposing its radical beliefs on people everywhere.

United States Documents

The terrorists practice a fringe form of Islamic extremism that has been rejected by Muslim scholars and the vast majority of Muslim clerics—a fringe movement that perverts the peaceful teachings of Islam. The terrorists' directive commands them to kill Christians and Jews, to kill all Americans, and make no distinction among military and civilians, including women and children.

This group and its leader—a person named Osama bin Laden—are linked to many other organizations in different countries, including the Egyptian Islamic Jihad and the Islamic Movement of Uzbekistan. There are thousands of these terrorists in more than 60 countries. They are recruited from their own nations and neighborhoods and brought to camps in places like Afghanistan, where they are trained in the tactics of terror. They are sent back to their homes or sent to hide in countries around the world to plot evil and destruction.

The leadership of al Qaeda has great influence in Afghanistan and supports the Taliban regime in controlling most of that country. In Afghanistan, we see al Qaeda's vision for the world.

Afghanistan's people have been brutalized—many are starving and many have fled. Women are not allowed to attend school. You can be jailed for owning a television. Religion can be practiced only as their leaders dictate. A man can be jailed in Afghanistan if his beard is not long enough.

The United States respects the people of Afghanistan—after all, we are currently its largest source of humanitarian aid—but we condemn the Taliban regime. It is not only repressing its own people, it is threatening people everywhere by sponsoring and sheltering and supplying terrorists. By aiding and abetting murder, the Taliban regime is committing murder.

And tonight, the United States of America makes the following demands on the Taliban: Deliver to United States authorities all the leaders of al Qaeda who hide in your land. Release all foreign nationals, including American citizens, you have unjustly imprisoned. Protect foreign journalists, diplomats and aid workers in your country. Close immediately and permanently every terrorist training camp in Afghanistan, and hand over every terrorist, and every person in their support structure, to appropriate authorities. Give the United States full access to terrorist training camps, so we can make sure they are no longer operating.

These demands are not open to negotiation or discussion. The Taliban must act, and act immediately. They will hand over the terrorists, or they will share in their fate.

I also want to speak tonight directly to Muslims throughout the world. We respect your faith. It's practiced freely by many millions of Americans, and by millions more in countries that America counts as friends. Its teachings are good and peaceful, and those who commit evil in the name of Allah blaspheme the name of Allah. The terrorists are traitors to their own faith, trying, in effect, to hijack Islam itself. The enemy of America is not our many Muslim friends; it is not our many Arab friends. Our enemy is a radical network of terrorists, and every government that supports them.

Our war on terror begins with al Qaeda, but it does not end there. It will not end until every terrorist group of global reach has been found, stopped and defeated.

Americans are asking, why do they hate us? They hate what we see right here in this chamber—a democratically elected government. Their leaders are self-appointed. They hate our freedoms—our freedom of religion, our freedom of speech, our freedom to vote and assemble and disagree with each other.

They want to overthrow existing governments in many Muslim countries, such as Egypt, Saudi Arabia, and Jordan. They want to drive Israel out of the Middle East. They want to drive Christians and Jews out of vast regions of Asia and Africa.

These terrorists kill not merely to end lives, but to disrupt and end a way of life. With every atrocity, they hope that America grows fearful, retreating from the world and forsaking our friends. They stand against us, because we stand in their way.

We are not deceived by their pretenses to piety. We have seen their kind before. They are the heirs of all the murderous ideologies of the 20th century. By sacrificing human life to serve their radical visions—by abandoning every value except the will to power—they follow in the path of fascism, and Nazism, and totalitarianism. And they will follow that path all the way, to where it ends: in history's unmarked grave of discarded lies.

Americans are asking: How will we fight and win this war? We will direct every resource at our command—every means of diplomacy, every tool of intelligence, every instrument of law enforcement, every financial influence, and every necessary weapon of war—to the disruption and to the defeat of the global terror network.

This war will not be like the war against Iraq a decade ago, with a decisive liberation of territory and a swift conclusion. It will not look like the air war above Kosovo two years ago, where no ground troops were used and not a single American was lost in combat.

Our response involves far more than instant retaliation and isolated strikes. Americans should not expect one battle, but a lengthy campaign, unlike any other we have ever seen. It may include dramatic strikes, visible on TV, and covert operations, secret even in success. We will starve terrorists of funding, turn them one against another, drive them from place to place, until there is no refuge or no rest. And we will pursue nations that provide aid or safe haven to terrorism. Every nation, in every region, now has a decision to make. Either you are with us, or you are with the terrorists. From this day forward, any nation that continues to harbor or support terrorism will be regarded by the United States as a hostile regime.

Our nation has been put on notice: We are not immune from attack. We will take defensive measures against terrorism to protect Americans. Today, dozens of federal departments and agencies, as well as state and local governments, have responsibilities affecting homeland security. These efforts must be coordinated at the highest level. So tonight I announce the creation of a Cabinet-level position reporting directly to me—the Office of Homeland Security.

And tonight I also announce a distinguished American to lead this effort, to strengthen American security: a military veteran, an effective governor, a true patriot, a trusted friend—Pennsylvania's Tom Ridge. He will lead, oversee and coordinate a comprehensive national strategy to safeguard our country against terrorism, and respond to any attacks that may come.

These measures are essential. But the only way to defeat terrorism as a threat to our way of life is to stop it, eliminate it, and destroy it where it grows.

Many will be involved in this effort, from FBI agents to intelligence operatives to the reservists we have called to active duty. All deserve our thanks, and all have our prayers. And tonight, a few miles from the damaged Pentagon, I have a message for our military: Be ready. I've called the Armed Forces to alert, and there is a reason. The hour is coming when America will act, and you will make us proud.

This is not, however, just America's fight. And what is at stake is not just America's freedom. This is the world's fight. This is civilization's fight. This is the fight of all who believe in progress and pluralism, tolerance and freedom.

We ask every nation to join us. We will ask, and we will need, the help of police forces, intelligence services, and banking systems around the world. The United States is grateful that many nations and many international organizations have already responded—with sympathy and with support. Nations from Latin America, to Asia, to Africa, to Europe, to the Islamic world. Perhaps the NATO Charter reflects best the attitude of the world: An attack on one is an attack on all.

The civilized world is rallying to America's side. They understand that if this terror goes unpunished, their own cities, their own citizens may be next. Terror, unanswered, cannot only bring down buildings, it can threaten the stability of legitimate governments. And you know what—we're not going to allow it.

Americans are asking: What is expected of us? I ask you to live your lives, and hug your children. I know many citizens have fears tonight, and I ask you to be calm and resolute, even in the face of a continuing threat.

I ask you to uphold the values of America, and remember why so many have come here. We are in a fight for our principles, and our first responsibility is to live by them. No one should be singled out for unfair treatment or unkind words because of their ethnic background or religious faith.

I ask you to continue to support the victims of this tragedy with your contributions. Those who want to give can go to a central source of information, libertyunites.org, to find the names of groups providing direct help in New York, Pennsylvania, and Virginia.

The thousands of FBI agents who are now at work in this investigation may need your cooperation, and I ask you to give it.

I ask for your patience, with the delays and inconveniences that may accompany tighter security; and for your patience in what will be a long struggle.

I ask your continued participation and confidence in the American economy. Terrorists attacked a symbol of American prosperity. They did not touch its source. America is successful because of the hard work, and creativity, and enterprise of our people. These were the true strengths of our economy before September 11th, and they are our strengths today.

And, finally, please continue praying for the victims of terror and their families, for those in uniform, and for our great country. Prayer has comforted us in sorrow, and will help strengthen us for the journey ahead.

Tonight I thank my fellow Americans for what you have already done and for what you will do. And ladies and gentlemen of the Congress, I thank you, their representatives, for what you have already done and for what we will do together.

Tonight, we face new and sudden national challenges. We will come together to improve air safety, to dramatically expand the number of air marshals on domestic flights, and take new measures to prevent hijacking. We will come together to promote stability and keep our airlines flying, with direct assistance during this emergency.

We will come together to give law enforcement the additional tools it needs to track down terror here at home. We will come together to strengthen our intelligence capabilities to know the plans of terrorists before they act, and find them before they strike.

We will come together to take active steps that strengthen America's economy, and put our people back to work.

Tonight we welcome two leaders who embody the extraordinary spirit of all New Yorkers: Governor George Pataki, and Mayor Rudolph Giuliani. As a symbol of America's resolve, my administration will work with Congress, and these two leaders, to show the world that we will rebuild New York City.

After all that has just passed—all the lives taken, and all the possibilities and hopes that died with them—it is natural to wonder if America's future is one of fear. Some speak of an age of terror. I know there are struggles ahead, and dangers to face. But this country will define our times, not be defined by them. As long as the United States of America is determined and strong, this will not be an age of terror; this will be an age of liberty, here and across the world.

Great harm has been done to us. We have suffered great loss. And in our grief and anger we have found our mission and our moment. Freedom and fear are at war. The advance of human freedom—the great achievement of our time, and the great hope of every time—now depends on us. Our nation—this generation—will lift a dark threat of violence from our people and our future. We will rally the world to this cause by our efforts, by our courage. We will not tire, we will not falter, and we will not fail.

It is my hope that in the months and years ahead, life will return almost to normal. We'll go back to our lives and routines, and that is good. Even grief recedes with time and grace. But our resolve must not pass. Each of us will remember what happened that day, and to whom it happened. We'll remember the moment the news came—where we were and what we were doing. Some will remember an image of a fire, or a story of rescue. Some will carry memories of a face and a voice gone forever.

And I will carry this: It is the police shield of a man named George Howard, who died at the World Trade Center trying to save others. It was given to me by his mom, Arlene, as a proud memorial to her son. This is my reminder of lives that ended, and a task that does not end.

I will not forget this wound to our country or those who inflicted it. I will not yield; I will not rest; I will not relent in waging this struggle for freedom and security for the American people.

The course of this conflict is not known, yet its outcome is certain. Freedom and fear, justice and cruelty, have always been at war, and we know that God is not neutral between them.

Fellow citizens, we'll meet violence with patient justice—assured of the rightness of our cause, and confident of the victories to come. In all that lies before us, may God grant us wisdom, and may He watch over the United States of America.

Thank you.

Source: CNN.com. "Transcript of President Bush's Address to a Joint Session of Congress on Thursday Night, September 20, 2001." Available online. URL: http://edition.cnn.com/2001/US/09/20/gen.bush.transcript/. Accessed November 25, 2009.

President George W. Bush, Address to Congress and the Nation (October 7, 2001)

On October 7, 2001, just 26 days after the September 11 attacks on the United States, President George W. Bush announced on television that the United States had begun military strikes against Taliban and al-Qaeda targets in Afghanistan. It was the start of a campaign aimed at overthrowing the Taliban regime, which had given support and protection to al-Qaeda. The speech contains hints that the U.S. campaign may extend beyond Afghanistan, particularly in the paragraph that begins: "Today we focus on Afghanistan, but the battle is broader. . . ." Osama bin Laden released his own statement concerning the U.S. attacks on Afghanistan the same day, which is included in chapter 5 of this volume (See Statement by Osama bin Laden on October 7, 2001.)

Good afternoon. On my orders, the United States military has begun strikes against al Qaeda terrorist training camps and military installations of the Taliban regime in Afghanistan. These carefully targeted actions are designed to disrupt the use of Afghanistan as a terrorist base of operations, and to attack the military capability of the Taliban regime.

We are joined in this operation by our staunch friend, Great Britain. Other close friends, including Canada, Australia, Germany and France, have pledged forces as the operation unfolds. More than 40 countries in the Middle East, Africa, Europe and across Asia have granted air transit or landing rights. Many more have shared intelligence. We are supported by the collective will of the world.

More than two weeks ago, I gave Taliban leaders a series of clear and specific demands: Close terrorist training camps; hand over leaders of the al Qaeda network; and return all foreign nationals, including American citizens, unjustly detained in your country. None of these demands were met. And now the Taliban will pay a price. By destroying camps and disrupting communications, we will make it more difficult for the terror network to train new recruits and coordinate their evil plans.

Initially, the terrorists may burrow deeper into caves and other entrenched hiding places. Our military action is also designed to clear the way for sustained, comprehensive and relentless operations to drive them out and bring them to justice.

At the same time, the oppressed people of Afghanistan will know the generosity of America and our allies. As we strike military targets, we'll also drop food, medicine and supplies to the starving and suffering men and women and children of Afghanistan.

The United States of America is a friend to the Afghan people, and we are the friends of almost a billion worldwide who practice the Islamic faith. The United States of America is an enemy of those who aid terrorists and of the barbaric criminals who profane a great religion by committing murder in its name.

This military action is a part of our campaign against terrorism, another front in a war that has already been joined through diplomacy, intelligence, the freezing of financial assets and the arrests of known terrorists by law enforcement agents in 38 countries. Given the nature and reach of our enemies, we will win this conflict by the patient accumulation of successes, by meeting a series of challenges with determination and will and purpose.

Today we focus on Afghanistan, but the battle is broader. Every nation has a choice to make. In this conflict, there is no neutral ground. If any government sponsors the outlaws and killers of innocents, they have become outlaws and murderers, themselves. And they will take that lonely path at their own peril.

I'm speaking to you today from the Treaty Room of the White House, a place where American Presidents have worked for peace. We're a peaceful nation. Yet, as we have learned, so suddenly and so tragically, there can be no peace in a world of sudden terror. In the face of today's new threat, the only way to pursue peace is to pursue those who threaten it.

We did not ask for this mission, but we will fulfill it. The name of today's military operation is Enduring Freedom. We defend not only our precious freedoms, but also the freedom of people everywhere to live and raise their children free from fear.

I know many Americans feel fear today. And our government is taking strong precautions. All law enforcement and intelligence agencies are working aggressively around America, around the world and around the clock. At my request, many governors have activated the National Guard to strengthen airport security. We have called up Reserves to reinforce our military capability and strengthen the protection of our homeland.

In the months ahead, our patience will be one of our strengths—patience with the long waits that will result from tighter security; patience and understanding that it will take time to achieve our goals; patience in all the sacrifices that may come.

Today, those sacrifices are being made by members of our Armed Forces who now defend us so far from home, and by their proud and worried families. A Commander-in-Chief sends America's sons and daughters into a battle in a foreign land only after the greatest care and a lot of prayer. We ask a lot of those who wear our uniform. We ask them to leave their loved ones, to travel great distances, to risk injury, even to be prepared to make the ultimate sacrifice of their lives. They are dedicated, they are honorable; they represent the best of our country. And we are grateful.

To all the men and women in our military—every sailor, every soldier, every airman, every coastguardsman, every Marine—I say this: Your mission is defined; your objectives are clear; your goal is just. You have my full confidence, and you will have every tool you need to carry out your duty.

I recently received a touching letter that says a lot about the state of America in these difficult times—a letter from a 4th grade girl, with a father in the military: "As much as I don't want my Dad to fight," she wrote, "I'm willing to give him to you."

This is a precious gift, the greatest she could give. This young girl knows what America is all about. Since September 11, an entire generation of young Americans has gained new understanding of the value of freedom, and its cost in duty and in sacrifice.

The battle is now joined on many fronts. We will not waver; we will not tire; we will not falter; and we will not fail. Peace and freedom will prevail.

Thank you. May God continue to bless America.

Source: Americanrhetoric.com. "Address on Initial Operations in Afghanistan." Available online. URL: http://www.americanrhetoric.com/speeches/gwbush911intialafghanistanops.htm. Accessed November 25, 2009.

Azizah al-Hibri on the Islamic Legal Rights of Married Women (2002)

Azizah al-Hibri is a leading Muslim-American academic specializing in the study of feminism and, particularly, Islamic marriage. She also founded KARAMAH: Muslim Women Lawyers for Human Rights, a charity concerned with human rights for Muslim women. In this extract Azizah al-Hibri argues that basic human rights have been denied to Muslim women who marry because of traditions that have emerged from unjustified patriarchal interpretations of Islam.

Marriage Relations in Islam

Historically, marriage has been an institution that favored men over women. Through this institution, basic women's rights such as the right to education, financial independence, and freedom of self-fulfillment were usually denied. A fulfilled woman was, in fact, viewed as one who married, served her husband well, and bore him children. This view, although less common today, continues to exist both in the West and in Muslim countries. Yet it is in total contradiction to the Islamic view of women and marriage.

Islam guarantees for women, among other things, the right to an education similar to that of the male, the right to financial independence, and even the right to engage in *ijtihad* [independent legal reasoning]. Islam also views marriage as an institution in which human beings find tranquility and affection with each other. It is for this reason that some prominent traditional Muslim scholars have argued that a woman is not required to serve her husband, prepare his food, or clean his house. In fact, the husband is obligated to bring his wife prepared food, for example. This assertion is based on the recognition that the Muslim wife is a companion to her husband and not a maid. Many jurists also defined the purpose of marriage institution in terms of sexual enjoyment (as distinguished from reproduction). They clearly stated that a Muslim woman has a right to sexual enjoyment within the marriage. This view has important consequences in areas such as contraception and divorce.

It is these rights and views, which are derived from the Qur'an and classical *ijtihad*, that we must actively reclaim. . . . So long as patriarchal (hierarchal/authoritarian) logic prevails, Muslim women will be denied their God-given rights. Qur'anic concepts of family relations must be more adequately recognized and enforced in Muslim countries and communities to abolish the authoritarian structure of the marriage institution.

In striving for this result we must recognize the fact that patriarchal logic is deeply entrenched in all societies and is quite resistant to being uprooted. If we, however, follow the Qur'anic approach to change, we will receive the support of many Muslim men and achieve a great measure of success without sacrificing the social cohesion of Muslim communities.

In fostering change the Qur'an resorts to what has been known recently in the West as affirmative action. In a patriarchal society even a general declaration of equal rights is not sufficient to protect women. Consequently, divine wisdom gave women further protections. Paramount among these protections is the ability of the Muslim woman to negotiate her marriage contract and place in it any conditions that do not contradict its purpose. For example, she could place in her marriage contract a condition forbidding her husband from moving her away from her own city or town. She could also insert a condition requiring him to support her in the pursuit of her education after marriage. She could also use the marriage contract to ensure that her marriage would foster, rather than destroy, her financial independence. This goal is usually achieved by requiring a substantial *mahr* [the dower].

The *Mahr* Requirement

Despite many patriarchal and Orientalist [stereotypical] interpretations that have distorted and even damaged the Muslim woman's rights in this area, the law of *mahr* was made clear quite early. The *mahr* is a requirement imposed by God upon men entering marriage as a sign of their serious commitment and a gesture of goodwill, a matter of great concern to women living in this patriarchal world. In fact, the giving of *mahr* is not much different from the Western custom of giving an engagement ring to signal commitment. Islamic law, however, preserved for the prospective wife the right to specify to her prospective husband the type of *mahr* she prefers. One woman may prefer cash, another property, depending on her relative needs or even taste. A third woman may choose something intangible (nonmaterial) as her *mahr,* such as education. That is acceptable also. A woman of meager means may prefer to ask for capital that she could immediately invest in a business. In fact, she could even use that capital to start her own business. Her husband would have no access to either the capital or income from that business even if he were in need because legally, her *mahr* belongs to her alone. . . .

Mahr, therefore, is not a "bride price" as some have erroneously described it. It is not money the woman pays to obtain a husband nor money [that] the husband pays to obtain a wife. It is part of a civil contract that specifies the conditions under which a woman is willing to abandon her status as a single woman and its related opportunities in order to marry a prospective husband and start a family. Consequently, as in Western prenuptial and nuptial agreements, the contract addresses matters of concern to the prospective wife and provides her with financial and other assurances. In short, it is a vehicle for ensuring the continued well-being of women entering matrimonial life in a world of patriarchal injustice and inequality. . . .

Family Planning

Another measure for guarding the interests of women in particular and the Muslim community in general is provided in the area of family planning. Islam values the family structure and, like Judaism and Christianity, encourages procreation. Islamic law, nevertheless, differs from both traditions in its liberal approach to family planning. It shares with some Judeo-Christian traditions the view that contraception is permissible. Coitus interruptus *(al-'azl)* was practiced by members of the Muslim community during the time of Prophet Muhammad. Indeed, the Prophet knew that some of his companions, including his cousin Ali, practiced it, yet he did not prohibit it.

Al-Ghazali, a prominent fifteenth-century jurist, argues that contraception is always permitted. He makes an analogy between intercourse and a contract. A contract consists of an offer and acceptance. So long as the offer has not been accepted, he notes, it can be withdrawn. He even suggests that a woman can engage in contraception to preserve her beauty but adds that it is disliked *(makrouh)* if used to avoid female offspring. Jurists have, however, conditioned the practice of *al-'azl* upon the consent of the wife. Some even argue that if the husband practices *al-'azl* without the wife's permission, he has to pay her a fine because he has detracted from her sexual enjoyment, her established right.

Until recently, the majority of traditional jurists have taken a relatively liberal view toward abortion that properly balances the rights of the mother and the rights of the child. They recognized a period of early pregnancy that could be terminated at will and a subsequent period in which the embryo became ensouled. The jurists argued that when the embryo became ensouled, increasingly stringent criteria should be used to justify abortion (such as the health of the mother). More recently, relying on medical data, jurists have adopted the view that the embryo is ensouled soon after conception. It is desirable that Muslim women physicians and jurists reexamine this recent conclusion to determine its validity.

Maintenance

Classical Islamic jurisprudence entitles the woman to maintenance by her husband. Even if fully financially independent, she is not required to spend any of her money except as she wishes. Furthermore, the wife is under no duty to do any housework although she may engage in such work on a volunteer basis. Some traditional jurists suggested that the wife was entitled to monetary compensation for her volunteer housework activity.

The law of maintenance is based on the Qur'an, but unfortunately it has been used to assert the general superiority of men over women. The relevant Qur'anic verse simply states that men may gain *qiwamah* (advisory, caretaking status) vis-à-vis women if only they satisfy two preconditions.

First, the male must be the (financial) maintainer of the woman. In other words, if he is not carrying her financial responsibility, then he has no standing to interfere in her affairs by providing unsolicited advice. Second, the male must also possess qualities (such as financial acumen, real estate expertise, etc.) that the advised woman needs to reach a particular decision but lacks (at that point). Without these two qualifications (which, incidentally, may change from time to time and from one decision to another), men may not even presume to provide advice or be caretakers *(qawwamun)*.

Because the Qur'an was revealed in a world that was and continues to be highly patriarchal, it engaged in affirmative action to protect women. The revelation about maintenance provided women against poverty. It also made clear that maintenance alone does not suffice for a man to claim *qiwamah* over a woman. . . .

Despite all the rights and guarantees offered by Islam to women, most men still use women as uncompensated laborers in their households. Furthermore, they not only expect them to produce heirs but also to nurse these heirs. . . . Yet most Muslim jurists do not require Muslim women to nurse their children except to save the life of the child. Instead, the husband is required to hire a wet nurse (or buy milk formula) if the mother does not want to nurse. If the husband divorces the wife, and she nurses the child after the divorce, jurists agree that she is entitled to monetary compensation for that nursing. Hence, while masquerading as Islamic family law, a significant amount of the present family law in Muslim countries is influenced by local custom and patriarchal tradition.

Polygyny

Western writers have treated polygyny as one of the most controversial Islamic practices. Thus, it may be surprising to discover that Qur'anic reasoning clearly favors monogamy. The major Qur'anic verses at issue are two. One *ayah* [verse] states: "If you fear that you shall not be able to deal justly with the orphans, marry women of your choice, two, or three, or four; But if you fear that you shall not be able to deal justly (with them), then only one or that which your right hand possesses. That will be more suitable to prevent you from doing injustice." The other *ayah* states that men cannot deal justly with their wives when they marry more than one woman [4:129].

Some Muslim jurists have interpreted the first *ayah* to mean that a man has the right to marry up to four wives as long as he is equally just with each of them. In providing this interpretation, these jurists ignored the first part of the *ayah* which conditions the permission upon a certain context that obtained at the time of its revelation, namely, one of justice and fairness concerning the treatment of orphaned wives. Secondly, these jurists ignored that last part of the *ayah*, which states that (even in that context) justice considerations make it preferable to marry only one wife. Consequently, this highly conditional and fact-specific verse was interpreted as if it articulated a general rule. Of the two conditions, the first was ignored altogether, whereas the second was reduced to the duty of exercising fairness in treatment and maintenance among the wives. These same jurists also ignored the second *ayah*, which flatly states that men are incapable of satisfying the condition precedent for engaging in polygyny, namely, justice and fairness.

Other traditional jurists, however, concluded that the Qur'an is clear in advocating monogamy as the general rule. They also added that insofar as polygyny causes the first wife harm, it is forbidden altogether *(haram)*. Several traditional jurists also recognized the right of the woman to place in the marriage contract a condition barring the prospective husband from additional (polygynous) marriages.

Yet practices of polygyny continue in some Muslim societies as a sign of economic or sexual power. As such, they are similar to the Western practice of having concubines or extramarital lovers. It is part of patriarchal custom and not religion. But religious scholars who attempt to criticize the practice or change the law are criticized for succumbing to Western influences.

Western neoorientalist critiques of Islam, thinly disguised as "feminist" critiques, have managed only to complicate the task of Muslim women. These critiques tend to be motivated more by a feeling of superiority and a desire for cultural hegemony than by a desire to help the female "Other" (in this case, the Muslim woman). The neoorientalist attitude is evidenced by the fact that only negative and distorted stereotypes of Muslim women are propagated in international fora. Furthermore, these Western "liberators" have taken it upon themselves to "explain" Islam, criticize the Qur'an, and redefine and prioritize the demands of Muslim women over these women's objections. This attack on Islam by unqualified biased commentators offends the religious sensibilities of all Muslims, male and female, regardless of their points of view.

Significantly, while Muslim women struggled repeatedly in international fora to raise basic issues of survival and development, such as hunger, water, war, and disease, patriarchal Western women have insisted on making the veil, clitoridectomy, and polygyny their primary preoccupations instead. They have even selected and funded some secular "Muslim" women to act as spokeswomen for the rest of the Muslim women. Needless to say, this neoorientalist attack on Islam had adversely impacted the civil rights of Muslims in Western countries and has poisoned the well for Muslim women seeking to regain their God-given Islamic rights in their own societies. Unfortunately, this state of affairs has alienated many Muslim women from the Western feminist movement.

Source: Azizah al-Hibri. "An Introduction to Muslim Women's Rights." In *Windows of Faith: Muslim Women Scholar-Activists in North America,* edited by Gisela Webb. Syracuse, N.Y.: Syracuse University Press, 2002, 57–60, 62–68.

Iraq Survey Group Final Report (September 30, 2004)

The Iraq Survey Group (ISG) was a commission charged with investigating allegations that the Iraqi government had been stockpiling chemical, biological, and radiological weapons (so-called weapons of mass destruction) before the 2003 U.S.-led invasion. The ISG consisted of more than a thousand personnel from the United States, the United Kingdom, and Australia and began its investigations shortly after the invasion. Since the alleged presence of weapons of mass destruction in Iraq was one of the principal justifications for the war, the work of the ISG was politically very important to the governments that had supported the invasion. In January 2004, the head of the ISG, David Kay, resigned, stating that he did not believe any weapons of mass destruction would be found in Iraq. The ISG's final report, published in September 2004, stated that no evidence of an active weapons of mass destruction program had been found in Iraq but that it believed Saddam Hussein would have restarted such a program given the opportunity.

Key Findings

Saddam never abandoned his intentions to resume a CW effort when sanctions were lifted and conditions were judged favorable:

* Saddam and many Iraqis regarded CW as a proven weapon against an enemy's superior numerical strength, a weapon that had saved the nation at least once already—during the Iran-Iraq war—and contributed to deterring the Coalition in 1991 from advancing to Baghdad.

169

While a small number of old, abandoned chemical munitions have been discovered, ISG judges that Iraq unilaterally destroyed its undeclared chemical weapons stockpile in 1991. There are no credible indications that Baghdad resumed production of chemical munitions thereafter, a policy ISG attributes to Baghdad's desire to see sanctions lifted, or rendered ineffectual, or its fear of force against it should WMD be discovered.

* The scale of the Iraqi conventional munitions stockpile, among other factors, precluded an examination of the entire stockpile; however, ISG inspected sites judged most likely associated with possible storage or deployment of chemical weapons.

Iraq's CW program was crippled by the Gulf war and the legitimate chemical industry, which suffered under sanctions, only began to recover in the mid-1990s. Subsequent changes in the management of key military and civilian organizations, followed by an influx of funding and resources, provided Iraq with the ability to reinvigorate its industrial base.

* Poor policies and management in the early 1990s left the Military Industrial Commission (MIC) financially unsound and in a state of almost complete disarray.

* Saddam implemented a number of changes to the Regime's organizational and programmatic structures after the departure of Husayn Kamil.

* Iraq's acceptance of the Oil-for-Food (OFF) program was the foundation of Iraq's economic recovery and sparked a flow of illicitly diverted funds that could be applied to projects for Iraq's chemical industry.

The way Iraq organized its chemical industry after the mid-1990s allowed it to conserve the knowledge-base needed to restart a CW program, conduct a modest amount of dual-use research, and partially recover from the decline of its production capability caused by the effects of the Gulf war and UN-sponsored destruction and sanctions. Iraq implemented a rigorous and formalized system of nationwide research and production of chemicals, but ISG will not be able to resolve whether Iraq intended the system to underpin any CW-related efforts.

* The Regime employed a cadre of trained and experienced researchers, production managers, and weaponization experts from the former CW program.

* Iraq began implementing a range of indigenous chemical production projects in 1995 and 1996. Many of these projects, while not weapons-related, were designed to improve Iraq's infrastructure, which would have enhanced Iraq's ability to produce CW agents if the scaled-up production processes were implemented.

* Iraq had an effective system for the procurement of items that Iraq was not allowed to acquire due to sanctions. ISG found no evidence that this system was used to acquire precursor chemicals in bulk; however documents indicate that dual-use laboratory equipment and chemicals were acquired through this system.

Iraq constructed a number of new plants starting in the mid-1990s that enhanced its chemical infrastructure, although its overall industry had not fully recovered from the effects of sanctions, and had not regained pre-1991 technical sophistication or production capabilities prior to Operation Iraqi Freedom (OIF).

* ISG did not discover chemical process or production units configured to produce key precursors or CW agents. However, site visits and debriefs revealed that Iraq maintained its ability for reconfiguring and 'making-do' with available equipment as substitutes for sanctioned items.

* ISG judges, based on available chemicals, infrastructure, and scientist debriefings, that Iraq at OIF probably had a capability to produce large quantities of sulfur mustard within three to six months.

* A former nerve agent expert indicated that Iraq retained the capability to produce nerve agent in significant quantities within two years, given the import of required phosphorous precursors. However, we have no credible indications that Iraq acquired or attempted to acquire large quantities of these chemicals through its existing procurement networks for sanctioned items.

In addition to new investment in its industry, Iraq was able to monitor the location and use of all existing dual-use process equipment. This provided Iraq the ability to rapidly reallocate key equipment for proscribed activities, if required by the Regime.

* One effect of UN monitoring was to implement a national level control system for important dual-use process plants.

Iraq's historical ability to implement simple solutions to weaponization challenges allowed Iraq to retain the capability to weaponize CW agent when the need arose. Because of the risk of discovery and consequences for ending UN sanctions, Iraq would have significantly jeopardized its chances of having sanctions lifted or no longer enforced if the UN or foreign entity had discovered that Iraq had undertaken any weaponization activities.

* ISG has uncovered hardware at a few military depots, which suggests that Iraq may have prototyped experimental CW rounds. The available evidence is insufficient to determine the nature of the effort or the timeframe of activities.

* Iraq could indigenously produce a range of conventional munitions, throughout the 1990s, many of which had previously been adapted for filling with CW agent. However, ISG has found ambiguous evidence of weaponization activities.

Saddam's Leadership Defense Plan consisted of a tactical doctrine taught to all Iraqi officers and included the concept of a "red-line" or last line of defense. However, ISG has no information that the plan ever included a trigger for CW use.

* Despite reported high-level discussions about the use of chemical weapons in the defense of Iraq, information acquired after OIF does not confirm the inclusion of CW in Iraq's tactical planning for OIF. We believe these were mostly theoretical discussions and do not imply the existence of undiscovered CW munitions.

Discussions concerning WMD, particularly leading up to OIF, would have been highly compartmentalized within the Regime. ISG found no credible evidence that any field elements knew about plans for CW use during Operation Iraqi Freedom.

* Uday—head of the Fedayeen Saddam—attempted to obtain chemical weapons for use during OIF, according to reporting, but ISG found no evidence that Iraq ever came into possession of any CW weapons.

ISG uncovered information that the Iraqi Intelligence Service (IIS) maintained throughout 1991 to 2003 a set of undeclared covert laboratories to research and test various chemicals and poisons, primarily for intelligence operations.

The network of laboratories could have provided an ideal, compartmented platform from which to continue CW agent R&D or small-scale production efforts, but we have no indications this was planned. (See Annex A.)

* ISG has no evidence that IIS Directorate of Criminology (M16) scientists were producing CW or BW agents in these laboratories. However, sources indicate that M16 was planning to produce several CW agents including sulfur mustard, nitrogen mustard, and Sarin.

* Exploitations of IIS laboratories, safe houses, and disposal sites revealed no evidence of CW-related research or production, however many of these sites were either sanitized by the Regime or looted prior to OIF. Interviews with key IIS officials within and outside of M16 yielded very little information about the IIS' activities in this area.

* The existence, function, and purpose of the laboratories were never declared to the UN.

* The IIS program included the use of human subjects for testing purposes.

ISG investigated a series of key pre-OIF indicators involving the possible movement and storage of chemical weapons, focusing on 11 major depots assessed to have possible links to CW. A review of documents, interviews, available reporting, and site exploitations revealed alternate, plausible explanations for activities noted prior to OIF which, at the time, were believed to be CW-related.

* ISG investigated pre-OIF activities at Musayyib Ammunition Storage Depot—the storage site that was judged to have the strongest link to CW. An extensive investigation of the facility revealed that there was no CW activity, unlike previously assessed.

Source: Globalsecurity.org. "Iraq Survey Group Final Report." Available online. URL: http://www.globalsecurity. org/wmd/library/report/2004/isg-final-report/isg-final-report_vol3_c w_key-findings.htm. Accessed November 25, 2009.

Souhail Mulla, Online Advice for Muslim Parents (2004–2005)

This extract comes from an online forum incorporated into the Web site of the Muslim American Society. It is typical of a large number of similar forums in which American Muslims discuss the problems of reconciling their faith and traditions with U.S. secular society, in this case the difficulties of raising children as Muslims in the United States. The question of how far Muslim parents should encourage their children to integrate with mainstream U.S. society and how far they should attempt to shield them from influences that may weaken their Muslim identity are raised several times here.

Q. I don't feel comfortable to send my daughter to a public middle school. I am so worried of doing so. Her older brothers are in public schools. But I am worry she might suffer with her *hijab* [scarf]. The problem is that there are no other options. We don't have Islamic middle or high schools in our area. What do you suggest?

A. We love to hear about young sisters who carry themselves as upright Muslims from a young age. The younger our children practice Islam, the stronger their Islam will develop as they grow older. This is something that you as a parent should be pleased with. At some point, sister, all of our daughters must step out into an environment where they will stick out because of their dress. On a positive note, we have numerous young girls who have gone to public schools in our community and have reported very few problems. More likely than not, your daughter will fit right in and make friends and these friends will be there to stand up for her if she ever does have any problems. Also you, as the mother, should always follow up with your daughter to see how things are going at school. There is a lot she will not tell you if you don't ask. It is possible that your daughter will be looked at differently because of the *hijab*. But this is what we want, we want the general public to know a Muslim woman when they see one and we don't want our women to be looked at the way other women are looked at (i.e., sex objects, etc.). It may also happen that she will be treated differently, possibly made fun of, etc. I don't say these things to scare you or your daughter, but only to get you mentally prepared for what you may or may not face as she begins middle school. After saying all that, you should take this as an opportunity to teach your daughter a very valuable life lesson. And that is that we do our best to follow the commandments of Allah and after that we leave the results up to Him and after taking all of the necessary steps, we leave ourselves under His protection.

Q. I would like to hear your opinion concerning the home schooling. Do you recommend this idea for our daughters? My husband insists on moving our daughter to home schooling believing that he is protecting her from the outside society, which could affect her in a negative way. I feel that by doing so, my daughter will loose a lot and her chance for a better education will decrease. This is in addition to the other side effects, such as isolating her from the outside society, community and friends. Please help me because I am so confused.

A. Dear Sister, you have raised an issue that almost every Muslim family struggles with; that is, "What type of school should I send my children to?" The options include public, private, Islamic, and home schooling. Home schooling is the least frequently chosen option. I am personally not a big proponent of home schooling. I believe that a child's full potential can be brought out best in a regular school setting where the child can interact with teachers, other students and other school staff. Cooperative learning is becoming a more commonly used method in teaching, and this is something that cannot take place in a one-on-one teacher/student relationship. Also, there are valuable social and life skills that are learned in a regular school setting that cannot be taught in a home schooling situation. Besides, to be involved with and to interact with other people, is closer to the experiences of life after school and is not something that can be taught as theory but is something that must be experienced. Some people think they are shielding their children from certain negative elements in society by home schooling their children. They may be shielding them from certain elements for the time-being, but what is going to happen when their children have to face these same negative elements after they leave the protective home environment? They will not have the same ability to cope with these issues as those who have encountered and learned to deal with these issues throughout their life. In addition, if home schooling is decided as the course a family is going to take with their children, all parties involved should be in *agreement* and *capable* for it to be an optimal learning situation. 95+% of the time the mother is the primary teacher when a child is home schooled and it can be an immense burden for her if she is not ready for task. Therefore, she should be doing it of her own free will and she should be scholastically capable of teaching all the material that any regular teacher must have command of. The mother must also be capable of transforming her home into a school and providing a strict, compartmentalized daily schedule of study just as a regular school provides. Allah knows best.

Q. I allowed my son to get out with his non-Muslim friends to play. He is not a young kid and I trust him, but I feel that there is a bad influence. As a father, when I think about it, I feel that they don't have the same background and they can't meet at one point. I mean someone should be influenced by the other and would try to meet with the other in the middle. I don't want my son to sacrifice his principles for the sake of friendship, but meanwhile I feel sorry for him for not having friends. What do you think?

A. Dear Brother, we share your concerns that you have for your son. The parental instinct that makes you feel that there is a bad influence among his friends is not something that should be ignored because it is something that comes from Allah. Parents know their children better than anyone else, and Allah has endowed them with the ability to know when they are going astray. You are absolutely correct about the fact that when two people are involved in a relationship or friendship they influence each other. Usually, the stronger personality has a greater influence and in this case it sounds like your son is being influenced by these stronger influences. There are numerous steps you can take to try to improve your son's situation. First of all, you should invite your son's friends over so that you can see who they are and get to know them. Have a BBQ, or some other activity that your son's friends would enjoy. After this meeting, you can discuss your son's relationship with his friends and you will be able to better gauge the extent of his friendship with particular individuals. Also, make sure you know your son's whereabouts at all times. You are the father and must regulate when and where he goes. One other very, very important step you must take is to try and connect your son with other Muslim youth. You should look to a local youth group, try to find a local *halaqa* [an Islamic study group] or find some outlet where he can connect with other Muslim youth. There is nothing else that can guarantee your son staying on the right track more than having good Muslim companionship.

Q. As parents, we need to encourage our kids when they do good things, but sometimes we need to punish them. In this country it is too hard to use your hands with your kids, although it helps them learning and to never forget what they learned. Do you believe that we could raise our kids well without using our hands?

A. Thank you for bringing up a very important point. My answer: We can *definitely* raise good children without having to raise our hands towards them. In fact, I believe that it is best not to punish our children with our hands. There is much debate as to whether or not physical punishment should be used with children. Most of this research tells us that we are much better off having a discipline system that doesn't include physical punishment. Our Prophet, peace be upon him, was never known to raise his hand against any of his children, nor against anyone else in his household. He is our example in all aspects of life, including his role as a parent. Shouldn't we follow his example?

Q. Dear Respected Brother: I am father of two boys. My old son wants to be an artist. I tried to convince him to select medicine, engineering or law, but he doesn't accept. He is very talented, but art is not a job. He could draw whenever he has extra time, but our nation doesn't need artists at this time. The problem is that his mother doesn't see any problem with her old son being an artist. I know art is good as a talent, but not as a career. Could you give me some tips on how to convince him or whom could convince from our Muslim scholars?

A. Dear Brother, May Allah bless you and your family and may Allah make your children from among our future leaders. Ameen. ["Amen" in Arabic.] This scenario that you bring forth is a common scenario that plays out . . . in this society. In this society, there are many opportunities in many different fields, which is in stark contrast to the opportunities that exist in many Muslim countries. At any given university, you can find up to one hundred different majors; educational opportunities are not just confined to law, medicine, teaching, and engineering, as they may be in certain Muslim countries. This same opportunity also plays itself out in the actual real world—the work world. There are many opportunities in many different fields. I advise you to do some research with your son. See what opportunities art may afford him. For example, in today's technological world, computer graphic art is a very respectable field into which many artists go into and do very well for themselves, may I add. Art is more than just drawing and painting pictures and, Allah knows best, there may be something out there for your son. Allah gives different talents and abilities to whomsoever he wishes. The good thing is that this society embraces creativity in the arts. At least, explore the possibilities and see if there are any viable avenues for him in this field. Three last comments: 1) Please look at my bio on the website and see what I got my bachelor's degree in (if you knew my ethnicity you would be even more surprised!). Even with that I was able to eventually find a field for myself in which now I do quite well for myself, *alhamdulillah* [praise be to God]! 2) We have enough Muslim doctors and engineers (there is an unfortunate need now for more Muslim lawyers though). It is about time Muslims started spreading themselves out into other fields. 3) At least he did not say that he wants to be an actor!

Source: Souhail Mulla. Online Advice about Muslim Youth. Muslim American Society Web site. November 2, 2004; December 7, 2004; December 28, 2004; and March 15, 2005. Available online. URL: http://www.masnet.org/discussion_archive.asp. Accessed August 23, 2006.

Council on American-Islamic Relations, "The Status of Muslim Civil Rights in the United States" (2005)

The Council on American-Islamic Relations (CAIR) is one of the largest Islamic advocacy groups in North America. Founded in 1994, it describes its purpose as to "enhance understanding of Islam, encourage dialogue, protect civil liberties, empower American Muslims, and build coalitions that promote justice and mutual understanding." This extract from the executive summary of a report entitled "The Status of Muslim Civil Rights in the United States" gives an overview of what CAIR sees as a disturbing trend toward the victimization and intimidation of American Muslims in the wake of the September 11, 2001, attacks on the United States.

Nearly four years removed from the 9/11 terror attacks, the greatest tragedy to befall our nation in modern history, our country has learned certain lessons that will hopefully lead us to a stronger, safer and more vibrant society for people of all races, faiths and cultures.

Since the 9/11 attacks, the most disturbing legal trend is the growing disparity in how American Muslims are being treated under the law on many different levels.

In order to fully understand the status of civil rights in the post-9/11 era, it is essential that this report offer a documented historical overview of major federal law enforcement initiatives, high-profile national cases and statistical evidence of anti-Muslim discrimination in the United States, particularly those incidents that occurred during the last calendar year of 2004.

In 2004, CAIR processed a total of 1,522 incident reports of civil rights cases compared to 1,019 cases reported to CAIR in 2003. This constitutes a 49 percent increase in the reported cases of harassment, violence and discriminatory treatment from 2003 and marks the highest number of Muslim civil rights cases ever reported to CAIR in our eleven year history.

In addition, CAIR received 141 reports of actual and potential violent anti-Muslim hate crimes, a 52 percent increase from the 93 reports received in 2003.

Overall, 10 states alone accounted for almost 79 percent of all reported incidents to CAIR in 2004. These ten states include: California (20.17%), New York (10.11%), Arizona (9.26%), Virginia (7.16%), Texas (6.83%), Florida (6.77%), Ohio (5.32%), Maryland (5.26%), New Jersey (4.53%) and Illinois (2.96%). . . .

United States Documents

Background and Findings

In the months directly following 9/11, Attorney General John Ashcroft, using his powers under section 412 of the now infamous USA PATRIOT Act, rounded up and imprisoned well over 1,200 Muslim and Arab men based solely on pretextual immigration violations. The most disconcerting fact about these mass round-ups was the fact that the Justice Department refused to disclose the detainees' identities, give them access to lawyers or allow them to have contact with their families.

In April 2003, Inspector General Glenn A. Fine reported that at least 1,200 men from predominantly Muslim and Arab countries were detained by law enforcement officials nationwide. An August 2002 Human Rights Watch report documents cases of prolonged detention without any charge, denial of access to bond release, interference with detainees' right to legal counsel and unduly harsh conditions of confinement for the over 1,200 detainees. Georgetown University law professor David Cole said that, "Thousands were detained in this blind search for terrorists without any real evidence of terrorism, and ultimately without netting virtually any terrorists of any kind."

In addition to the indiscriminate immigrant dragnet after September 11, several high profile cases against American Muslims further stigmatized the American Muslim community.

For example, after spending seventy-six days in solitary confinement and being labeled a 'spy' in most media circles, where can Army chaplain and West Point graduate Captain James Yee go to regain his respectability after being falsely accused of treasonous crimes that could have resulted in the death penalty? Where might Oregon attorney Brandon Mayfield reclaim his good name after being falsely linked by the FBI to the Madrid train bombings of March 11, 2004? How does Sami Al-Hussayen resume a normal life with his family after being found not guilty of 'aiding terrorists' while serving as a webmaster and exercising his First Amendment right to free speech?

The American Muslim community has always categorically condemned acts of terrorism and believes that those who break the law should be prosecuted to the fullest extent of the law. However, in order to remain consistent with the constitutional hallmarks of due process and 'equal protection' under the law, it is essential that our law enforcement agencies enforce and apply the law in a consistent manner to all people rather than selectively target people based on their religious or ethnic affiliation.

It is time once again for American society to reclaim its true legal tradition and judge a person on the criminality of their acts, not on the color of his skin or the religion to which she adheres.

The Dragnets of John Ashcroft

Under United States immigration law, an 'absconder' is defined as an "alien who, though subject to . . . [deportation], has failed to surrender for removal or to otherwise comply with the order." According to a January 2002 memorandum sent to federal immigration and law enforcement officials, the Deputy Attorney General of the United States estimated that there are approximately 314,000 absconders, or deportable illegal aliens, living in the United States today. Of these 314,000, only about 6,000, less than 2 percent, originate from Muslim or Arab nations. Although over 90 percent of absconders are from Latin American countries, the Justice Department began selectively targeting absconders only from predominantly Muslim and Arab countries in the past few years. However, their selective targeting of Muslims and Arabs after September 11 bore almost no criminal fruits. By the end of May 2002, the Justice Department admitted that out of 314,000 absconders, only 585 had been located. More embarrassingly, not a single terrorist had been apprehended.

Whereas all Americans have been greatly affected by 9/11 and its aftermath, young males from Arab and Muslim countries have been most profoundly affected by the dragnet conducted by the Department of Justice in our ongoing "war on terror." In addition to the law enforcement dragnets conducted by the Justice Department after 9/11, certain congressional legislation has also been passed which has stirred great debate in all American circles as to how to best balance national security interests whilst still safeguarding the civil liberties guaranteed to every American by our Constitution.

The Secret Roundup

Glenn A. Fine, Inspector General for the Department of Justice, officially reported that at least 1,200 men from predominantly Muslim and Arab countries were detained by law enforcement officials nationwide within two months of 9/11. The Inspector General conceded in his official report that a senior officer in the Office of Public Affairs stopped reporting the cumulative count of detainees after 1,200 because the "statistics became too confusing."

In August 2002, Human Rights Watch (HRW) released a 95-page report, entitled *Presumption of Guilt,* which documented cases of prolonged detention without any charge, denial of access to bond release, interference with detainees' right to legal counsel, and unduly harsh conditions of confinement for the over 1,200 detainees. HRW's findings were later confirmed by Inspector General Fine's report, which also identified a pattern of "physical and verbal abuse" by correctional staff at the Metropolitan Detention Center (MDC) in Brooklyn, New York.

The September 11 detainees comprised citizens from more than 20 countries. The largest number, 254 (or 33 percent), were from Pakistan, more than double the number of any other country. The second largest number (111) was from Egypt and there were also substantial numbers of detainees from Jordan, Turkey, Yemen and India. The ages of the detainees varied, but by far the greatest number, 479 (or 63 percent), were between the ages of 26 and 40.

The fruits of these legally suspect and egregiously overarching dragnets was succinctly summed up by Georgetown University law professor David Cole when he said that, "Thousands were detained in this blind search for terrorists without any real evidence of terrorism, and ultimately without netting virtually any terrorists of any kind."

. . .

Sample Cases [of Civil Rights Abuses]

March 21, 2003—A Muslim American family of Palestinian descent became victim of property damage when their van was bombed outside their home in the Chicago suburb of Burbank, Illinois. The individual responsible for the crime had been convicted earlier of criminal damage to property in 2001 for vandalizing an Arab-owned furniture store two days after the 9/11 attacks.

December 12, 2003—A Muslim woman was shopping in a New York toy store when a man followed her, verbally accosted and assaulted her. She reported the incident to the police and the attacker was arrested.

March 2, 2004—In San Diego, a man of Portuguese descent was beaten by a group of four white men who mistook him for being Middle Eastern. They yelled racial slurs at him and told him to go back to Iraq.

March 3, 2004—A San Antonio, Texas, man was sentenced to 30 years in prison for setting a series of fires at Muslim-owned convenience stores and other businesses in the city. The County District Attorney referred to the man as a 'terrorist' for his connection with another attack against a Muslim-owned business when the arsons began in 2003.

April 24, 2004—A Muslim woman and her son were harassed, threatened and attacked by another woman while shopping in Pennsylvania. The woman yelled that American troops were fighting in Iraq and Afghanistan so that women did not have to dress like her and also hit her with her cart repeatedly. Employees of the store refused to call security when she requested that they do so and did not assist her in finding a phone to call the police.

May 27, 2004—A Muslim man and his family were verbally harassed by a patron while eating at a restaurant in Florida. The offender called them 'terrorists'. When the Muslim man complained, the manager elected to remove him from the premises instead of the offender.

June 21, 2004—A Muslim man reported that while riding on a van that runs from New York to his home in Paterson, New Jersey, a group of Latino males harassed him. They hit him on his arm and made comments like, "take the bombs off before I kill you." The driver did not say anything until they began cursing him in Spanish at which point she asked them to stop.

June 26, 2004—While driving home in Illinois, a Muslim woman was harassed and physically assaulted. Three individuals asked her for a lighter. When she replied that she did not have one, they became angry and said, "Stupid Muslims, F-cking Muslims" as they surrounded her car and repeatedly kicked it. When the victim stepped out of her car to confront them, one of the individuals punched her in the face and tore her *hijab* from her head.

July 14, 2004—A Muslim-owned grocery store was torched and completely destroyed. Anti-Arab slurs that read, "F-ck you Arab" were found spray-painted on the scene.

July 30, 2004—A Muslim woman from New York was soliciting donations on behalf of a charitable organization when she was verbally and physically attacked.

August 13, 2004—A cabbie in New York was punched in the face while driving a cab near Ground Zero after the offender said to him, "You are Muslim." The offender was drunk and later charged with third degree assault and harassment.

United States Documents

August 23, 2004—In Tucson, Arizona, a Muslim family of Jordanian origin reported that their car was vandalized in the parking lot of their apartment building. Allegedly the car's tires were slashed and the windshield was smashed. A note taped to the vehicle read, "You are not welcome here. Go back home you stupid f-ckers."

September 12, 2004—In California, a Muslim man and his children placed an order at a drive through Burger King, when he overheard an employee say to his co-workers, "Look, Osama Bin Laden" is here.

October 27, 2004—A community member filed a report of graffiti on a METRA stop in Illinois that read, "Kill all Muslims B4 they kill U."

October 29, 2004—Two Staten Island men were arrested and charged with hate crimes for allegedly hitting a Muslim student at Stony Brook University while shouting anti-Muslim slurs. Suffolk County police charged the 19 and 20-year old with criminal trespass in the second degree and aggravated harassment in the second degree as a hate crime. The two men allegedly knocked on a student's door and awoke him at about 4 a.m. The victim said he opened the door and the two men went into his room and began throwing items at him, hitting him and overturning furniture, all the while calling him anti-Muslim names.

December 1, 2004—In Chesterfield, Virginia, a Sikh-owned gas station was destroyed by fire and anti-Muslim graffiti was found on a nearby trash container and shed. The fire is being investigated as an arson and possible hate crime.

December 21, 2004—A fire that took place at a used car lot in Nebraska is being investigated as arson and a hate crime. Swastikas were spray-painted on the walls. Most of the graffiti involves derogatory references to Latinos and Arabs.

Source: Council on American-Islamic Relations. "The Status of Muslim Civil Rights in the United States" (2005). Available online. URL http://www.cair-net.org/asp/2005CivilRightsReport.pdf. Accessed April 10, 2006.

A Muslim Congressman Supports Israel (2008)

André D. Carson was elected to Congress in 2008 as U.S. representative for Indiana's Seventh Congressional District, becoming only the second Muslim representative in the House. Raised a Christian, Carson converted to Islam as a teenager. In this extract, Carson expresses his support on the floor of the House for a resolution recognizing the 60th anniversary of the founding of the state of Israel in May 1948. The United States's early recognition of Israel in 1948 was extremely unpopular among the Arab-Muslim states of the Middle East, and its continuing political and military support of the country remains controversial in the Muslim world. Democratic congressman Carson's recognition of Israel's anniversary can be seen as part of efforts by President Barack Obama's administration to foster peaceful relations between the Muslim world and Israel.

Mr. CARSON of Indiana. Mr. Speaker, I rise in strong support of House Concurrent Resolution 322, a resolution recognizing the 60th anniversary of the founding of the State of Israel. Mr. Speaker, beyond just being an influential world leader, the State of Israel has been a staunch and ardently loyal ally of the United States over the last several decades. This great nation's commitment to protecting it citizens and securing its homeland are simply unmatched. Since the founding of the modern State of Israel in 1948, the bond between the United States and our Middle East partner has grown and remained strong. It is incumbent that we as Members of Congress do all we can to make sure that this relationship continue to flourish.

Mr. Speaker, the United States must make every effort possible to safeguard our relationship with the Middle East's only democracy, Israel. Now more than ever, we must diligently advance our shared interests and goals as it pertains to promoting peace and combating terrorism.

Mr. Speaker, in closing I would like to congratulate the State of Israel, the Israeli citizens, and the Jewish community on reaching this milestone. This great nation has much to celebrate and be proud of on its 60th birthday.

Source: U.S. Congress. *Congressional Record* (House), 110th Cong., 2nd sess. April 22, 2008, p. H2522. Available online. URL: http://thomas.loc.gov. Accessed January 26, 2009.

President Barack Obama, "Remarks by the President on a New Beginning" (June 4, 2009)

In June 2009, recently elected U.S. president Barack Obama gave a speech at Cairo University, Egypt, in which he described his wish to build a new relationship with the Muslim world. The speech was widely promoted as a "new beginning" in U.S. policy and addressed many of the issues that had caused great tension between the United States and many Muslim-majority states in the previous decade. The speech did not include any specific policy announcements, but it did contain several statements that were seen as highly significant. Obama referred to Israeli settlements in the Occupied Territories as illegitimate and called for them to stop. He also indicated that he favored women's right to wear hijab *and acknowledged the role of the United States in the overthrow of Iran's Mossadeq government in 1953.*

Thank you very much. Good afternoon. I am honored to be in the timeless city of Cairo, and to be hosted by two remarkable institutions. For over a thousand years, Al-Azhar has stood as a beacon of Islamic learning; and for over a century, Cairo University has been a source of Egypt's advancement. And together, you represent the harmony between tradition and progress. I'm grateful for your hospitality, and the hospitality of the people of Egypt. And I'm also proud to carry with me the goodwill of the American people, and a greeting of peace from Muslim communities in my country: Assalaamu alaykum.

We meet at a time of great tension between the United States and Muslims around the world—tension rooted in historical forces that go beyond any current policy debate. The relationship between Islam and the West includes centuries of coexistence and cooperation, but also conflict and religious wars. More recently, tension has been fed by colonialism that denied rights and opportunities to many Muslims, and a Cold War in which Muslim-majority countries were too often treated as proxies without regard to their own aspirations. Moreover, the sweeping change brought by modernity and globalization led many Muslims to view the West as hostile to the traditions of Islam.

Violent extremists have exploited these tensions in a small but potent minority of Muslims. The attacks of September 11, 2001 and the continued efforts of these extremists to engage in violence against civilians has led some in my country to view Islam as inevitably hostile not only to America and Western countries, but also to human rights. All this has bred more fear and more mistrust.

. . .

I've come here to Cairo to seek a new beginning between the United States and Muslims around the world, one based on mutual interest and mutual respect, and one based upon the truth that America and Islam are not exclusive and need not be in competition. Instead, they overlap, and share common principles—principles of justice and progress; tolerance and the dignity of all human beings.

I do so recognizing that change cannot happen overnight. I know there's been a lot of publicity about this speech, but no single speech can eradicate years of mistrust, nor can I answer in the time that I have this afternoon all the complex questions that brought us to this point. But I am convinced that in order to move forward, we must say openly to each other the things we hold in our hearts and that too often are said only behind closed doors. There must be a sustained effort to listen to each other; to learn from each other; to respect one another; and to seek common ground. As the Holy Koran tells us, "Be conscious of God and speak always the truth." That is what I will try to do today—to speak the truth as best I can, humbled by the task before us, and firm in my belief that the interests we share as human beings are far more powerful than the forces that drive us apart.

Now part of this conviction is rooted in my own experience. I'm a Christian, but my father came from a Kenyan family that includes generations of Muslims. As a boy, I spent several years in Indonesia and heard the call of the azaan at the break of dawn and at the fall of dusk. As a young man, I worked in Chicago communities where many found dignity and peace in their Muslim faith.

. . .

I also know that Islam has always been a part of America's story. The first nation to recognize my country was Morocco. In signing the Treaty of Tripoli in 1796, our second President, John Adams, wrote, "The United States has in itself no character of enmity against the laws, religion or tranquility of Muslims." And since our founding, American Muslims have enriched the United States. They have fought in our wars, they have served in our government, they have stood for civil rights, they have started businesses, they have taught at our universities, they've excelled in our sports arenas, they've won Nobel Prizes, built our tallest building, and lit the Olympic Torch. And when the first Muslim American was recently elected to Congress, he took the oath to defend our Constitution using the same Holy Koran that one of our Founding Fathers—Thomas Jefferson—kept in his personal library.

So I have known Islam on three continents before coming to the region where it was first revealed. That experience guides my conviction that partnership between America and Islam must be based on what Islam is, not what it isn't. And I consider it part of my responsibility as President of the United States to fight against negative stereotypes of Islam wherever they appear.

But that same principle must apply to Muslim perceptions of America. Just as Muslims do not fit a crude stereotype, America is not the crude stereotype of a self-interested empire. The United States has been one of the greatest sources of progress that the world has ever known. We were born out of revolution against an empire. We were founded upon the ideal that all are created equal, and we have shed blood and struggled for centuries to give meaning to those words—within our borders, and around the world. We are shaped by every culture, drawn from every end of the Earth, and dedicated to a simple concept: E pluribus unum—"Out of many, one."

. . .

So let there be no doubt: Islam is a part of America. And I believe that America holds within her the truth that regardless of race, religion, or station in life, all of us share common aspirations—to live in peace and security; to get an education and to work with dignity; to love our families, our communities, and our God. These things we share. This is the hope of all humanity.

. . .

The first issue that we have to confront is violent extremism in all of its forms.

In Ankara, I made clear that America is not—and never will be—at war with Islam. We will, however, relentlessly confront violent extremists who pose a grave threat to our security—because we reject the same thing that people of all faiths reject: the killing of innocent men, women, and children. And it is my first duty as President to protect the American people.

The situation in Afghanistan demonstrates America's goals, and our need to work together. Over seven years ago, the United States pursued al Qaeda and the Taliban with broad international support. We did not go by choice; we went because of necessity. I'm aware that there's still some who would question or even justify the events of 9/11. But let us be clear: Al Qaeda killed nearly 3,000 people on that day. The victims were innocent men, women and children from America and many other nations who had done nothing to harm anybody. And yet al Qaeda chose to ruthlessly murder these people, claimed credit for the attack, and even now states their determination to kill on a massive scale. They have affiliates in many countries and are trying to expand their reach. These are not opinions to be debated; these are facts to be dealt with.

Now, make no mistake: We do not want to keep our troops in Afghanistan. We see no military—we seek no military bases there. It is agonizing for America to lose our young men and women. It is costly and politically difficult to continue this conflict. We would gladly bring every single one of our troops home if we could be confident that there were not violent extremists in Afghanistan and now Pakistan determined to kill as many Americans as they possibly can. But that is not yet the case.

. . .

Let me also address the issue of Iraq. Unlike Afghanistan, Iraq was a war of choice that provoked strong differences in my country and around the world. Although I believe that the Iraqi people are ultimately better off without the tyranny of Saddam Hussein, I also believe that events in Iraq have reminded America of the need to use diplomacy and build international consensus to resolve our problems whenever possible. Indeed, we can recall the words of Thomas Jefferson, who said: "I hope that our wisdom will grow with our power, and teach us that the less we use our power the greater it will be."

Today, America has a dual responsibility: to help Iraq forge a better future—and to leave Iraq to Iraqis. And I have made it clear to the Iraqi people that we pursue no bases, and no claim on their territory or resources. Iraq's sovereignty is its own. And that's why I ordered the removal of our combat brigades by next August. That is why we will honor our agreement with Iraq's democratically elected government to remove combat troops from Iraqi cities by July, and to remove all of our troops from Iraq by 2012. We will help Iraq train its security forces and develop its economy. But we will support a secure and united Iraq as a partner, and never as a patron.

And finally, just as America can never tolerate violence by extremists, we must never alter or forget our principles. Nine-eleven was an enormous trauma to our country. The fear and anger that it provoked was understandable, but in some cases, it led us to act contrary to our traditions and our ideals. We are taking concrete actions to change course. I have unequivocally prohibited the use of torture by the United States, and I have ordered the prison at Guantanamo Bay closed by early next year.

. . .

The second major source of tension that we need to discuss is the situation between Israelis, Palestinians and the Arab world.

America's strong bonds with Israel are well known. This bond is unbreakable. It is based upon cultural and historical ties, and the recognition that the aspiration for a Jewish homeland is rooted in a tragic history that cannot be denied.

Around the world, the Jewish people were persecuted for centuries, and anti-Semitism in Europe culminated in an unprecedented Holocaust. Tomorrow, I will visit Buchenwald, which was part of a network of camps where Jews were enslaved, tortured, shot and gassed to death by the Third Reich. Six million Jews were killed—more than the entire Jewish population of Israel today. Denying that fact is baseless, it is ignorant, and it is hateful. Threatening Israel with destruction—or repeating vile stereotypes about Jews—is deeply wrong, and only serves to evoke in the minds of Israelis this most painful of memories while preventing the peace that the people of this region deserve.

On the other hand, it is also undeniable that the Palestinian people— Muslims and Christians—have suffered in pursuit of a homeland. For more than 60 years they've endured the pain of dislocation. Many wait in refugee camps in the West Bank, Gaza, and neighboring lands for a life of peace and security that they have never been able to lead. They endure the daily humiliations—large and small—that come with occupation. So let there be no doubt: The situation for the Palestinian people is intolerable. And America will not turn our backs on the legitimate Palestinian aspiration for dignity, opportunity, and a state of their own.

. . .

Now is the time for Palestinians to focus on what they can build. The Palestinian Authority must develop its capacity to govern, with institutions that serve the needs of its people. Hamas does have support among some Palestinians, but they also have to recognize they have responsibilities. To play a role in fulfilling Palestinian aspirations, to unify the Palestinian people, Hamas must put an end to violence, recognize past agreements, recognize Israel's right to exist.

At the same time, Israelis must acknowledge that just as Israel's right to exist cannot be denied, neither can Palestine's. The United States does not accept the legitimacy of continued Israeli settlements. This construction violates previous agreements and undermines efforts to achieve peace. It is time for these settlements to stop.

And Israel must also live up to its obligation to ensure that Palestinians can live and work and develop their society. Just as it devastates Palestinian families, the continuing humanitarian crisis in Gaza does not serve Israel's security; neither does the continuing lack of opportunity in the West Bank. Progress in the daily lives of the Palestinian people must be a critical part of a road to peace, and Israel must take concrete steps to enable such progress.

And finally, the Arab states must recognize that the Arab Peace Initiative was an important beginning, but not the end of their responsibilities. The Arab-Israeli conflict should no longer be used to distract the people of Arab nations from other problems. Instead, it must be a cause for action to help the Palestinian people develop the institutions that will sustain their state, to recognize Israel's legitimacy, and to choose progress over a self-defeating focus on the past.

. . .

Too many tears have been shed. Too much blood has been shed. All of us have a responsibility to work for the day when the mothers of Israelis and Palestinians can see their children grow up without fear; when the Holy Land of the three great faiths is the place of peace that God intended it to be; when Jerusalem is a secure and lasting home for Jews and Christians and Muslims, and a place for all of the children of Abraham to mingle peacefully together as in the story of Isra, when Moses, Jesus, and Mohammed, peace be upon them, joined in prayer.

The third source of tension is our shared interest in the rights and responsibilities of nations on nuclear weapons.

This issue has been a source of tension between the United States and the Islamic Republic of Iran. For many years, Iran has defined itself in part by its opposition to my country, and there is in fact a tumultuous history between us. In the middle of the Cold War, the United States played a role in the overthrow of a democratically elected Iranian government. Since the Islamic Revolution, Iran has played a role in acts of hostage-taking and violence against U.S. troops and civilians. This history is well known. Rather than remain trapped in the past, I've made it clear to Iran's leaders and people that my country is prepared to move forward. The question now is not what Iran is against, but rather what future it wants to build.

. . .

I understand those who protest that some countries have weapons that others do not. No single nation should pick and choose which nation holds nuclear weapons. And that's why I strongly reaffirmed America's commitment to seek a world in which no nations hold nuclear weapons. (Applause.) And any nation—including Iran—should have the right to access peaceful nuclear power if it complies with its responsibilities under the nuclear Non-Proliferation Treaty. That commitment is at the core of the treaty, and it must be kept for all who fully abide by it. And I'm hopeful that all countries in the region can share in this goal.

The fourth issue that I will address is democracy.

I know there has been controversy about the promotion of democracy in recent years, and much of this controversy is connected to the war in Iraq. So let me be clear: No system of government can or should be imposed by one nation by any other.

That does not lessen my commitment, however, to governments that reflect the will of the people. Each nation gives life to this principle in its own way, grounded in the traditions of its own people. America does not presume to know what is best for everyone, just as we would not presume to pick the outcome of a peaceful election. But I do have an unyielding belief that all people yearn for certain things: the ability to speak your mind and have a say in how you are governed; confidence in the rule of law and the equal administration of justice; government that is transparent and doesn't steal from the people; the freedom to live as you choose. These are not just American ideas; they are human rights. And that is why we will support them everywhere.

THE MUSLIM WORLD

. . .

The fifth issue that we must address together is religious freedom.

Islam has a proud tradition of tolerance. We see it in the history of Andalusia and Cordoba during the Inquisition. I saw it firsthand as a child in Indonesia, where devout Christians worshiped freely in an overwhelmingly Muslim country. That is the spirit we need today. People in every country should be free to choose and live their faith based upon the persuasion of the mind and the heart and the soul. This tolerance is essential for religion to thrive, but it's being challenged in many different ways.

Among some Muslims, there's a disturbing tendency to measure one's own faith by the rejection of somebody else's faith. The richness of religious diversity must be upheld—whether it is for Maronites in Lebanon or the Copts in Egypt. And if we are being honest, fault lines must be closed among Muslims, as well, as the divisions between Sunni and Shia have led to tragic violence, particularly in Iraq.

Freedom of religion is central to the ability of peoples to live together. We must always examine the ways in which we protect it. For instance, in the United States, rules on charitable giving have made it harder for Muslims to fulfill their religious obligation. That's why I'm committed to working with American Muslims to ensure that they can fulfill zakat.

Likewise, it is important for Western countries to avoid impeding Muslim citizens from practicing religion as they see fit—for instance, by dictating what clothes a Muslim woman should wear. We can't disguise hostility towards any religion behind the pretence of liberalism.

. . .

The sixth issue that I want to address is women's rights. I know—and you can tell from this audience, that there is a healthy debate about this issue. I reject the view of some in the West that a woman who chooses to cover her hair is somehow less equal, but I do believe that a woman who is denied an education is denied equality. And it is no coincidence that countries where women are well educated are far more likely to be prosperous.

Now, let me be clear: Issues of women's equality are by no means simply an issue for Islam. In Turkey, Pakistan, Bangladesh, Indonesia, we've seen Muslim-majority countries elect a woman to lead. Meanwhile, the struggle for women's equality continues in many aspects of American life, and in countries around the world.

I am convinced that our daughters can contribute just as much to society as our sons. Our common prosperity will be advanced by allowing all humanity—men and women—to reach their full potential. I do not believe that women must make the same choices as men in order to be equal, and I respect those women who choose to live their lives in traditional roles. But it should be their choice. And that is why the United States will partner with any Muslim-majority country to support expanded literacy for girls, and to help young women pursue employment through micro-financing that helps people live their dreams.

· · ·

The issues that I have described will not be easy to address. But we have a responsibility to join together on behalf of the world that we seek—a world where extremists no longer threaten our people, and American troops have come home; a world where Israelis and Palestinians are each secure in a state of their own, and nuclear energy is used for peaceful purposes; a world where governments serve their citizens, and the rights of all God's children are respected. Those are mutual interests. That is the world we seek. But we can only achieve it together.

I know there are many—Muslim and non-Muslim—who question whether we can forge this new beginning. Some are eager to stoke the flames of division, and to stand in the way of progress. Some suggest that it isn't worth the effort—that we are fated to disagree, and civilizations are doomed to clash. Many more are simply skeptical that real change can occur. There's so much fear, so much mistrust that has built up over the years. But if we choose to be bound by the past, we will never move forward. And I want to particularly say this to young people of every faith, in every country—you, more than anyone, have the ability to reimagine the world, to remake this world.

· · ·

We have the power to make the world we seek, but only if we have the courage to make a new beginning, keeping in mind what has been written.

The Holy Koran tells us: "O mankind! We have created you male and a female; and we have made you into nations and tribes so that you may know one another."

The Talmud tells us: "The whole of the Torah is for the purpose of promoting peace."

The Holy Bible tells us: "Blessed are the peacemakers, for they shall be called sons of God."

The people of the world can live together in peace. We know that is God's vision. Now that must be our work here on Earth.

Thank you. And may God's peace be upon you. Thank you very much. Thank you.

Source: Whitehouse.gov. "Remarks by the President on a New Beginning." Available online. URL: http://www.whitehouse.gov/the_press_office/Remarks-by-the-President-at-Cairo-University-6-04-09/. Accessed November 25, 2009.

5

International Documents

GENERAL

The Covenant of Umar (637)

In 637, Arab-Muslim forces besieged and captured the city of Jerusalem as part of their campaign against the Christian Byzantine Empire. Caliph Umar I, then the ruler of the Muslim world, visited the city and concluded an agreement with the Christian patriarch of Jerusalem, Sophronius, guaranteeing the religious freedoms of Christians under Muslim rule. Christians were required to pay the Jizia tax, a poll tax levied on all non-Muslims living under Muslim rule. The covenant is notable for its insistence that no Jews should be allowed to live in the city. Although this agreement is now more than 1,400 years old, some Palestinians still regard it as the basis of Christian-Muslim relations in Jerusalem to the present day.

In the Name of Allah, the Most Merciful, the Most Compassionate

This is an assurance of peace and protection given by the servant of Allah Omar, Commander of the Believers to the people of Ilia' (Jerusalem). He gave them an assurance of protection for their lives, property, church and crosses as well as the sick and healthy and all its religious community.

Their churches shall not be occupied, demolished nor taken away wholly or in part. None of their crosses nor property shall be seized. They shall not be coerced in their religion nor shall any of them be injured. None of the Jews shall reside with them in Ilia'.

The people of Ilia, shall pay Jizia tax as inhabitants of cities do. They shall evict all Romans and thieves.

He whoever gets out shall be guaranteed safety for his life and property until he reach his safe haven. He whoever stays shall be (also) safe, in which case he shall pay as much tax as the people of Ilia' do. Should any of the people of Ilia, wish to move together with his property along with the Romans and to clear out of their churches and crosses, they shall be safe for their lives, churches and crosses, until they have reached their safe haven. He whoever chooses to stay he may do so and he shall pay as much tax as the people of Ilia' do. He whoever wishes to move along with the Roman, may do so, and whoever wishes to return back home to his kinsfolk, may do so. Nothing shall be taken from them, their crops have been harvested. To the contents of this convent here are given the Covenant of Allah, the guarantees of His Messenger, the Caliphs and the Believers, provided they (the people of Ilia') pay their due Jizia tax.

Witnesses hereto are:

Khalid Ibn al-Waleed Amr Ibn al-Ass Abdul-Rahman Ibn'Auf Mu'awiya Ibn abi-Sifian Made and executed in the year 15 AH.

Source: Mideastweb.org. "The Covenant of Omar." Available online. URL: http://www.mideastweb.org/coven antofomar.htm. Accessed November 25, 2009.

The Balfour Declaration (November 2, 1917)

The Balfour Declaration is a critical document in the history of the Arab-Muslim world and Israel. The declaration takes the form of a letter written by then British foreign secretary Arthur James Balfour to Walter Rothschild (second baron Rothschild), a wealthy Jewish financier involved in the Zionist movement, in November 1917. The letter was intended to inform the Zionist Federation of Great Britain and Ireland of the British government's favorable opinion of the establishment of a Jewish homeland in Palestine. Britain's approval of the Zionist idea for a Jewish homeland was important because Britain was bound to have a powerful influence over the future of the Middle East following the expected collapse of the Ottoman Empire in World War I. The document deliberately referred to a "national home for the Jewish people" rather than a "Jewish state," although some commentators have claimed the terms are synonymous, and to its establishment "in" Palestine rather than the establishment "of" Palestine as a homeland.

Foreign Office

Dear Lord Rothschild,

I have much pleasure in conveying to you, on behalf of His Majesty's Government, the following declaration of sympathy with Jewish Zionist aspirations which has been submitted to, and approved by, the Cabinet.

"His Majesty's Government view with favour the establishment in Palestine of a national home for the Jewish people, and will use their best endeavours to facilitate the achievement of this object, it being clearly understood that nothing shall be done which may prejudice the civil and religious rights of existing non-Jewish communities in Palestine, or the rights and political status enjoyed by Jews in any other country."

I should be grateful if you would bring this declaration to the knowledge of the Zionist Federation.

Yours sincerely,
Arthur James Balfour

Source: Jewishvirtuallibrary.org. "The Balfour Declaration." Available online. URL: http://www.jewishvirtual library.org/jsource/History/balfour.html. Accessed November 25, 2009.

Statement by the Arab League upon the Declaration of the State of Israel (May 15, 1948)

The League of Arab States (often known as the Arab League) was formed in Cairo, Egypt, on March 22, 1945, with six members: Egypt, Iraq, Transjordan (renamed Jordan after 1946), Lebanon, Saudi Arabia, and Syria. When Israel declared its independence on May 14, 1948, the Arab League responded the next day with this statement making clear its strong objections. Egypt, Iraq, Transjordan, Lebanon, and Syria launched an assault on Israel the same day, starting the 1948 Arab-Israeli War. Although this document is now more than 60 years old and does not reflect the current policies of the Arab League, the issues it raises remain at the core of ongoing conflicts between Israel and the Muslim world.

Palestine was part of the former Ottoman Empire subject to its law and represented in its parliament. The overwhelming majority of the population of Palestine were Arabs. There was in it a small minority of Jews that enjoyed the same rights and bore the same responsibilities as the [other] inhabitants, and did not suffer any ill-treatment on account of its religious beliefs. The holy places were inviolable and the freedom of access to them was guaranteed.

The Arabs have always asked for their freedom and independence. On the outbreak of the First World War, and when the Allies declared that they were fighting for the liberation of peoples, the Arabs joined them and fought on their side with a view to realizing their national aspirations and obtaining their independence. England pledged herself to recognize the independence of the Arab countries in Asia, including Palestine. The Arabs played a remarkable part in the achievement of final victory and the Allies have admitted this.

In 1917 England issued a declaration in which she expressed her sympathy with the establishment of a National Home for the Jews in Palestine. When the Arabs knew of this they protested against it, but England reassured them by affirming to them that this would not prejudice the right of their countries to freedom and independence or affect the political status of the Arabs in Palestine. Notwithstanding the legally void character of this declaration, it was interpreted by England to aim at no more than the establishment of a spiritual centre for the Jews in Palestine, and to conceal no ulterior political aims, such as the establishment of a Jewish State. The same thing was declared by the Jewish leaders.

When the war came to an end England did not keep her promise. Indeed, the Allies placed Palestine under the Mandate system and entrusted England with [the task of carrying it out], in accordance with a document providing for the administration of the country, in the interests of its inhabitants and its preparation for the independence which the Covenant of the League of Nations recognized that Palestine was qualified to have.

England administered Palestine in a manner which enabled the Jews to flood it with immigrants and helped them to settle in the country. [This was so] notwithstanding the fact that it was proved that the density of the population in Palestine had exceeded the economic capacity of the country to absorb additional immigrants. England did not pay regard to the interests or rights of the Arab inhabitants, the lawful owners of the country. Although they used to express, by various means, their concern and indignation on account of this state of affairs which was harmful to their being and their future, they [invariably] were met by indifference, imprisonment and oppression.

As Palestine is an Arab country, situated in the heart of the Arab countries and attached to the Arab world by various ties—spiritual, historical, and strategic—the Arab countries, and even the Eastern ones, governments as well as peoples, have concerned themselves with the problem of Palestine and have raised it to the international level; (they have also raised the problem) with England, asking for its solution in accordance with the pledges made and with democratic principles. The Round Table Conference was held in London in 1939 in order to discuss the Palestine question and arrive at the just solution thereof. The Governments of the Arab States participated in (this conference) and asked for the preservation of the Arab character of Palestine and the proclamation of its independence. This conference ended with the issue of a White Paper in which England defined her policy towards Palestine, recognized its independence, and undertook to set up the institutions that would lead to its exercise of the characteristics of (this independence). She (also) declared that her obligations concerning the establishment of a Jewish national home had been fulfilled, since that home had actually been established. But the policy defined in the (White) Paper was not carried out. This, therefore, led to the deterioration of the situation and the aggravation of matters contrary to the interests of the Arabs.

While the Second World War was still in progress, the Governments of the Arab States began to hold consultations regarding the reinforcement of their cooperation and the increasing of the means of their collaboration and their solidarity, with a view to safeguarding their present and their future and to participating in the erection of the edifice of the new world on firm foundations. Palestine had its (worthy) share of consideration and attention in these conversations. These conversations led to the establishment of the League of Arab States as an instrument for the cooperation of the Arab States for their security, peace and wellbeing. The Pact of the League of Arab States declared that Palestine has been an independent country since its separation from the Ottoman Empire, but the manifestations of this independence have been suppressed due to reasons which were out of the control of its inhabitants. The establishment of the United Nations shortly afterwards was an event about which the Arabs had the greatest hopes. Their belief in the ideals on which that organization was based made them participate in its establishment and membership.

Since then the Arab League and its (member) Governments have not spared any effort to pursue any course, whether with the Mandatory Power or with the United Nations, in order to bring about a just solution of the Palestine problem: (a solution) based upon true democratic principles and compatible with the provisions of the Covenant of the League of Nations and the (Charter) of the United Nations, and which would (at the same time) be lasting, guarantee peace and security in the country and prepare it for progress and prosperity. But Zionist claims were always an obstacle to finding such a solution, (as the Zionists), having prepared themselves with armed forces, strongholds and fortifications to face by force anyone standing in their way, publicly declared (their intention) to establish a Jewish State.

When the General Assembly of the United Nations issued, on 29 November 1947, its recommendation concerning the solution of the Palestine problem, on the basis of the establishment of an Arab State and of another Jewish (State) in (Palestine) together with placing the City of Jerusalem under the trusteeship of the United Nations, the Arab States drew attention to the injustice implied in this solution (affecting) the right of the people of Palestine to immediate independence, as well as democratic principles and the provisions of the Covenant of the League of Nations and (the Charter) of the United Nations. (These States also) declared the Arabs' rejection of (that solution) and that it would not be possible to carry it out by peaceful means, and that its forcible imposition would constitute a threat to peace and security in this area. The warnings and expectations of the Arab States have, indeed, proved to be true, as disturbances were soon widespread throughout Palestine. The Arabs clashed with the Jews, and the two (parties) proceeded to fight each other and shed each other's blood. Whereupon the United Nations began to realize the danger of recommending the partition (of Palestine) and is still looking for a way out of this state of affairs.

Now that the British mandate over Palestine has come to an end, without there being a legitimate constitutional authority in the country, which would safeguard the maintenance of security and respect for law and which would protect the lives and properties of the inhabitants, the Governments of the Arab States declare the following:

First: That the rule of Palestine should revert to its inhabitants, in accordance with the provisions of the Covenant of the League of Nations and (the Charter) of the United Nations and that (the Palestinians) should alone have the right to determine their future.

Second: Security and order in Palestine have become disrupted. The Zionist aggression resulted in the exodus of more than a quarter of a million of its Arab inhabitants from their homes and in taking refuge in the neighbouring Arab countries. The events which have taken place in Palestine have unmasked the aggressive intentions and the imperialist designs of the Zionists, including the atrocities committed by them against the peace-loving

Arab inhabitants, especially in Dayr Yasin, Tiberias and others. Nor have they respected the inviolability of consuls, as they have attacked the consulates of the Arab States in Jerusalem. After the termination of the British mandate over Palestine the British authorities are no longer responsible for security in the country, except to the degree affecting their withdrawing forces, and (only) in the areas in which these forces happen to be at the time of withdrawal as announced by (these authorities). This state of affairs would render Palestine without any governmental machinery capable of restoring order and the rule of law to the country, and of protecting the lives and properties of the inhabitants.

Third: This state of affairs is threatening to spread to the neighbouring Arab countries, where feeling is running high because of the events in Palestine. The Governments of the Member States of the Arab League and the United Nations are exceedingly worried and deeply concerned about this state of affairs.

Fourth: These Governments had hoped that the United Nations would have succeeded in finding a peaceful and just solution of the problem of Palestine, in accordance with democratic principles and the provisions of the Covenant of the League of Nations and (the Charter) of the United Nations, so that peace, security and prosperity would prevail in this part of the world.

Fifth· The Governments of the Arab States, as members of the Arab League, a regional organization within the meaning of the provisions of Chapter VIII of the Charter of the United Nations, are responsible for maintaining peace and security in their area. These Governments view the events taking place in Palestine as a threat to peace and security in the area as a whole and (also) in each of them taken separately.

Sixth: Therefore, as security in Palestine is a sacred trust in the hands of the Arab States, and in order to put an end to this state of affairs and to prevent it from becoming aggravated or from turning into (a state of) chaos, the extent of which no one can foretell; in order to stop the spreading of disturbances and disorder in Palestine to the neighbouring Arab countries; in order to fill the gap brought about in the governmental machinery in Palestine as a result of the termination of the mandate and the non-establishment of a lawful successor authority, the Governments of the Arab States have found themselves compelled to intervene in Palestine solely in order to help its inhabitants restore peace and security and the rule of justice and law to their country, and in order to prevent bloodshed.

Seventh: The Governments of the Arab States recognize that the independence of Palestine, which has so far been suppressed by the British Mandate,
has become an accomplished fact for the lawful inhabitants of Palestine.
They alone, by virtue of their absolute sovereignty, have the right to provide
their country with laws and governmental institutions. They alone should
exercise the attributes of their independence, through their own means and
without any kind of foreign interference, immediately after peace, security,
and the rule of law have been restored to the country. At that time the intervention of the Arab states will cease, and the independent State of Palestine
will cooperate with the (other member) States of the Arab League in order
to bring peace, security and prosperity to this part of the world. The Governments of the Arab States emphasize, on this occasion, what they have
already declared before the London Conference and the United Nations,
that the only solution of the Palestine problem is the establishment of a unitary Palestinian State, in accordance with democratic principles, whereby
its inhabitants will enjoy complete equality before the law, (and whereby)
minorities will be assured of all the guarantees recognized in democratic
constitutional countries and (whereby) the holy places will be preserved and
the rights of access thereto guaranteed.

Eighth: The Arab States most emphatically declare that (their) intervention
in Palestine was due only to these considerations and objectives, and that
they aim at nothing more than to put an end to the prevailing conditions in
(Palestine). For this reason, they have great confidence that their action will
have the support of the United Nations; (that it will be) considered as an
action aiming at the realization of its aims and at promoting its principles,
as provided for in its Charter.

Source: Jewishvirtuallibrary.org. "Arab League Declaration on the Invasion of Palestine." Available online. URL:
http://www.jewishvirtuallibrary.org/jsource/History/arab_invasion.html. Accessed November 11, 2009.

Mahathir Mohamad at the
Tenth Islamic Summit Conference (2003)

*Several voices within the Muslim world agree that the whole Muslim com-
munity suffers from a malaise. The words "weak" and "backward" were used
by Mahathir Mohamad, prime minister of Malaysia, at the Tenth Islamic
Summit Conference in 2003, soon after the U.S. invasion of Iraq.*

The whole world is looking at us. Certainly 1.3 billion Muslims, one-sixth of
the world's population are placing their hopes in us, in this meeting, even

though they may be cynical about our will and capacity to even decide to restore the honor of Islam and the Muslims, much less to free their brothers and sisters from the oppression and humiliation from which they suffer today.

I will not enumerate the instances of our humiliation and oppression, nor will I once again condemn our detractors and oppressors. It would be an exercise in futility, because they are not going to change their attitudes just because we condemn them. If we are to recover our dignity and that of Islam, our religion, it is we who must decide, it is we who must act.

To begin with, the governments of all the Muslim countries can close ranks and have a common stand; if not on all issues, at least on some major ones, such as on Palestine. We are all Muslims. We are all oppressed. We are all being humiliated. But we who have been raised by Allah above our fellow Muslims to rule our countries have never really tried to act in concert in order to exhibit at our level the brotherhood and unity that Islam enjoins upon us.

But, not only are our governments divided, the Muslim ummah is also divided, and divided again and again. Over the last 1,400 years the interpreters of Islam, the learned ones, the ulamas have interpreted and reinterpreted the single Islamic religion brought by Prophet Muhammad (Peace Be Upon Him), so differently that now we have a thousand religions which are often so much at odds with one another that we often fights and kill each other

From being a single ummah we have allowed ourselves to be divided into numerous sects, mazhabs and tarikats, each more concerned with claiming to be the true Islam than our oneness as the Islamic ummah. We fail to notice that our detractors and enemies do not care whether we are true Muslims or not. To them we are all Muslims, followers of a religion and a Prophet whom they declare promotes terrorism, and we are all their sworn enemies. They will attack and kill us, invade our lands, bring down our Governments whether we are Sunnis or Syiahs, Alawait or Druze or whatever. And we aid and abet them by attacking and weakening each other, and sometimes by doing their bidding, acting as their proxies to attack fellow Muslims. We try to bring down our governments through violence, succeeding to weaken and impoverish our countries.

We ignore entirely, and we continue to ignore, the Islamic injunction to unite and to be brothers to each other, we, the governments of the Islamic countries and the ummah. But this is not all that we ignore about the teachings of Islam. We are enjoined to Read, Iqra i.e., to acquire knowledge. The early Muslims took this to mean translating and studying the works of the Greeks and other scholars before Islam. And these Muslim scholars added to the body of knowledge through their own studies.

The early Muslims produced great mathematicians and scientists, scholars, physicians and astronomers, etc., and they excelled in all the fields of knowledge of their times, besides studying and practicing their own religion of Islam. As a result, the Muslims were able to develop and extract wealth from their lands and through their world trade, able to strengthen their defenses, protect their people and give them the Islamic way of life, Addin, as prescribed by Islam. At the time, the Europeans of the Middle Ages were still superstitious and backward, the enlightened Muslims had already built a great Muslim civilization, respected and powerful, more than able to compete with the rest of the world and able to protect the ummah from foreign aggression. The Europeans had to kneel at the feet of Muslim scholars in order to access their own scholastic heritage.

. . .

But halfway through the building of the great Islamic civilization came new interpreters of Islam, who taught that acquisition of knowledge by Muslims meant only the study of Islamic theology. The study of science, medicine, etc., was discouraged. Intellectually, the Muslims began to regress. With intellectual regression, the great Muslim civilization began to falter and wither. But for the emergence of the Ottoman warriors, Muslim civilization would have disappeared with the fall of Granada in 1492.

The early successes of the Ottomans were not accompanied by an intellectual renaissance. Instead, they became more and more preoccupied with minor issues, such as whether tight trousers and peak caps were Islamic, whether printing machines should be allowed or electricity used to light mosques. The Industrial Revolution was totally missed by the Muslims. And the regression continued until the British and French instigated rebellion against Turkish rule, brought about the downfall of the Ottomans, the last Muslim world power, and replaced it with European colonies and not independent states as promised. It was only after World War II that these colonies became independent.

Apart from the new nation-states, we also accepted the western democratic system. This also divided us because of the political parties and groups that we form, some of which claim Islam for themselves, reject the Islam of other parties and refuse to accept the results of the practice of democracy if they fail to gain power for themselves. They resort to violence, thus destabilizing the weakening Muslim countries.

With all these developments over the centuries, the ummah and the Muslim civilization became so weak that, at one time, there was not a single Muslim country which was not colonized or hegemonized by the Europeans. But regaining independence did not help to strengthen the Muslims. Their states were weak and badly administered, constantly in a state of turmoil. The Europeans could do what they liked with Muslim territories. It is not surprising that they should excise Muslim land to create the state of Israel to solve their Jewish problem. Divided, the Muslims could do nothing effective to stop the Balfour and Zionist transgression.

. . .

Allah has said in Surah Ar-Ra'd, verse 11 that He will not change the fate of a community until the community has tried to change its fate itself. The early Muslims were as oppressed as we are presently. But after their sincere and determined efforts to help themselves in accordance with the teachings of Islam, Allah had helped them to defeat their enemies and to create a great and powerful Muslim civilization. But what effort have we made, especially with the resources that He has endowed us with?

We are now 1.3 billion strong. We have the biggest oil reserve in the world. We have great wealth. We are not as ignorant as the Jahilliah who embraced Islam. We are familiar with the workings of the world's economy and finances. We control 57 out of the 180 countries in the world. Our votes can make or break international organizations. Yet we seem more helpless than the small number of Jahilliah converts who accepted the Prophet as their leader. Why? Is it because of Allah's will or is it because we have interpreted our religion wrongly, or failed to abide by the correct teachings of our religion, or done the wrong things?

. . .

This is what comes from the superficial interpretation of the Qur'an, stressing not the substance of the Prophet's sunnah and the Qur'an's injunctions, but rather the form, the manner and the means used in the 1st Century of the Hijrah. And it is the same with the other teachings of Islam. We are more concerned with the forms rather than the substance of the words of Allah and adhering only to the literal interpretation of the traditions of the Prophet.

We may want to recreate the first century of the Hijrah, the way of life in those times, in order to practice what we think to the be true Islamic way of life. But we will not be allowed to do so. Our detractors and enemies will take advantage of the resulting backwardness and weakness in order to dominate us. Islam is not just for the 7th Century A.D. Islam is for all times. And times have changed.

Whether we like it or not, we have to change, not by changing our religion, but by applying its teachings in the context of a world that is radically different from that of the first century of the Hijrah. Islam is not wrong, but the interpretations by our scholars, who are not prophets even though they may be very learned, can be wrong. We have a need to go back to the fundamental teachings of Islam to find out whether we are indeed believing in and practicing the Islam that the Prophet preached. It cannot be that we are all practicing the correct and true Islam, when our beliefs are so different from one another.

Today we, the whole Muslim ummah, are treated with contempt and dishonor. Our religion is denigrated. Our holy places desecrated. Our countries are occupied. Our people starved and killed. None of our countries are truly independent. We are under pressure to conform to our oppressors' wishes about how we should behave, how we should govern our lands, how we should think, even.

. . .

Our only reaction is to become more and more angry. Angry people cannot think properly. And so we find some of our people reacting irrationally. They launch their own attacks, killing just about anybody, including fellow Muslims, to vent their anger and frustration. Their Governments can do nothing to stop them. The enemy retaliates and puts more pressure on the governments. And the governments have no choice but to give in, to accept the directions of the enemy, literally to give up their independence of action.

With this their people and the ummah become angrier and turn against their own governments. Every attempt at a peaceful solution is sabotaged by more indiscriminate attacks calculated to anger the enemy and prevent any peaceful settlement. But the attacks solve nothing. The Muslims simply get more oppressed.

There is a feeling of hopelessness among the Muslim countries and their people. They feel that they can do nothing right. They believe that things can only get worse. The Muslims will forever be oppressed and dominated by the Europeans and the Jews. They will forever be poor, backward and weak. Some believe, as I have said, this is the Will of Allah, that the proper state of the Muslims is to be poor and oppressed in this world.

But is it true that we should do and can do nothing for ourselves? Is it true that 1.3 billion people can exert no power to save themselves from the humiliation and oppression inflicted upon them by a much smaller enemy? Can they only lash back blindly in anger? Is there no other way than to ask our young people to blow themselves up and kill people and invite the massacre of more of our own people?

. . .

Surely the 23-years struggle of the Prophet can provide us with some guidance as to what we can and should do.

We know he and his early followers were oppressed by the Qhuraish. Did he launch retaliatory strikes? No. He was prepared to make strategic retreats. He sent his early followers to a Christian country and he himself later migrated to Madinah. There he gathered followers, built up his defense capability and ensured the security of his people. At Hudaibiyah he was prepared to accept an unfair treaty, against the wishes of his companions and followers. During the peace that followed he consolidated his strength and eventually he was able to enter Mecca and claim it for Islam. Even then he did not seek revenge. And the peoples of Mecca accepted Islam and many became his most powerful supporters, defending the Muslims against all their enemies.

That briefly, is the story of the struggle of the Prophet. We talk so much about following the sunnah of the Prophet. We quote the instances and the traditions profusely. But we actually ignore all of them.

If we use the faculty to think that Allah has given us, then we should know that we are acting irrationally. We fight without any objective, without any goal other than to hurt the enemy because they hurt us. Naively we expect them to surrender. We sacrifice lives unnecessarily, achieving nothing other than to attract more massive retaliation and humiliation.

It is surety time that we pause to think. But will this be wasting time? For well over half a century we have fought over Palestine. What have we achieved? Nothing. We are worse off than before. If we had paused to think then we could have devised a plan, a strategy that can win us final victory. Pausing and thinking calmly is not a waste of time. We have a need to make a strategic retreat and to calmly assess our situation.

We are actually very strong. 1.3 billion people cannot be simply wiped out. The Europeans killed six million Jews out of 12 million. But today, the Jews rule this world by proxy. They get others to fight and die for them.

We may not be able to do that. We may not be able to unite all the 1.3 billion Muslims. We may not be able to get all the Muslim governments to act in concert. But even if we can get a third of the ummah and a third of the Muslim states to act together, we can already do something. Remember that the Prophet did not have many followers when he went to Madinah. But he united the Ansars and the Muhajirins and eventually he became strong enough to defend Islam.

· · ·

We also know that not all non-Muslims are against us. Some are well-disposed towards us. Some even see our enemies as their enemies. Even among the Jews there are many who do not approve of what the Israelis are doing.

We must not antagonize everyone. We must win their hearts and minds. We must win them to our side not by begging for help from them but by the honorable way that we struggle to help ourselves. We must not strengthen the enemy by pushing everyone into their camps through irresponsible and un-Islamic acts.

· · ·

We must build up our strength in every field, not just in armed might. Our countries must be stable and well administered, must be economically and financially strong, industrially competent and technologically advanced. This will take time, but it can be done and it will be time well spent. We are enjoined by our religion to be patient.

. . .

We know that the Jahilliah Arabs were given to feuding, to killing each other simply because they were from different tribes. The Prophet preached the brotherhood of Islam to them and they were able to overcome their hatred for each other, become united and help toward the establishment of the great Muslim civilization. Can we say that what the Jahilliah (the ignorant) could do, we, the modern Muslims, cannot do? If not all, at least some of us can do. If not the renaissance of our great civilization, at least ensuring the security of the ummah.

To do things that are suggested will not even require all of us to give up our differences with each other. We need only to call a truce, so we can act together in tackling only certain problems of common interests, the Palestine problem for example.

In any struggle, in any war, nothing is more important that concerted and coordinated action. A degree of discipline is all that is needed. The Prophet lost in Jabal Uhud because his forces broke rank. We know that, yet we are unwilling to discipline ourselves and to give up our irregular and uncoordinated actions. We need to be brave, but not foolhardy. We need to think, not just of our reward in the afterlife, but also of the worldly results of our mission.

The Qur'an tells us that when the enemy sues for peace, we must react positively. True, the treaty offered is not favorable to us. But we can negotiate. The Prophet did, at Hudaibiyah. And, in the end, he triumphed.

. . .

The enemy will probably welcome these proposals and we will conclude that the promoters are working for the enemy. But think. We are up against a people who think. They survived 2000 years of pogroms not by hitting back, but by thinking. They invented and successfully promoted Socialism, Communism, human rights and democracy so that persecuting them would appear to be wrong, so they may enjoy equal rights with others. With these they have now gained control of the most powerful countries and they, this tiny community, have become a world power. We cannot fight them through brawn alone. We must use our brains also.

Of late because of their power and their apparent success they have become arrogant. And arrogant people, like angry people will make mistakes, will forget to think. They are already beginning to make mistakes. And they will make more mistakes. There may be windows of opportunity for us now and in the future. We must seize these opportunities.

But to do so, we must get our acts right. Rhetoric is good. It helps us to expose the wrongs perpetrated against us, perhaps win us some sympathy and support. It may strengthen our spirit, our will and resolve, to face the enemy. We can and should pray to Allah (S.W.T.), for in the end, it is He Who will determine whether we succeed or fail. We need His blessings and His help in our endeavors.

. . .

As I said at the beginning, the whole world is looking at us, the whole Muslim ummah is placing their hopes in this conference of the leaders of Islamic nations. They expect us not just to vent our frustrations and anger, through words and gestures; not just to pray for Allah's blessings. They expect us to do something, to act. We cannot say we cannot do anything, we, the leaders of the Muslim nations. We cannot say we cannot unite, even when faced with the destruction of our religion and the ummah.

We know we can. There are many things that we can do. There are many resources that we have at our disposal. What is needed is merely the will to do it. As Muslims, we must be grateful for the guidance of our religion, we must do what needs to be done, willingly and with determination. Allah has not raised us, the leaders, above the others so we may enjoy power for ourselves only. The power we wield is for our people, for the ummah, for Islam. We must have the will to make use of this power judiciously, prudently, concertedly. Insyaallah we will triumph in the end.

Source: Final Call News. Available Online. URL: Finalcall.com/artman/publish/perspectives_1/Malaysian_prime_ minister_address_the_organizati on_1089.shtml. Accessed January 26, 2010.

Muslim Nation Discusses the GDP of all Muslim-Majority Countries (2006)

This extract is from a blog written by a Muslim advocating the unification of all Muslim-majority nations into a super state. The idea of a unified state encompassing all Muslims, the ummah *or world community of Muslims, has a long history and harks back to the time shortly after the establishment of Islam when the great majority of Muslims lived in a single, rapidly expanding empire. The author of this blog bemoans the apparent economic and political weakness of the world's Muslim-majority states despite the fact that Muslims make up more than 20 percent of the global population.*

Yet how do Muslims figure in the world arena? Sad to say it's nothing less than pathetic. The Gross Domestic Product (GDP) of ALL the Muslim countries combined is less than or equal to that of France. 15 years ago when 50,000 Muslim women are raped by Christian Serbs in Bosnia, Muslims watched as spectators. Now when country after country falls to the hands of American and other neo-colonialists Muslims look on helplessly. When Lebanon is bombed to Stone Age and Palestine is no more we heat our seats. Millions starving in Africa, many more oppressed by cruel dictators in Central Asia does not disturb the Muslim peace of mind. YaAllah! I dare say they'll be heating their chairs even if Mecca is vaporized or millions butchered in Saudi Arabia and Iran. "The less we think about the Muslims the happier we'll be," seems the thought of the day.

Source: 1 Muslim Nation "A Proposal to Unite Muslim World—A Union of Muslim Countries (UMC)." August 13, 2006. Available online. URL: http://1muslimnation.wordpress.com/2006/08/13/a-proposal-to-unite-muslim-world-a-union-of-muslim-countries-umc/. Accessed August 30, 2009.

INDONESIA

Declaration of Independence of Aceh (1976)

The Free Aceh Movement (GAM), also known as the Aceh Sumatra National Liberation Front (ASNLF), began its campaign to achieve independence for the Indonesian province in 1976 with the following declaration. Although government forces militarily defeated the GAM by the end of 1977, the movement did not die. Fighting broke out again many times over the next 30 years, ending finally with a 2005 peace agreement in which Aceh achieved limited self-rule as a "special territory." The distinction made in the document between the people of "Acheh," which is on the island of Sumatra, and the "Javanese" is a reminder of the great cultural and historical diversity of the people of Indonesia.

To The peoples Of The World:

We, the people of Acheh, Sumatra, exercising our right of self-determination, and protecting our historic right of eminent domain to our fatherland, do hereby declare ourselves free and independent from all political control of the foreign regime of Jakarta and the alien people of the island of Java.

Our fatherland, Acheh, Sumatra, had always been a free and independent sovereign State since the world begun. Holland was the first foreign power to attempt to colonize us when it declared war against the sovereign State of Acheh, on March 26, 1873, and on the same day invaded our territory, aided by Javanese mercenaries. The aftermath of this invasion was duly recorded on the front pages of contemporary newspapers all over the world. The London, TIMES, on April 22, 1873, wrote: "A remarkable incident in modern colonial history is reported from East Indian Archipelago. A considerable force of Europeans has been defeated and held in check by the army of native state . . . the State of Acheh. The Achehnese have gained a decisive victory. Their enemy is not only defeated, but compelled to withdraw."

. . .

On Christmas day, 1873, the Dutch invaded Acheh for the second time, and thus begun what HARPER'S MAGAZINE had called "A Hundred Years War of Today", one of the bloodiest, and longest colonial war in human history, during which one-half of our people had laid down their lives defending our sovereign State. It was being fought right up to the beginning of World War II. Eight immediate forefathers of the signer of this Declaration died in the battlefields of that long war, defending our sovereign nation, all as successive rulers and supreme commanders of the forces of the sovereign and independent State of Acheh, Sumatra.

However, when, after World War II, the Dutch East Indies was supposed to have been liquidated,—an empire is not liquidated if its territorial integrity is preserved,—our fatherland, Acheh, Sumatra, was not returned to us. Instead, our fatherland was turned over by the Dutch to the Javanese—their ex-mercenaries,—by hasty fiat of former colonial powers. The Javanese are alien and foreign people to us Achehnese Sumatrans. We have no historic, political, cultural, economic or geographic relationship with them. When the fruits of Dutch conquests are preserved, intact, and then bequeathed, as it were, to the Javanese, the result is inevitable that a Javanese colonial empire would be established in place of that of the Dutch over our fatherland, Acheh, Sumatra. But, colonialism, either by white, Dutch, Europeans or by brown Javanese, Asians, is not acceptable to the people of Acheh, Sumatra.

This illegal transfer of sovereignty over our fatherland by the old, Dutch, colonialists to the new, Javanese colonialists, was done in the most appalling political fraud of the century: the Dutch colonialist was supposed to have turned over sovereignty over our fatherland to a "new nation" called "indonesia". But "indonesia" was a fraud: a cloak to cover up Javanese colonialism. Since the world began, there never was a people, much less a nation, in our part of the world by that name. No such people existed in the Malay Archipelago by definition of ethnology, philology, cultural anthropology, sociology, or by any other scientific findings. "Indonesia" is merely a new label, in a totally foreign nomenclature, which has nothing to do with our own history, language, culture, or interests; it was a new label considered useful by the Dutch to replace the despicable "Dutch East Indies", in an attempt to unite administration of their ill-gotten, far-flung colonies; and the Javanese neo-colonialists knew its usefulness to gain fraudulent recognition from the unsuspecting world, ignorant of the history of the Malay Archipelago. If Dutch colonialism was wrong, then Javanese colonialism which was squarely based on it cannot be right. The most fundamental principle of international Law states: Ex injuria jus non oritur. Right cannot originate from wrong!

The Javanese, nevertheless, are attempting to perpetuate colonialism which all the Western colonial powers had abandoned and all the world had condemned. During these last thirty years the people of Acheh, Sumatra, have witnessed how our fatherland has been exploited and driven into ruinous conditions by the Javanese neo-colonialists: they have stolen our properties; they have robbed us from our livelihood; they have abused the education of our children; they have exiled our leaders; they have put our people in chains of tyranny, poverty, and neglect: the life-expectancy of our people is 34 years and is decreasing—compare this to the world's standard of 70 years and is increasing! While Acheh, Sumatra, has been producing a revenue of over 15 billion US dollars yearly for the Javanese neo-colonialists, which they used totally for the benefit of Java and the Javanese.

We, the people of Acheh, Sumatra, would have no quarrel with the Javanese, if they had stayed in their own country, and if they had not tried to lord it over us. From now on, we intend to be the masters in our own house: the only way life is worth living; to make our own laws: as we see fit; to become the guarantor of our own freedom and independence: for which we are capable; to become equal with all the peoples of the world: as our forefathers had always been. In short, to become sovereign in our own fatherland!

Our cause is just! Our land is endowed by the Almighty with plenty and bounty. We covet no foreign territory. We intend to be a worthy contributor to human welfare the world over. We extend the hands of friendship to all peoples and to all governments from the four corners of the earth.

In the name of the sovereign people of Acheh, Sumatra.
Tengku Hasan M.di Tiro
Chairman, National Liberation Front of Acheh, Sumatra, and Head of State.
Acheh, Sumatra, December 4, 1976

Source: "Declaration of Independence of Aceh." Available online. URL: http://acehnet.tripod.com/declare.htm. Accessed February 2, 2010.

Suharto, Resignation Speech (excerpt) (1998)

Suharto, the second president of Indonesia, held office for 30 years from 1967 to 1998. Indonesia flourished economically under Suharto's reign, but his administration became increasingly dictatorial and unpopular. A severe economic crisis across East Asia in 1997 coupled with the growing international criticism of Suharto's human rights record weakened the regime and emboldened its opponents. After six months of civil disorder and mounting pressure from previously loyal elements of Indonesia's political and military elite, Suharto agreed to step down. In his resignation speech, reproduced here, Suharto made reference to the first constitution of an independent Indonesia, promulgated in 1945, and to the political doctrine of Pancasila created by his predecessor Sukarno.

In the name of God the All-Mighty,
Fellow members of the nation and the motherland,
Assalamualaikum Warrachmatullahi Wabarakatu,

During these recent times, I have been following carefully the development of our national situation, especially the aspirations of the people for reforms in all sectors in the life of our nation and state.

Based on my deep understanding of these aspirations and prompted by the conviction that these reforms need to be implemented in an orderly, peaceful and constitutional manner for the sake of maintaining the unity and cohesion of the nation, and the continuity of the national development, I declared a plan to form the committee for reform and to change the composition of the Seventh Development Cabinet.

But, the reality to date has shown that the said committee for reform cannot be materialized because there was no adequate response to the plan to form that committee.

In the wish of implementing these reforms in the best manner possible, I deem that faced with the impossibility of forming the committee, changes in the composition of the Seventh Development Cabinet are no longer necessary.

Considering the above development, I am of the opinion that it would be very difficult for me to implement in a good manner, duties in governing the state and in development.

Therefore, in line with article 8 of the 1945 constitution and after earnestly taking into consideration the views of the leadership of People's Representatives Council and the leadership of the factions in it, I have decided to declare that I have ceased to be the president of the Republic of Indonesia as of the time I read this on this day, Thursday, May 21, 1998.

I have conveyed this statement, about me stepping down from the post of president of the Republic of Indonesia, to you, leaders of the People's Representatives Council who are also the leaders of the People's Consultative Assembly, during the opportunity for a meeting.

In line with article 8 of the 1945 constitution, the vice president of the Republic of Indonesia, professor, doctor, engineer B. J. Habibie is the one who will conclude the remainder of the presidential term, holder of the mandate of the MPR, for 1998–2003.

For the assistance and support of the people while I led the nation and state of Indonesia, I express my thanks and I seek forgiveness if there was any mistakes and shortcomings.

May the Indonesian nation remain victorious with Pancasila and the 1945 constitution.

As of this day too, the Seventh Development Cabinet is outgoing and to the ministers I express my thanks.

Because conditions do not allow the taking of oath in front of the People's Representative Council, to prevent a vacuum of leadership in implement-

ing the governing of the state, the vice president should now take his oath
before the Supreme Court of the Republic of Indonesia.

Source: Suharto's Resignation Speech. English translation by Agence France-Presse. Available online. URL: http://partners.nytimes.com/library/world/asia/052198indonesia-suharto-text.html. Accessed March 5, 2010.

Laskar Jihad Commander Ustadz Ja'far Umar Thalib, Declaration of War (2002)

Laskar Jihad is an Islamist militia based in Indonesia. It emerged during violence between Muslims and Christians on the Moluccan Islands in 2000 and 2001 and later broadened its operations to include Sulawesi, Aceh, and Papua. Laskar Jihad has been accused of killing not only thousands of Christians but also Muslims whom it regards as having failed to fulfill their obligations under Islam. The text reproduced here is a translation of a statement issued in May 2002 by Laskar Jihad leader Ustadz Ja'far Umar Thalib on an Indonesian radio station calling itself the Voice of the Maluku Muslim Struggle. Following the bomb attacks on the island of Bali carried out by Indonesian terrorist group Jemaah Islamiyah in October 2002, Laskar Jihad claimed to have disbanded, but strong evidence exists that the group was still active in 2006 and probably remains so to the present day.

May peace and His mercy and blessing be upon you. Beloved and honoured Muslim faithful. Teachers, imams prayer leaders of mosques, community figures and all Muslim faithful wherever they are who are listening to my call.

We are grateful to Allah God Subhanahu Wataala praise be to the Almighty who has chosen us as His soldiers. Allah's soldiers have received a military obligation as stated by Allah: "Jihad is ordained for you though you dislike it and it may be that you dislike a thing which is good for you and that you like a thing which is bad for you. And Allah knows but you do not know!" Koranic verses quoted throughout. Therefore, Allah has ordained the military obligation to us as Allah's soldiers.

Beloved and honoured Muslim faithful. For those who are still doubtful about going to war, listen to Allah's advice on how we should carry out this mission of war. Allah Subhanahu Wataala has warned us: "And what is wrong with you that you don't fight in the cause of Allah? And those oppressed among them cry to Allah: Our Lord! Rescue us from this town whose people are oppressors. Our Lord! Raise for us from You one who will help."

Beloved and honoured Muslim Faithful, listeners of SPMM radio. What law in this world can oppose Allah's law when Allah states that we are obliged to fight to defend the oppressed people who cannot defend themselves? And what earthly law can prohibit the religious obligation expressed in the command of Allah, "And if they, your brothers in faith, ask you for your help, then you are ordained to help them." Therefore, I state emphatically that all laws and regulations that oppose Allah's commandments are actually invalid.

Beloved and honoured Muslim faithful. Because of this, then, we face the reality of the oppression, crimes and treason of the Maluku provincial administration, which has been given the title Civil Emergency Authority. For more than three years the Muslim faithful have been toyed with and mocked with various kinds of fraud, evil play and treasonous evil carried out by the Maluku provincial administration, together with the Church, which is the command headquarters of the RMS South Maluku Republic movement.

The Maluku provincial administration, led by Saleh Latuconsina, and the Church led by perpetrators of crimes against humanity, priests who have stolen the proscribed wealth of the people, have conspired to carry out an evil and treasonous plot against the Muslim faithful, namely that of expelling the Muslim faithful and then proclaiming the establishment of the RMS state.

We have tried lobbying to resist the evil that is continuously perpetrated. We have lobbied the central government, TNI/Polri Indonesian National Military Forces/National Police personnel, both at TNI Headquarters and Polri Headquarters and in the Maluku provincial administration.

We have been trying more than adequately to do this for more than three years. And yet all these efforts have not helped the condition of the Muslim faithful, who are constantly subject to the games of the perpetrators of crimes against humanity.

Moreover, the PDS Civil Emergency Authority has apparently been taken over and is now controlled by the Church which is actually the command headquarters of the RMS movement. So this movement is no longer mere talk, but it has been realized in the form of political manoeuvres at the national and international level.

It also exists in the form of military manoeuvres and mass mobilization through insulting state symbols such as the DPRD Provincial House of Representatives and the Governor's Office.

Apart from that, they also dare to disregard the prohibition of the central government and regional administration concerning the RMS anniversary and raising of the RMS flag. Saleh Latuconsina, in his capacity as Civil Emergency Authority, has done nothing whatsoever in response to all these insults. Saleh has now positioned himself as the civil emergency traitor.

The climax was when we Muslim faithful warned the government by threatening a people's war that stern action must be taken against all plans of RMS figures within and without the Church who wanted to commemorate the RMS anniversary.

Beloved and honoured Muslim faithful. We have done all this in the name of exercising our duty and obligation as citizens of the Republic of Indonesia to defend it. Moreover, we have done all this in the name of exercising our religious obligations, namely defending the integrity of the Unitary Republic of Indonesia.

But all the ultimatums that we issued were ignored by the PDS. In fact, the PDS actually approved and allowed the RMS anniversary to be commemorated throughout Maluku. In some places, based on photographic evidence that we have received, there were official ceremonies of RMS flag-raising. It all shows what a cruel traitor Saleh Latuconsina is towards the Islamic faithful and the Republic of Indonesia.

Because of all of this, we don't want to eventually be categorized by Allah as a group that is good at talking but does nothing. As Allah Subhanahu Wataala warned in his Word: "O you who believe! Why do you say that which you do not do? Most hateful it is with Allah that you only talk, but do not do what you say." Therefore, in view of the current situation, we declare our determination to conduct universal people's warfare against the treason of the Civil Emergency Traitor led by Saleh Latuconsina. And we Muslim faithful must prove this declaration by taking action.

In the current situation, it would be extremely strange if Saleh Latuconsina decided tomorrow on 2 May 2002, large-scale sweeping would commence across Maluku.

He's incapable of defending the Indonesian government from the under-mining of the RMS rebellion, in which the Maluku Governor's Office and Ambon City DPRD Building have been burnt down. He's also inca-pable of defending his political decisions such as the prohibition of RMS anniversary celebrations. What's more, he's incapable of protect-ing the Muslim faithful from the subsequent threat posed by the RMS rebellion.

Then he issued orders that all Muslims must be disarmed. He's unable to disarm the RMS rebels, either in Kudamati, Passo or other places.

Therefore, we Muslim faithful firmly reject all forms of sweeping or other excuses similar to that, which certainly have the ultimate objective of dis-arming the Muslim faithful. And then he, Saleh Latuconsina, will provoke the anger of the Muslim faithful in order to create clashes with TNI/Polri. This is another crime of Saleh Latuconsina.

O Saleh Latuconsina, if you hear my voice then listen to my final piece of advice. Be afraid of Allah knowing that the Church leaders, both national and international, cannot protect you from Allah's curse, damnation and wrath when you oppress the Muslim faithful.

O Saleh Latuconsina, listen to my advice. Don't continuously deceive the Muslim faithful. If you don't immediately repent of your deeds, Allah will disgrace you as low as possible, because the prayers of the oppressed are heard by Allah.

Remember. You won't live forever. Soon you will die because you're already old. Maybe you'll be a weak old man soon and a disgraced person if you don't immediately repent to Allah, or you'll enter your grave with Allah's wrath and be proscribed from His blessing.

Don't be too confident about all your crimes. O Saleh Latuconsina, if there is still a speck of faith in your heart, then you'd better think about the here-after. All your ambition in this world to be elected governor again will in fact just result in more Muslim blood being spilt and multiply your sins and Allah's curse on you.

Are you going to live another hundred years O Saleh Latuconsina? Be afraid of Allah!!! Fear Allah!

Now my advice to the Pangdam commander of XVI Pattimura Military Area Command, Brother Moestopo. Fear Allah and His curse. Verily, the prayers of oppressed Muslims will get you. Be afraid of the prayers of the oppressed. The Muslim faithful have been oppressed by the ploys of your leader, Saleh Latuconsina. You should know that TNI is the tool of the state, not the tool of the ruler. Therefore, you should put the interests of the state before those of the ruler.

To Provincial Police Chief Sunarko, fear Allah! Be afraid of Allah! Do you still remember that you will die one day? Then you'll regret the responsibility of the Muslim blood on your hands because of what you have done.

Be afraid of Allah, O servants of Allah. You will be defeated if you oppose Allah's greatness. You will be destroyed if you are determined to oppose Allah's power. Don't be over confident of the physical power that you have.

Remember! Allah has soldiers whose numbers are infinite. If you are proud of your tens of thousands of soldiers and police, remember Allah has an infinite number of soldiers.

Allah's angels are always observing you. Remember you three Allah's angels are Allah's servants who were given great power. If the tip of an angel's wing touched the face of the earth, the earth and its contents would be destroyed. What armoured vehicles and Kopassus army special forces troops would you use to oppose Allah's angels?

Remember that the supreme commander is actually Allah. Therefore, if you remember this, you will repent from the rotten games that you play.

Beloved and honoured Muslim faithful. Prepare yourselves for the disarmament operations to be conducted by security personnel led by their superiors who are making themselves the dogs of the RMS.

Beloved and honoured Muslim faithful. Fear not the threats of the Civil Emergency Authority, or to be more precise the Civil Emergency Traitor. Allah Subhanahu Wataala has told us about the mentality of the believers in saying: "They the believers are the ones whom the others fear, and they have gathered against you (a great army), therefore fear them." But it only strengthened their Faith and they said, "Allah alone is Sufficient for us, and He is the Best Disposer of affairs (for us)."

That is the mentality of the believers. We are advised and called on by Allah to have such a mentality. We won't retreat in the face of their bluffing such as threats to carry out repressive action if we refuse sweeping.

Beloved and honoured Muslim faithful. Continue preparing all manner of opposition against all attempts of the PDS aimed at tricking the security personnel into confronting us. We will prepare everything necessary. Get the bombs that we have ready. Get our ammunition ready to spew forth the weapons that we have.

And we swear by Allah! . . . In the name of Allah! . . ellipses as published In the name of Allah! If one Muslim is killed by the security personnel, then Kudamati and Passo Christian areas of Ambon will be a sea of fire. In Allah's name we declare it.

We don't want to deal with messengers the security forces paid to clash with us. We want revenge for all the evil deeds committed against us by annihilating those giving the orders in Kudamati and Passo. This is our resolve.

We don't care about this constant flattery and deception. We are already far too disappointed in the government, both provincial and central, for its continuous deception.

O Saleh Latuconsina. Don't take this ultimatum for granted. You are apparently making plans to distract attention from the danger posed by the RMS treason which is undermining the dignity of the Unitary Republic of Indonesia by creating clashes between Muslims and security personnel.

I swear by Allah! We are determined that we will not clash with the TNI/Polri. However, if they attack us on the grounds of sweeping or for any other reasons, we will fight back until the last drop of blood. We will also carry on the resistance up to Kudamati, Passo and until we free Maluku from the dirty hands of the RMS. This is our resolution. Don't mess with these tigers of Allah. We will not retreat from this principle.

Therefore, I order all members of the Laskar Jihad of Ahlussunnah Wal Jamaah to write their will and testament and prepare themselves to take up the position of martyrs. Get all the weaponry out.

Because of this state of war, I am forced to announce to all Muslim faithful that the activities of SDIP Islamic Elementary School, TKIP Islamic Kindergarten, and TPQ Koran Reciting Course are temporarily suspended in order to allow for preparations for the people's war. And to all medical workers, they'd better make all preparation for providing services to those injured in battle.

To all the Muslim faithful I advise that they close the ranks and prepare themselves to take part in the people's resistance against the attempted betrayal of the nation and state.

We all place our trust in Allah Subhanahu Wataala, rejecting all forms of sweeping and the like. We are prepared to confront any type of armoured vehicles. In fact, we are prepared to confront jet fighters or combat helicopters. We don't care. This is all part of a warning to the world.

Listen, you accomplices of the United States. Listen, you accomplices of the World Church Council. Listen, you accomplices of Zionist evangelists. Listen, you Jews and Christians: We Muslims are inviting the US military to prove its power in Maluku. Let us fight to the finish. Let us prove for the umpteenth time that the Muslim faithful cannot be conquered by over-exaggerated physical power.

The second Afghanistan war will take place in Maluku if you are determined to carry out the threat, O America. Now you, the US, are suffering defeats, various terrifying strikes in Afghanistan. Let us meet gallantly on the field of battle.

We will bequeath our fighting spirit to our descendants because we have been appointed by Allah as His soldiers. And we hope that Allah includes us among His servants that are favoured by Him and His servants who uphold the dignity of His religion.

May Allah Subhanahu Wataala help us and save us from all forms of arrogance, ambition for compliments and the desire to seek popularity. May Allah continue saving us from such things. May Allah also endow us with pure intentions in worshipping Allah.

We remind all Muslim faithful that there is no power and no struggle without the help of Allah. Only Allah can help us. Therefore, increase prayers for forgiveness, prayers of repentance to Allah and multiply deeds of obedience to Allah to obtain Allah's favour so Allah makes us victorious because of that. Only Allah knows this matter. Until we meet in the battlefield. Allahu Akbar God is Great,

And may His peace, mercy and blessings be upon you!

Source: Ambon Information Website. "Text of the 'Declaration of War' by Laskar Jihad Commander Ustadz Ja'far Umar Thalib, broadcast on Radio SPMM (Voice of the Maluku Muslim Struggle) on 1–3, May 2002"; as published by Indonesian newspaper Berdarah web site on 8 May." Available online. URL: http://www.websitesrcg.com/ambon/documents/laskar-jihad-010502. Accessed January 26, 2010.

Abu Bakar Bashir on the Struggle for Islamic Law in Indonesia (2006)

Abu Bakar Bashir is an Indonesian Muslim cleric with a long and controversial history of advocating the establishment of sharia law in the country. Bashir spent 17 years in exile during the Suharto regime and returned to Indonesia shortly after his resignation. The United Nations and many Western states believe Bashir to be deeply involved in the Islamist terrorist organization Jemaah Islamiyah.

Keep on fighting for the application of Islamic law. If this state and nation wants to become great, safe, and at peace then it has to return to Islam one hundred percent without bargaining. If not, then it will be destroyed.

Source: "The Religion of Peace." Available online. URL: http://www.thereligionofpeace.com/Pages/In-The-Name-of-Allah.htm. Accessed January 26, 2010.

Persecution of Ahmadiyya Community Indonesia Continues as Religious Authority Calls for It to Be Banned (2008)

Ahmadiyya is a religious movement that emerged from mainstream Islam. It was founded in India in the last decades of the 19th century by Mirza Ghulam Ahmad, who claimed to be the prophesied Mahdi. Most Muslims do not regard members of the Ahmadiyya as coreligionists largely because of their belief in the divine status of the movement's founder. Ahmadis have lived peacefully in Indonesia for more than a century, but since the fall of Suharto in 1998, conservative Muslim elements have pushed for the movement to be banned or for Ahmadis to be subject to social restrictions. Ahmadis have also been attacked and their places of worship burned by radicals. This document is a press release issued by the Ahmadiyya detailing what they see as the severe threat to their continued existence in Indonesia.

The organisation regarded as Indonesia's highest religious authority the Majlis Ulema Indonesia (MUI) has submitted what it calls a 'Fatwa' against the Ahmadiyya Community in the Office of the Attorney-General. The MUI has called for the Ahmadiyya Community to be completely banned from the country.

The Head of the MUI has said *"We hope to settle the matter once and for all by getting the group banned."*[1] He went onto say that the Ahmadiyya Community should not regard themselves as Muslim.

The Assistant Attorney-General has stated that a decision would be made next week at a meeting to be held by his Office. In relation to this the Press Secretary of the Ahmadiyya Jama'at Abid Khan has said:

"We urge the Office of the Attorney-General to reject the so called 'Fatwa' against the Ahmadiyya Community. If allowed the decision would signal the end for the freedoms guaranteed to minority groups under both the State Constitution and the International Conventions that Indonesia is party to.

The Ahmadiyya Community wishes no harm to anyone and simply desires that its members are able to practice their faith in a safe and peaceful environment."

The main objection of the MUI is that the Ahmadiyya Community does not believe the Holy Prophet Muhammad (peace be upon him) to be the last Prophet. Clarifying the Ahmadiyya Community's position on this matter, Abid Khan said:

"The Holy Prophet Muhammad was the greatest of all Prophets and the final law bearing prophet. Any Prophet who comes after him must be from amongst his believers and subservient. Hadhrat Mirza Ghulam Ahmad, the Founder of the Ahmadiyya Community, was such a person, who we believe was sent by God to re-establish the true peaceful teachings of Islam as taught by the Holy Prophet Muhammad (peace be upon him)."

---

[1] "Kiayi Haji Ma'ruf—Interview" *The Strait Times,* January 2, 2008.

Over the past months the Ahmadiyya Community in Indonesia has been subjected to severe persecution. Members of the Community have been attacked, others have been forced to leave their homes and Mosques have been destroyed. If the Attorney General's Office passes the proposed law then this would no doubt add a stamp of Government approval to the atrocities that have recently occurred and members of the Ahmadiyya Community would be at severe risk of further attacks.

Source: International Press and Media Desk Ahmadiyya Muslim Association. Available online. URL: http://www.alislam.org/press-release/indonesia_jan03-08.pdf. Accessed January 26, 2010.

Open Letter to the Indonesian Government on the Implementation of Islamic Law in Aceh Province (2009)

Indonesia's overwhelmingly Muslim Aceh province has a long tradition of religious conservatism. One of the aims of some of those who fought for the Free Aceh Movement was to achieve the freedom to implement sharia law. As early as 2002, as fighting with government troops continued, sharia courts and police were established in the area. In 2009, with the province now enjoying the freedoms of a "special territory," Aceh's regional parliament passed a series of sharia-inspired laws that made adultery punishable by stoning to death and homosexual acts punishable by caning. This document is an open letter to the Indonesian government from the human rights advocacy group Amnesty International condemning Aceh's sharia laws.

Dear Minister,

RE: The Islamic Criminal Code in Aceh

I would like to take this opportunity to welcome you in your new position and bring to your attention some of our recent concerns regarding a new Indonesian bylaw in Aceh, the Islamic Criminal Code (Qanun Hukum Jinayat), which provides for stoning to death for adultery and caning of up to 100 lashes for homosexuality.

We would like to call on your ministry to take immediate measures to ensure that this law, which contravenes the Indonesian constitution and the 1999 Law on Human Rights, be repealed immediately so that the criminalization of adultery and homosexuality contained in this bylaw are abolished.

Of particular concern are the inclusions of provisions allowing for caning which constitutes cruel, inhuman and degrading treatment and may amount to torture, and the inclusion for the first time in Indonesia of stoning to death (rajam) as a penalty for those who commit adultery.

Punishments by caning are not new in Aceh, in violation of international human rights standards on cruel, inhuman and degrading treatment. Victims of caning experience pain, fear and humiliation, and caning can cause long-term or permanent injuries. The provision of caning as a penalty violates the UN Convention against Torture and other Cruel, Inhuman or Degrading Treatment or Punishment which Indonesia ratified in 1998.

Stoning to death violates the right to life provided for in the Indonesian Constitution, and in international human rights treaties such as the International Covenant on Civil and Political Rights which Indonesia ratified in 2006. International human rights law and standards oppose the extension of the death penalty to new crimes. Moreover this punishment is particularly cruel and constitutes torture, which is absolutely forbidden under all circumstances in international law.

Amnesty International is also concerned by provisions that criminalize adultery and homosexuality, consensual sexual acts outside marriage. We urge you to ensure that such provisions are repealed in conformity with international law and standards relating to physical and mental integrity and the right not to be discriminated against, the right to privacy, and freedom of expression.

We also request that your ministry undertake a review of all local regulations that have been put in place in the last decade in Indonesia to ensure that they are in full conformity with international human rights law and standards, and other human rights provisions set out in the Indonesian Constitution and in the 1999 Law on Human Rights. The decentralization process and regional autonomy should not come at the expense of human rights. Local regulations should conform to international human rights law and standards at all times.

Please do let us know if you have any questions. We would be pleased to discuss with you the Aceh Criminal Code and other areas of mutual concern.

Yours sincerely,
Donna Guest
Asia Pacific Programme Deputy Director

226

ALGERIA

Proclamation of the Algerian National Liberation Front (November 1, 1954)

The Algerian National Liberation Front (FLN) was the leading force in the struggle to win Algeria's independence from French rule that took place from 1954 to 1962. This proclamation was broadcast by radio from Cairo, Egypt, on the eve of the anticolonial war.

After decades of struggle, the National Movement has reached its final phase of fulfilment. At home, the people are united behind the watchwords of independence and action. Abroad, the atmosphere is favourable, especially with the diplomatic support of our Arab and Moslem brothers. Our National Movement, prostrated by years of immobility and routine, badly directed was disintegrating little by little. Faced with this situation, a youthful group, gathering about it the majority of wholesome and resolute elements, judged that the moment had come to take the National Movement out of the impasse into which it had been forced by the conflicts of persons and of influence and to launch it into the true revolutionary struggle at the side of the Moroccan and Tunisian brothers. We are independent of the two factions that are vying for power. Our movement gives to compatriots of every social position, to all the purely Algerian parties and movements, the possibility of joining in the liberation struggle.

GOAL. National independence through:

1. the restoration of the Algerian state, sovereign, democratic, and social, within the framework of the principles of Islam;
2. the preservation of fundamental freedoms, without distinction of race or religion.

INTERNAL Objective Political house-cleaning through the destruction of the last vestiges of corruption and reformism

EXTERNAL Objectives:

1. The internationalization of the Algerian problem;
2. The pursuit of North African unity in its national Arabo-Islamic context;
3. The assertion, through United Nations channels, of our active sympathy toward all nations that may support our liberating action.

MEANS OF STRUGGLE: Struggle by every means until our goal is attained. Exertion at home and abroad through political and direct action, with a view to making the Algerian problem a reality for the entire world. The struggle will be long, but the outcome is certain. To limit the bloodshed, we propose an honourable platform for discussion with the French authorities:

1. The opening of negotiations with the authorized spokesmen the Algerian people, on the basis of a recognition of Algerian sovereignty, one and indivisible.
2. The inception of an atmosphere of confidence brought about freeing all those who are detained, by annulling all measures without exception, and by ending all legal action against the combatant forces.
3. The recognition of Algerian nationhood by an official declaration abrogating all edicts, decrees, and laws by virtue of which Algeria was "French soil."

In return for which:

1. French cultural and economic interests will be respected, as well as persons and families.
2. All French citizens desiring to remain in Algeria will be allowed to opt for their original nationality, in which case they will be considered as foreigners, or for Algerian nationality, in which case they will be considered as Algerians, equal both as to rights and as to duties.
3. The ties between France and Algeria will be the object of agreement between the two Powers on the basis of equality and mutual respect.

Algerians: The F. L. N. is your front; its victory is your victory. For our part, strong in your support, we shall give the best of ourselves to the Fatherland.

Source: Historicaltextarchive.com. "Proclamation of the Algerian National Front, Liberation Front, (FLN) November 1954." Available online. URL: http://historicaltextarchive.com/sections.php?action=read&artid=10. Accessed November 25, 2009.

Report on the Status of Women in Algeria (1999)

This report, compiled by the women's human rights advocacy group the International Women's Human Rights Clinic (IWHRC), addresses many of the hardships faced by women living in a country that has been wracked by decades of war and in which conservative Muslim elements have repeatedly attempted to impose restrictions on women's freedoms. The 1984 Algerian Family Code is a particular target for criticism. Debated for many years between elements of Algerian society who wanted to model family law along Western secular lines and those who wanted a structure conforming to conservative Muslim ethics, the report provoked mass demonstrations on the streets of Algiers and a walk-out of female members of the National People's Assembly.

Summary

The fundamentalist movement in Algeria has been active at least since the 1970's. Throughout the 1970's and 1980's, fundamentalists organized politically as well as used violence as a means of imposing their agenda. In particular, fundamentalists attacked feminist activists, female university students, women workers in state owned factories, and single women living without a male relative which qualifies under the law as a guardian (walii). In the late 1980's, arson attacks against single women resulted in the death of a child. In 1984, the fundamentalist scored a substantial political victory in pressuring the State to enact a highly regressive family code which essentially treats women as minors. In 1989, in the wake of broad popular protest against the one party, military backed government, it amended the Constitution to be amended to allow for the formation of political parties. The fundamentalists united under the party of the Islamic Salvation Front (FIS). The FIS had an armed wing known as AIS. The leaders of FIS, from its birth, declared their opposition to democracy and their ideology of gender-apartheid. The fundamentalist political violence against women continued and escalated after the formation of FIS.

In the June 1990 municipal elections, FIS won control electorally over a large number of municipalities. During their official tenure until early 1992, FIS sought to impose discrimination amounting to gender-apartheid through both legal means and through threats of force. They decreed, for example, the separation of boys and girls in the schools, men and women on buses, and in some workplaces. After the cancellation of the second phase of the national legislative elections in December 1991, the violence against women and other civilians escalated severely. The State banned the FIS, and the fundamentalists formed additional armed groups, such as the Armed

Islamic Group (GIA), which systematically attacked civilians as a method of war, in particular women who deviated from their prescribed roles.

The first group of civilians assassinated, raped, and otherwise tortured by the armed groups were female relatives of members of the security forces, police, and government. In 1993, the fundamentalists then began to assassinate and threaten feminists, journalists, artists, foreigners, intellectuals, other professionals and any visible member of civil society who represented an alternative vision to the FIS ideology. The overwhelming number of these victims has no association to the government, and in fact many were known opponents of the State. Leading feminists were personally threatened; one was killed and others forced to live in hiding or go into exile. The armed groups also regularly abducted young women from the streets, neighborhoods and houses and held them in camps as sexual and domestic slaves (called mutaa marriages). The fundamentalists posted communiqués promising death to ordinary women who did not follow their dictates—such as unveiled women, hairdressers, working women and single women. In a number of cases, they carried out these threats.

In 1994–1995, the attacks on civilians became even more indiscriminate. The armed groups bombed public places causing unprecedented casualties. In 1997, particularly in connection with Ramadan, they began to massacre whole villages, resulting in large numbers of casualties, disproportionately women and children.

Despite the fact that the years of terror and imposed gender subordination have negatively affected the culture in terms of gender equality, many segments of civil society provide strong resistance to the fundamentalist agenda. Women have been in the leadership. Feminists activists and women's organizations, journalists and others continue to demonstrate against the fundamentalists and document the abuses despite the risk to their own lives. Moreover, ordinary women and men continue to work and maintain social institutions, such as schools, despite the terror. Teachers, hairdressers and seamstresses (women whose occupation involved the beautification of women) unveiled women as well as veiled women who wear a touch of lipstick all resist the fundamentalist's terror and totalitarian agenda by continuing their everyday lives. Recently, the number of unveiled women has increased.

Despite the State's military and violent opposition to the fundamentalist movement, the fundamentalists have had a profound influence on State policies. Accommodation to the fundamentalist pressure underlies the States reservations to the Women's Convention and the current regressive family code which violates the fundamental rights of women. Moreover, the State has not adequately responded to the need for social and health services and economic support for the victims of fundamentalist violence. In particular, the State has not provided adequate support to the survivors of rape. Finally, while the State has rejected some of the more egregious fundamentalist demands for gender apartheid, such as segregated education and transportation, it has not taken sufficient steps to address the cultural damage to gender equality wrought by the fundamentalist agenda.

The Committee has the authority to, and should, address the extreme obstacles presented by the fundamentalist campaign of violence and terror as well as its influence on state power to reaching the goals of gender equality and women's human rights. The Committee should question the State on these issues and urge the State to prevent and protect against the violence; redress the damage caused to women by fundamentalism; and adhere and vigorously implement the Convention. In particular, we recommend that the Committee:

- Urge the State, and exact its commitment to withdraw its reservations to the Convention, reservations which legitimize and perpetuate inequality—especially in family life—for women and which violate the object and purpose of the Convention.
- Urge the State, and exact its commitment to accept and support legislation to enact the full series of amendments to the Family Code formulated and agreed upon by the NGO women's consultation as well as to support enactment and implement other measures necessary to eliminate discrimination and ensure equality.
- Urge the State, and exact its commitment to take immediate steps to ensure that victims of fundamentalist violence, including women who have been raped and subjected to sexual slavery receive adequate social services, including abortion services, and counseling to enable them to regain their self esteem and rebuild their lives.
- Urge the State, and exact its commitment to take immediate steps to ensure that all women have equal preparation for, access to and enjoyment of employment, education, and healthcare rights in accordance with the Convention, and that women victims of fundamentalist as well as state violence be provided economic and other assistance necessary to enable them to rebuild their lives and support their families and themselves.

- Urge the State, and exact its commitment, to take measures, directed at both women and men, through support of media and community education and arts, to overcome the gender-discriminatory stereo-types and fears fostered by the fundamentalist terror as a cultural matter.
- Urge the State, and exact its commitment to provide resources to and protect and ensure the flourishing of an autonomous NGO community, independent of the State,—in particular NGO's pro-moting and protecting women's human rights, in order to facilitate the building of civil society and respect for human rights.

Source: Mujeresred Shadow Report on Algeria. "To The Committee on the Elimination of Discrimination against Women" submitted by International Women's Health Rights Law Clinic and Women Living under Muslim Laws. Available online. URL: http://www.nodo50.org/mujeresred/argelia-shadowreport.html#11. Accessed February 23, 2010.

THE UNITED ARAB EMIRATES

UAE Constitution (excerpt) (1971)

The constitution of the United Arab Emirates (UAE) came into effect in December 1971, the day after the creation of the UAE itself. The articles of the constitution reproduced here concern the rights and duties of UAE citizens and are closely modeled on the constitutions and laws of democratic Western states. The UAE has frequently come under attack, however, for not extending these same rights to the millions of migrant workers in the country who make up 80 percent of the population and 90 percent of the workforce.

Part Three Freedom, Rights and Public Duties

Article 25

All persons are equal before the law, without distinction between citizens of the Union in regard to race, nationality, religious belief or social status.

Article 26

Personal liberty is guaranteed to all citizens. No person may be arrested, searched, detained or imprisoned except in accordance with the provisions of law.

No person shall be subjected to torture or to degrading treatment.

Article 27
Crimes and punishments shall be defined by the law. No penalty shall be imposed for any act of commission or omission committed before the relevant law has been promulgated.

Article 28
Penalty is personal. An accused shall be presumed innocent until proved guilty in a legal and fair trial. The accused shall have the right to appoint the person who is capable to conduct his defence during the trial. The law shall prescribe the cases in which the presence of a counsel for defence shall be assigned.

Physical and moral abuse of an accused person is prohibited.

Article 29
Freedom of movement and residence shall be guaranteed to citizens within the limits of law.

Article 30
Freedom of opinion and expressing it verbally, in writing or by other means of expression shall be guaranteed within the limits of law.

Article 31
Freedom of communication by post, telegraph or other means of communication and the secrecy thereof shall be guaranteed in accordance with law.

Article 32
Freedom to exercise religious worship shall be guaranteed in accordance with established customs, provided that it does not conflict with public policy or violate public morals.

Article 33
Freedom of assembly and establishing associations shall be guaranteed within the limits of law.

Article 34
Every citizen shall be free to choose his occupation, trade or profession within the limits of law. Due consideration being given to regulations organising some of such professions and trades. No person may be subjected to forced labour except in exceptional circumstances provided for by the law and in return for compensation.

No person may be enslaved.

11 All rights are reserved for the Federal National Council 2003.

Article 41
Every person shall have the right to submit complaints to the competent authorities, including the judicial authorities. concerning the abuse or infringement of the rights and freedom stipulated in this Part.

Article 42
Payment of taxes and public charges determined by law is a duty of every citizen.

Article 43
Defence of the Union is a sacred duty of every citizen and military service is an honour for citizens which shall be regulated by law.

Article 44
Respect of the Constitution. laws and orders issued by public authorities in execution thereof, observance of public order and respect of public morality are duties incumbent upon all inhabitants of the Union.

Source: Federal National Council. Available online. URL: http://www.worldstatesmen.org/uae_const.doc. Accessed January 26, 2010.

General Authority for Islamic Affairs and Endowments Permits

The General Authority for Islamic Affairs and Endowments is a department of the government of the United Arab Emirates (UAE). It is responsible for overseeing many aspect of religious life in the country including appointing the majority of imams, approving the construction of new mosques, and licensing travel agents to offer Hajj tours. The authority also issues weekly guidelines on the content of sermons delivered in mosques across the country. This extract from the Abu Dhabi government Web site outlines the process for obtaining a license to offer Hajj and Umrah tours. (Umrah is a pilgrimage to Mecca undertaken at a time other than the specific dates for the Hajj.)

Hajj & Umrah Travel Agent Permit
Only authorised travel agents can conduct Hajj and Umrah tours.

International Documents

Please follow these steps:

1. Fill the required application.
2. Present the required supporting documents.

Required Document Special Consideration

A no objection letter from the employer to be submitted to the department of Hajj and Umrah notifying no objection to practice the Hajj and Umrah business.

A certificate of good conduct

Academic Qualifications

Valid passport and I/D

An open bank warranty from an accredited bank in the UAE.

Special conditions

The applicant must:

- Be a UAE National.
- Between 25 and 70 Years old
- Be competent to practice their profession as per the regulations.
- Have no prior convictions of a dishonoring crime or felony. Exemption will be made for those who had their honor restored by an official pardon.
- Be physically fit as certified by a competent authority in the Ministry of Health. These conditions apply to all employees in the campaign.
- Have a good conduct and behaviour.
- Not be banned from practicing this profession by a specialised agency permanently or for a period not yet completed.
- Not to be one of the Authority's employees.
- Not to be a partner with a banned or suspended contractor.
- Pass the interview.
- Have previously performed his Hajj duties.

Application must be submitted during the Arabic month of Rabei Awal.

Source: Web site of the Government of Abu Dhabi. Available online. URL: http://www.abudhabi.ae/egovPoolPortal_WAR/appmanager/ADeGP/Citizen?_nfpb=true&_pageLabel=p_citizen_departments&did=15030&lang=en. Accessed March 6, 2010.

"Building Towers, Cheating Workers" (2006)

These extracts, from a 2006 Human Rights Watch report entitled "Building Towers, Cheating Workers," describe the most widespread illegal practices and abuses in the treatment of the United Arab Emirates huge immigrant workforce. Following repeated accusations of human rights abuses, particularly with regard to migrant workers, the government of the UAE has made efforts to improve conditions, including holding an open forum with Asian labor-exporting countries in January 2008 known as the Abu Dhabi Dialogue.

The Recruitment Process

UAE law explicitly forbids UAE recruiters from collecting any fees from prospective migrant workers.[32] However, UAE recruitment agents appear to openly flout this law, charging workers these fees instead of requiring the prospective employer to bear the cost. Our researchers talked to five recruitment agencies in the UAE regarding the recruitment of construction workers. Four of these five agencies confirmed that they expect workers to pay for the visa and travel fees that UAE law requires only employers to pay. One recruiter told our researcher that prospective "candidates [migrant workers] will bear the visa and travel costs. We will collect these fees from candidates and pay it to construction companies who apply for their visa. It is of course illegal and I can't put it on a written contract; it is done in cash. We do it all the time."[33] According to another recruitment agency in Dubai, "We [the agency] will take care of transportation, advertisement, and other costs. We can charge the candidates. People who are candidates will cover all the costs including visa fees and air tickets."[34] A third agent said, "I can provide a company with ten, hundred, or even a thousand workers. We will interview and select them in India and Pakistan. For unskilled workers, we don't charge the employers anything. The candidates will pay for visa and transportation costs."[35]

Workers Human Rights Watch interviewed confirmed the same facts: every single construction worker interviewed said he had been required to pay up-front travel and visa fees to his recruiting agent.

Nataranjan works for a construction and landscaping company in Dubai. He is from the state of Kerala in India. Human Rights Watch interviewed him and 19 other Indian workers who are employed by the same company. Nataranjan said,

I paid 100,000 Indian rupees ($2,200) to an agency in India to get a visa to come here and work. Each of us owes a lot of money to recruiting agents back home.[36]

International Documents

Sattar is a construction worker from India who also described the same recruitment process:

I am 42 years [old] and come from Rajasthan in India. I am married with three children. In 2003, I saw a posting by an agency advertising jobs in Dubai. I paid a recruitment agency in India 80,000 Indian rupees ($1,788). This money covered my visa fee, airline ticket, and medical fees. I borrowed the money from friends and family.[37]

. . .

Unpaid Wages

The most common complaint from construction workers in the UAE, which also appears to form the basis of the vast majority of labor disputes reviewed by the Ministry of Labor and the Dubai labor agencies (see below, "Government Mechanisms Addressing Labor Disputes"), is the withholding of wages by employers. All 60 of the workers interviewed by Human Rights Watch said that their employers routinely withheld their wages, and many of the workers we spoke to were owed back wages at the time of the interview. The impact on workers whose wages are withheld for even one month is very serious: they immediately fall into arrears on the debt they owe recruiting agencies in their home countries; they incur additional interest; and they are unable to send money home to their families, who depend on the income earned in the UAE. In some cases, the non-payment of wages means that workers do not have money to buy food or basic goods and end up borrowing money just to survive.

Withholding one-and-a-half or two months' wages as "security" to prevent workers from "running away" to a better job appears to be accepted as a "custom" among construction companies in the UAE.[42] When workers protest or complain about withheld wages, their complaint is not based on this "customary" withholding, but about wages withheld beyond that period. Of course, there is no basis in law for either practice; indeed, to withhold wages violates UAE law requiring employers to pay workers in a timely fashion and keep verifiable records.[43] Construction business officials and workers have explained that construction companies withhold wages beyond the two-month "security withholding" when they run into cash flow problems, although that explanation may not be uniformly credible, particularly in the context of Dubai's booming construction sector.[44]

. . .

Confiscation of Passports

While employers in the UAE are prohibited from confiscating the passports of their employees, employers routinely do this, retaining the passports for the duration of their workers' employment, typically to ensure that the employees do not abscond. All of the 107 migrant workers interviewed by Human Rights Watch (construction workers and others-see "Methodology," above), said that their employers had confiscated their passports upon their arrival in the UAE.[71]

Lt. Col. Rashid Bakhit Al Jumairi, assistant director of follow up and investigation at the Dubai Naturalization and Residency Administration, told Human Rights Watch that according to the law, "they [the employers] should not hold passports." But he justified the practice by saying, "sometimes workers lose their passports so the safest place to keep it is at the company offices."[72] Maj. Aref Mohammad Baqer, deputy director of the Human Rights Department at Dubai Police, told Human Rights Watch that companies justify this as customary and also to protect their own interests:

The companies say that holding of passports is part of the business culture. They justify it by saying it would prevent the workers from stealing money or trade secrets and information from the company. Also employers say that by holding on to their workers' passports, they can guarantee they will get a return on the money they invest on each worker in visa fees and other expenses.[73]

Death and injury in site accidents

The extent of death and injury of migrant workers is one of the most troubling, if poorly documented, aspects of the construction sector in the UAE. As described below, there appear to be no official countrywide government figures on cases of death and injury of construction workers. The few figures available from government sources cover only Dubai, and even these figures appear to be well below the figures compiled by private sources. This discrepancy in numbers can be attributed in part to the extremely low incidence of companies reporting deaths and injuries to the government.

Dubai Municipality recorded 34 deaths of construction workers at their workplaces in 2004 and 39 deaths in 2005.[75] Independent research by a construction trade publication, Construction Week, found that a total of 880 migrant construction workers died in the UAE in 2004: 460 from India, 375 from Pakistan and approximately forty-five from Bangladesh.[76] While the Construction Week report did not provide information regarding the cause of death so it is unclear how many were work-related accidents, an official with the Indian Community Welfare Committee, K. Kumar, told Construction Week that he believed up to 30 percent of the deaths of the Indians in the report were related to site accidents.[77]

. . .

Illegal workers particularly vulnerable

Some migrant construction workers are in the UAE illegally, and are particularly vulnerable because their employers do not want to take responsibility for them when they are injured at the workplace. According to a local Indian social activist who tracks injured workers:

Private foremen, working on behalf of manpower supply companies, hire a van and drive around hiring illegal construction workers. Because there is a high demand for labor in the construction sector, contractors turn to manpower supply companies to address labor shortages. Local government officials are very helpful in fining companies who hire illegal workers but it is a problem. Manpower supply companies are mostly run by expats [expatriates] who employ illegal workers. They are a big part of the problem. Accidents should be reported to the police, but these employers avoid doing so because they don't want to pay for proper compensation.[97]

In a visit to the government-run Kuwaiti Hospital in Sharjah on February 21, 2006, Human Rights Watch found two men, one an illegal worker and the status of the other worker unknown, hospitalized due to accidents at construction sites. Both had been "dumped" at the hospital by their employers who did not identify themselves to the hospital authorities.

One, an Indian construction worker named Chekelli, was hospitalized for back injuries. According to an Indian businessman who was helping Chekelli to return to India:

Chekelli was working for a manpower supply company who employed him illegally. Chekelli is from Nizamuddin in Andhra Pradesh in India. He arrived in the UAE on a tourist visa and was subsequently employed by a manpower supply company. He worked at a construction site in Dubai. A large cement bucket fell on his back from a crane, pinning him to the ground. He was admitted to the Kuwaiti Hospital on January 22, 2006. His employer disappeared after dumping the injured man at the hospital. The employer claimed that he had fallen from a staircase.[98]

The seriousness of Chekalli's injuries meant that he was paralyzed. He would be returning to India without receiving any compensation for his work-related injuries.

[32] Ministerial order No. (57) states, in art. 2, "In order to be granted permission for mediation in the recruitment and supply of labor from abroad, the following pre-conditions must be met: 2. The applicant shall submit an undertaking to the ministry to the effect that it shall not get any commission or remuneration from the labor in consideration of their recruitment whether before or after the acceptance of such labor to work." Federal Law No. 8 For 1980, On Regulation of Labor Relations, http://www.mol.gov.ae/Pages-EN/documents-en/rule-labour.HTML (accessed August 30, 2006) art. 18 states: "No licensed employment agent or labour supplier shall demand or accept from any worker, whether before or after the latter's admission to employment, any commission or material reward in return for employment, or charge him for any expenses thereby incurred, except as may be prescribed or approved by the Ministry of Labour and Social Affairs.

[33] Telephone Interview with recruitment agency official, identity withheld, Dubai, September 5, 2006.

[34] Telephone Interview with recruitment agency official, identity withheld, Dubai, September 6, 2006.

[35] Telephone interview with head of a labor supply company, identity withheld, Dubai, September 6, 2006.

[36] Human Rights Watch interview with Nataranjan, Dubai, February 19, 2006.

[37] Human Rights Watch interview with Sattar, Dubai, February 24, 2006.

[42] Following a recent protest by hundreds of unpaid workers for a Sharjah-based company, a company official was quoted in the local media as saying "We only hold back salary for 45 days as surety in case of runaways." See Mahmoud Saberi, "Hundreds Protest Over Non-payment of Wages," Gulf News, August 29, 2006.

International Documents

[43] Federal Law No. 8 for 1980, On Regulation of Labor Relations, article 56 states, "Workers employed on yearly or monthly wage basis shall be paid at least once a month; all other workers shall be paid at least once every two weeks." Article 58 of the same law states, "Evidence of payment to workers of their due wages, irrespective of their amount or nature, shall not be admissible unless it is in the form of documentary proof, admission or oath." See Ministry of Labor website, http://www.mol.gov.ae/Pages-EN/documents-en/rule-labour.HTML (accessed August 30, 2006).

[44] The managing director of a construction company in the UAE told our researcher that "depending on the type and size of the companies, some contractors find themselves facing cash flow problems due to a variety of reasons. During the nineties, contractors worked on very low margins (2–3 % of revenue) and thus maintaining cash flow was essential for their survival. It has often been that contractors working for the government sector found themselves waiting for 120 to 180 days to get paid which meant a major cash squeeze. To add insult to injury, contractors were not regulated properly in terms of financial ability and there are still no credit ratings for companies in this part of the world. All this has since changed in the UAE as of 2004 when the construction boom started in Dubai creating perhaps an unprecedented oasis for contractors. Demand has outstripped supply to such a large extent that every contractor I am aware of is working on very high margins. Long gone are the days that contractors wait for payments." Email correspondence with managing director of a construction company, identity withheld, August 25, 2006.

[71] Human Rights Watch interviewed 107 migrant workers including 60 construction workers.

[72] Human Rights Watch interview with Lt. Col. Rashid Bakhit Al Jumairi, February 21, 2006.

[73] Human Rights Watch interview with Maj. Aref Mohammad Baqer, Dubai, February 25, 2006.

[74] Ruling by Dubai Court of Cassation, Case # 268 (2001), October 27, 2001.

[75] Diaa Hadid, "Construction deaths and accidents leap," Gulf News, January 17, 2006.

[76] "Site worker death toll exceeds 800," Construction Week, No. 83, August 6–19, 2005. Their investigation calculated fatality figures for migrant workers by compiling data recorded by the embassies of India, Pakistan and Bangladesh, countries that have the largest number of workers in the construction sector.

[77] Ibid.

[97] Human Rights Watch interview with Indian social activist, identity withhold, February 21, 2006.

[98] Human Rights Watch interview with Indian businessman who wished to remain anonymous, Kuwaiti Hospital, Sharjah, February 21, 2006.

Source: Human Rights Watch. "Building Towers, Cheating Workers." Available online. URL: http://www.hrw.org/en/reports/2006/11/11/building-towers-cheating-workers. Accessed March 2, 2010.

Expensive Cars Abandoned at the Airport (2009)

The global economic crisis of 2008–09 hit Dubai hard. Thousands of foreign workers in the construction and property sectors found themselves out of a job and unable to pay mortgages and bank loans for cars. Under UAE law people who fail to keep up payments on debts can find themselves sentenced to prison. To avoid this fate thousands simply fled the country, leaving their apartments empty and their cars sitting in the car park in the Dubai International Airport. This extract is from A Cry for Help! *a book written by Omani journalist Majid al Suleimany and describes the abandoned car phenomenon.*

Fleeing Dubai

Wednesday, January 14, 2009

Local police have found at least 3,000 automobiles—sedans, SUVs, regulars—abandoned outside Dubai International Airport in the last four months. Police say most of the vehicles had keys in the ignition, a clear sign they were left behind by owners in a hurry to take flight.

The global economic crisis has brought Dubai's economic progress, mirrored by its soaring towers and luxurious resorts, to a stuttering halt. Several people have been laid off in the past months after the realty boom started unraveling. On the night of December 31, 2008 alone more than 80 vehicles were found at the airport. "Sixty cars were seized on the first day of this year," director general of Airport Security, Mohammad Bin Thani told DNA over the phone. On the same day, deputy director of traffic, colonel Saif Mohair Al Mazroui, said they seized 22 cars abandoned at a prohibited area in the airport.

Faced with a cash crunch and a bleak future ahead, there were no goodbyes for the migrants—overwhelmingly South Asians, mostly Indians—just a quiet abandoning of the family car at the airport and other places.

While 2,500 vehicles have been found dumped in the past four months outside Terminal III, which caters to all global airlines, Terminal II, which is only used by Emirates Airlines, had 160 cars in the same period.

Source: Suleimany, Majid al. *A Cry for Help!* IUniverse, 2009.

THE TALIBAN

Soviet Intervention in Afghanistan (1979)

Afghanistan's decades-long history of war and privation began with the crisis that prompted the Soviet invasion of the country. In 1978 the communist government of President Nur Muhammad Taraki undertook a series of reforms of traditional Islamic laws that enraged conservative Muslim elements in the country. The resulting rebellion by mujahideen guerrillas threatened to unseat the government and prompted Taraki to ask the Soviet Union for military assistance. The extract reproduced here is from a translation of the transcript of a telephone conversation between Afghan president Taraki and Chairman of the Council of Ministers of the USSR Alexei Kosygin that took place in March 1979.

Kosygin: Ask Comrade Taraki, perhaps he will outline the situation in Afghanistan.

Taraki: The situation is bad and getting worse.

Kosygin: Do you have support among the workers, city dwellers, the petty bourgeoisie, and the white collar workers in Herat? Is there still anyone on your side?

Taraki: There is no active support on the part of the population. It is almost wholly under the influence of Shiite slogans—follow not the heathens, but follow us. The propaganda is underpinned by this.

Kosygin: Are there many workers there?

Taraki: Very few—between 1,000 and 2,000 people in all.

Kosygin: What are the prospects?

Taraki: We are convinced that the enemy will form new units and will develop an offensive.

Kosygin: Do you not have the forces to rout them?

Taraki: I wish it were the case.

Kosygin: What, then, are your proposals on this issue?

Taraki: We ask that you extend practical and technical assistance, involving people and arms.

Kosygin: It is a very complex matter.

Taraki: Iran and Pakistan are working against us, according to the same plan. Hence, if you now launch a decisive attack on Herat, it will be possible to save the revolution.

Kosygin: The whole world will immediately get to know this. The rebels have portable radio transmitters and will report it directly.

Taraki: I ask that you extend assistance.

Kosygin: We must hold consultations on this issue. Do you not have connections with Iran's progressives? Can't you tell them that it is currently the United States that is your and their chief enemy? The Iranians are very hostile toward the United States and evidently this can be put to use as propaganda. What foreign policy activities or statements would you like to see coming from us? Do you have any ideas on this question, propaganda-wise?

Taraki: Propaganda help must be combined with practical assistance. I suggest that you place Afghan markings on your tanks and aircraft and no one will be any the wiser. Your troops could advance from the direction of Kushka and from the direction of Kabul. In our view, no one will be any the wiser. They will think these are Government troops.

Kosygin: I do not want to disappoint you, but it will not be possible to conceal this. Two hours later the whole world will know about this. Everyone will begin to shout that the Soviet Union's intervention in Afghanistan has begun. If we quickly airlift tanks, the necessary ammunition and make mortars available to you, will you find specialists who can use these weapons?

Taraki: I am unable to answer this question. The Soviet advisers can answer that.

Kosygin: Hundreds of Afghan officers were trained in the Soviet Union. Where are they all now?

Taraki: Most of them are Moslem reactionaries. We are unable to rely on them, we have no confidence in them.

Kosygin: Can't you recruit a further 50,000 soldiers if we quickly airlift arms to you? How many people can you recruit?

Taraki: The core can only be formed by older secondary school pupils, students, and a few workers. The working class in Afghanistan is very small, but it is a long affair to train them. But we will take any measures, if necessary.

Kosygin: We have decided to quickly deliver military equipment and property to you and to repair helicopters and aircraft. All this is for free. We have also decided to deliver to you 100,000 tons of grain and to raise gas prices from $21 per cubic meter to $37.

Taraki: That is very good, but let us talk of Herat. Why can't the Soviet Union send Uzbeks, Tajiks, and Turkmens in civilian clothing? No one will recognize them. We want you to send them. They could drive tanks, because we have all these nationalities in Afghanistan. Let them don Afghan costume and wear Afghan badges and no one will recognize them. It is very easy work, in our view. If Iran's and Pakistan's experience is anything to go by, it is clear that it is easy to do this work, they have already shown how it can be done.

Kosygin: You are, of course, oversimplifying the issue. It is a complex political and international issue, but, irrespective of this, we will hold consultations again and will get back to you.

Taraki: Send us infantry fighting vehicles by air.

Kosygin: Do you have anyone to drive them?

Taraki: We will find drivers for between 30 and 35 vehicles.

Kosygin: Are they reliable? Won't they flee to the enemy, together with their vehicles? After all, our drivers do not speak the language.

Taraki: Send vehicles together with drivers who speak our language—Tajiks and Uzbeks.

Kosygin: I expected this kind of reply from you. We are comrades and are waging a common struggle and that is why we should not stand on ceremony with each other. Everything must be subordinate to this.

Source: "Transcript of Telephone Conversation between Soviet Premier Alexei Kosygin and Afghan Prime Minister Nur Mohammed Taraki." Available online. URL: http://www.wilsoncenter.org/index.cfm/news/index.cfm?topic_id=1409&fuseaction=va 2.browse&sort=Collection&item=Soviet%20Invasion%20of%20Afghanistan. Accessed March 5, 2010.

Taliban Human Rights Violations (2000)

These extract from Human Rights Watch World Report of 2000 describe the severe human rights abuses practiced by the Taliban against non-Muslims, ethnic minorities, and, especially, women in the parts of Afghanistan that they controlled at that time.

Human Rights Developments

Fighting continued for control of the central part of the country which had fallen to the Taliban in 1998. On April 21, United Front faction Hizb-i Wahdat took control of Bamiyan city, only to relinquish it after heavy fighting in early May. Following the Hizb-i Wahdat victory, relief workers reported that Hizb-i Wahdat forces had beaten and detained residents suspected of supporting the Taliban, and burned their houses. When Taliban forces retook the city, they reportedly took reprisals by shooting suspected Hizb-i

Wahdat supporters, primarily ethnic Shi'a Hazaras, burning hundreds of homes and deporting men to unknown locations.

In late July, at peace talks held in Tashkent, the Taliban and the United Front agreed to the "Tashkent declaration," which called on all parties to resolve the conflict through "peaceful political negotiation." Almost immediately afterwards, both the Taliban and the United Front resumed fighting, with the Taliban focusing its efforts on United Front Commander Ahmad Shah Massoud's territory north of Kabul. As they pushed north, the Taliban forced civilians from their homes and then set fire to houses and crops, and destroyed irrigation canals and wells, ostensibly to rout opposition sympathizers but effectively preventing the residents' return. In the Shomali region, men believed to be loyal to Massoud were arrested or shot, and women and children were taken by truck to Pakistan or made to walk to Kabul. Some one thousand ethnic Tajik men were reportedly separated from their families during the exodus and held by the Taliban. Over four days in August the U. N. estimated that over twenty thousand people fled to Kabul, bringing the total to close to forty thousand in a two-week period.

The influx of displaced people into Kabul further strained relief efforts in the city. Some 850 families took refuge in the abandoned Soviet diplomatic compound. A further one hundred thousand displaced were thought to have taken refuge in the Massoud-held Panjshir valley, fifteen thousand of them without shelter. In September, officials with the U.N. World Food Programme stated that 145,000 people were at risk of malnutrition in the coming winter.

. . .

Taliban officials continued to beat women on the streets of Kabul for dress code violations and for venturing outside the home without the company of a close male relative. In Kabul, girls were not permitted to attend school, although primary schools for girls were permitted in other parts of the country. Women's employment remained severely restricted and was generally limited to health care. To ensure that religious practices were strictly enforced, Taliban police continued to arrest men for having beards that were too short, for not attending prayers, and for having shops open during scheduled prayer times.

As in previous years, the Taliban enforced its laws according to its interpretation of Islamic Sharia, with weekly public executions, floggings, and amputations in Kabul stadium and other cities under its control. Several men accused of sodomy were punished by having walls pushed on them by a tank. In one case, a man who survived the ordeal after being left under the rubble for two hours was reportedly allowed to go free.

In September, the Taliban issued new decrees aimed at non-Muslims that forbade them from building places of worship but allowed them to worship at existing holy sites, banned non-Muslims from criticizing Muslims, ordered non-Muslims to identify their houses by placing a yellow cloth on their rooftops, forbade non-Muslims from living in the same residence as Muslims, and required that non-Muslim women wear a yellow dress with a special mark so that Muslims could keep their distance.

. . .

United Nations

The special rapporteur on Afghanistan, Dr. Kamal Hossain, visited the country in March. In April, the United Nations Commission on Human Rights passed a resolution condemning human rights violations by all parties in Afghanistan, citing in particular the mass killings that accompanied the Taliban's taking of Mazar-i Sharif in August 1998 and the continuing violations of women's rights. It also denounced both sides in the conflict for continuing the civil war and urged other nations to refrain from supplying military support to any of the factions. The commission also specifically condemned the Taliban for violations of women's and girls' human rights. The mandate of the special rapporteur on Afghanistan was extended for another year.

Shortly after the start of the Taliban's July offensive, the U.N. Security Council called for an immediate stop to hostilities. Once again, countries were urged not to aid any of the factions militarily. U.N. Secretary-General Kofi Annan implored the Afghan factions to stop their "senseless self-destruction." He criticized all the parties for committing "criminal acts" and then relying on "the U.N. and the international community . . . to help save their own people from disasters provoked by those who claim to be their country's leaders." He also denounced the use of child soldiers in the conflict.

In August, the U.N. Subcommission on Human Rights adopted a resolution condemning the Taliban for violations of the most fundamental rights of women and girls, stating that Afghan women were "cheated of their rights to health, employment, freedom of movement and security."

International Documents

In September, U.N. Special Rapporteur for Violence against Women Radhika Coomaraswamy visited Afghanistan. She condemned the Taliban militia for its "widespread systematic violation of the human rights of women." She stated that public beatings of women continued and she urged the Taliban authorities to respect international conventions on human rights and dismantle the Ministry for Promotion of Virtue and Prevention of Vice, the religious police responsible for the beatings.

In January, UNICEF reported that 90 percent of the girls in Afghanistan and 75 percent of the boys were not attending school in Taliban-controlled areas, a drop from previous statistics. In a July UNICEF report on children at risk, Afghanistan ranked behind only Angola and Sierra Leone. The study analyzed environmental conditions, mortality rates, nutrition, primary education, security, and health.

Afghanistan remained one of the most densely mined countries in the world, with approximately six million mines, most of them remnants of the war with the Soviet Union from 1979–1992. In 1999 it was estimated that there were ten to twelve victims of landmines per day in the country, 30 percent of them children and 50 percent of them fatalities due to inadequate or nonexistent medical facilities. In July and August, the U.N. reported that the United Front was laying mines north of Kabul to repulse the Taliban offensive.

The U.N. High Commissioner for Refugees (UNHCR) reported in February that the 2.6 million refugees from Afghanistan living in Pakistan and Iran remained the largest group of refugees in the world. Over two million remained internally displaced due to fighting and forced evictions and relocations. Although some fifteen thousand refugees returned from Iran, and fifty-one thousand from Pakistan during the first half of the year, renewed fighting deterred many from going back.

Source: Human Rights Watch. "Human Rights Watch World Report 2000." Available online. URL: http://www.hrw.org/legacy/wr2k/Asia.htm. Accessed March 5, 2010.

Osama bin Laden, Declaration of War against the Americans Occupying the Land of the Two Holy Places (August 1996)

This text, often described as Osama bin Laden's fatwa (here: declaration of war), first appeared in the London-based newspaper Al Quds Al Arabi *in August 1996. At that time Osama bin Laden was largely unknown outside his home country of Saudi Arabia, and this article received little attention. A shortened version of this article signed by Osama bin Laden and four others also appeared in* Al Quds Al Arabi *in February 1998. The five signatories described themselves as the "World Islamic Front for Jihad against Jews and Crusaders." The bomb attacks on the U.S. embassies in Dar es Salaam, Tanzania, and Nairobi, Kenya, that occurred a few months later made Osama bin Laden and his al-Qaeda organization notorious.*

The extracts reproduced here represent less than a third of the original document but include its main points. Osama bin Laden urges all Muslims to oppose the United States and Israel by any means available to them, including guerrilla warfare. The prime justification for this campaign is the presence of U.S. forces in Saudi Arabia, which Osama bin Laden describes as "the country of the two Holy Places" in reference to Mecca and Medina—the two holiest shrines in Islam. The document also makes reference to the defeat of the Soviet forces in Afghanistan ("the largest infidel military force of the world") by the mujahideen and boasts that Osama bin Laden and his group have found "a safe base . . . in the high Hindukush mountains in Khurasan."

Praise be to Allah, we seek His help and ask for his pardon. We take refuge in Allah from our wrongs and bad deeds. Who ever been guided by Allah will not be misled, and who ever has been misled, he will never be guided. I bear witness that there is no God except Allah—no associates with Him—and I bear witness that Muhammad is His slave and messenger.

. . .

It should not be hidden from you that the people of Islam had suffered from aggression, iniquity and injustice imposed on them by the Zionist-Crusaders alliance and their collaborators; to the extent that the Muslims blood became the cheapest and their wealth as loot in the hands of the enemies. Their blood was spilled in Palestine and Iraq. The horrifying pictures of the massacre of Qana, in Lebanon are still fresh in our memory. Massacres in Tajakestan, Burma, Cashmere, Assam, Philippines, Fatani, Ogadin, Somalia, Erithria, Chechnia and in Bosnia-Herzegovina took place, massacres that send shivers in the body and shake the conscience. All of this and the world watch and hear, and not only didn't respond to these atrocities, but also with a clear conspiracy between the USA and its allies and under the cover of the iniquitous United Nations, the dispossessed people were even prevented from obtaining arms to defend themselves.

The people of Islam awakened and realised that they are the main target for the aggression of the Zionist-Crusaders alliance. All false claims and propaganda about "Human Rights" were hammered down and exposed by the massacres that took place against the Muslims in every part of the world.

The latest and the greatest of these aggressions, incurred by the Muslims since the death of the Prophet (ALLAH'S BLESSING AND SALUTATIONS ON HIM) is the occupation of the land of the two Holy Places—the foundation of the house of Islam, the place of the revelation, the source of the message and the place of the noble Ka'ba, the Qiblah of all Muslims—by the armies of the American Crusaders and their allies. (We bemoan this and can only say: "No power and power acquiring except through Allah").

. . .

We, myself and my group, have suffered some of this injustice ourselves; we have been prevented from addressing the Muslims. We have been pursued in Pakistan, Sudan and Afghanistan, hence this long absence on my part. But by the Grace of Allah, a safe base is now available in the high Hindukush mountains in Khurasan; where—by the Grace of Allah—the largest infidel military force of the world was destroyed. And the myth of the super power was withered in front of the Mujahideen cries of Allahu Akbar (God is greater). Today we work from the same mountains to lift the iniquity that had been imposed on the Ummah by the Zionist-Crusader alliance, particularly after they have occupied the blessed land around Jerusalem, route of the journey of the Prophet (ALLAH'S BLESSING AND SALUTATIONS ON HIM) and the land of the two Holy Places. We ask Allah to bestow us with victory, He is our Patron and He is the Most Capable.

From here, today we begin the work, talking and discussing the ways of correcting what had happened to the Islamic world in general, and the Land of the two Holy Places in particular.

. . .

Injustice had affected the people of the industry and agriculture. It affected the people of the rural and urban areas. And almost everybody complains about something. The situation at the land of the two Holy places became like a huge volcano at the verge of eruption that would destroy the Kufr and the corruption and its sources. The explosion at Riyadh and Al-Khobar is a warning of this volcanic eruption emerging as a result of the sever oppression, suffering, excessive iniquity, humiliation and poverty.

People are fully concerned about their every day livings; every body talks about the deterioration of the economy, inflation, ever increasing debts and jails full of prisoners. Government employees with limited income talk about debts of ten thousands and hundred thousands of Saudi Riyals. They complain that the value of the Riyal is greatly and continuously deteriorating among most of the main currencies. Great merchants and contractors speak about hundreds and thousands of million Riyals owed to them by the government. More than three hundred forty billions of Riyal owed by the government to the people in addition to the daily accumulated interest, let alone the foreign debt. People wonder whether we are the largest oil exporting country?! They even believe that this situation is a curse put on them by Allah for not objecting to the oppressive and illegitimate behaviour and measures of the ruling regime: Ignoring the divine Shari'ah law; depriving people of their legitimate rights; allowing the American to occupy the land of the two Holy Places; imprisonment, unjustly, of the sincere scholars. The honourable Ulamah and scholars as well as merchants, economists and eminent people of the country were all alerted by this disastrous situation.

Quick efforts were made by each group to contain and to correct the situation. All agreed that the country is heading toward a great catastrophe, the depth of which is not known except by Allah. One big merchant commented: "the king is leading the state into a 'sixty-six' fold disaster," (We bemoan this and can only say: "No power and power acquiring except through Allah"). Numerous princes share with the people their feelings, privately expressing their concerns and objecting to the corruption, repression and the intimidation taking place in the country. But the competition between influential princes for personal gains and interest had destroyed the country. Through its course of actions the regime has torn off its legitimacy:

(1) Suspension of the Islamic Shari'ah law and exchanging it with man made civil law. The regime entered into a bloody confrontation with the truthful Ulamah and the righteous youths (we sanctify nobody; Allah sanctify Whom He pleaseth).

(2) The inability of the regime to protect the country, and allowing the enemy of the Ummah—the American crusader forces—to occupy the land for the longest of years. The crusader forces became the main cause of our disastrous condition, particularly in the economical aspect of it due to the unjustified heavy spending on these

252

forces. As a result of the policy imposed on the country, especially in the field of oil industry where production is restricted or
expanded and prices are fixed to suit the American economy ignoring the economy of the country. Expensive deals were imposed on
the country to purchase arms. People asking what is the justification for the very existence of the regime then?

· · ·

Therefore every one agreed that the situation cannot be rectified (the
shadow cannot be straighten when its source, the rod, is not straight either)
unless the root of the problem is tackled. Hence it is essential to hit the main
enemy who divided the Ummah into small and little countries and pushed
it, for the last few decades, into a state of confusion. The Zionist-Crusader
alliance moves quickly to contain and abort any "corrective movement"
appearing in the Islamic countries. Different means and methods are used to
achieve their target; on occasion the "movement" is dragged into an armed
struggle at a predetermined unfavourable time and place. Sometime officials
from the Ministry of Interior, who are also graduates of the colleges of the
Shari'ah, are leashed out to mislead and confuse the nation and the Ummah
(by wrong Fatwas) and to circulate false information about the movement.
At other occasions some righteous people were tricked into a war of words
against the Ulama and the leaders of the movement, wasting the energy of
the nation in discussing minor issues and ignoring the main one that is the
unification of the people under the divine law of Allah.

· · ·

Under such circumstances, to push the enemy—the greatest Kufr—out of
the country is a prime duty. No other duty after Belief is more important.
Utmost effort should be made to prepare and instigate the Ummah against
the enemy, the American-Israeli alliance-occupying the country of the two
Holy Places and the route of the Apostle (Allah's Blessings and Salutations
may be on him) to the Furthest Mosque (Al-Aqsa Mosque). Also to remind
the Muslims not to be engaged in an internal war among themselves, as that
will have grieve consequences namely:

1 Consumption of the Muslims human resources as most casualties
   and fatalities will be among the Muslims people.
2 Exhaustion of the economic and financial resources.
3 Destruction of the country infrastructures.

4 Dissociation of the society.
5 Destruction of the oil industries. The presence of the USA Crusader military forces on land, sea and air of the states of the Islamic Gulf is the greatest danger threatening the largest oil reserve in the world. The existence of these forces in the area will provoke the people of the country and induces aggression on their religion, feelings and prides and push them to take up armed struggle against the invaders occupying the land; therefore spread of the fighting in the region will expose the oil wealth to the danger of being burned up. The economic interests of the States of the Gulf and the land of the two Holy Places will be damaged and even a greater damage will be caused to the economy of the world. I would like here to alert my brothers, the Mujahideen, the sons of the nation, to protect this (oil) wealth and not to include it in the battle as it is a great Islamic wealth and a large economical power essential for the soon to be established Islamic state, by Allah's Permission and Grace. We also warn the aggressors, the USA, against burning this Islamic wealth . . .
6 Division of the land of the two Holy Places, and annexing of the northerly part of it by Israel. Dividing the land of the two Holy Places is an essential demand of the Zionist-Crusader alliance. The existence of such a large country with its huge resources under the leadership of the forthcoming Islamic State, by Allah's Grace, represent a serious danger to the very existence of the Zionist state in Palestine. The Nobel Ka'ba—the Qiblah of all Muslims—makes the land of the two Holy Places a symbol for the unity of the Islamic world. Moreover, the presence of the world largest oil reserve makes the land of the two Holy Places an important economical power in the Islamic world . . .
7 An internal war is a great mistake, no matter what reasons there are for it. The presence of the occupier's—the USA—forces will control the outcome of the battle for the benefit of the international Kufr.

I address now my brothers of the security and military forces and the national guards may Allah preserve you hoard for Islam and the Muslims people:

. . .

Today your brothers and sons, the sons of the two Holy Places, have started their Jihad in the cause of Allah, to expel the occupying enemy from of the country of the two Holy places. And there is no doubt you would like to carry out this mission too, in order to re-establish the greatness of this Ummah and to liberate its occupied sanctities. Nevertheless, it must be obvious to you that, due to the imbalance of power between our armed forces and the enemy forces, a suitable means of fighting must be adopted i.e. using fast moving light forces that work under complete secrecy. In other word to initiate a guerrilla warfare, were the sons of the nation, and not the military forces, take part in it. And as you know, it is wise, in the present circumstances, for the armed military forces not to be engaged in a conventional fighting with the forces of the crusader enemy (the exceptions are the bold and the forceful operations carried out by the members of the armed forces individually, that is without the movement of the formal forces in its conventional shape and hence the responses will not be directed, strongly, against the army) unless a big advantage is likely to be achieved; and great losses induced on the enemy side (that would shaken and destroy its foundations and infrastructures) that will help to expel the defeated enemy from the country.

The Mujahideen, your brothers and sons, requesting that you support them in every possible way by supplying them with the necessary information, materials and arms. Security men are especially asked to cover up for the Mujahideen and to assist them as much as possible against the occupying enemy; and to spread rumours, fear and discouragement among the members of the enemy forces.

· · ·

The regime is fully responsible for what had been incurred by the country and the nation; however the occupying American enemy is the principle and the main cause of the situation. Therefore efforts should be concentrated on destroying, fighting and killing the enemy until, by the Grace of Allah, it is completely defeated. The time will come—by the Permission of Allah—when you'll perform your decisive role so that the word of Allah will be supreme and the word of the infidels (Kaferoon) will be the inferior. You will hit with iron fist against the aggressors. You'll re-establish the normal course and give the people their rights and carry out your truly Islamic duty. Allah willing, I'll have a separate talk about these issues.

· · ·

Before closing my talk, I have a very important message to the youths of Islam, men of the brilliant future of the Ummah of Muhammad (ALLAH'S

BLESSING AND SALUTATIONS ON HIM). Our talk with the youths about their duty in this difficult period in the history of our Ummah. A period in which the youths and no one else came forward to carry out the variable and different duties. While some of the well known individuals had hesitated in their duty of defending Islam and saving themselves and their wealth from the injustice, aggression and terror—exercised by the government—the youths (may Allah protect them) were forthcoming and raised the banner of Jihad against the American-Zionist alliance occupying the sanctities of Islam. Others who have been tricked into loving this materialistic world, and those who have been terrorised by the government choose to give legitimacy to the greatest betrayal, the occupation of the land of the two Holy Places (We bemoan this and can only say: "No power and power acquiring except through Allah"). We are not surprised from the action of our youths.

. . .

A few days ago the news agencies reported that the Defence Secretary of the Crusading Americans had said that the explosion at Riyadh and Al-Khobar had taught him one lesson: that is not to withdraw when attacked by coward terrorists.

We say to the Defence Secretary that his talk can induce a grieving mother to laughter and shows the fears that has enshrined you all. Where was this false courage of yours when the explosion in Beirut took place on 1983 A.D. (1403 A.H). You were turned into scattered bits and pieces at that time; 241 mainly marines solders were killed. And where was this courage of yours when two explosions made you to leave Aden in less than twenty four hours!

But your most disgraceful case was in Somalia; where—after vigorous propaganda about the power of the USA and its post cold war leadership of the new world order—you moved tens of thousands of international force, including twenty eight thousand American solders into Somalia. However, when tens of your soldiers were killed in minor battles and one American Pilot was dragged in the streets of Mogadishu you left the area carrying disappointment, humiliation, defeat and your dead with you. Clinton appeared in front of the whole world threatening and promising revenge, but these threats were merely a preparation for withdrawal. You have been disgraced by Allah and you withdrew; the extent of your impotence and weaknesses became very clear. It was a pleasure for the heart of every Muslim and a remedy to the chests of believing nations to see you defeated in the three Islamic cities of Beirut, Aden and Mogadishu.

I say to the Secretary of Defence: The sons of the land of the two Holy Places had come out to fight against the Russian in Afghanistan, the Serb in Bosnia-Herzegovina and today they are fighting in Chechenia and—by the Permission of Allah—they have been made victorious over your partner, the Russians. By the command of Allah, they are also fighting in Tajakistan.

I say: Since the sons of the land of the two Holy Places feel and strongly believe that fighting (Jihad) against the Kuffar in every part of the world, is absolutely essential; then they would be even more enthusiastic, more powerful and larger in number upon fighting on their own land—the place of their births—defending the greatest of their sanctities, the noble Ka'ba (the Qiblah of all Muslims). They know that the Muslims of the world will assist and help them to victory. To liberate their sanctities is the greatest of issues concerning all Muslims; it is the duty of every Muslims in this world.

. . .

Those youths know that their rewards in fighting you, the USA, is double than their rewards in fighting some one else not from the people of the book. They have no intention except to enter paradise by killing you. An infidel, and enemy of God like you, cannot be in the same hell with his righteous executioner.

. . .

Terrorising you, while you are carrying arms on our land, is a legitimate and morally demanded duty. It is a legitimate right well known to all humans and other creatures. Your example and our example is like a snake that entered into a house of a man and was killed by him. The coward is the one who lets you walk, while carrying arms, freely on his land and provides you with peace and security.

Those youths are different from your soldiers. Your problem will be how to convince your troops to fight, while our problem will be how to restrain our youths to wait for their turn in fighting and in operations. These youths are commendation and praiseworthy.

THE MUSLIM WORLD

. . .

The youths hold you responsible for all of the killings and evictions of the Muslims and the violation of the sanctities, carried out by your Zionist brothers in Lebanon; you openly supplied them with arms and finance. More than 600,000 Iraqi children have died due to lack of food and medicine and as a result of the unjustifiable aggression (sanction) imposed on Iraq and its nation. The children of Iraq are our children. You, the USA, together with the Saudi regime are responsible for the shedding of the blood of these innocent children. Due to all of that, whatever treaty you have with our country is now null and void.

. . .

These youths know that: if one is not to be killed one will die (anyway) and the most honourable death is to be killed in the way of Allah. They are even more determined after the martyrdom of the four heroes who bombed the Americans in Riyadh. Those youths who raised high the head of the Ummah and humiliated the Americans—the occupier—by their operation in Riyadh.

Our women had set a tremendous example of generosity in the cause of Allah; they motivated and encouraged their sons, brothers and husbands to fight—in the cause of Allah—in Afghanistan, Bosnia-Herzegovina, Chechenia and in other countries. We ask Allah to accept from them these deeds, and may He help their fathers, brothers, husbands and sons. May Allah strengthen the belief—Imaan—of our women in the way of generosity and sacrifice for the supremacy of the word of Allah. Our women weep not, except over men who fight in the cause of Allah; our women instigate their brothers to fight in the cause of Allah.

. . .

My Muslim Brothers of The World:

Your brothers in Palestine and in the land of the two Holy Places are calling upon your help and asking you to take part in fighting against the enemy—your enemy and their enemy—the Americans and the Israelis. They are asking you to do whatever you can, with one's own means and ability, to expel the enemy, humiliated and defeated, out of the sanctities of Islam . . .

Source: Freepublic.com. "Declaration of War by Usama bin Ladin." Available online. URL: http://www.freerepublic. com/focus/news/824916/posts. Accessed November 25, 2009.

Statement by Osama bin Laden (October 7, 2001)

On the same day that U.S. attacks against Taliban targets in Afghanistan began, and less than six weeks after the September 11, 2001, attacks on the United States, the Qatar-based Al Jazeera television network aired what it described as a statement from al-Qaeda leader Osama bin Laden. The reference to "Andalucia" at the beginning of the statement refers to "Al-Andalus"; the Arabic name for the parts of present-day Spain and Portugal ruled by North African Muslims between the eighth and 15th centuries. The mention of an unspecified event that occurred 80 years previously is thought to refer to the Sykes-Picot agreement of 1916, which divided the Arab provinces of the Ottoman Empire between the British and the French after World War I, or to the British mandate over Palestine that lasted from 1922 until 1948 and which was immediately followed by the establishment of the state of Israel.

Let the whole world know that we shall never accept that the tragedy of Andalucia would be repeated in Palestine. We cannot accept that Palestine will become Jewish.

And with regard to you, Muslims, this is the day of question. This is a new (inaudible) against you, all against the Muslims and Medina. So be like the followers of the prophet, peace be upon him, and all countrymen, lovers of God and the prophet within, and a new battle, great battle, similar to the great battles of Islam, like the conqueror of Jerusalem. So, hurry up to the dignity of life and the eternity of death. Thanks to God, he who God guides will never lose. And I believe that there's only one God. And I declare I believe there's no prophet but Hammed.

This is America, God has sent one of the attacks by God and has attacked one of its best buildings. And this is America filled with fear from the north, south, east and west, thank God.

And what America is facing today is something very little of what we have tasted for decades. Our nation, since nearly 80 years is tasting this humility. Sons are killed, and nobody answers the call.

And when God has guided a bunch of Muslims to be at the forefront and destroyed America, a big destruction, I wish God would lift their position.

And when those people have defended and retaliated to what their brothers and sisters have suffered in Palestine and Lebanon, the whole world has been shouting.

And there are civilians, innocent children being killed every day in Iraq without any guilt, and we never hear anybody. We never hear any (inaudible) from the clergymen of the government.

And every day we see the Israeli tanks going to Jeanine, Ramallah, Beit Jalla and other lands of Islam. And, no, we never hear anybody objecting to that.

So when the swords came after eight years to America, then the whole world has been crying for those criminals who attacked. This is the least which could be said about them. They are people. They supported the murder against the victim, so God has given them back what they deserve.

I say the matter is very clear, so every Muslim after this, and after the officials in America, starting with the head of the infidels, Bush. And they came out with their men and equipment and they even encouraged even countries claiming to be Muslims against us. So, we run with our religion. They came out to fight Islam with the name of fighting terrorism.

People (inaudible) event of the world (inaudible) in Japan, hundreds of thousands of people got killed. This is not a war crime. Or in Iraq, what our (inaudible) who are being killed in Iraq. This is not a crime. And those, when they were attacked in my Nairobi, and Dar Es Salaam, Afghanistan, and Sudan were attacked.

I say these events have split the whole world into two camps: the camp of belief and the disbelief. So every Muslim shall take (inaudible) shall support his religion.

And now with the winds of change has blown up now, has come to the Arabian Peninsula.

And to America, I stay to it and to its people this: I swear by God the Great, America will never dream nor those who live in America will never taste security and safety unless we feel security and safety in our land and in Palestine.

Source: ABCnews.com. "Transcript of Osama bin Laden." Available online. URL: http://abcnews.go.com/International/story?id=80490&page=1. Accessed November 25, 2009.

Islamic Emirate of Afghanistan (2009)

During the period of their rule over the majority of Afghanistan the Taliban referred to the country as the Islamic Emirate of Afghanistan. Only Pakistan, Saudi Arabia, and the United Arab Emirates recognized the Taliban government. Although the Taliban regime was overthrown by a U.S.-led military invasion in 2001 the Taliban and their allies continue to use the term Islamic Emirate of Afghanistan and do not recognize the current Afghan government. This extract is from a Web site that claims to represent the views of those who are fighting Afghan government troops and their NATO allies. It refers to these groups collectively as "mujahideen" rather than as the Taliban.

The Aims of Mujahideen

As an Islamic liberation force, the Mujahideen of the Islamic Emirate represent aspirations of the Afghan masses who want to free themselves from the claws of colonialism. This is the only force, the people look to for realization of their noble aims.

Therefore, to live up to the expectation of the people, the Mujahideen's objectives are clear. They want to establish an Islamic system based on justice and equality and gain independence of the country where the Afghans will be owners of their own country and fate. Education, spiritual and material uplift and reconstructions are other aims of the Islamic Emirate. It has declared time and again that it will implement these goals upon gaining independence. However, the intelligence agencies of the invading countries and the biased media are trying to mar the good name of Mujahideen. Under the notorious name of terrorism, they want to create hatred among the people against the true sons of this land (Afghanistan). Even some time, these agencies resort to perpetrating gruesome crimes like explosions in congested places where hundreds of innocent people lose their lives. Some time, they flare up sectarian violence as per the old divide and rule formula of colonialism. Then, they accuse Mujahideen of being involved these crimes. The Mujahideen are free from all such charges. No Mujahid will ever want to kill an innocent Muslim or Muslima.

261

But the biased media constantly publish the official story and the people under the influence of the partial reports are confused and some time, misjudge the events because they do not know to tell facts from lies. On the other hand, the mainstream media do not publish the stand of Mujahideen regarding every event, fearing the invading Americans will accuse them of helping the so-called terrorists. In fact, the world has now been taken hostage by the media suffocation unleashed by the colonialism.

Pentagon has a psychological war department. This department is charged with spreading lies against Mujahideen. They spend millions of dollars to make it possible that the lies fabricated in Pentagon reach every ear in the world. They pay high sum of money to journalists who is ready to publish maligning stories against Mujahideen. According to a media report, a CIA cell in one of the neighboring countries of Afghanistan pay a journalist $1000 for a story against Mujahideen. They put on air dramas aimed at marring the image of Mujahideen. Ironically, the colonialists have taken this war from the battle fields to the fields of media, labor unions, business circles and scholar forums. So they should be confronted in all these fields.

Those journalists who are committed to human dignity, liberation, and justice should form Mujahideen Support Groups and wage an unwavering and constant campaign against the black propaganda launched by the colonialists because in the final analysis, this is not the war of Taliban. This is the war of all freedom-loving and justice-loving people all over the world who want to live as free people without the sword of colonialism hanging over their heads in this 21st century.

Source: "The Aims of Mujahideen." Available online. URL: http://www.alemarah.info/english/. Accessed February 27, 2010.

PART III

Research Tools

6

How to Research
the Muslim World

The Muslim world is a vast topic. The world's 1.5 billion Muslims live in every nation on every continent. The history of Islam stretches back 1,400 years and encompasses a bewildering array of empires, states, and communities. Taken together these factors can make the task of researching the Muslim world an intimidating prospect. The amount of information available is just as enormous. This section will help create a focus for research, give guidelines on the best places to look for information, and help evaluate the nature and quality of that information.

CHOOSING A SUBJECT

Unless one has been given a very specific subject to research, the most difficult first step is choosing a single strand to investigate from the vast and complex tapestry that makes up the Muslim world. Before even considering a specific topic, get an overview of the Muslim world. Become familiar with the broad sweep of the history of Islam, the geographical extent of those parts of the world that have Muslim-majority populations, the parts of the world that have significant numbers of Muslim minorities, and the broad scope of Muslim culture. If looking for a contemporary subject, be aware that understanding the history of that subject may take in centuries of past development. If looking for a cultural topic, be aware that, though all Muslims share some customs, the culture of Muslims living thousands of miles apart is likely to be very different.

CHALLENGE ASSUMPTIONS

Before trying to chose a specific subject, it is very important to be aware of the full range of possible subjects. This means the researcher should give himself an overview of the entire field rather than relying on what he thinks he knows. He may have assumptions about the Muslim world that are completely untrue, and these must be challenged before he can make an intelligent choice of subject. For example, he might imagine that most Muslims are Arabs and live in the Middle East. This is untrue: The world's four largest Muslim populations live in Indonesia, Pakistan, India, and Bangladesh; none of these nations are Arab countries and none are in the Middle East. Challenge this assumption further: What exactly is an Arab? Are all Arabs Muslim? He should ask himself what else he thinks he knows about the Muslim world and check to see if it is true before proceeding.

The Muslim world is not homogeneous. There are countries where Muslims make up the great majority of the population and others where they make up a tiny minority. Both are an integral part of the Muslim world in the broadest sense. There are wealthy, technologically developed Muslim-majority states, and Muslim-majority states with some of the worst standards of living in the world. There are secular states where most people are Muslims, and Muslim theocracies where not everybody is Muslim. A Muslim might be a wealthy businessman living in Seattle, the prince of a conservative Middle Eastern emirate, or a penniless farmer in Malaysia. The opinions and beliefs of such a wide variety of people in such diverse societies means that there is no such thing as the Muslim point of view or the average life of a Muslim. The researcher must be aware that, for any opinion or point of view expressed by a Muslim, there is another Muslim somewhere who believes the opposite. The researcher must also be aware that non-Muslims who come into contact with the Muslim world are likely to have highly diverse experiences and opinions. An expat European living in Dubai will have a completely different impression of the Muslim world from a Christian farmer in Indonesia who has been in gunfights with his Muslim neighbors.

Becoming familiar with the historical and cultural diversity of the Muslim world is an excellent way to uncover potential topics for research. Original subjects that may never have been considered are more likely to present themselves when the researcher looks into aspects of the Muslim world she is unfamiliar with.

STAY ON TARGET

Keeping the goal of one's research clear is a challenge in a subject as vast as the Muslim world. Although it is important to look into and understand topics that impact the chosen area of research, one should beware of wandering too far from the chosen path. For example, a researcher may decide to research education in the Muslim world only to find herself delving into the problems of poverty or censorship in particular Muslim-majority states. These issues should be understood and mentioned, but do not let them distract you from the original goal: A project that sets out to discuss education and ends up discussing the causes of poverty is unlikely to be useful as a study of either education or poverty.

UNDERSTANDING SOURCES

There are literally millions of possible sources of information on the Muslim world. Hundreds of books are published every year on one aspect of the Muslim world or another, tens of thousands of articles are written, and some part of the Muslim world is always in the news headlines. In addition to these mainstream sources, countless blogs and Web sites are available on the Internet that present every conceivable point of view on a wide range of subjects directly or indirectly connected to the Muslim world. How can a researcher begin to make sense of this bewildering array of information, and even more importantly, how much faith can be placed in them?

Online Sources

Any one who has spent more than five minutes using the Internet knows that not everything it contains can be taken at face value. Having said that, the Internet does feature many Web sites that contain high quality nonbiased information. Even Web sites that advocate specific points of view can be of great value to the researcher as a source of quotes and ideas.

In general a Web site's credibility can be judged by its transparency. Credible Web sites are usually just one aspect of a larger organization with a clear and documented "real-world" presence. A credible Web site will give the author or author's real names, a physical postal address or office, and a statement of its aims and any sources of funding. Tying a Web site to the name of an organization or individual means that organization or individual is legally responsible for its content in the same way that the author and publisher of a book is responsible for its content. This provides some guarantee that the content has at least been checked and approved. One should also normally expect a credible Web site to cite its sources and back up its facts with references in the same way a published book or article would.

Governmental Web Sites

Almost all national governments have Web sites that can be a highly valuable source of information. In the United States, government Web sites have URLs that end with the suffix, or top-level domain, .gov. Only U.S.

government agencies are able to set up Web sites with this top-level domain, although some federal agencies use *.fed.us* and many U.S. military agencies use *.mil.* In all other countries a second-level domain is used for the Web sites of government agencies. In the United Kingdom, for example, government Web sites have a *.gov.uk* suffix and in France *.gouv.fr.* Checking for these top- and second-level domain names is a guarantee that the Web site visited is an official portal. Government Web sites are often extremely good sources for statistics, full and original texts of laws, speeches or reports made by officials, and detailed histories of policy decisions. The researcher must always remember, however, that government Web sites cannot be considered free of bias.

Web Sites of International Organizations

International organizations can be conveniently divided into international governmental organizations (IGOs) and international nongovernmental organizations (INGOs). IGOs are usually made up of groups of sovereign states, while INGOs are made up of profit or nonprofit private organizations operating internationally.

The United Nations is the largest and best-known IGO. Almost every sovereign nation on Earth belongs to the United Nations, and the organization's vast Web presence includes reams of information and statistics on all of them. The United Nations consists of many specialized agencies set up to deal with particular issues, such as the International Atomic Energy Agency; the United Nations Educational, Scientific and Cultural Organization; the International Monetary Fund; and the World Health Organization, all of which are deeply involved in the Muslim world as they are in all parts of the world. Because the United Nations has such a diverse membership, some of whose members may be in open conflict with others at any particular time, its standards of impartiality have to be very high. This makes it a great source of raw, unbiased factual data, but less useful as a source of opinion.

There are a large number of IGOs other than the United Nations, some of which are geographically or economically focused on the major centers of the Muslim world. The Organization of the Islamic Conference, for example, is an IGO of 57 member states, most of which are Muslim-majority. The League of Arab States (also known as the Arab League) is a large and important ethnocultural IGO also made up of Muslim-majority states. Other important IGOs in which Muslim-majority states play a major role include the economic trade bloc known as the Organization of the Petroleum Exporting Countries (OPEC) and regional diplomatic and trade forums such as the Association of Southeast Asian Nations (ASEAN) and the African Union. All of these organizations have extensive Web sites containing invaluable information for research into the Muslim world.

There are a great many more INGOs than IGOs. Any company that operates internationally is, technically, an INGO, but the Web sites of multinational corporations are likely to be useful only in highly specific instances of research. International nonprofit organizations are usually a richer source of cultural, economic, and political information. These include charities, such as the International Red Cross and Red Crescent Movement, and cooperative organizations, such as the Union of NGOs of the Muslim world. Many thousands of charities and cultural organizations operate in the Muslim world that may be of use to researchers. When looking at the Web sites of INGOs bear in mind that all of them have a specific agenda. Read the *about us* or *mission statement* section of these Web sites to find out what the organization's purpose is and take this into account when weighing the value and bias of any information found there. A Web site that does not provide a statement of this kind should be treated with great wariness as a source of reliable information.

Political groups are another large category of INGOs or, more often, country- or region-specific nongovernmental organizations (NGOs). These include political parties, which aim to influence through gaining direct political power, and advocacy groups, which seek to influence political developments by lobbying. Today almost all sizable political parties and advocacy groups have Web sites, even those in developing countries. Although these Web sites may not always be in English, those that seek to influence world opinion will usually, as a matter of necessity, have a mission statement, background information, or a manifesto in English. Political parties and advocacy groups are, by nature, partisan and likely to present information in a manner that is biased toward their own point of view.

News Agencies and News Outlets

The Web sites of international news agencies are one of the most useful sources of information for the online researcher. News agencies are essentially organizations of journalists that supply news stories to media companies such as television stations, newspapers, magazines, and online news sites. Some news agencies, such as CNN in the United States, the BBC in the United Kingdom, and Al Jazeera in the Middle East, are also media companies that print or broadcast news as well; in other words, they are both news agencies and news outlets. Other respected news agencies covering worldwide news include the Associated Press, the Press Association, and Reuters, although there are many others specializing in particular geographical areas. The Web portals provided by companies such as the BBC or Al Jazeera give access to the latest news from all over the Muslim world, archives of related stories stretching back many years, and in-depth articles that provide details about the history and cultural background to current events. Every major, and most minor, news outlets have Web sites. News outlets range from large media companies that publish internationally famous newspapers and magazines to local news sites across the globe. News outlets are a prime source of material for any research project involving current events. The great advantage of online portals for well-established news outlets is that they frequently offer the facility to read earlier stories on the same or related subjects. This can be an invaluable way of tracking the progress of an issue over many years up to the present day and uncovering the emergence of new themes and points of view on that issue. The reliability of different types of journalism is discussed below in the section entitled *Evaluating Sources.*

Blogs, Chat Rooms, and other Web Sites

Web sites on which private individuals express their personal views and experiences can be a huge, if unwieldy, resource for the researcher. First-person accounts of life in parts of the world where censorship laws prevent the free reporting of events by mainstream media provide insights that would have been impossible just a decade ago. During dramatic events in regions where foreign journalists find it difficult or impossible to gain access, local bloggers are sometimes the only source of current information. In some Muslim-majority states blogging has become a powerful political and cultural phenomenon in itself. In Iran, for example, tens of thousands of bloggers have used the relative freedom of the Internet to communicate their views to each other and the rest of the world in a culture in which other forms of reporting are heavily censored. Blogs are not the only form of individual expression on the Internet. Chat rooms, photo and video sites, and podcasts (online audio transmissions) are all used by individuals to publish their views and experiences. Taken together these forms of expression are sometimes referred to as citizen media, and they form an enormous and easily accessible research resource that is increasingly being taken seriously by professional researchers.

The factor that makes citizen media so immediate, namely, the complete lack of editorial or expert review, is of course also the factor that makes it highly unreliable as a source of facts. There is nothing to prevent an individual publishing inaccurate or deliberately misleading information via citizen media. As a source of pure opinion, however, citizen media is unparalleled.

270

How to Research the Muslim World

Traditional Sources

Traditional sources include material that was originally published or broadcast through established media such as books, magazines, television, film, and radio. Today much traditional media is also broadcast or published on the Internet as well as in its original form, which makes accessing it from another country much easier.

National Newspapers and Magazines

Mass circulation newspapers and general-interest magazines remain one of the leading sources of international news, in-depth reports, and expert opinion. The biggest newspapers in the United States include the *New York Times, Washington Post, Chicago Tribune,* and *Los Angeles Times.* Major general-interest magazines include *Time, Newsweek,* the *New Yorker,* the *Economist,* and *National Geographic.* In recent years all of these newspapers and magazines have published thousands of stories and reports concerning the Muslim world, many of which are available through their Web sites or in public library archives.

Specialist and Peer-Reviewed Journals

Specialized journals that publish original research by academics or professionals are one of the most valuable sources for the researcher. Many of these journals are peer reviewed or refereed, which means that their contents are checked and edited by other academics or professionals who have expert knowledge of the subject. There are many journals of this kind dedicated to research and study into the past and present of the Muslim world or specific parts of it, including the *International Journal of Middle East Studies, Critique: Critical Middle Eastern Studies, Bulletin of the School of Oriental and African Studies, British Journal of Middle East Studies, Journal of Near Eastern Studies, Middle East Report, Middle East Review of International Affairs,* and *Journal of Islamic Studies.* Material published in specialist journals is often available online, but it can be accessed usually only after paying a subscription. Some libraries and academic institutions are able to offer students and researchers free access to these archives.

Books

Books are probably the single most important source of reliable, in-depth information on most topics of academic interest, and the Muslim world is no exception. However, even in a relatively narrow topic such as the Muslim world, there are a very wide range of types of book with varying levels of usefulness and reliability.

271

ACADEMIC BOOKS

At the top of this range are academic books written by experts in their field. These books may be based on years or even decades of research and are frequently an extension or a consolidation of papers written by the author for peer-reviewed journals. They are aimed primarily at an academic readership and are often published by specialist publishers. Books of this kind cite their sources the same way academic papers do and go through an extensive process of expert review before being published. The one disadvantage of academic books of this kind is that they tend to cover extremely narrow and specialized topics in great detail. This is great if the topic happens to fit exactly the researcher's own topic, but it can be prohibitively time-consuming to read through an entire volume just for a few pieces of information if it does not. Generalized introductions aimed at a wider readership are often a better place to start. These are also often written by respected academics, but they are meant to give an overview to the nonspecialist or the student rather than presenting cutting-edge research to other specialists. Biographies of prominent figures from the Muslim world can also provide an overview of an historical period in a particular country or region.

FIRST-HAND ACCOUNTS

Books written by nonacademics who have expert firsthand knowledge of their topic are next in line. Their authors may be journalists or other professionals who have spent considerable time intimately involved with their subject matter. They are usually aimed at a wider readership than either specialist or introductory academic volumes and rarely cite sources in a rigorous way, if at all. In essence, they represent the opinions of trained and knowledgeable observers based on years of firsthand experience and, as such, are a valuable and legitimate source of information for the researcher.

ADVOCACY AND SENSATIONALIST TITLES

A third category of book with less value as a source of reliable information, but still useful to the researcher, includes titles advocating a particular point of view and sensationalist titles. Advocacy books usually aim to persuade the reader that the author's point of view is the correct one rather than to present several different points of view and examine their merits and drawbacks. Books of this kind can be difficult for the nonexpert to identify because they sometimes cite academic and other sources in a way that looks superficially similar to the citations in academic volumes. The difference is that only sources that support the authors claims are included while others are ignored. Reviews in academic journals or respected newspapers can usually be relied upon to identify advocacy titles. Despite their unhelpfulness as sources of factual information, books of this kind can still be valuable to the researcher as a source of opinion.

Video and Audio Sources

Television and radio programs and films are often overlooked as potential sources for research, which is unfortunate because they can be a treasure store of unique material. Public and private broadcast news programs usually present short reports of stories that are covered in more depth in national newspapers, but sometimes they air special reports featuring exclusive interviews with prominent figures or eyewitnesses to dramatic events. These can be legitimately quoted and referenced in the same way as statements in books, newspapers, or journals. Both private and public broadcasters also transmit in-depth documentaries, which can also be a unique source of information. Many of these documentaries are available through libraries or online for research purposes.

EVALUATING SOURCES

All information is valuable, but the researcher needs to be able to differentiate between different kinds of information and to use these different kinds for disparate purposes. Facts are vital, but opinions about the interpretation of those facts will always differ. It is the responsibility of the researcher to discover the facts and to come to a comprehensive understanding of the numerous interpretations that are made of them.

Primary and Secondary Sources

One of the most crucial distinctions the researcher must understand is between primary and secondary sources. At the simplest level primary sources are raw information, and secondary sources are studies of that information. For example, a speech made by the president is a primary source. An article written some time later that examines the content and consequences of that speech is a secondary source. Secondary sources refer to primary sources, but primary sources very rarely refer to secondary sources. Typical primary sources include eyewitness accounts, speeches, legal documents, letters, works of art, statistics, surveys, photographs, diaries, and, in some cases, news reports. Typical secondary sources include most books, but particularly academic studies, papers in academic journals, documentaries, and some newspaper or magazine articles. Journalism often sits confusingly in the grey area between primary and secondary sources. On one hand a newspaper article is usually about, or refers to, primary sources, but it may be regarded as a primary source in itself because its publication may be treated as an event or action that is itself commented on in secondary sources such as books or academic papers. A journalistic piece that comments on an event and brings in references to other past events or any other knowledge beyond the immediate circumstances of the event is likely to qualify as a secondary source. By contrast a piece of journalism that simply reports an event and conveys a sense of immediacy should probably be classified as a primary source.

Both primary and secondary sources have their value. Primary sources are the main source of facts. A properly conducted public-opinion survey, for example, is an indisputable reference for the actual beliefs of the people included in that survey. A professionally prepared transcript of a presidential speech or, even better, a video recording of the speech being made is a factual record of precisely what was said. No piece of research can stand up without citing proper references to primary sources. If, for example, a researcher wishes to state in her piece that President Obama said "I've come here . . . to seek a new beginning between the United States and Muslims around the world," she would be wise to look at the primary source to see if he actually did say it. Secondary sources are the main source of opinion. An academic or journalist writing a secondary source presents his own opinions and interpretations of the facts found in primary sources or, more often, a mixture of his own and other people's opinions and interpretations. Academics usually try to justify their interpretations by referring to supporting interpretations made by other respected academics, but this does not make them facts; only the information incontrovertibly contained in primary sources are facts.

Evaluating Primary and Secondary Sources

Primary sources are, by their nature, usually reliable, but a good researcher should never take this for granted. It is possible for primary sources to be faked or to be presented in such a way as to distort reality. Remember, for example, that the text of a speech or a document that has been translated effectively becomes a secondary source since the process of translation inevitably requires a degree of interpretation.

Secondary sources are more troublesome. How is a nonexpert to distinguish between a good interpretation of the facts and a bad one? Several key questions can help in this task. The first step is to ask about the motivation of the writer or creator of the secondary source. Journalists, for example, often rely on developing a reputation for truthfulness and impartiality. Academics, too, usually strive to be accurate and comprehensive if they want to make professional progress. Some authors, however, may be more interested in generating sales by being sensational and, consequently, sacrifice accuracy.

In some cases secondary sources are created to promote or advocate a specific point of view. Find out as much as possible about the author or creator to uncover any strong biases or political affiliations. The second question concerns the scope of the author's arguments. Does the author present and examine a range of arguments or just one? Does the author admit complexities that make his interpretations difficult to support in some cases, or does he make it seem like a black-and-white argument in which he is always in the right? The third step is to look at the citations in the work. For academic books this is a straightforward process, and a researcher can be confident that references will have been checked before publication. If the author references primary sources to back up facts and numerous secondary sources to demonstrate a range of views among other academics, that work should be considered a safe source of useful opinion on the subject. Newspaper and magazine articles are less simple to evaluate because they almost never give formal citations. Often the primary sources for news stories are eyewitness accounts, interviews with individuals involved in the story, or the journalist's own experiences. In this case it is a matter of journalistic integrity as to how accurately these sources are followed.

Balancing Opinions

Balance and comprehensiveness are the hallmarks of good research, and one flows from the other. Comprehensiveness is important to put together an overview of a subject but also to construct a compelling argument for one particular point of view. For a useful overview, gather as many different interpretations as possible and distinguish between those that fit the facts and those that do not. For a truly convincing argument, examine opposing arguments and point out their weaknesses. Both of these objectives benefit from gathering as much good research material as possible and evaluating it effectively. Putting together a collection of 10 secondary sources that support a point of view is useful, but showing why the conclusions of 10 secondary sources that do not support a point of view are wrong is far more compelling.

A SPECIAL NOTE ABOUT PERCEPTIONS OF THE MUSLIM WORLD

Seen through the lens of the Western media the Muslim world can look like a violent and dangerous place. This is not generally the case. The vast majority of Muslims go about their daily lives in peace and security. However, issues in some Muslim-majority states are among the most contentious in the modern world. Issues such as the future of the Palestinian people, U.S. military involvement in parts of the Middle East, and extremist violence and terrorism arouse strong emotions. For the researcher, two things flow from this. First, it is important to remember that these, sometimes violently contested, issues are only a tiny part of the modern Muslim world. A myriad a Muslim world topics can be cited that have nothing to do with these problems. Do not make the mistake of assuming your research into the Muslim world must be about violence and conflict. Second, if the chosen topic does encompass one or more of these controversial issues, take special care to look out for bias in secondary sources and to strive for impartiality. The researcher needs to be acutely aware of the biases of her own culture. She should not dismiss the motivations and arguments of elements of the Muslim world that are opposed to her own culture just because a tiny percentage of their number have committed acts of violence. She does not have to support these points of view, but an effort must be made to examine and understand them by referring to primary sources and a range of responsible and coherent secondary sources. Equally, she should not discount the responses of her own culture to perceived threats as overreactions.

7

Facts and Figures

INTRODUCTION

1.1 Estimated World Oil Reserves by Region, 2009

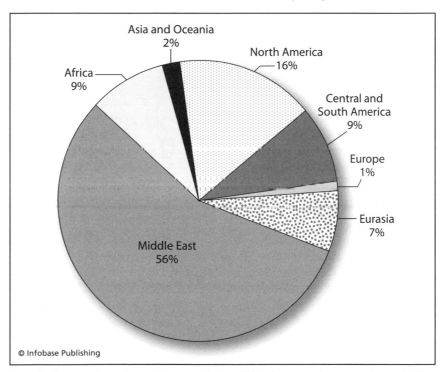

A graph showing the estimated amount of oil available for extraction across the world. The Middle East contains more than half of all known oil reserves.

Source: Based on U.S. Energy Information Administration, *Oil and Gas Journal,* 2009. Available online. URL: http://www.eia.doe.gov/emeu/international/reserves.html. Accessed August 3, 2010.

1.2 Ottoman Empire, 1683–1914

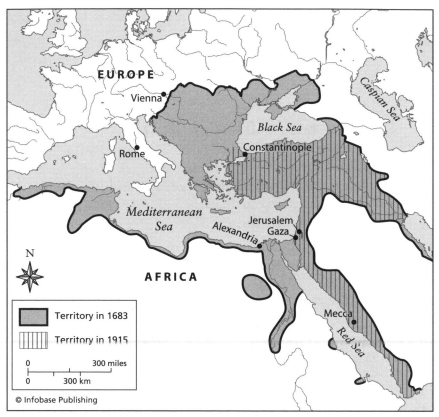

This map shows the extent of the Ottoman Empire between 1683 and the start of World War I in 1914, shortly before the empire's official demise. Throughout its existence, the empire encompassed modern Turkey and spanned most of the Middle East, parts of North Africa, and as far west as the Balkans and eastern Europe.

1.3 Muslim-Majority States

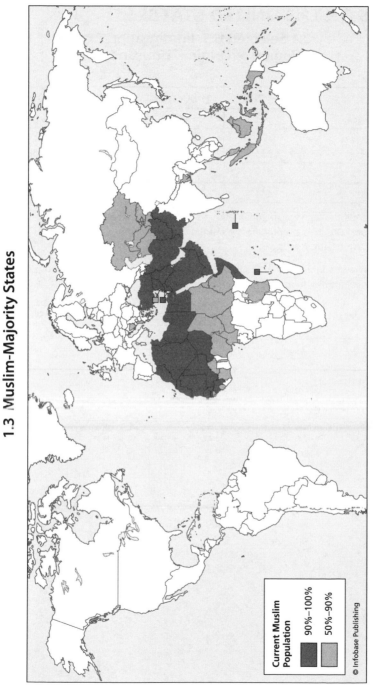

Parts of the world where more than 50 percent of the population is Muslim.

Source: CIA World Factbook.

FOCUS ON THE UNITED STATES
2.1 Selected U.S. Immigration
by Region of Origin (Thousands)

	PRE-1980	1980–89	1990–99	2000–07
Latin America	3,443	4,442	6,467	6,015
East/Southeast Asia	1,233	1,720	1,922	1,682
South Asia	249	388	680	727
Middle East	344	398	324	244

A table showing the increase in immigration to the United States from parts of the world where the population is predominantly Muslim and comparing it to the much greater immigration from Latin American.

Source: "Immigrants in the United States, 2007: A Profile of America's Foreign-Born Population." Center For Immigration Studies, November, 2007.

2.2 Muslim-American Views of U.S. Military Force in Iraq and Afghanistan

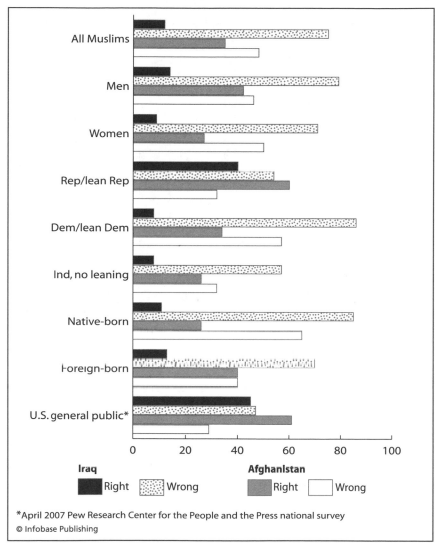

A graph showing the opinion of Muslim Americans when asked if they believed it was wrong or right for the United States to use military force in Iraq and Afghanistan.

Source: "Muslim Americans: Middle Class and Mostly Mainstream." Pew Research Center. May 22, 2007. Available online. URL: http://pewresearch.org/pubs/483/muslim-americans. Accessed April 17, 2010.

2.3 Muslim Opinion of the Influence of the United States

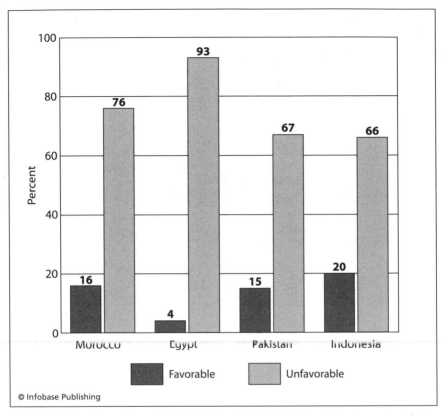

A graph showing the opinions of Muslims in four Muslim-majority states when asked if they believed the influence of the United States on the world was favorable or unfavorable.

Source: "Muslim Public Opinion on U.S. Policy, Attacks on Civilians, and al Qaeda." World-publicopinion.org, a project of the Program on International Policy Attitudes at the University of Maryland. April 24, 2007.

2.4 Muslim Belief That the United States Intends to Weaken Islam

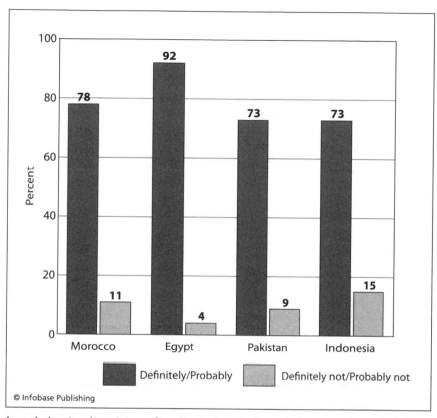

© Infobase Publishing

A graph showing the opinions of Muslims in four Muslim-majority states when asked if they believed it was the intention of the United States to weaken Islam.

Source: "Muslim Public Opinion on U.S. Policy, Attacks on Civilians, and al Qaeda." World-publicopinion.org, a project of the Program on International Policy Attitudes at the University of Maryland. April 24, 2007.

2.5 Muslim Support for Attacks on Civilians

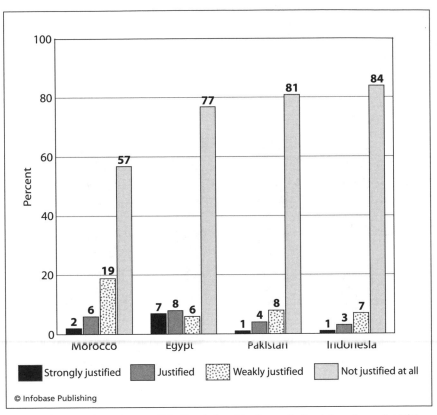

A graph showing the opinions of Muslims in four Muslim-majority states when asked if they believed attacks on civilians were ever justified.

Source: "Muslim Public Opinion on U.S. Policy, Attacks on Civilians, and al Qaeda." Worldpublicopinion.org, a project of the Program on International Policy Attitudes at the University of Maryland. April 24, 2007.

2.6 U.S. Oil Imports v. Domestic Oil Production, 1960–2009

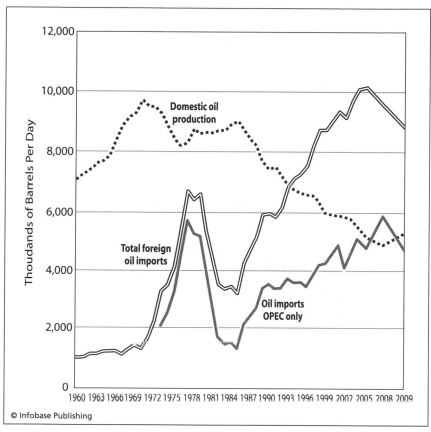

A graph showing U.S. oil production against U.S. oil imports. U.S. oil production has dropped steadily since 1985, and in 1994 the amount of oil imported by the United States exceeded the amount that it produced for the first time.

Source: U.S. Energy Information Administration. Available online. URL: http://www.eia.doe.gov/energyexplained/index.cfm?page=oil_home#tab2. Accessed August 3, 2010.

2.7 Origin of U.S. Oil Imports, 2009

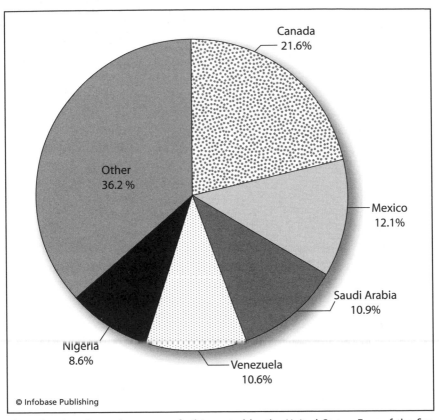

Canada
21.6%

Other
36.2 %

Mexico
12.1%

Saudi Arabia
10.9%

Nigeria
8.6%

Venezuela
10.6%

© Infobase Publishing

Chart showing the main sources of oil imported by the United States. Four of the five greatest sources of U.S. oil imports are non-Arab states. The United States imported 9,013,000 barrels per day in 2009.

Source: U.S. Energy Information Administration. Available online. URL: http://tonto.eia.doe.gov/dnav/pet/pet_move_impcus_a2_nus_epc0_im0_mbblpd_a.htm.

2.8 The Golan Heights, West Bank, and Gaza Strip

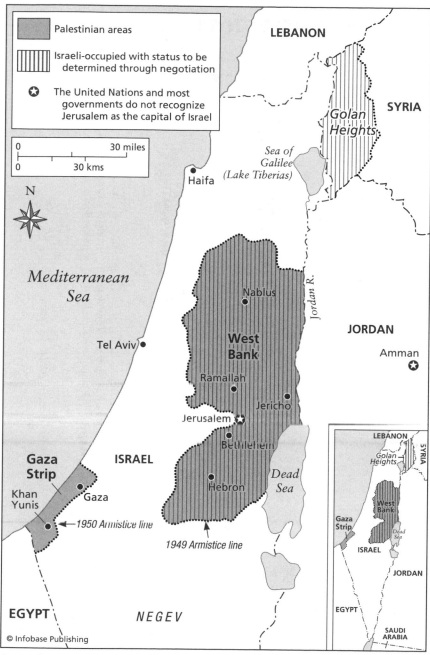

A map showing the Israeli-occupied territories of the Golan Heights and the West Bank, as well as the Gaza Strip. The future of these areas remains one of the most contentious issues in the relationship between Israel and the Muslim world.

GLOBAL PERSPECTIVES

3.1 Religious Distribution of Indonesia's Population

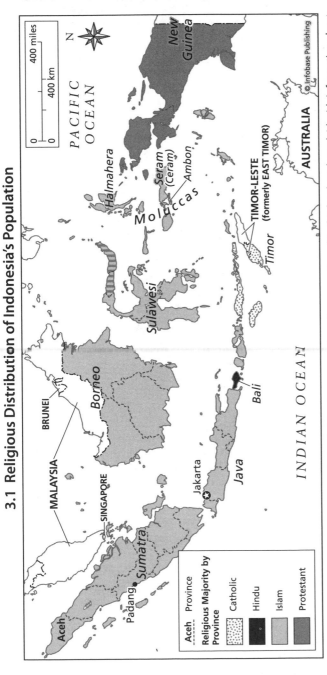

A map of Indonesia showing the principal islands, island groups, and provinces mentioned in this book and overlaid with information about the broad religious affiliations of its inhabitants. Most parts of Indonesia have a Muslim-majority population, but there are significant pockets of Hindus and Christians on certain islands.

Source: Map based on "Indonesia Religious Majority by Province," Encyclopaedia Britannica, Inc.

3.2A Ottoman Empire in Northern Africa, 1830–1881

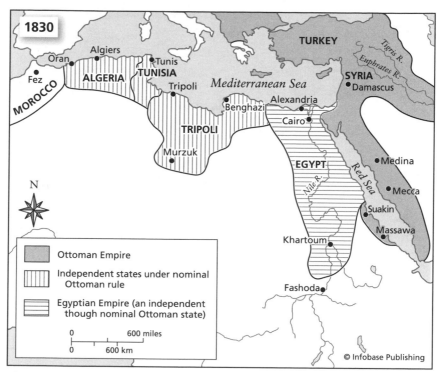

These two maps of North Africa in 1830 and 1881 show the shifting borders of Ottoman influence in the face of increasing French control. France had become a presence in the region during the 1790s, when wheat from the Algerian hinterland supplied France during the Napoleonic Wars. France invaded Algiers in 1830. In 1848 Algeria became part of France, and over the course of the next 30-plus years France expanded its state, invading Tunisia—nominally controlled by the Ottomans—in 1881.

3.2B

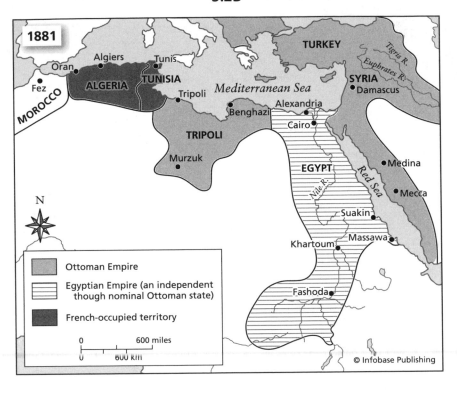

3.3 Value of Property Sales in Dubai in Billions of Arab Emirates Dihram (AED), January 2005–March 2009

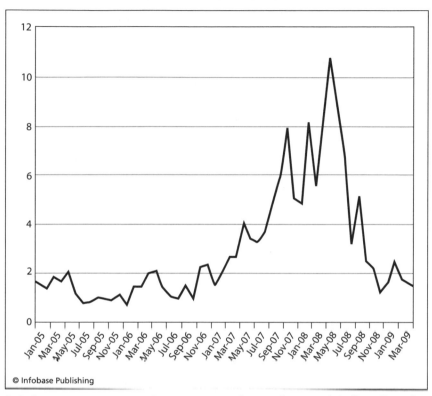

© Infobase Publishing

Dubai's attempts to restructure its economy away from a reliance on dwindling oil supplies focused on the construction of real estate to attract foreign investors. The resulting real estate investment boom collapsed in 2008, leaving companies engaged in ongoing construction projects unable to service their debts.

Source: Arabianbusiness.com. "Green Shoots of Recovery Are Right under Our Noses." Available online. URL: http://www.arabianbusiness.com/blogs/404-green-shoots-of-recovery-are-right-under-our-noses. Accessed February 3, 2010.

3.4 Federally Administered Tribal Areas of Pakistan

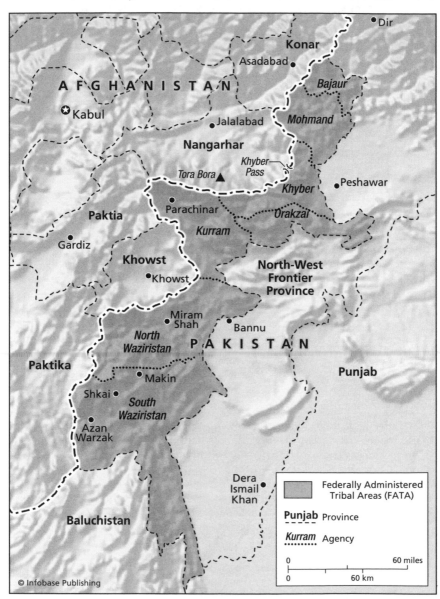

The Federally Administered Tribal Areas (FATA) are a region of Pakistan bordering Afghanistan. Following the 2001 U.S.-led invasion of Afghanistan, many Taliban and al-Qaeda fighters are believed to have found refuge in the FATA, and since 2004 the region has seen escalating conflict between these elements and Pakistani government forces.

Source: CIA World Factbook.

8

Key Players: A to Z

MUHAMMAD IBN ABD AL-WAHHAB (1703–92) Muslim scholar whose teachings led to the development of the so-called Wahhabi branch of Sunni Islam. Born in the Najd region of the Arabian Peninsula (then part of the Ottoman Empire) Abd al-Wahhab became a prominent Muslim scholar allied with Muhammad ibn Saud, the founder of the future ruling dynasty of Saudi Arabia. Abd Al-Wahhab wanted to return Islam to a "pure" state that he believed had existed in the time of Muhammad. His teachings became the policy of the first Saudi state (1744–1818) and the form of Islam followed by almost all modern Saudis. Wahhabi doctrine has been adopted by, or has influenced, many Muslim extremists in the present day.

ABU BAKR (ca. 573–634) father-in-law and close companion of MUHAMMAD, the founder and prophet of Islam. Following Muhammad's death in 632 Abu Bakr became the leader of the Muslim community, establishing the tradition of the caliph. For Sunni Muslims Abu Bakr was the first of the righteously guided caliphs. Shia Muslims, however, regard Abu Bakr as an opportunist who usurped Muhammad's cousin and son-in-law ALI.

MAHMOUD AHMADINEJAD (1956–   ) Iranian politician and president of Iran (2005–   ). Ahmadinejad made a dramatic leap into the political limelight in 2005 when he won the presidency after previously having served as mayor of Tehran. Once in power Ahmadinejad gained a reputation as a fierce and outspoken critic of Israel and the West. Relations between Iran and the West were severely strained during his presidency over the issue of Iran's nuclear power program.

ALI IBN ABI TALIB (ca. 600–661) cousin, son-in-law, and close companion of MUHAMMAD, the founder and prophet of Islam. He ruled much of the Muslim world as caliph (656–661), but his succession to this position split the Muslim community into Sunni and Shia branches. Sunni Muslims regard Ali as the fourth and last of the righteously guided caliphs. Shia Mus-

293

lims regard him as the first imam (leader of the Muslim community) and the first of the rightful successors to Muhammad. Shia Muslims believe that Muhammad designated Ali as his successor and that ABU BAKR, the first caliph, was a usurper.

YASSER ARAFAT (1929–2004)   Palestinian politician. A leading figure in the Palestinian movement for self-determination Arafat led the Palestine Liberation Organization (PLO) and the Fatah political party. Many Palestinians regarded him as a national hero, but in the West he was often described as a terrorist. Later in his career he changed his lifelong opposition to the existence of Israel and represented the Palestinian people in a series of negotiations with Israel aimed at achieving a peaceful resolution. Arafat served as the first president of the Palestinian National Authority (1996–2004); an administrative organization created in the 1993 Oslo Accords to govern part of the Palestinian territories.

KEMAL MUSTAFA ATATÜRK (1881–1938)   Turkish independence leader and first president of the Republic of Turkey (1923–38). Serving as an army officer in the last years of the Ottoman Empire Atatürk became involved in the movement to modernize and reform the empire. Following the collapse of the Ottoman Empire at the end of World War I Atatürk led Turkish nationalist forces in their successful campaign to eject Allied and Greek forces from Anatolia. He became the first president of independent Turkey on its foundation in 1923. As president Atatürk undertook a radical and far-reaching program of social, political, and economic reforms that transformed Turkey into a secular democratic state.

AHMED HASAN AL-BAKR (1914–82)   president of Iraq (1968–79). He organized the 1963 coup that briefly brought the Baath Party to power in Iraq and also led the 1968 coup that returned the party to power and elevated him to the presidency. In power he pursued a pan-Arabist foreign policy and opposed Israel. His vice president, SADDAM HUSSEIN, became president when al-Bakr retired.

ARTHUR BALFOUR (1848–1930)   British politician and statesmen. Balfour served as prime minister of the United Kingdom (1902–05) and later as foreign secretary (1916–19) during World War I. In the context of the Muslim world Balfour is best known for the Balfour Declaration of 1917—a letter to a prominent British Zionist in which he expressed the British government's support for the establishment of a Jewish homeland in Palestine. The Balfour Declaration was later incorporated into the postwar peace treaty with Turkey and the League of Nations's Mandate for Palestine, which gave Britain control over the former Ottoman Empire territory.

Key Players: A to Z

HASAN AL-BANNA (1906–49)   Egyptian Islamic and social reformer and founder of the Muslim Brotherhood. Concerned about what he saw as the erosion of Muslim traditions by Western influences, al-Banna became convinced that a return to a "pure" form of Islam was the only hope for Muslim civilization. He founded the Society of the Muslim Brothers (also known as the Muslim Brotherhood) in 1928, and under his leadership it grew into a mass organization opposed to British and other foreign influence in Egypt and the wider Muslim world. After his assassination in 1949 the Muslim Brotherhood went on to become one of the world's largest Muslim political groups with branches in most Muslim states.

ABU BAKAR BASHIR (1938–   )   Indonesian Muslim cleric and religious leader. During the presidency of SUHARTO, Bashir spent 17 years exiled in Malaysia to avoid arrest for political activities, including advocating the establishment of sharia law in Indonesia. Returning to Indonesia in 1999 Bashir once again became involved in politics, calling for a strengthening of Muslim traditions. The United Nations and several Western governments regard Bashir as the spiritual leader of Jemaah Islamiyah, a militant Islamic organization thought to be responsible for the 2002 Bali bombings and numerous other terrorist attacks in Indonesia and across Southeast Asia.

ALI BELHAJ (1956–   )   Muslim cleric and vice president of the Islamic Salvation Front in Algeria (FIS). Ali Belhaj founded the FIS, an Islamist party, along with Abbas Madani when opposition political parties became legal in Algeria in 1989. The FIS advocated the establishment of an Islamic state in the country and gained mass popular support before being banned in 1991. Ali Belhaj was arrested and remained imprisoned during the Algerian civil war (1991 2002).

ABD AL-HAMID BEN BADIS (1889–1940)   Algerian political and religious thinker who had a strong influence on the Algerian nationalist and Muslim revivalist movements in the period between World War I and World War II. His father and grandfather held prominent positions in the French colonial administration, and one of his brothers was educated in France, but Ben Badis had a traditional religious education in Algeria and completed his studies at the Zeitouna Mosque in Tunis. He then made a pilgrimage to Mecca and spent time in various cities in the Middle East, where he became interested in the Islamic reform movement, a school of religious thought that wanted to return to what they saw as a purer form of Islam. Ben Badis returned to Algeria in 1913. Through his work as a journalist and teacher he strove to bring the central teachings of Islam to ordinary Algerians and also argued strongly against the influence of French secular culture. Ben Badis was a well-known figure in the interwar period and remains a national hero and an inspiration to Islamic reformers in Algeria.

AHMED BEN BELLA (1918–   )   a leader of Algeria's struggle for independence from France and the first president of independent Algeria (1963–65).
Ben Bella served in the French army before and during World War II. After
the war he became involved in anticolonial activities, eventually becoming
a leading figure in the National Liberation Front (FLN). Arrested in 1951
he escaped from prison and fled to Egypt, where he continued to organise
FLN activities. During the war for Algerian independence (1954–62) Ben
Bella was captured and imprisoned in France. Released in 1962 he returned
to Algeria and was elected as its first president. His increasingly autocratic
rule alienated FLN colleagues, and he was deposed in 1965 by HOUARI BOU-
MEDIENNE. He lived under house arrest in Algeria until 1980 and was then
exiled to Switzerland. Ben Bella returned to Algeria in 1990 and later became
a leading Arab voice against the U.S. invasion of Iraq.

CHADLI BENDJEDID (1929–   )   president of Algeria (1979–92). A
member of the National Liberation Front during the Algerian war of independence (1954–62) he rose through the ranks of the party in the post-
independence period and won the presidency as something of a compromise
candidate during a period of infighting. As president he eased the political
repression that had been practiced by his predecessors and, in the face of
growing public unrest, allowed the formation of opposition parties for the
first time. Bendjedid was forced out of office when the Algerian military
stepped in to prevent elections that looked likely to bring the radical Islamic
Salvation Front to power in 1991.

OSAMA BIN LADEN (1957–   )   reputed founder and leader of the Muslim
terrorist group al-Qaeda. Born Osama bin Mohammed bin Awad bin Laden to
a wealthy Saudi Arabian family he traveled to Afghanistan in 1979 to help the
mujahideen fight the Soviet invasion and occupation. Bin Laden helped raise
funds and recruit fighters for the mujahideen across the Arab-Muslim world.
By the late 1980s he is reputed to have created the al-Qaeda organization that
would later become notorious for terrorist attacks against the United States and
other Western nations. Based in Sudan in the mid-1990s Bin Laden is believed
to have been involved in planning attacks in Egypt, Algeria, and Yemen.
Returning to the safe haven of Taliban-ruled Afghanistan in the late 1990s he
organized the 1998 bombings of U.S. embassies in Kenya and Tanzania and the
September 11, 2001, attacks on the United States. Bin Laden is believed to have
escaped into Pakistan during the 2001 U.S.-led invasion of Afghanistan.

HOUARI BOUMEDIENNE (1932–78)   Algerian politician and president
of Algeria (1965–78). Born Mohamed Ben Brahim Boukharouba he adopted
the name Houari Boumedienne while fighting for the National Liberation
Front (FLN) in the war for Algerian independence from France. He served

as defense minister under Algeria's first president AHMED BEN BELLA but became disillusioned with Ben Bella's increasingly autocratic rule and headed a military coup that deposed him in 1965. Boumedienne maintained a firm grip on power by ruthlessly undermining potential opponents. The lack of qualified successors led to a period of political chaos in Algeria after Boumedienne's death that resulted in the establishment of a military government.

ZBIGNIEW BRZEZINSKI (1928–) U.S. politician and National Security Advisor to president JIMMY CARTER (1977–81). Known as an uncompromising realist in foreign policy Brzezinski's term in office coincided with the Camp David Accords that resulted in a peace agreement between Israel and Egypt, the Iranian hostage crisis and the breakdown in relations between Iran and the United States, and early efforts to aid Afghan mujahideen against Soviet forces.

GEORGE H. W. BUSH (1924–) 41st president of the United States (1989–93), vice president (1981–89) under RONALD REAGAN, and father of 43rd U.S. president GEORGE W. BUSH. George H. W. Bush served as a pilot in the U.S. Navy during World War II, graduated from Yale University, and made his fortune in the oil business. His political career brought him many posts in government, including the directorship of the CIA in 1976. After serving as Ronald Reagan's vice president Bush won the presidency on a conservative agenda. During his one term in office Bush authorized the use of U.S. forces to liberate Kuwait from Iraqi occupation during the Persian Gulf War. After the war Bush pursued an Arab-Israeli peace process that resulted in the ground breaking Madrid Conference of 1991.

GEORGE W. BUSH (1946–) 43rd president of the United States (2001–09). The eldest son of the 41st U.S. president, GEORGE H. W. BUSH, George W. Bush graduated from Yale University and Harvard Business School before working for his father's oil company. He was elected governor of Texas in 1995 and held the office until 2000. The September 11, 2001, attacks on the United States occurred just eight months into Bush's first term as president. His response was to declare a war on terror that included the invasion of Afghanistan in 2001 and of Iraq in 2003. His strong military response to the attacks was initially popular, but the insurgency that followed the invasion and occupation of Iraq severely damaged his popularity among some Americans. Bush's second term in office was dominated by U.S. accusations that Iran was developing nuclear weapons, further straining the poor relations between the two countries. In collaboration with the European Union, Russia, and the United Nations Bush engaged in the Palestinian-Israeli peace process by contributing to the "road map for peace" plan, which called for the establishment of a Palestinian state and led to the election of the first Palestinian prime minister in 2003.

JIMMY CARTER (1924–) 39th president of the United States (1977–81). After serving in the U.S. Navy Carter ran his family's farm in Georgia and began his political career in the 1960s in the Georgia state senate. He became governor of Georgia in 1971 and held the office until 1975. As president Carter faced a number of challenges in relations between the United States and the Muslim world. In 1978 Carter sponsored negotiations between Israel and Egypt that led to the groundbreaking Camp David Accords and a peace treaty between the two countries in 1979. The Iran hostage crisis, in which Iranian militants held 52 U.S. citizens hostage following the Iranian revolution of 1979, was a major turning point in U.S.-Iranian relations, and Carter's failure to resolve the crisis greatly damaged his reputation. At the same time Carter's administration began the policy of sending money and arms to anti-communist mujahideen rebels in Afghanistan.

BILL CLINTON (1946–) 42nd president of the United States (1993–2001). A graduate of Yale Law School Clinton started his political career at the age of 32 when he became governor of Arkansas, an office he held until 1992 with an interruption from 1981–83. As president Clinton was heavily involved in attempts to achieve a peace settlement between Arabs and Israelis. In 1993 Clinton was instrumental in the signing of the Oslo Accords between Israeli prime minister Yitzhak Rabin and Palestine Liberation Organization chairman Yasser Arafat. In 1994 he was involved in the negotiations that led to a peace settlement between Jordan and Israel. Clinton's policy toward Iraq was dominated by accusations that Iraq was attempting to build weapons of mass destruction and misleading United Nations weapons inspectors. He authorized a four-day intensive bombing campaign against Iraqi military targets in 1998.

KING FAHD (1921–2005) king of the Kingdom of Saudi Arabia (1982–2005). King Fahd (full name: Fahd bin Abdul Aziz al-Saud) ruled Saudi Arabia during one of the most difficult periods in its history. As head of state he agreed to the deployment of U.S. and other foreign troops in Saudi Arabia during the buildup to the Persian Gulf War in 1991 and the U.S.-led invasion of Iraq in 2003, decisions that caused resentment among many in the Muslim world. After suffering a stroke in 1995 King Fahd delegated much of the business of ruling the kingdom to Crown Prince Abdullah, who later became king.

KING FAISAL (1904–75) king of the Kingdom of Saudi Arabia (1964–75). King Faisal (full name: Faisal ibn Abdul Aziz al-Saud) ruled Saudi Arabia for much of the cold war period and was a key ally of the United States in the Middle East. Rejecting any association with the Soviet bloc because he believed communism was incompatible with Islam King Faisal built on the strong economic and military ties that had begun in the 1950s. His relations with the United States were sometimes strained because of his firm opposition to Israel.

RASHID ALI AL-GAILANI (1892–1965)   Iraqi politician and three-time prime minister (1933, 1940–41, 1941). A committed Arab nationalist Rashid Ali al-Gailani sought to reverse British influence over Iraq during his short terms in office. During World War II he attempted to form an alliance with the Axis powers, prompting a British invasion and occupation of Iraq. Rashid Ali al-Gailani fled to Germany and created an Iraqi government in exile.

HUSAYN IBN ALI (628–680)   son of ALI IBN ABI TALIB and an important figure in the history of Shia Islam. Ali refused to accept the authority of the Umayyad Caliphate and was subsequently killed at the Battle of Karbala, in present-day Iraq. Regarded as a martyr by Shia Muslims, Husayn's death is celebrated every year.

SADDAM HUSSEIN (1937–2006)   president of Iraq (1979–2003). As a member of the secular, socialist, and pan-Arabist Baath Party Saddam Hussein played a prominent role in the 1968 coup that brought the party to power in Iraq. As vice president under Ahmed Hasan al-Bakr, Hussein created a formidable internal security force and spearheaded the nationalization of Iraq's foreign-owned oil industry. As president Hussein committed Iraq to a series of disastrous wars and violently oppressed all opposition to his regime. During the Iran-Iraq War (1980–88) Hussein was supported by the United States, but his 1990 invasion and occupation of Kuwait was met by a large U.S.-led military response that liberated the country in 1991 and devastated Iraq's armed forces. Hussein's contravention of the cease-fire agreements signed at the end of the Persian Gulf War during the 1990s led ultimately to the 2003 U.S.-led invasion of Iraq that removed him from power.

IBN SAUD (ABDUL AZIZ AL-SAUD) (1876–1953)   founder and first ruler of the Kingdom of Saudi Arabia (1932–53). Between 1913 and 1926 Abdul Aziz al-Saud led the al-Saud clan in a series of wars that brought the group control over most of the Arabian Peninsula. Britain recognized Ibn Saud as the ruler of the Kingdom of Hejaz and Nejd in 1927, and the name of the kingdom was changed to Saudi Arabia in 1932. The kingdom's vast oil wealth was discovered and began to be exploited during Ibn Saud's reign.

JAFAR UMAR THALIB (ca. 1963)   Indonesian cleric and head of the Islamist anti-Christian militia Laskar Jihad. Born in Indonesia to parents of Yemeni descent Jafar Umar Thalib claims to have fought in Afghanistan against Soviet occupation in the 1980s and ran a chain of Koranic boarding schools in Indonesia in the 1990s. He created Laskar Jihad in 1999 or 2000 and used its fighters to promote anti-Christian violence on the Indonesian island of Ambon and later in other parts of the country. A proponent of founding an Islamic state in the country Jafar Umar Thalib was arrested in 2001 for allegedly organizing an illegal sharia court that sentenced a rapist to death by stoning, but he was not prosecuted. Laskar Jihad was disbanded following the 2002 Bali bombings and Jafar Umar Thalib was later controversially cleared of inciting religious violence.

AYATOLLAH ALI KHAMENEI (1939–)   Iranian Muslim cleric and politician. One of the most influential figures in Iranian politics since the establishment of the Islamic Republic in 1979 Ayatollah Ali Khamenei served as president of Iran (1981–89) and became the supreme leader of Iran in 1989. Ali Khamenei was a close ally of Ayatollah Khomeini during the Islamic revolution and was the first cleric to hold the presidency. Shortly after his election he narrowly escaped an assassination attempt that left his right arm disabled. He became Iran's second supreme leader following the death of Ayatollah Khomeini in 1989. Regarded as a conservative defender of the Islamic revolution he has strongly opposed attempts to introduce democratic reforms.

RUHOLLAH MUSAVI KHOMEINI (1902–89)   Iranian political and religious leader and Supreme Leader of the Islamic Republic of Iran (1979–89). After decades in exile Khomeini returned to Iran at the height of the 1979 Iranian revolution that overthrew the shah, MOHAMMAD REZA PAHLAVI, and engineered the establishment of an Islamic republic with himself as head of state. Best known in the West as Ayatollah Khomeini he was the absolute ruler of Iran for a decade during which relations between Iran and the United States plummeted.

ABBAS MADANI (1931–)   Algerian political leader and president of the Islamic Salvation Front. As a young man Madani joined the National Liberation Front (FLN) and took part in the opening stages of the Algerian War of Independence. He was captured by the French within days and spent the rest of the war in prison. After his release in 1962 Madani studied educational psychology and became a professor of education sciences at the University of Algiers. In 1989, following a change in the Algerian constitution allowing the formation of new political parties, Madani cofounded the Islamic Salvation Front (FIS) with Ali Belhadj. The FIS rapidly gained mass support on a platform promising the establishment of an Islamic state ruled by sharia and radical reform of Algeria's economy. Madani was arrested in 1991 for his role in organizing massive demonstrations against the government, and the FIS was banned. He remained under arrest throughout the Algerian civil war, finally being released in 2003.

MOHAMMED BIN RASHID AL-MAKTOUM (1947–) emir (ruler) of Dubai (2006–) and prime minister of the United Arab Emirates (2006–). Appointed crown prince and de facto ruler of Dubai in 1995 by his father the emir MAKTOUM BIN RASHID AL-MAKTOUM he was the driving force between the radical program of economic restructuring that transformed Dubai in the first decade of the 21st century.

RASHID BIN SAEED AL-MAKTOUM (1912–90) emir (ruler) of Dubai (1979–90) and prime minister and vice president of the United Arab Emirates (1979–90). During his reign Dubai was transformed from a poor, largely rural kingdom into a wealthy industrialized state thanks to oil revenues. Rashid bin Saeed al-Maktoum was credited with using Dubai's sudden influx of wealth to greatly improve the living standards of its citizens. His son MOHAMMED BIN RASHID AL-MAKTOUM became emir after his death.

MEGAWATI SUKARNOPUTRI (1947–) the second president of Indonesia (2001–04) following the dictatorial SUHARTO era. The daughter of Indonesia's first president, SUKARNO, Megawati was the country's first female head of state. She was elected by Indonesia's parliament following the removal of ABDURRAHMAN WAHID from power and failed to achieve a second term in the general election of 2004. She was criticized for being too passive in office and did little to push forward the democratic and legal reforms begun under Wahid.

MOHAMED EL-MOKRANI (1815–1871) Algerian freedom fighter and tribal leader. In 1871 he led a revolt against the extension of direct French rule over rural parts of Algeria. After winning several battles against the French el-Mokrani was killed while fighting, and the revolt was crushed in 1872.

MOHAMMED MOSSADEQ (1882–1967) Iranian politician and prime minister of Iran (1951–53). Educated in France and Switzerland Mossadeq began his political career during the Iranian constitutional revolution (1905–11), a period of political upheaval that led to the establishment of the first Iranian parliament. As prime minister Mossadeq pushed through the nationalization of Iran's oil industry, taking it out of the hands of British oil companies. A long time opponent of the Pahlavi dynasty, and the shah, MOHAMMAD REZA PAHLAVI, Mossadeq attempted to wrest powers away from the monarchy leading to a constitutional crisis. The United States and Britain conspired with conservative elements in Iran to organize a coup that removed Mossadeq from power in 1953.

MOHAMMAD REZA PAHLAVI (1919–1980) shah (ruler) of Iran (1941–79). The second and last monarch of the Iranian Pahlavi dynasty, Mohammad Reza Pahlavi ruled Iran for almost four decades before being deposed in the 1979 Islamic revolution that brought RUHOLLAH MUSAVI KHOMEINI to power. Mohammad Reza Pahlavi was a vital strategic ally of the United States during the cold war period, and successive U.S. administrations supported his regime even when it became extremely unpopular in Iran. In the first decades of his reign Mohammad Reza Pahlavi pursued ambitious modernization plans, but his rule became increasingly corrupt and oppressive later on.

MUHAMMAD (570-632) the founder and prophet of Islam. Both a prophet and a statesman, Muhammad delivered the Quran's message to the people of Mecca and Medina. Believed to be a descendant of Abraham and Ishmael, two major figures in the Hebrew Bible, Muhammad created a religious community that would grow into a great civilization after his death. Muhammad's own words and deeds (the Hadith) are known to Muslims everywhere, and Muslims follow his example in their spiritual and worldly affairs. Known by many names, including "God's Messenger" (Rasul Allah) and "Beloved" (al-Habib), he is also recognized in the Quran as the Seal of the Prophets (*khatam al-nabiyyin*), which, according to Islamic belief, means that he is the last one to bring God's word to humankind.

ELIJAH MUHAMMAD (1897–1975) leader of the controversial American religious organization the Nation of Islam. Born Elijah Poole, the son of poor African-American sharecroppers in Georgia, Muhammad witnessed racial lynchings in his childhood and converted to Islam in 1931 after hearing a speech by WALLACE FARD MUHAMMAD in Detroit. Elijah Muhammad joined Fard's Nation of Islam, a politico-religious organization drawing on elements of Islam and black nationalism, and he became its leader from 1935 until his death in 1975. Under Elijah Muhammad's leadership the Nation of Islam attracted criticism from Muslim groups for claiming that Wallace Fard Muhammad had been a prophet and from many other quarters for advocating black separatism in the United States.

BARACK OBAMA (1961–) 44th president of the United States (2009–) and the first African American to hold that office. Graduating from Columbia University and Harvard Law School Obama worked as a civil rights attorney in Chicago and taught constitutional law at the University of Chicago Law School until being elected to the U.S. Senate from Illinois in 2004. As President Obama has concentrated on relations between the United States and the Muslim world in his foreign policy. He announced the closure of the controversial Guantánamo Bay detention camp and proposed to withdraw all U.S. combat troops from Iraq by mid-2010, but he has also committed the United States to the deployment of extra forces in Afghanistan. Obama was awarded the 2009 Nobel Peace Prize for his commitment to nuclear nonproliferation and his efforts to improve U.S. relations with the Muslim world.

COLIN POWELL (1937–) U.S. soldier and secretary of state (2001–04) under president GEORGE W. BUSH. Powell served in the U.S. army for 35 years, eventually rising to the rank of general in 1989. He served as President Ronald Reagan's National Security Advisor and as chairman of the Joint Chiefs of Staff (1989–93), the most senior military position in the United States, during the presidency of GEORGE H. W. BUSH, a period that included the Persian Gulf War. Powell's term as secretary of state coincided with the September 11, 2001, attacks on the United States and the subsequent U.S.-led invasions of Afghanistan and Iraq.

ABDUL KARIM QASSIM (1914–63) Iraqi soldier and prime minister of Iraq (1958–63). As a member of the Free Officers movement, a pan-Arabist group opposed to foreign influence in the Arab world, Qassim was a prominent figure in the 1958 revolution that overthrew Iraq's British-backed monarchy. He ruled the country as prime minister until deposed by a Baath Party coup in 1963.

SAYYID QUTB (1906–66) Egyptian author and Islamist. During the 1950s and 1960s Qutb was the leading intellectual voice of the Muslim Brotherhood. He disapproved of the influence of Western values and practices on Egyptian society and believed that Islam should play a central role in the political and social life of Muslim-majority nations. He was arrested in 1965, convicted of plotting to overthrow the Egyptian government, and executed in 1966. His writings remain highly influential among some Muslim groups.

RONALD REAGAN (1911–2004) 40th president of the United States (1981–89). A former film and television actor from Illinois Reagan began his political career in the 1960s and held the office of governor of California from 1967 to 1975. The 1980 presidential election that brought Reagan to power coincided with the Iranian hostage crisis that severely damaged the reputation of the incumbent JIMMY CARTER. The central concern of Reagan's foreign policy was the defeat of the Soviet Union and the containment of communism around the world. This program include the provision of money and sophisticated weapons to the anticommunist mujahideen opposing the Soviet invasion of Afghanistan. The Iranian hostage crisis was resolved within days of Reagan taking office, but relations between Iran and the United States remained poor because the Unitd States aided Iraq during the Iran-Iraq War (1980–88).

REZA SHAH PAHLAVI (1878–1944) shah (ruler) of Iran (1925–41) and founder of the Pahlavi dynasty. Growing up in a period of political turmoil in

Iran Reza Pahlavi came from humble beginnings to establish the last dynasty of Iranian monarchs. Many Iranians regard him as the father of modern Iran because of his ambitious efforts to modernize and industrialize the country. He was forced to abdicate during the Anglo-Soviet invasion of Iran (1941) in favor of his son MOHAMMAD REZA PAHLAVI.

DONALD RUMSFELD (1932–) U.S. politician and twice holder of the office of secretary of defense (1975–77 and 2001–06). After serving in the U.S. Navy as a pilot he entered politics and became secretary of defense under president Gerald Ford. After a long and successful business career he again became secretary of defense under president GEORGE W. BUSH a few months before the September 11, 2001, attacks on the United States. As secretary of defense he was intimately involved in the planning and execution of the U.S. invasions of Afghanistan (2001) and Iraq (2003). The insurgency that followed the invasion of Iraq led many to blame Rumsfeld for failing to plan for the post-invasion period.

SUHARTO (1921–2008) president of Indonesia (1967–98). After fighting in Indonesia's independence struggle against the Netherlands Suharto rose through the ranks of the army in the post-independence period. A loyal supporter of independent Indonesia's first president, SUKARNO, he was elected president himself after Sukarno's political downfall. Suharto built a highly centralized, military-dominated regime that assured stability but at the cost of political freedom and growing corruption. Growing popular dissent during the 1990s resulted in Suharto's 1998 resignation.

SUKARNO (1901–70) president of Indonesia (1945–67). A prominent figure in Indonesia's early independence movement Sukarno founded the Indonesian National Party in 1927 while the country was still under Dutch rule. During World War II he organized assistance to support the invading Japanese forces against the Dutch, seeing the war as an opportunity to achieve independence. Following the Japanese surrender Sukarno unilaterally declared Indonesian independence and was appointed as the nation's first president. In power Sukarno became increasingly dictatorial. He believed that full democracy was unsuitable for Indonesia and advocated a system known as "guided democracy" based on a mix of Indonesian traditions.

HARRY S. TRUMAN (1884–1972) 33rd president of the United States (1945–53) and vice president (1945) under Franklin D. Roosevelt. Becoming president on the death of Franklin D. Roosevelt just a few months into his term as vice president Truman faced the enormous difficulty of taking over the administration of the country in the closing months of World War II. His most significant actions in relation to the Muslim world were his recognition of the new state of Pakistan in 1947 and his strong support for the establishment of Israel in 1948.

ABDURRAHMAN WAHID (1940–) president of Indonesia (1999–2001). Wahid was Indonesia's first democratically elected president after the fall of the dictatorial SUHARTO regime. In office he began a series of reforms that opened Indonesian society to democracy, but his time in power was blighted by serious religious violence and economic woes.

CASPAR WEINBERGER (1917–2006) U.S. politician and secretary of defense under President RONALD REAGAN (1981–87). Weinberger served in the U.S. Army during World War II and worked in a law firm after the war. As secretary of defense he implemented Ronald Reagan's policy of massive investment in the U.S. armed forces to counter the perceived threat from the Soviet Union. He was implicated in the Iran-contra affair, which involved the sale by the administration of arms to Iran in contravention of a U.S. trade embargo with the country, and using the profits to fund anticommunist rebels in Nicaragua. He resigned over his involvement. During his term in office the United States was also involved in supplying aid to Saddam Hussein in his war against Iran and arms and weapons to the mujahideen fighting Soviet forces in Afghanistan.

SUSILO BAMBANG YUDHOYONO (1949–) president of Indonesia (2004–). Serving with great distinction in the Indonesian army during the rule of dictatorial president SUHARTO, Yudhoyono seemed an unlikely choice for president in the period of democratic freedom that followed his fall from power. A reputation for honorable conduct, even at the cost of his own career, and the role he played in reducing the influence of the military in national politics, however, made Yudhoyono a popular choice following the chaotic and corrupt administrations of ABDURRAHMAN WAHID and MEGAWATI SUKARNOPUTRI.

ABU MUSAB AL-ZARQAWI (1966–2006) Jordanian-born militant Islamist who became notorious during the Iraq War for his involvement in a series of bombing and shootings and the execution of Western hostages. Al-Zarqawi met OSAMA BIN LADEN in Afghanistan and spent five years in a Jordanian jail in the 1990s for conspiring to overthrow the monarchy. In the late 1990s al-Zarqawi set up a militant training camp in Afghanistan and was involved in planning attacks in Jordan. Following the 2003 U.S. invasion of Iraq al-Zarqawi became a prominent figure in the insurgency against U.S. occupation. In 2004 he was identified by U.S. security forces as the person shown killing U.S. civilian hostage Nicholas Berg in a propaganda video. Al-Zarqawi was killed in a U.S. airstrike in Iraq.

9

Organizations and Agencies

There are tens of thousands of Muslim organizations around the world. It is possible to present only a tiny fraction of them here. This list includes the largest and most influential as well as a representative selection of smaller, more specialized organizations. The Web sites of many of the larger agencies themselves have lists of smaller, local organizations.

ORGANIZATIONS AND AGENCIES BASED WITHIN NORTH AMERICA

American-Arab Anti-Discrimination Committee
httpı//www.adc.org/
1732 Wisconsin Avenue NW
Washington, DC 20007
Phone: (202) 244-2990

An organization dedicated to "defending the civil rights of all people of Arab heritage in the United States." Founded in 1980 the organization has chapters across the United States.

American Islamic Congress
http://www.aicongress.org/
1718 M Street NW, #243
Washington, DC 20036
Phone: (202) 457-5892

A civil rights organization promoting tolerance and the exchange of ideas between Muslims and non-Muslims.

American Moslem Foundation
http://www.oz.net/~msarram/
15004 SE 256th Street

Covington, WA 98042
Phone: (253) 638-9989

A charity organization bringing together American Muslims in Washington State and the Pacific Northwest in general.

American Muslim Alliance
http://www.amaweb.org/
Suite 220 E
39675 Cedar Blvd.
Newark, CA 94560
Phone: (510) 252-9858

An organization committed to improving the participation of Muslim Americans in the democratic process at all levels and increasing the number of Muslim Americans elected to public office.

American Muslim Association of North America
http://al-amana.net/
183 NE 166 Street
North Miami Beach, FL 33162
Phone: (305) 898-9314

News, contacts, civil rights, and educational links from an organization with branches across the United States.

American Task Force on Palestine
http://www.americantaskforce.org/
1634 Eye St. NW, Suite 725
Washington, DC 20006
Phone: (202) 887-0177

An organization dedicated to advocating an "end to the conflict in the Middle East through a negotiated agreement that provides for two states—Israel and Palestine—living side by side in peace and security."

Amila (American Muslims Intent on Learning and Activism)
http://www.amila.org/
PO Box 420 614
San Francisco, CA 94142
An organization bringing together American Muslims from many different branches of Islam and from many different ethnicities and national origins.

Association of Muslim Social Scientists of North America
http://208.106.208.252/
PO Box 5502
Herndon, VA 20172
A forum for the discussion and promotion of Islamic positions on academic disciplines, particularly in the humanities and social sciences.

Al-Awda, The Palestine Right to Return Coalition
http://al-awda.org/
PO Box 131352
Carlsbad, CA 92013
Phone: (760) 918-9441
Fax: (760) 918-9442
E-mail: info@al-awda.org

A U.S.-based organization dedicated to raising public awareness about the issue of the Palestinian Right to Return.

Canadian Council of Muslim Theologians
http://ccmt.jucanada.org/
1562 Danforth Avenue
PO Box 72031
Toronto, Ontario M4J 1P0
Canada
Phone: (416) 731-2247

An organization to support and inform the Muslim community of Canada.

Center for the Study of Islam and Democracy
https://www.csidonline.org/
1625 Massachusetts Avenue NW, Suite 601
Washington, DC 20036
Phone: (202) 265-1200

Founded by a group of Muslim and non-Muslim U.S. academics, professionals, and activists the CSID is dedicated to the study of the interaction between Islamic ideas and democratic political thought.

Council on American-Islamic Relations
http://www.cair.com/
453 New Jersey Avenue SE
Washington, DC 20003
Phone: (202) 488-8787

One of the largest Muslim organizations in the United States. Founded in 1994 it has offices across North America and says its mission is to: "enhance understanding of Islam, encourage dialogue, protect civil liberties, empower American Muslims, and build coalitions that promote justice and mutual understanding."

Council on Islamic Education
http://www.cie.org/
10055 Slater Avenue
Suite 250
Fountain Valley, CA 92708
Phone: (714) 839-2929

An organization concentrating on the role of Islam in the U.S. education system that includes an extensive research arm and a strong media platform.

Foundation for Democracy in Iran
http://www.iran.org/
11140 Rockville Pike, Suite 100
Rockville, MD 20852
Phone: (301) 946-2918

Founded with grants from the U.S.-based National Endowment for Democracy the Foundation for Democracy in Iran is dedicated to promoting "democracy and internationally-recognized standards of human rights in Iran."

Foundation for Islamic Education
http://www.fiesite.org/

1860 Montgomery Avenue
Villanova, PA 19085
Phone: (610) 520-9624

A Muslim education and community support organization based in the Philadelphia region.

Free Muslims Coalition
http://www.freemuslims.org/
1050 17th Street NW, Suite 1000
Washington, DC 20036
Phone: (202) 776-7190

An association of American Muslims dedicated to rejecting the use of violence and terrorism in the worldwide Muslim community.

International Association of Sufism
http://www.ias.org/
14 Commercial Boulevard, Suite 101
Novato, CA 94949
Phone: (415) 382-7834

A "nongovernmental organization of the United Nations, Department of Public Information" dedicated to explaining, promoting, and encouraging the discussion of Sufism.

Islamic Circle of North America
http://www.icna.org/
166-26 89th Avenue
Jamaica, NY 11432
Phone: (718) 658-1199

A Muslim proselytizing organization that works through various media and activities to bring the message of Islam to Americans. Its annual convention is one of the largest Muslim gatherings in the United States.

IslamiCity
http://www.islamicity.com/
P.O. Box 3030
Culver City, CA 90231
Phone: (310) 642-0006

A California-based Muslim organization offering a large online community and a range of educational and community support services.

Islamic Medical Association of North America
http://www.imana.org/
101 W 22nd Street, Suite 106
Lombard, IL 60148
Phone: (630) 932-0000

A prominent organization for Muslim Americans who are healthcare professionals providing: "a forum and resource for Muslim physicians and other health care professionals, to promote a greater awareness of Islamic medical ethics and values among Muslims and the community-at-large."

Islamic School's League of America
http://www.4islamicschools.org/
PO Box 1265
Falls Church, VA 22041
Phone: (517) 303-3905

An organization promoting cooperation between Islamic schools across the United States and abroad.

Islamic Society of North America
http://www.isna.net/
PO Box 38
Plainfield, IN 46168
Phone: (317) 839-8157

One of the largest Muslim organizations in North America the ISNA was founded in 1963 and provides a national framework to which many smaller Muslim groups are affiliated. Its annual conference is one of the most significant gatherings of U.S. and Canadian Muslims.

Karamah: Muslim Women Lawyers for Human Rights
http://karamah.org/
1420 16th Street NW
Washington, DC 20036
Phone: (202) 234-7302

An educational and advocacy group describing itself as "a human rights organization of Muslim women lawyers dedicated to promoting dignity for all human beings through education and legal outreach."

Minaret of Freedom Institute
http://www.minaret.org/
4323 Rosedale Avenue
Bethesda, MD 20814
Phone: (301) 907-0947

An organization dedicated to educating non-Muslims about the values of Islam and to correcting misconceptions.

Muslim Public Affairs Council
http://www.mpac.org/
110 Maryland Avenue NE Suite 210

Washington, DC 20002
Phone: (202) 547-7701

An American-Muslim advocacy and public policy organization.

Muslim Students Association of the United States and Canada
http://www.msanational.org/
PO Box 1096
Falls Church, VA 22041
Phone: (703) 820-7900

An umbrella organization with affiliated chapters in educational establish-
ments across the United States and Canada, it is the largest Islamic student
organization in North America.

Muslim Women's League
http://www.mwlusa.org/
3010 Wilshire Boulevard, Suite 519
Los Angeles, CA 90010
Phone: (626) 358-0335

An organization that supports Muslim women in the United States and aims
to "implement the values of Islam and thereby reclaim the status of women
as free, equal and vital contributors to society."

North American Bangladeshi Islamic Community
http://www.nabic.org/
PO Box 6631
Oak Ridge, TN 37831
Phone: (865) 481-8988

An organization promoting the interests of American Muslims of Bangladeshi heritage.

ORGANIZATIONS AND AGENCIES BASED OUTSIDE NORTH AMERICA

Africa Muslims Agency
http://www.africamuslimsagency.co.za/
2 Central Road, (Off Main Reef Road)

Fordsburg, Gauteng 2033
South Africa
Phone: (011-27) 834-8685

A Muslim missionary and aid agency largely sponsored by Kuwaiti sources that concentrates on distributing financial aid to Africans in need. The African Muslims Agency says that its aim is to "uplift the standard of life, morality and education of the most deserving and needy in the Continent of Africa."

Ahlus Sunnah wal Jama'ah Association of Australia
http://www.aswj.com.au/
132 Haldon Street
Lakemba, New South Wales 2195
Australia
Phone: (011-61-2) 9758-3406

A large Muslim organization with centers across Australia.

Association of Muslim Professionals
http://www.amp.org.sg/
Pasir Ris Drive 4
#05-11
Singapore 519457
Phone:(011-65) 6416-3966

Founded in 1991 the Association of Muslim Professionals describes itself as playing an "active role in the development and long term transformation of Malay/Muslim Singaporeans into a dynamic community taking its pride of place in the larger Singaporean society."

Association of Muslim Researchers
http://www.amr.org.uk/
P.O. Box 8715
London SE23 3ZB
United Kingdom
Phone: (011-44-020) 8699-1887

A U.K.-based organization that describes itself as an "independent and inclusive association of people promoting a critical pursuit of knowledge within a coherent Islamic framework to provide alternative models for a just society."

Channel Islam International
http://www.ciibroadcasting.com/
53 Crownwood Road
Crownwood Centre
Ormonde
South Africa
Phone: (011-27-11) 494-7000

A South Africa–based audio broadcaster concentrating on stories from around the world concerning the Muslim community.

Islamic Foundation for Ecology and Environmental Science
http://www.ifees.org.uk/
93 Court Road
Birmingham B12 9LQ
United Kingdom
Phone: (011-44-121) 440-3500

A U.K.-based Muslim organization concentrating on ecological and environmental issues from the point of view of Islam. It calls its campaign to improve the environment of Muslim-majority communities across the world an "eco-jihad."

Islamic Aid
http://www.islamicaid.org.uk/
47 Theydon Street
London E17 8EN
United Kingdom
Phone: (011- 44-20) 8503-7649

A U.K.-based organization dedicated to distributing Islamic aid across the world.

Islamic Educational, Scientific and Cultural Organization
Avenue des F.A.R
Hay Ryad
PO Box 2275
PC Code 10104
Rabat
Morocco
Phone: (011-212-53) 756-6052

Established in 1979 the ISESCO is one of the world's largest Muslim organizations. It provides information and support in the fields of education, science, and culture. The ISESCO was founded at the Ninth Islamic Conference of Foreign Ministers—an organization of 57 member states.

Islamic Foundation
http://www.islamic-foundation.org.uk/
Markfield Conference Centre
Ratby Lane
Markfield
Leicestershire LE67 9SY
United Kingdom
Phone: (011-44-1530) 244-944

A U.K.-based Muslim organization founded in 1979 and dedicated to building links between the Muslim and non-Muslim communities.

Islamic Human Rights Commission
http://www.ihrc.org/
PO Box 598
Wembley HA9 7XH
United Kingdom
Phone: (011- 44-20) 8904-4222

A U.K. based human rights advocacy agency holding consultative status with the United Nations Economic and Social Council.

Islamic Information and Services Network of Australasia
http://www.iisna.com/
1/995 Sydney Road
Coburg North, 3058
Melbourne, Victoria
Australia
Phone: (011-61-3) 9354-7500

An Australian organization to support and inform the Muslim community of Australia and the wider Australasian region.

Islamic Party of Britain
http://www.islamicparty.com/
PO Box 844

Oldbrook, Milton Keynes MK6 2YT
United Kingdom

Describing itself as the "first national Islamic political organisation in the UK and the only Islamic political party in the non-Muslim Western world."

Islamic Research Foundation
http://www.irf.net/
56/58 Tandel Street North
Dongri
Mumbai 400009
India
Phone: (011-91-22) 2373-6875

An online organization promoting Islam through video telecasts.

Jaamat-e-Islami
http://www.jamaat-e-islami.org/
505 Elephant Road
Bara Moghbazar
Dhaka-1217
Bangladesh
Phone: (011-880-2) 933-1581

Describing itself as "a religious, political, social and cultural movement" Jaamat-e-Islami is strongly engaged in Bangladeshi politics.

Leeds New Muslims
http://www.leedsnewmuslims.org.uk/
PO Box 48
Harehills, Leeds LS8 2ZP
United Kingdom

A U.K.-based organization that concentrates on supporting recent converts to Islam or those interested in learning more about Islam.

Mazlumder: The Association of Human Rights and Solidarity for
Oppressed People
http://www.mazlumder.org/
Mithatpaşa Cad. 21/14
Kizilay/Ankara
Turkey
Phone: (011-90-312) 435-7795

Organizations and Agencies

An organization campaigning for and supporting oppressed people around the world and based in Turkey.

Minhaj-ul-Quran International
http://www.minhaj.org/
365 M, Model Town
Lahore
Pakistan
Phone: (092-42) 516-9111

A Pakistan-based organization addressing global issues and news stories from an Islamic perspective.

Muslim Hands
http://www.muslimhands.org/
148 Gregory Boulevard
Nottingham NG7 5JE
United Kingdom
Phone: (011-44-115) 911-7222

A U.K.-based international charity working in more than 40 countries to distribute aid donated primarily by Muslims.

Organisation of the Islamic Conference
http://www.oic-un.org/
20 Route de Pré-Bois
CP1818
1215 Geneva 15
Switzerland
Phone: (011-41-22) 788-6000

One of the world's largest intergovernmental organizations the OIC has 57 member states and was founded at a summit of representatives from Muslim-majority states in Rabat, Morocco, in 1969.

Palestinian Centre for Human Rights
http://www.pchrgaza.org/
29 Omar El Mukhtar Street
Near Amal Hotel
PO Box 1328
Gaza City
Phone: (011-972-8) 2824-776

A Muslim human rights organization based in Gaza City and with Special Consultative Status with the Economic and Social Council of the United Nations.

Sisters in Islam
http://www.sistersinislam.org.my/
No. 7, Jalan 6/10
Petaling Jaya
Selangor Darul Ehsan
46000
Malaysia
Phone: (011-60-3) 7785-6121

An organization run by a group of Muslim Malaysian women dedicated to "promoting the rights of women within the framework of Islam."

World Muslim Congress
http://www.motamaralalamalislami.org/
SITE 9-A, Block-7, Gulshan-e-Iqbal
PO Box No. 5030
Karachi–74000
Pakistan
Phone: (011-92-21) 496-9423

One of the oldest and most prominent Muslim associations the World Muslim Congress (or Motamar al-Alam al-Islami) was founded in 1924 and currently has consultative status at the United Nations. Its goal is "to promote solidarity and cooperation among the global Islamic community."

10

Annotated Bibliography

This section lists selections of recent books, articles, and movies that may be consulted to find more information on the topics discussed in this book. The material is divided into five themed sections and each item is accompanied by a short description of its content.

> *Political and Economic Reform in the Muslim World*
>
> *U.S. Foreign Policy and the Muslim World*
>
> *General Background on Islam and the Muslim World*
>
> *Historical and Contemporary Islam*
>
> *Islamic Militancy*

POLITICAL AND ECONOMIC REFORM IN THE MUSLIM WORLD

Books

Abou El Fadl, Khaled M., et al. *Democracy and Islam in the New Constitution of Afghanistan.* Santa Monica, Calif.: Rand Corporation, 2004. A report on a conference held to identify and discuss ways in which a new constitution for Afghanistan could encourage democracy and stabilize the country.

Afary, Janet. *The Iranian Constitutional Revolution: Grassroots Democracy, Social Democracy, and the Origins of Feminism.* New York: Columbia University Press, 1996. A detailed account of the social and political conditions that led to the creation of Iran's first constitution and, especially, the role played by women in this process.

Albright, Madeleine, and Vin Weber. *In Support of Arab Democracy: Why and How: Report of an Independent Task Force.* New York: Council on Foreign Relations, 2005. A report sponsored by the Council on Foreign Relations, a U.S. nonpartisan think tank, that argues in favor of the United States working to encourage democracy across the Arab world despite the inherent risks of such a policy. One of its authors, Madeleine Albright, was the first woman to serve as U.S. secretary of state (1997–2001).

Al-Sulami, Misham. *The West and Islam: Western Liberal Democracy versus the System of Shura.* Oxford: Taylor & Francis, 2003. An analysis of the relationship between Western and Islamic political ideologies with particular reference to the Islamic system of *shura*—an ancient method of consultation and decision making in Muslim tradition.

Amin, Galal A., and David Wilmsen. *Illusion of Progress in the Arab World.* New York: American University in Cairo Press, 2006. A critical analysis of western views of economic and political progress in the Muslim World showing how Western concepts sometimes fail to apply to Muslim-majority states.

Anderson, Lisa, et al., eds. *Islam, Democracy and the State in North Africa.* Bloomington: Indiana University Press, 1997. A collection of essays looking at the pressures for social and political change coming from Islamist movements in North Africa in the last decades of the 20th century.

Ansari, Ali M. *Iran, Islam, and Democracy: The Politics of Managing Change.* London: Royal Institute of International Affairs, 2001. An analysis of the conflicting social and political conditions during the presidency of Mohammad Khatami.

Arat, Yesim. *Rethinking Islam and Liberal Democracy: Islamist Women in Turkish Politics.* New York: State University of New York Press, 2007. An examination of the struggles of Muslim women activists in Turkey.

Azra, Azyumardi. *Indonesia, Islam, and Democracy: Dynamics in a Global Context.* Canada: Solstice Publishing, 2006. An overview of the influence of Islam on Indonesia's fledgling democracy, tracing the origins and development of Islamic political thought in the post-Suharto era.

Bayat, Assef. *Making Islam Democratic: Social Movements and the Post-Islamist Turn.* Stanford, Calif.: Stanford University Press, 2007. Focusing on the experience of Egypt and Iran this volume offers insights into perceptions of democracy in the Muslim world and how they are shaped by the twin evils of authoritarian rule at home and the threat of military intervention by the West.

Benard, Cheryl. *Civil Democratic Islam: Partners, Resources, and Strategies.* Santa Monica, Calif.: Rand Corporation, 2004. An attempt to provide a framework through which the West can better understand and interact meaningfully with Muslim societies.

Bin Talal, El Hassan, and Alain Elkann. *To Be a Muslim: Islam, Peace, and Democracy.* Eastbourne, East Sussex, England: Sussex Academic Press, 2004. Written in part by prince Hassan bin Talal of Jordan this book is an attempt to explain the basic tenets of Islam to a non-Muslim Western audience and to encourage interfaith dialogue.

Bonner, Michael. *Islam, Democracy, and the State in Algeria: Lessons for the Western Mediterranean and Beyond.* Abingdon, Oxford: Routledge, 2005. An examination of the implications for the Muslim states of North Africa and the Middle East of the traumatic events that led up to the Algerian civil war that began in the early 1990s.

Annotated Bibliography

Browers, Michaelle. *Democracy and Civil Society in Arab Political Thought: Transcultural Possibilities.* New York: Syracuse University Press, 2006. An overview of the currents of Muslim political thought concerning democracy and civil societies that argues that many of the Muslim world's conflicts involve, at root, homegrown attempts to reform authoritarian governments rather than emerging from a collision between Western ideas and Islam.

Carothers, Thomas, and Marina Ottaway. *Uncharted Journey: Promoting Democracy in the Middle East.* Washington, D.C.: Carnegie Endowment for International Peace, 2005. A collection of essays examining the impact on the Muslim world of the 2003 U.S.-led invasion of Iraq and the possibilities for building democracy in the region.

Cesari, Jocelyne. *When Islam and Democracy Meet: Muslims in Europe and in the United States.* New York: Palgrave Macmillan, 2006. An exploration of the place of Islam and Muslims in U.S. and European society.

Charfi, Mohamed, and Patrick Camiller. *Islam and Liberty: The Historical Misunderstanding.* New York: Palgrave Macmillan, 2004. An attempt to solve the problem of how to reconcile Islam with Western notions of democracy and the state.

Cole, Juan. *The Ayatollahs and Democracy in Contemporary Iraq.* Amsterdam: Amsterdam University Press, 2006. An examination of the participation of Iraq's religious leaders in attempts to introduce democracy to Iraq in the post-invasion period.

Cotran, Eugene. *Democracy: The Rule of Law and Islam.* New York: Springer, 1999. A collection of essays written by legal professionals focusing on various questions surrounding the relationship between the law and Islam.

Dallmayr, Fred R. *The Promise of Democracy: Political Agency and Transformation.* Albany: State University of New York Press, 2010. A wide-ranging survey of the roots of the principles of democracy and the application of these principles to the contemporary Muslim world.

Diamond, Larry, Marc F. Plattner, and Daniel Brumberg, eds. *Islam and Democracy in the Middle East.* Baltimore, Md.: Johns Hopkins University Press, 2003. A comprehensive overview of the origins and health of autocratic governments in the Muslim world and the attempts of reformers to change them.

El Fadl, Khaled Abou, Deborah Chasman, and Joshua Cohen. *Islam and the Challenge of Democracy.* Princeton, N.J., and Oxford: Princeton University Press, 2004. An attempt to construct a framework for democracy from the principles of Islamic law.

Feldman, Noah. *After Jihad: America and the Struggle for Islamic Democracy.* New York: Farrar, Straus & Giroux, 2004. The author argues that the Islamist violence of the last 20 years is the last gasp of a dying tradition rather than the opening of a new chapter in the history of the Muslim world.

Hale, William M., and Ergun Özbudun. *Islamism, Democracy and Liberalism in Turkey: The Case of the AKP.* London: Routledge, 2010. An analysis of the Islamist AKP, Justice and Development Party in Turkey and its role in the transformation of Turkish politics.

Hasan, Zoja. *Democracy in Muslim Societies: The Asian Experience*. Thousand Oaks, Calif.: Sage Publications, 2007. An examination of the progress of attempts to create democratic reforms in Bangladesh, Indonesia, Iran, Malaysia, Pakistan, and Turkey.

Howard, Philip N. *The Digital Origins of Dictatorship and Democracy: Information Technology and Political Islam*. Oxford: Oxford University Press, 2010. The influence of digital communications and the Internet on political developments in the Muslim world.

Hunter, Shireen T., Huma Malik, and Ahmedou Ould-Abdallah. *Modernization, Democracy, and Islam*. Westport, Conn.: Greenwood Publishing Group, 2005. A collection of essays on the multitude of challenges facing attempts to modernize and democratize the Muslim world.

Ibrahim, Saad Eddin. *Egypt, Islam, and Democracy: Critical Essays*. New York: American University in Cairo Press, 2002. A collection of essays on the political, religious, economic, and social issues of contemporary Egypt written over a 15-year period.

Inglehart, Ronald. *Islam, Gender, Culture, and Democracy*. Whitby, Canada: De Sitter Publications, 2003. A collection of articles exploring the relationship between Islam and democracy, Islamic worldviews, culture and democratic institutions, and the changing role of gender.

Jamal, Amaney J. *Barriers to Democracy: The Other Side of Social Capital in Palestine and the Arab World*. Princeton, N.J.: Princeton University Press, 2007. An analysis of the role of civil associations, such as interest groups and nonpolitical clubs, in the development of democracy among Palestinians.

Jazouli, Ahmed. *Islam, Democracy, and Governance in the North African Countries: The Zero Stage of States*. Bloomington, Ind.: IUniverse, 2006. An examination of the peculiar political, economic, and cultural problems undermining the fight for democracy in North African nations.

Jung, Dietrich. *Democratization and Development: New Political Strategies for the Middle East*. Basingstoke, Hampshire, England: Palgrave Macmillan, 2006. An insight into the role played by external initiatives for the support of good governance in Arab states, new satellite broadcasting, and Islamist organizations.

Kamrava, Mehran. *The New Voices of Islam: Rethinking Politics and Modernity: A Reader*. Berkeley and Los Angeles: University of California Press, 2007. A collection of writings from prominent Muslim thinkers arguing for reforms in Islamic theology and jurisprudence.

Kassab, Elizabeth Suzanne. *Contemporary Arab Thought: Cultural Critique in Comparative Perspective*. New York: Columbia University Press, 2010. A survey of the state of political thought in the contemporary Muslim world.

Khan, M. A. *Islamic Democratic Discourse: Theory, Debates, and Philosophical Perspectives*. Lanham, Md.: Rowman & Littlefield Publishers, 2006. A collection of essays concentrating on different aspects of the relationship between Islamic political thought and Western democracy.

Annotated Bibliography

Mernissi, Fatima. *Islam and Democracy: Fear of the Modern World.* Reading, Mass.: Perseus Publishing, 1992. Regarded as an established classic in the field of Islamic political thought, this book examines the way in which reformers in the Muslim world attempt to use the same religious texts as conservatives to justify opposing aims.

Moussalli, Ahmad. *Islamic Quest for Democracy, Pluralism and Human Rights.* Gainesville: University Press of Florida, 2003. An examination of the writings of important Muslim thinkers that attempts to show their development of theories of limited government, civil society, and individual liberty.

Nasr, Vali. *The Shia Revival: How Conflicts within Islam Will Shape the Future.* New York and London: W. W. Norton, 2007. An examination of the shifting relationship between Shia and Sunni communities in Iraq during and after the 2003 U.S.-led invasion and occupation.

Nasr, Vali, and Ali Gheissari. *Democracy in Iran: History and the Quest for Liberty.* Oxford: Oxford University Press, 2006. An investigation into the progress and setbacks experienced by the idea of democracy in the complex and hidden world of Iranian politics before and after the 1979 revolution.

Quandt, William B., and Michael H. Armacost. *Between Ballots and Bullets: Algeria's Transition from Authoritarianism.* Washington, D.C.: Brookings Institution Press, 1998. A history of the social pressures that undermined the authoritarian regime in Algeria and the difficulties of making the transition to democracy.

Qureshi, P. *Islamic Democracy.* New Delhi: MD Publications Ltd, 2009. A history of the tradition of Islamic democracy known as Faisalism.

Riaz, Ali *Religion and Politics in South Asia.* London: Routledge, 2010. A comprehensive analysis of the interaction of religion and politics in Afghanistan, Bangladesh, India, Nepal, Pakistan, and Sri Lanka.

Robinson, Kathryn May. *Gender, Islam and Democracy in Indonesia.* London: Routledge, 2009. An examination of the history of the relationships among gender, religion, and political action in Indonesia.

Roy, Olivier, and George Holoch. *Secularism Confronts Islam.* New York: Columbia University Press, 2007. An analysis and deconstruction of the myths surrounding the debate concerning the compatibility of democracy and Islam.

Rubin, Barry. *The Long War for Freedom: The Arab Struggle for Democracy in the Middle East.* Hoboken, N.J.: John Wiley & Sons, 2005. A portrait of the many and varied elements of Arab society engaged in attempts to introduce democratic reforms.

Sachedina, Abdulaziz. *The Islamic Roots of Democratic Pluralism.* Oxford: Oxford University Press, 2001. An investigation of Muslim teachings on pluralism, civil society, war, and peace that argues that Islam is a natural source of tolerance and pluralism.

———. *The Role of Islam in the Public Square: Guidance or Governance?* Amsterdam: Amsterdam University Press, 2006. A look at the critical role played by Islam in the political development of Iraq and Afghanistan.

323

Sadiki, Larbi. *The Search for Arab Democracy: Discourses and Counter-Discourses.* New York: Columbia University Press, 2004. An examination of the writings and opinions of a wide range of Muslim thinkers, ranging from medieval philosophers to contemporary Islamists, on the question of Islam and democracy.

Saroush, Abdolkarim, Mahmoud Sadri, and Ahmad Sadri. *Reason, Freedom, and Democracy in Islam: Essential Writings of Abdolkarim Saroush.* Oxford: Oxford University Press, 2002. Selected writings by the renowned Iranian religious philosopher Abdolkarim Soroush, who was named one of the world's 100 most influential people by *Time* magazine in 2005.

Viorst, Milton. *Storm from the East: The Struggle between the Arab World and the Christian West.* New York: Random House Publishing Group, 2007. A history of the difficult relationship between the United States and the Muslim world seen in the context of more than a thousand years of conflict between Muslims and Christians.

Volpi, Frédéric. *Islam and Democracy: The Failure of Dialogue in Algeria.* Sterling, Va.: Pluto Press, 2003. A history of the Algerian civil war and its relevance to the relationship between Islam and democratic reform across the Muslim world.

Wittes, Tamara Coffman. *Freedom's Unsteady March: America's Role in Building Arab Democracy.* Washington, D.C.: Brookings Institution Press, 2008. The author argues that promoting democracy in the Muslim world must remain a central pillar of U.S. foreign policy if the United States is to achieve any of its long-term aims in its relationship with the Middle East.

Yavuz, M. Hakan. *The Emergence of a New Turkey: Islam, Democracy, and the AK Parti.* Salt Lake City: University of Utah Press, 2006. An examination of the surprising political success of the Islamist AKP, Justice and Development Party in Turkey and its strong pro–European Union stance.

Articles and Web Documents

Anderson, J. L. "The Taliban's Opium War: The Difficulties and Dangers of the Eradication Program." *New Yorker*, July 9, 2007. An examination of the difficulties faced by the Afghan government in its attempts to eradicate the opium industry in the country.

Barlow, Rebecca, and Shahram Akbarzadeh. "Women's Rights in the Muslim World: Reform or Reconstruction?" *Third World Quarterly* 27, no. 8, 2006. An investigation into feminist thinking and action in the Muslim world.

Ben-Meir, Alon. "Challenges to Democracy in the Arab and Muslim World." *Political Quarterly* 77, no. 3, 2006. An overview of the difficulties facing attempts to democratize Muslim-majority states.

Bhimji, Fazila. "Identities and Agency in Religious Spheres: A Study of British Muslim Women's Experience." *Gender, Place & Culture* 16, no. 4, 2009. Examining the role of Islamic study circles in the lives of Muslim women in contemporary British society.

Annotated Bibliography

Bleich, Erik. "Muslims and the State in the Post-9/11 West: Introduction." *Journal of Ethnic and Migration Studies* 35, no. 3, 2009. An examination of the position of Muslims in Western societies.

Dorman, W. J. "Informal Cairo: Between Islamist Insurgency and the Neglectful State?" *Security Dialogue* 40, no. 4–5, 2009. The role of grassroots Islamist groups in the daily lives of the citizens of Cairo, Egypt.

Editorial. "Science in the Muslim World." *Nature*, no. 7097, 2006. The state of the sciences in the Muslim world.

Emmett, Chad. "The Siting of Churches and Mosques as an Indicator of Christian-Muslim Relations." *Islam and Christian-Muslim Relations* 20, no. 4, 2009. A study of local Christian-Muslim relations through the physical locations of churches and mosques.

Gillespie, Michael. "Bill Moyers, Modernity and Islam." Available online. URL: http://www.mediamonitors.net/gillespie6.html. Accessed December 19, 2009. A critical analysis of a television program in which Bill Moyers discussed the clash between Islam and the West with a panel of Muslim and non-Muslim journalists and scholars.

Gulen, Fethullah. "A Comparative Approach to Islam and Democracy." Available online. URL: http://theamericanmuslim.org/tam.php/features/articles/a_comparative_approach_to_islam_and_democracy/. Accessed December 19, 2009. The author describes the difficulties of comparing the mutable norms of democracy with the unchanging principles of Islam and lists what he sees as the underlying principles of Islam that apply to the political arena.

Jamaal al-din Zarabozo. "Modernism in Islam." Available online. URL: http://www.islaam.com/Article.aspx?id=119. Accessed December 19, 2009. A critical history of the modernizing strand in the history of Islam.

Levey, Geoffrey, and Tariq Modood. "The Muhammad Cartoons and Multicultural Democracies." *Ethnicities* 9, no. 3, 2009. An examination of the implications for multicultural societies of the controversy surrounding the publication of political cartoons depicting Muhammad in Denmark.

Mujani, S., and R. W. Liddle. "Muslim Indonesia's Secular Democracy." *Asian Survey* 49, no. 4, 2009. A survey of the state of democracy in Indonesia.

Powers, Shawn, and Mohammed el-Nawawy. "Al-Jazeera English and Global News Networks: Clash of Civilizations or Cross-Cultural Dialogue?" *Media, War & Conflict* 2, no. 3, 2009. An examination of the role of global news agencies in cross-cultural understanding.

Volpi, Frédéric. "Political Islam in the Mediterranean: The View from Democratization Studies." *Democratization* 16, no. 1, 2009. An overview of Islamist groups and ambitions around the Mediterranean.

—— "Pseudo-Democracy in the Muslim World." *Third World Quarterly* 25, no. 6, 2004. The author argues that attempts to democratize certain Muslim-majority states have resulted in pseudo-democracies.

Television/Film/Video

ABC-TV (Australia), and Majelis Ulama Indonesia. *Islam in Indonesia.* 66 min. Sydney, Australia: ABC, 2006. DVD. An investigative report from Australian television on the political situation in Indonesia and the powerful influence of Islam in the country.

Jenkins, Paul, and Ziauddin Sardar. *The Battle for Islam.* Produced and directed by Paul Jenkins. 63 min. Princeton, N.J.: Films for the Humanities & Sciences, 2006. DVD. A film that argues for moderation and tolerance as the solution to the Muslim world's problems.

Mahmood, Jamal, Marc Zuber, and Ziauddin Sardar. *Islamic State? Islamic Conversations.* 30 min. Princeton, N.J.: Films for the Humanities & Sciences, 2003. DVD. Dr. Hassan Turabi, a conservative Muslim religious leader in Sudan, describes his vision of an ideal Islamic state and the state of human rights in Sudan.

U.S. FOREIGN POLICY AND THE MUSLIM WORLD
Books

Bahgat, Gawdat. *American Oil Diplomacy in the Persian Gulf and the Caspian Sea.* Gainesville: University Press of Florida, 2003. A study of U.S. relations with the major oil producers of the Middle East.

Barrett, Roby C. *The Greater Middle East and the Cold War: U.S. Foreign Policy under Eisenhower and Kennedy.* New York: I. B. Tauris, 2007. An insight into another period of sustained crisis in the Middle East that has implications for U.S. foreign policy today.

Bass, Warren. *Support Any Friend: Kennedy's Middle East and the Making of the U.S.-Israel Alliance.* New York: Oxford University Press, 2003. The author argues that the administration of John F. Kennedy marked a major turning point in relations between Israel and the United States and, consequently, between the Arab world and the United States.

Baxter, Kylie, and Shahram Akbarzadeh. *U.S. Foreign Policy in the Middle East: The Roots of Anti-Americanism.* London: Routledge, 2008. The author traces the origins of anti-Americanism in among Muslims of the Middle East directly to U.S. foreign policy in the region, rejecting the idea that it is inherent to the Muslim political culture.

Blank, Stephen. *Russia and the U.S. in the Middle East: Policies and Contexts.* Swindon, England: Defence Academy of the United Kingdom, Conflict Studies Research Centre, June 2006. This academic paper argues that Russian foreign policy in the Middle East is being driven by a desire to counter growing U.S. influence in the region.

Carter, Jimmy. *Palestine: Peace Not Apartheid.* New York: Simon & Schuster, 2006. A personal view of attempts to reach an Palestinian-Israeli peace settlement by former U.S. president Jimmy Carter.

Annotated Bibliography

Chomsky, Noam. *Perilous Power: The Middle East & U.S. Foreign Policy: Dialogues on Terror, Democracy, War, and Justice.* Boulder, Colo.: Paradigm Publishers, 2007. A wide-ranging survey of U.S. foreign policy in relation to terrorism, fundamentalism, oil, democracy, self-determination, anti-Semitism, anti-Arab racism, as well as the war in Afghanistan, the invasion and occupation of Iraq, and the Palestinian-Israeli conflict.

Chubin, Shahram. *The United States, Europe, and the Wider Middle East.* Santa Monica, Calif.: Rand Center for Middle East Public Policy, 2004. The proceedings of a conference on the insurgency in Iraq, the Arab-Israeli conflict, terrorism, internal security in Saudi Arabia, and Iran and the proliferation of weapons of mass destruction.

Dershowitz, Alan M. *Preemption: A Knife That Cuts Both Ways.* New York: W. W. Norton, 2006. An examination of the perils and potential rewards of preemptive actions such as Israel's strike against Egypt and Syria at the beginning of the 1967 Arab-Israeli War.

Fuller, Graham E. *The Youth Factor: The New Demographics of the Middle East and the Implications for U.S. Policy.* Washington, D.C.: The Saban Center for Middle East Policy at the Brookings Institution, June 2003. An examination of the social, economic, and political problems arising from the fact that most Middle Eastern nations have rapidly growing populations.

Hadar, Leon. *Sandstorm: Policy Failure in the Middle East.* New York: Palgrave Mac-Millan, 2005. The author argues that the United States has consistently failed to understand the consequences of its actions in the Middle East and that a policy of disengagement is the way forward.

Hahn, Peter L. *Historical Dictionary of United States–Middle East Relations.* Lanham, Md.: Scarecrow Press, 2007. A comprehensive history of diplomatic relations between the United States and the Middle East from the onset of the cold war up to the present.

Halabi, Yakub. *U.S. Foreign Policy in the Middle East: From Crises to Change.* Farnham, Surrey, England: Ashgate, 2009. An analysis of U.S. foreign policy in the Middle East from the end of World War II to the present.

Henderson, Simon. *The New Pillar: Conservative Arab Gulf States and U.S. Strategy.* Washington, D.C.: Washington Institute for Near East Policy, 2003. The author identifies a trend in U.S. foreign policy toward a closer relationship with the smaller Arab Gulf States of Kuwait, Qatar, Bahrain, Oman, and the United Arab Emirates and the implications for peace and security in the region.

Indyk, Martin. *Innocent Abroad: An Intimate Account of American Peace Diplomacy in the Middle East.* New York: Simon & Schuster, 2009. The author, who served as U.S. ambassador to Israel and assistant secretary of state for Near East affairs under President Bill Clinton, describes his experience of the Clinton administration's efforts to achieve peace in the Middle East.

Laham, Nicholas. *Crossing the Rubicon: Ronald Reagan and U.S. Policy in the Middle East.* U.S. Foreign Policy and Conflict in the Islamic World series. Aldershot,

Hants, England: Ashgate, 2004. The author argues that the Reagan administration set the tone for U.S. foreign policy in the Middle East up to the present day.

Miller, Aaron David. *The Much Too Promised Land: America's Elusive Search for Arab-Israeli Peace.* New York: Bantam Books, 2008. An account of U.S. efforts to broker Arab-Israeli peace written by a career diplomat.

Oren, Michael B. *Power, Faith, and Fantasy: America in the Middle East, 1776 to the Present.* New York: W. W. Norton, 2007. Tracing commonalities in U.S. foreign policy in the Middle East over more than two centuries.

Pintak, Lawrence. *Seeds of Hate: How America's Flawed Middle East Policy Ignited the Jihad.* Sterling, Va.: Pluto Press, 2003. The author traces the roots of the hatred shown by some Muslim elements toward the West to U.S. policy in Lebanon in the 1980s.

Pollack, Kenneth M. *A Path out of the Desert: A Grand Strategy for America in the Middle East.* New York: Random House, 2008. The author, who was a strong advocate for the 2003 U.S. invasion of Iraq, sets out his strategies for U.S. foreign policy in the aftermath of that war.

Rugh, William A. *American Encounters with Arabs: The "Soft Power" of U.S. Public Diplomacy in the Middle East.* Westport, Conn.: Praeger Security International, 2006. The author argues in favor of greater "public diplomacy" in relations between the United States and the Arab world.

Shannon, Vaughn P. *Balancing Act: U.S. Foreign Policy and the Arab-Israeli Conflict.* Burlington, Vt.: Ashgate Publishing Company, 2003. The author explores the roles played by strategic considerations, domestic politics, and the decisions of powerful individuals in the evolution of U.S. foreign policy with regard to the Arab-Israeli conflict.

Terry, Janice J. *U.S. Foreign Policy in the Middle East: The Role of Lobbies and Special Interest Groups.* Ann Arbor, Mich.: Pluto Press, 2005. An investigation into the role of pro-Israeli lobbyists in influencing U.S. foreign policy.

Tyler, Patrick. *A World of Trouble: The White House and the Middle East—from the Cold War to the War on Terror.* New York: Farrar, Straus & Giroux, 2009. A wide-ranging history of U.S. involvement in the Middle East from Dwight Eisenhower to George W. Bush.

Vaughan, James R. *The Failure of American and British Propaganda in the Arab Middle East, 1945–1957: Unconquerable Minds.* New York: Palgrave Macmillan, 2005. A study into the use and effectiveness of Western propaganda in Arab states in the decade after World War II.

Wise, Harold Lee. *Inside the Danger Zone: The U.S. Military in the Persian Gulf 1987–1988.* Annapolis, Md.: Naval Institute Press, 2007. The story of U.S. military engagement in the Persian Gulf during a tense period that included the Iranian attack on the USS *Stark* and missions to protect oil tanker traffic.

Yaqub, Salim. *Containing Arab Nationalism: The Eisenhower Doctrine and the Middle East.* Chapel Hill: University of North Carolina Press, 2004. An examination of U.S. foreign policy toward the Middle East at the height of the cold war.

Yetiv, Steve A. *Crude Awakenings: Global Oil Security and American Foreign Policy.* Ithaca, N.Y.: Cornell University Press, 2004. The authors argue that, contrary to popular perceptions, oil supplies from the Middle East are more, rather than less, stable and secure than they have been for decades.

Zunes, Stephen. *Tinderbox: U.S. Foreign Policy and the Roots of Terrorism.* Monroe, Maine: Common Courage Press, 2003. The author asks whether the desire for economic dominance or the traditional values of U.S. society will triumph in its developing policy toward the Muslim world.

Articles and Web Documents

Abbas, Hassan. "Hillary Clinton on Pakistan and U.S. Relations with the Muslim World." Available online. URL: http://www.asiasociety.org.policy-politics/inter national-relations/us-asia/hillary-clinton-pakistan-and-us-relations-muslim-wor. Accessed April 19, 2010. Extracts from an interview with U.S. secretary of state Hillary Clinton that includes discussion of U.S. support for Pakistan's military campaign against the Taliban and for women's rights in the Muslim world.

Ahmad, Imad-ad-Dean, and Alejandro J. Beutel. "U.S. Foreign Policy, Not Islamic Teachings Account for al-Qaeda's Draw." Available online. URL: http://www.the americanmuslim.org/tam.php/features/articles/us_foreign_policy_not_islamic_ teachings_account_for_al_qaedas_draw/. Accessed April 19, 2010. An article about the negative impact of U.S. foreign policy on Muslim public opinion and a detailed examination of the content of statements made by bin Laden showing that they are more focused on political concerns than religious concerns.

"Barack Obama Speaks to the Muslim World—Let's Be Friends." *Economist* 391, no. 8634, 2009. A review of U.S. president Barack Obama's speech promising a new era in relations between the United States and the Muslim world.

BBC.co.uk. "Obama Reaches Out to Muslim World." Available online. URL: http:// news.bbc.co.uk/2/hi/7984762.stm. Accessed April 19, 2010. A report on Barack Obama's speech to the Turkish parliament in 2009 in which the president declared that the United States "is not at war with Islam."

Bishara, Marwan. "An Obstacle to Better U.S.-Muslim Relations." Available online. URL: http://blogs.aljazeera.net/imperium/2010/02/14/obstacle-better-us-muslim -relations. Accessed April 9, 2010. Al Jazeera's senior political analyst discusses the Saban Center for Middle East Policy, an element of the U.S. Brookings Institution, and its possible impact on U.S.-Muslim relations.

Cherribi, Sam. "U.S. Public Diplomacy in the Arab World." *American Behavioral Scientist* 52, no. 5, 2009. An examination of Arab media coverage of U.S. undersecretary for state and public diplomacy Karen Hughes and her attempts to rebrand the image of the United States in the Muslim world.

Hasan, Mehdi. "Can Obama Woo the Muslim World?" *New Statesman* 26, 2009. A report on U.S. president Barack Obama's attempts to forge a new relationship with the Muslim world.

Nasir, S. "Bungling Democracy in the Muslim World." *Peace Research Abstracts Journal* 43, no. 1, 2006. A critical review of U.S. attempts to promote democracy in the Muslim world.

Yacoubian, Mona. "Bridging the Divide: U.S. Efforts to Engage the Muslim World." *Middle East Journal* 63, no. 3, 2009. An investigation into U.S. attempts to build bridges with the Muslim world after the administration of George W. Bush.

Zaharna, R. S. "Improving U.S.-Muslim Relations: Obama's Other Audience." Foreign Policy in Focus, June 5, 2009. Available online. URL: http://www.fpif.org/articles/improving_us-muslim_relations_obamas_other_audience. Accessed April 19, 2010. An examination of President Barack Obama's foreign policy with respect to the Muslim world.

Television/Film/Video

Jennings, Peter. *Minefield: The U.S. and the Muslim World.* 44 min. Princeton, N.J.: Films for the Humanities & Sciences, 2002. DVD. One of America's most prominent television journalists looks at the difficult relationship between the United States and the Muslim world.

Khan, Imran, John Purdie, and Bruno Sorrentino. *Islam and America: Through the Eyes of Imran Khan.* Produced by John Purdie. 25 min. New York: Filmakers Library, 2001. Pakistani politician and former cricketer Imran Khan presents a personal view of the sources of resentment of ordinary Pakistanis toward the United States.

GENERAL BACKGROUND ON ISLAM AND THE MUSLIM WORLD

Books

Allen, Mark. *Arabs.* New York: Continuum, 2006. A study of the worldview and psychology of modern Arab societies.

Boosahda, Elizabeth. *Arab-American Faces and Voices: The Origins of an Immigrant Community.* Austin: University of Texas Press, 2003. A study of more than 100 years of the Arab-American community.

Burke, Edmund, and David N. Yaghoubian. *Struggle and Survival in the Modern Middle East.* Los Angeles: University of California Press, 2006. The stories of ordinary men and women who have lived through the turbulent recent history of the Middle East.

Catherwood, Christopher. *A Brief History of the Middle East: From Abraham to Arafat.* New York: Carroll & Graf, 2006. A history of the Middle East before September 11, 2001, that attempts to show how many of the world's current geopolitical realities have their roots in the history of the region.

Chasdi, Richard J. *Tapestry of Terror: A Portrait of Middle East Terrorism, 1994–1999.* New York: Lexington Books, 2002. A detailed statistical and quantitative analysis of four Middle East terrorist organizations, in Algeria, Turkey, Egypt, and Israel.

Choueiri, Youssef M. *Modern Arab Historiography: Historical Discourse and the Nation-State.* New York: Routledge Curzon Taylor & Francis Group, 2003. A

Annotated Bibliography

study of the history of Arab writings about Arab nationalism and their relation to the development of Arab nation-states.

Collomb, Rodney. *The Rise and Fall of the Arab Empire and the Founding of Western Pre-Eminence.* Stroud, England: Spellmount, 2006. A study of the rise of the Muslim Arab empire, its strengths and weaknesses, and the circumstances under which Christian Europe came to dominate the Muslim lands of the Middle East.

Dombroski, Kenneth R. *Peacekeeping in the Middle East as an International Regime.* New York: Routledge, 2007. An investigation into the successes and failures of international peacekeeping efforts intended to promote Arab-Israeli peace from 1948 to 1994.

Dumper, Michael R. T., and Bruce E. Stanley, eds. *Cities of the Middle East and North Africa: A Historical Encyclopedia.* Santa Barbara, Calif.: ABC-CLIO, 2007. The histories, achievements, and problems of 100 cities in the Middle East and North Africa.

Florence, Ronald. *Lawrence and Aaronsohn: T. E. Lawrence, Aaron Aaronsohn, and the Seeds of the Arab-Israeli Conflict.* New York: Viking, 2007. A study of two flamboyant figures involved in the defeat of the Ottoman Empire in World War I.

Gerner, Deborah J., and Jillian Schwedler. *Understanding the Contemporary Middle East.* Boulder, Colo.: Lynne Rienner, 2004. An introduction to the core issues facing the Middle East at the beginning of the 21st century.

Gershoni, Israel, ed. *Middle East Historiographies: Narrating the Twentieth Century.* Seattle: University of Washington Press, 2006. A study of writings about Middle East history over the course of the 20th century.

Gresh, Alain, and Dominique Vidal. *The New A–Z of the Middle East.* New York. I. B. Tauris, 2004. General information about the Middle East.

Hiro, Dilip. *The Essential Middle East: A Comprehensive Guide.* New York: Carroll & Graf, 2003. An encyclopedic guide to the contemporary Middle East.

Hourani, Albert. *A History of the Arab Peoples.* New York: Warner Books, 1991. A highly influential concise history of the Arab peoples from the rise of Islam in the seventh century to the 1980s.

Kepel, Gilles. *Bad Moon Rising: A Chronicle of the Middle East Today.* Translated by Pascale Ghazaleh. London: Saqi Books, 2003. A personal view of the impact of the events of September 11, 2001, on public opinion in the Middle East and the United States.

Leeming, David. *Jealous Gods and Chosen People: The Mythology of the Middle East.* New York: Oxford University Press, 2004. An overview of the ancient religions and mythologies of the Middle East and their echoes in the present day.

Lewis, Bernard. *From Babel to Dragomans: Interpreting the Middle East.* New York: Oxford University Press, 2004. A collection of essays and speeches on a wide range of topics concerning the Middle East by one of the West's best-known scholars of the region.

Mattar, Philip, ed. *Encyclopedia of the Modern Middle East & North Africa.* New York: Thomson Gale, 2004. Featuring more then 3,000 entries covering topics in fields such as politics, history, economics, religion, sociology, and literature.

Melady, John. *Pearson's Prize: Canada and the Suez Crisis.* Toronto, Canada: Dundurn Group, 2006. A study of the role played by Canada's minister of external affairs Lester Pearson in the resolution of the Suez Crisis of 1956.

Milton-Edwards, Beverley, and Peter Hinchcliffe. *Conflicts in the Middle East since 1945.* New York: Routledge, 2004. An analysis of the racial, ethnic, political, cultural, religious, and economic factors of recent conflicts in the Middle East.

Nicholson, Helen, and David Nicolle. *God's Warriors: Crusaders, Saracens and the Battle for Jerusalem.* New York: Osprey, 2005. A history of the 12th-century wars fought between Muslims and Christians for control of the city of Jerusalem.

Peters, James. *The Arab World Handbook: Arabian Peninsula and Iraq Edition.* London: Stacey International, 2005. A guide to the language, etiquette, and customs of the Arab world.

Pryce-Jones, David. *Betrayal: France, the Arabs, and the Jews.* New York: Encounter Books, 2006. The author presents a negative view of the role of France in the early 20th-century history of the Middle East.

Salzman, Philip Carl. *Culture and Conflict in the Middle East.* Amherst, N.Y.: Humanity Books, 2008. An anthropologist's view of the sources of conflict and misunderstanding between Middle Eastern Muslims and the West.

Sartre, Maurice. *The Middle East under Rome.* Translated by Catherine Porter. Cambridge, Mass.: Belknap Press of Harvard University, 2005. A history of Roman power and influence in the Middle East, including the early development of Christianity and the destruction of Jewish communities.

Slack, Corliss K. *Historical Dictionary of the Crusades.* Lanham, Md.: Scarecrow Press, 2003. A survey of Christian attempts to wrest Jerusalem from Muslim control from the 11th to the 14th centuries.

Smith, Dan. *The State of the Middle East: An Atlas of Conflict and Resolution.* Los Angeles: University of California Press, 2006. A guide to Middle Eastern and global politics.

Spencer, William, ed. *Global Studies: The Middle East.* Guilford, Conn.: Dushkin Publishing Group, 2007. Featuring comprehensive background information and selected world press articles about the Middle East.

Stewart, Dona J. *The Middle East Today: Political, Geographical & Cultural Perspectives.* London: Routledge, 2009. An introductory textbook for students of Middle East studies covering a wide range of contemporary issues.

Stokes, Jamie, ed. *Encyclopedia of the Peoples of Africa and the Middle East.* New York: Facts On File, 2009. A comprehensive guide to the ethnic groups, nationalities, and historical peoples of Africa and the Middle East.

Tyerman, Christopher. *God's War: A New History of the Crusades.* Cambridge, Mass.: Belknap Press of Harvard University, 2006. A comprehensive history of the Crusades.

Television/Film/Video

Armstrong, Karen. *Karen Armstrong, Religious Scholar: Series of Lectures and TV Interviews on Islam.* 320 min. Karachi: His Highness The Agha Khan Shia Imami Ismaili Council for Pakistan, 2009. DVD. A collection of television interviews and lectures about the past and future of Islam given by a respected scholar of comparative religion.

Baig, Anila. *Great British Islam.* 49 min. Channel 4, England: Real Life Media Productions, 2009. DVD. A documentary about the role of Muslims in British society filmed against the background of the July 2007 suicide bombings in London.

Daniel, Isioma. *Of Fatwas & Beauty Queens.* Produced by the Canadian Broadcasting Corporation. 48 min. New York: Filmakers Library, 2004. DVD. An investigative report into riots in Nigeria caused by plans to hold the Miss World beauty pageant in the country and remarks made by journalist Isioma Daniel that led to her having to flee the country.

Dembowski, Nick. *T.V.'s Promised Land.* 75 min. Mafi Media Awareness Foundation International, 2003. DVD. A film about the portrayal of Muslims and the Arab world in Western television programs and films made between 2000 and 2003.

Hamid, Ruhi, and Samira Ahmed. *Women and Islam: Islam Unveiled.* Produced and directed by Ruhi Hamid. 100 min. New York: Filmakers Library, 2003. DVD. A British journalist travels through the Middle East, Asia, Malaysia, and Africa, talking to Muslim spiritual leaders, educators, and activists about the role of women in Islam.

Moyers, Bill D., and Zaid Shakir. *Zaid Shakir on Being Muslim in America.* Princeton, N.J.: Films for the Humanities & Sciences, 2002. DVD. Veteran broadcaster Bill Moyers talks to prominent Muslim-American scholar and writer Zaid Shakir about his experience as a Muslim in the United States after September 11, 2001.

Nurmohamed, Arif, and Andrew Scarborough. *Message in a Bottle.* 60 min. North Sydney: BBC Worldwide by BBC Active, 2003. DVD. A documentary about two companies attempting to replace Coca-Cola with their own brands in the Muslim world.

Soliman, Ahmed. *Born in the USA: Muslim Americans.* Produced and directed by Ahmed Soliman. 60 min. Sterling, Va.: Astrolabe Pictures, 2003. DVD. A film following the everyday lives of a Muslim-American doctor and teacher.

HISTORICAL AND CONTEMPORARY ISLAM
Books

Abd-Allah, Umar F. *A Muslim in Victorian America: The Life of Alexander Russell Webb.* New York: Oxford University Press, 2006. The biography of one of the earliest known U.S.-born converts to Islam who became a prominent figure in American society.

Abu-Rabi, Ibrahim M. Malden, ed. *The Blackwell Companion to Contemporary Islamic Thought.* Oxford: Blackwell Publishing, 2006. An overview of the many strands of Islamic philosophy and political thought.

Afsaruddin, Asma. *The First Muslims: History and Memory.* Oxford: Oneworld, 2008. A history of the formative era of Islam and Muslim society based on a wealth of contemporary documents.

Almond, Ian. *The New Orientalists: Postmodern Representations of Islam from Foucault to Baudrillard.* New York: I. B. Tauris, 2007. A controversial study of the use of Islamic ideas and symbols by postmodern thinkers.

Arkoun, Mohammed. *Islam: To Reform or to Subvert?* London: Saqi Books, 2006. A radical interpretation of Muslim thinking about their own history.

Aspinall, Edward. *Islam and Nation: Separatist Rebellion in Aceh, Indonesia.* Stanford, Calif.: Stanford University Press, 2009. A history of the origins, growth, and current condition of the nationalist movement in the Aceh region of Indonesia.

Bashir, Shahzad. *Fazlallah Astarabadi and the Hurufis.* Oxford: Oneworld, 2005. A history of a prominent historical Sufi thinker and the influence of his ideas on the Muslim world.

Biran, Michal. *The Empire of the Qara Khitai in Eurasian History: Between China and the Islamic World.* New York: Cambridge University Press, 2005. The history of a little-known empire that acted as a cultural bridge between Muslim western Asia and East Asia.

Cook, David. *Martyrdom in Islam.* New York: Cambridge University Press, 2007. A history of the concept of martyrdom in the Muslim world.

Coughlin, Kathryn M., ed. *Muslim Cultures Today: A Reference Guide.* Westport, Conn.: Greenwood Press, 2006. A review of current issues in 16 nations with large Muslim communities.

Curtis, Edward E. *Black Muslim Religion in the Nation of Islam, 1960–1975.* Chapel Hill: University of North Carolina Press, 2006. A comprehensive history of the Nation of Islam organization at the height of its notoriety.

Ende, Werner, and Udo Steinbach. *Islam in the World Today: A Handbook of Politics, Religion, Culture, and Society.* Ithaca, N.Y.: Cornell University Press, 2010. A comprehensive volume on every conceivable aspect of Islam in the modern world.

Geaves, Ron. *Aspects of Islam.* Washington, D.C.: Georgetown University Press, 2005. An overview of contemporary controversies in Islamic thought.

———. *Key Words in Islam.* Washington, D.C.: Georgetown University Press, 2006. A students' guide to the central concepts of Islam.

Ghazanfar, S. M. *Islamic Civilization: History, Contributions, and Influence: A Compendium of Literature.* Lanham, Md.: Scarecrow Press, 2006. Notes on more than 600 English-language books and articles about the history of Islam and the influence of its ideas.

Green, Dominic. *Three Empires on the Nile: The Victorian Jihad, 1869–1899.* New York: Free Press, 2007. A history of British imperial conquest and rule in the Nile Valley.

Grieve, Paul. *A Brief Guide to Islam: History, Faith and Politics: The Complete Introduction.* New York: Carroll & Graf, 2006. The author presents his personal interpretation of the history of faith and politics in the Muslim world.

Hassaballa, Hesham A., and Kabir Helminski. *The Beliefnet Guide to Islam.* New York: Doubleday–Three Leaves Press, 2006. An examination of the five pillars of Muslim faith in context with the historical circumstances in which they were written.

Annotated Bibliography

Jackson, Roy. *Fifty Key Figures in Islam.* New York: Routledge, 2006. An overview of the lives and beliefs of 50 prominent figures in the history of Islam.

Karsh, Efraim. *Islamic Imperialism: A History.* New Haven, Conn.: Yale University Press, 2006. An examination of the reality and mythology of empire building in the history of the Muslim world.

Kennedy, Hugh. *The Great Arab Conquests: How the Spread of Islam Changed the World We Live In.* Philadelphia: Da Capo Press, 2007. A history of the first century after the establishment of Islam and its dramatic military expansion across the Middle East.

Kenney, Jeffrey T. *Muslim Rebels: Kharijites and the Politics of Extremism in Egypt.* New York: Oxford University Press, 2006. An examination of the origins and influence of the Kharijite movement; described as "the first sectarian movement in Islamic history."

Kung, Hans. *Islam: Past, Present & Future.* Oxford: Oneworld, 2007. A comprehensive study of the history of Islam written by a leading theologian.

Lewis, David Levering. *God's Crucible: Islam and the Making of Europe, 570–1215.* New York: W. W. Norton, 2008. A history of the five centuries during which Islam and Christianity fought for supremacy in Europe.

Manji, Irshad. *The Trouble with Islam: A Muslim's Call for Reform in Her Faith.* New York: St. Martin's Press, 2003. A personal view of the shortcomings of modern Islam written by a Canadian journalist born to Muslim parents in South Africa.

Marable, Manning, and Hishaam D. Aidi. *Black Routes to Islam.* New York: Palgrave Macmillan, 2009. A history of the part played by Islam in the lives of African Americans over two centuries.

Nasr, Seyyed Hossein, ed. *Islamic Philosophy from Its Origin to the Present: Philosophy in the Land of Prophecy.* Albany: State University of New York Press, 2006. A comprehensive overview of Islamic philosophy from the ninth century to the present day.

O'Shea, Stephen. *Sea of Faith: Islam and Christianity in the Medieval Mediterranean World.* New York: Walker & Company, 2006. The history of Muslim and Christian conflict and peaceful coexistence during the medieval period.

Robinson, Francis. *The Mughal Emperors and the Islamic Dynasties of India, Iran and Central Asia.* New York: Thames & Hudson, 2007. An overview of seven centuries of rule by the Mongols and their cultural descendants in central and southern Asia.

Ruthven, Malise. *Islam in the World.* New York: Oxford University Press, 2006. An overview of Islam in its many and varied historical, geographic, and social settings.

Sanyal, Usha. *Ahmad Riza Khan Barelwi: In the Path of the Prophet.* Oxford: Oneworld, 2005. An investigation into the life and influence of the Indian Muslim scholar Ahmad Riza Khan Barelwi, who lived in the last decades of British rule.

Shepard, William E. *Introducing Islam.* London: Routledge, 2009. A students' introduction to the history of Islam and its place in the modern world.

Silverstein, Adam J. *Islamic History.* Oxford: Oxford University Press, 2010. An overview of the history of Islam in less than 150 pages.

Sonn, Tamara. *Islam: A Brief History.* Maldon, Mass.: Wiley-Blackwell, 2010. The key cultural, intellectual, social, and political developments in the history of Islam.

Trofimov, Yaroslav. *The Siege of Mecca: The Forgotten Uprising in Islam's Holiest Shrine and the Birth of Al Qaeda.* New York: Doubleday, 2007. An investigation into a little reported incident in 1979 when Islamist extremists occupied Islam's holiest site.

Waterson, James. *The Knights of Islam: The Wars of the Mamluks.* St. Paul, Minn.: MBI, 2007. The history of the slave soldiers known as Mamluks who formed one of the most formidable fighting formations in history.

Watt, W. Montgomery, and Pierre Cachia. *A History of Islamic Spain.* New Brunswick, N.J.: Aldine Transaction, 2007. A history of Muslim rule in the Iberian Peninsula from the eighth to the 15th centuries.

Wuthnow, Robert, ed. *Encyclopedia of Politics and Religion.* Washington, D.C.: CQ Press, 2007. More than 250 articles examining the role of religious concepts and traditions in the history and development of major political ideas.

Television/Film/Video

Aboul-Enein, Youssef H. *The Battles of Prophet Muhammad: An Analytic Perspective.* 137 min. Bethesda, Md.: Navy Medicine Support Command, Visual Information Directorate, Audiovisual Production Department, 2009. DVD. U.S. Navy commander Youssef Aboul-Enein discusses the history of the Arabian Peninsula immediately before and during the life of Muhammad.

ISLAMIC MILITANCY
Books

Abbas, Tahir. *Islamic Radicalism and Multicultural Politics: The British Experience.* Abingdon, Oxon, England: Routledge, 2010. A history of the phenomenon of Islamic radicalism in the United Kingdom, its origins and consequences.

Akbarzadeh, Shahram, and Fethi Mansouri. *Islam and Political Violence: Muslim Diaspora and Radicalism in the West.* London: I. B. Tauris, 2010. An examination of the deepening divide between Muslims and non-Muslims in Western societies.

Aksikas, Jaafar. *Arab Modernities: Islamism, Nationalism, and Liberalism in the Post-Colonial Arab World.* New York: Peter Lang, 2009. A look at three ideologies: liberalism, nationalism, and Islamism and the potential for reconciling them with each other in the context of the modern Arab world.

Ali, Ayaan Hirsi. *Infidel.* New York: Free Press, 2007. The autobiography of a woman raised as a Muslim who moved to the Netherlands in search of a freer life, was elected to parliament, and then moved to the United States in fear of her life from Islamic radicals.

Annotated Bibliography

Aslan, Reza. *How to Win a Cosmic War: Confronting Radical Islam.* London: William Heinemann, 2009. An alternative perspective on the war on terror that examines the ideological concepts of good and evil espoused by both sides.

Babbin, Jed. *In the Words of Our Enemies.* Washington, D.C.: Regnery, 2007. Written by a former deputy undersecretary of defense in the administration of George H. W. Bush, this book is an uncompromising account of threats issued against the United States by Islamists and other anti-Western elements.

Bawer, Bruce. *While Europe Slept.* New York: Doubleday, 2006. The author argues that liberal attitudes in Europe are allowing Islamists to form dangerous radical movements that threaten democracy and freedom.

Bostom, Andrew G., ed. *The Legacy of Jihad, Islamic Holy War and the Fate of Non-Muslims.* Amherst, N.Y.: Prometheus Books, 2005. A history of the Islamic concept of jihad and its role in the historical expansion of the Muslim world.

Brachman, Jarret. *Global Jihadism: Theory and Practice.* London: Routledge, 2009. An analysis of the ideologies that inspire and sustain al-Qaeda and other violent jihadi groups.

Cesari, Jocelyne. *Muslims in the West after 9/11: Religion, Politics, and Law.* Routledge studies in liberty and security. London: Routledge, 2010. A comprehensive analysis of the religious, political, and legal status of Muslims living in present-day Western societies.

Crooke, Alastair. *Resistance: The Essence of the Islamist Revolution.* London: Pluto Press, 2009. The author traces the origins and development of a trend toward Islamist thinking in the Muslim world that has become a mass movement with global implications.

Davis, Gregory. *Religion of Peace? Islam's War against the World.* Los Angeles: World Ahead, 2006. The author questions the belief that Islam is a religion of peace simply requiring reform to make it into a force for good in the world.

Emerson, Steven. *American Jihad: The Terrorists Living among Us.* New York: Simon & Schuster, 2003. An investigation into the presence of Muslim terrorist organizations in the United States.

Esposito, John. *The Islamic Threat: Myth or Reality?* New York: Oxford University Press, 1999. A comprehensive overview of the perceived threat from Islam in some Western points of view.

Euben, Roxanne Leslie, and Muhammad Qasim Zaman. *Princeton Readings in Islamist Thought: Texts and Contexts from Al-Banna to Bin Laden.* Princeton, N.J.: Princeton University Press, 2009. An anthology of primary texts providing an introduction to Islamist political thought from the early 20th century to the present.

Fair, C. Christine. *The Madrassah Challenge: Militancy and Religious Education in Pakistan.* Washington, D.C.: United States Institute of Peace Press, 2008. An examination of the huge network of Muslim religious schools (madrassas) in Pakistan and the often-repeated accusation that they are a major source of militants.

Gabriel, Mark A. *Islam and Terrorism.* Lake Mary, Fla.: Charisma House, 2002. An examination of the motivates of Muslim terrorists and how they use the Quran to justify their actions.

Gerges, Fawaz A. *America and Political Islam: A Clash of Cultures.* Cambridge and New York: Cambridge University Press, 1999. A history of U.S. attitudes and policies toward radical Islamism.

———. *The Far Enemy: Why Jihad Went Global.* Cambridge: Cambridge University Press, 2005. A history of the jihadist movement and an analysis of why elements of it seek to make war on the West while others concentrate on domestic campaigns.

———. *Journey of the Jihadist: Inside Muslim Militancy.* Orlando, Fla.: Harcourt, 2006. The author focuses on several key Muslim militant figures and analyzes their motives and aims.

Gold, Dore. *Hatred's Kingdom: How Saudi Arabia Supports the New Global Terrorism.* Washington, D.C.: Regnery, 2003. A former Israeli ambassador to the United Nations argues that Saudi Arabia is a prominent supporter of Muslim terrorism.

Habeck, Mary. *Knowing the Enemy: Jihadist Ideology and the War on Terror.* New Haven, Conn.: Yale University Press, 2006. A detailed examination of the history of jihadist ideology from the 14th century to the present day.

Harris, Lee. *The Suicide of Reason: Radical Islam's Threat to the West.* New York: Basic Books, 2007. An examination of the particular problems faced by Western democracies, founded on principles of Enlightenment values, when faced with the religious fanaticism of Muslim terror movements.

Ibrahim, Raymond. *The Al Qaeda Reader.* New York: Doubleday, 2007. A study of the true aims, motives, and beliefs of al-Qaeda based on a close examination of its propaganda.

Jensen, Michael Irving. *The Political Ideology of Hamas: A Grassroots Perspective.* London: I. B. Tauris, 2009. A study of the political activities of Hamas in grassroots Palestinian communities that attempts to explain the organization's surprising victory in the 2006 Palestinian elections.

Karsh, Efraim. *Islamic Imperialism.* New Haven, Conn.: Yale University Press, 2006. A history of Muslim expansionism from the time of the Muhammad to Osama bin Laden.

Khosrokhavar, Farhad. *Inside Jihadism: Understanding Jihadi Movements Worldwide.* Boulder, Colo.: Paradigm, 2009. The author identifies two main strands of political thought driving modern jihadi activists, one based in the old Muslim world and a second that emerged from Muslim communities living in the West.

Koppel, Nikolas J. *Combating Islamic Militancy and Terrorism in Pakistan's Border Region.* Hauppauge, N.Y.: Nova Science Publishers, 2009. An examination of the growing violence between Islamic militants and the government of Pakistan in the Afghan-Pakistani border region.

Lafraie, Najibullah. *Revolutionary Ideology and Islamic Militancy: The Iranian Revolution and Interpretations of the Quran.* London: Tauris Academic Studies, 2009. An examination of the ways in which the Quran was used to justify Iran's 1979 Islamic revolution and how this aids in understanding present-day radical Islamism.

Lewis, Bernard. *The Crisis of Islam: Holy War and Unholy Terror.* New York: Random House, 2004. Written by one of the world's leading historians of the Middle East, this volume explores the long history of conflict and misunderstanding between the West and the Muslim world.

Lutz, Brenda J., and James M. Lutz. *Global Terrorism.* Sage library of international relations. Los Angeles: Sage Publications, 2008. An introduction to the history, politics, ideologies, and strategies of both contemporary and older terrorist groups.

Marranci, Gabriele. *Understanding Muslim Identity: Rethinking Fundamentalism.* Basingstoke, England: Palgrave Macmillan, 2009. A broad survey of the various current theories on the origins of Islamic fundamentalism.

Miniter, Richard. *Losing Bin Laden: How Bill Clinton's Failures Unleashed Global Terror.* Washington, D.C.: Regnery, 2004. The author argues that the policies of U.S. president Bill Clinton allowed Osama bin Laden to escalate his campaign against the West with little hindrance.

Naff, Clay Farris. *Conflict in the Middle East.* Compact research series. San Diego, Calif.: ReferencePoint Press, 2008. A book for younger readers that outlines the history of recent conflicts in the Middle East and the role played by the United States in the region.

Pape, Robert A. *Dying to Win: The Strategic Logic of Suicide Terrorism.* New York: Random House, 2005. A groundbreaking analysis of the phenomenon of suicide bombings based on the stories of hundreds of real suicide bombers.

Pargeter, Alison. *The New Frontiers of Jihad: Radical Islam in Europe.* Philadelphia: University of Pennsylvania Press, 2008. The author rejects the idea that a single monolithic movement exists that might be called European jihad and that the attacks in London and Madrid were linked to al-Qaeda.

Peters, Ralph. *Wars of Blood and Faith.* Mechanicsburg, Pa.: Stackpole Books, 2007. The author argues that the world is entering a period that will be dominated by violent conflicts arising from ethnic and religious differences.

Phillips, David L. *From Bullets to Ballots: Violent Muslim Movements in Transition.* New Brunswick, N.J.: Transaction, 2009. The author considers several violent Muslim groups across the world and the degree to which they have tried and succeeded, or tried and failed, to make the transition to mainstream politics.

Phillips, Melanie. *Londonistan.* New York: Encounter Books (USA), 2006. The author argues that the July 2005 suicide bombings in London followed a period in which radical Islamists had been allowed to establish themselves in the city by a combination of social factors.

Ramakrishna, Kumar. *Radical Pathways: Understanding Muslim Radicalization in Indonesia.* Westport, Conn.: Praeger Security International, 2009. The author explores the ideological background of the Indonesian radical Islamist organization Jemmah Islamiyah that planned and carried out the Bali bombings of 2002 and other terrorist attacks in Indonesia.

Rashid, Ahmed. *Descent into Chaos: The World's Most Unstable Region and the Threat to Global Security.* London: Penguin, 2009. An examination of the growing phenomenon of radical Islamist violence in Central Asia.

Rubin, Barry M. *Guide to Islamist Movements.* Armonk, N.Y.: M. E. Sharpe, 2010. A comprehensive guide to political Islamism.

Shultz, Richard H., Jr., and Andrea J. Dew. *Insurgents, Terrorists, and Militias: The Warriors of Contemporary Combat.* New York: Columbia University Press, 2006. A comprehensive assessment of unconventional wars and the people who fight them.

Springer, Devin R., James L. Regens, and David N. Edger. *Islamic Radicalism and Global Jihad.* Washington, D.C.: Georgetown University Press, 2009. A survey of Islamic radicalism and its relationship to terrorism and the West.

Warraq, Ibn, ed. *Leaving Islam: Apostates Speak Out.* Amherst, N.Y.: Prometheus Books, 2003. In this follow-up to Warraq's earlier book *Why I Am Not a Muslim,* dozens of former Muslims explain why they left the religion of their birth.

———. *Why I Am Not a Muslim.* Amherst, N.Y.: Prometheus Books, 2003. A controversial volume first published in 1995 that outlines the author's personal views of the failings of Islam.

Weigel, George. *Faith, Reason and the War against Jihadism.* New York: Doubleday Random House, 2007. The author argues that the war against radical Islamism is a war of ideas rather than one arising from poverty or other social factors in the Muslim world.

Yemelianova, Galina M. *Radical Islam in the Former Soviet Union.* New York: Routledge, 2010. A comprehensive examination of Islamic radicalization in the Muslim regions of the former Soviet Union since the end of communism.

Articles and Web Documents

Abdulla, Rasha A. "Islam, Jihad, and Terrorism in Post-9/11 Arabic Discussion Boards." *Journal of Computer-Mediated Communication* 12, no. 3, 2007. A study of messages posted to three of the largest Arabic-language online message boards regarding the attacks of September 11, 2001.

Cammack, Mark. "Laskar Jihad: Islam, Militancy and the Quest for Identity in Post-New Order Indonesia." *Islamic Law and Society* 15, no. 3, 2008. An overview of the role of the terrorist group Laskar Jihad in the period since the fall of President Suharto.

Crooke, Alastair. "The Essence of Islamist Resistance: A Different View of Iran, Hezbollah and Hamas." *New Perspectives Quarterly* 26, no. 3, 2009. An examination of the anti-Western tradition in Iranian politics.

Euben, Roxanne L. "Killing (for) Politics: Jihad, Martyrdom, and Political Action." *Political Theory* 30, no. 1, 2002. An investigation into the role of jihad and suicide bombings in Muslim politics.

Fattah, Khaled, and K. M. Fierke. "A Clash of Emotions: The Politics of Humiliation and Political Violence in the Middle East." *European Journal of International Relations* 15, no. 1, 2009. The role of emotion as a spur to political violence.

Hasan, Noorhaidi, and Robert W. Hefner. "Southeast Asia—Laskar Jihad: Islam, Militancy, and the Quest for Identity in Post-New Order Indonesia." *Pacific Affairs* 80, no. 1, 2007. An investigation into the activities of the terrorist group Laskar Jihad across Southeast Asia.

Khaled Abou El Fadl. "Islam and the Theology of Power." Available online. URL: http://www.merip.org/mer/mer221/221_abu_el_fadl.html. Accessed December

17, 2009. The author asks is Islam is really facing a crises of identity as many commentators have reported.

Nasr, Seyyed Hossein. "Islam and the Question of Violence." Available online. URL: http://www.al-islam.org/al-serat/IslamAndViolence.htm. Accessed December 17, 2009. The author addresses the question of the use of violence by Muslims.

Ufen, Andreas. "Mobilising Political Islam: Indonesia and Malaysia Compared." *Commonwealth & Comparative Politics* 47, no. 3, 2009. A comparison between the rise of political Islam in Malaysia and Indonesia.

Yates, Joshua J. "The Resurgence of Jihad & the Specter of Religious Populism." *SAIS Review* 27, no. 1, 2007. The author examines the effects of globalism on popular religion and particularly the spread of Islamist ideas.

Zakaria, F. "In the Muslim World, the Extremists Are Getting Desperate." *Newsweek–American Edition*, 2004. A report on the perception of extremists in the Muslim world.

Television/Film/Video

Brokaw, Tom. *The Roots of Rage Inside Islam.* 45 min. Mount Kisco, N.Y.: Human Relations Media, 2004. DVD. One of America's leading television journalists investigates the origins of Muslim terrorism.

Bronson, Rachel, Steven Emerson, Gilles Kepel, and Dennis Ross. *Terrorism and the Muslim World.* 108 min. Washington, D.C.: National Cable Satellite Corp, 2004. DVD. Footage of a congressional hearing on Islam, jihad, terrorism, and the effect of U.S. policies in the Middle East held on July 9, 2003, before the National Commission on Terrorist Attacks upon the United States.

Eedle, Paul, and Huda Ali. *Jihad TV.* Produced and directed by Paul Eedle. 46 min. Princeton, N.J.: Films for the Humanities & Sciences, 2007. DVD. An investigative report into the use of the Internet and broadcast media by Islamist extremists and their effect on young Muslims.

Scheuer, Michael, Robert Anthony Pape, Alberto M. Fernandez, Zaki Chehab, and Syed Farooq Hasnat. *Understanding the Global Insurgency.* 87 min. New York: National Cable Satellite Corporation, 2006. DVD. A panel discussion about Islamic terrorism and how it can be defeated.

Streeter, Sabin. *The Road to 9/11.* Written and produced by Sabin Streeter. 60 min. Washington, D.C.: Distributed by PBS Home Video, 2006. DVD. A detailed look at the circumstances surrounding the September 11, 2001, attacks on the United States, featuring interviews with leading scholars and journalists, including Bernard Lewis, Fareed Zakaria, Thomas Friedman, Ishad Manji, Azar Nafisi, Kanan Makiya, Fawaz Gerges, and David Fromkin.

Walsh, Mark, and Detlef Siebert. *Between the Devil and the Deep Blue Sea: Salman Rushdie.* Produced and directed by Mark Walsh and Detlef Siebert. 45 min. New York: Filmakers Library, 2009. DVD. A documentary about reactions in the Muslim world to the publication of Salman Rushdie's book *Satanic Verses* and the subsequent death sentence on the author issued by Iran's Ayotollah Khomeini.

Chronology

570 C.E.

- Birth of Muhammad, the founder of Islam, in the Arabian Peninsula city of Mecca, in present-day Saudi Arabia. He is born into the Banu Hashim tribe, a prominent family in the city.

610

- According to Muslim tradition Muhammad receives the first of a series of revelations that will make up the text of the Quran. Members of Muhammad's immediate family become Muslims, and Muhammad begins preaching in Mecca soon after.

CA. 613–32

- Islam is accepted gradually by the majority of the tribes of the Arabian Peninsula through a series of wars and diplomatic missions. The Arabian Peninsula remains under the nominal overall authority of the Persian Sassanid Empire.

622

- By this date Muhammad and the majority of his followers have migrated to the city of Medina—an event known as the Hijra.

632

- Death of Muhammad. A century of rapid military expansion beyond the Arabian Peninsula by Muslim peoples begins.
- Abu Bakr becomes the administrative and military leader of the majority of the Muslim community, creating the office of the Muslim caliph and beginning the period known as the Rashidun Caliphate. His succession causes a split in the Muslim community that later become the Sunni and Shia branches of the faith. Sunni Muslims regard Abu Bakr as the first of the Rightly Guided Caliphs, Shia Muslims regard him as a usurper.

Chronology

632–61

- The period of the rule of the Rashidun Caliphate over the Muslim world. Four caliphs, known to Sunni Muslims as the Rightly Guided caliphs, rule the Rashidun Caliphate: Abu Bakr (r. 632–34), Umar (r. 634–44), Uthman (r. 644–56), and Ali (r. 656–61). During this period Arab-Muslim forces conquer the entire Persian Sassanid Empire, much of North Africa, the Middle East, the Caucasus, part of Anatolia, territories deep into Central Asia, and the islands of Cyprus, Rhodes, and Sicily.

644–56

- During the rule of the caliph Usman Muslim traders begin to make contact with communities living on the islands that will later make up the state of Indonesia. It is possible that some Muslims settle in the area, creating small Muslim enclaves.

656–61

- The First Islamic Civil War, also known as the First Fitna. During the rule of Ali, the fourth and final caliph of the Rashidun Caliphate, a series of revolts splits the Muslim community and solidifies the division of Islam into Sunni and Shia branches. The war begins following the assassination of the third caliph, Usman, and ends with the assassination of the fourth caliph, Ali.

661–750

- The period of the rule of the Umayyad Caliphate over the Muslim world. The Umayyad Caliphate begins with the rule of Muawiyah I (r. 661–80) during which time its capital is established in Damascus in present-day Syria. During this period the caliphate continues to expand geographically west into North Africa, across the Mediterranean Sea into the Iberian Peninsula, and east to the borders of present-day India. After being overthrown in 750, a branch of the Umayyad Dynasty continues to rule parts of Spain and Portugal until the end of the 15th century.

750–1258

- The period of the rule of the Abbasid Caliphate over parts of the Muslim world. Originally based in the city of Harran in present-day Turkey the capital of the caliphate was later moved to Baghdad in present-day Iraq. From 909 a major division of the Muslim world occurred as the Fatimid Dynasty established a new caliphate in North Africa.

EIGHTH TO 13TH CENTURIES

- The Islamic Golden Age (also known as the Islamic Renaissance). During this period the Islamic world is a leading center of technological and cultural achievement in the world. Advances made during this golden age influence all subsequent cultures and civilizations.

909–1171

- The period of the rule of the Fatimid Caliphate over parts of the Muslim world. The Fatimids build their capital in Cairo, Egypt, and rule over a territory that includes the whole of North Africa, Lebanon, parts of the Arabian Peninsula, and the island of Sicily at its greatest extent.

1136

- Founding of the Muslim Kedah Sultanate on the Malay Peninsula (part of present-day Malaysia). The earliest known Muslim state in Southeast Asia, the Kedah Sultanate resulted from the conversion of the king of the already established Kedah Kingdom to Islam.

1145–1269

- The Almohad dynasty rules much of North Africa.

1171–1341

- The period of the rule of the Ayyubid dynasty over parts of the Muslim world in the Middle East. Centered in Damascus and Cairo, the dynasty was founded by the great Muslim warrior known as Saladin.

1293–1923

- Period of the Ottoman Empire. Founded by Osman I (1258–1324) the Ottoman Empire grows from its center in Anatolia to encompass the entire Middle East, North Africa, and much of southeastern Europe by the end of the 17th century. After a long period of slow decline the Ottoman Empire is dissolved following its defeat in World War I.

1409

- Founding of the Muslim Sultanate of Malacca on the Malay Peninsula (part of present-day Malaysia) and the neighboring island of Sumatra (part of present-day Indonesia).

CA. 1450

- Founding of the Muslim Sultanate of Sulu on the islands of the Sulu Sea (part of present-day Philippines).

CA. 1475

- Founding of the Muslim Sultanate of Demak on the north coast of the island of Java (part of present-day Indonesia).

Chronology

CA. 1496

- Founding of the Muslim Sultanate of Aceh in the north of the island of Sumatra (part of present-day Indonesia).

1511–1641

- The Portuguese conquer and occupy the territory of the Sultanate of Malacca.

1516

- The area of present-day Algeria comes under the control of the Ottoman Empire. Algeria is to remain an Ottoman possession for almost 300 years.

CA. 1526

- Founding of the Muslim Sultanate of Banten in the northwest of the island of Java (part of present-day Indonesia).

1528

- Founding of the Muslim Sultanate of Johor on the Malay Peninsula (part of present-day Malaysia) and the neighboring island of Sumatra (part of present-day Indonesia) following the Portuguese conquest of the Sultanate of Malacca.

1603–1800

- The Dutch East India Company runs trade posts throughout the territory of present-day Indonesia. The Dutch compete fiercely for influence over the islands with the British East India Company.

1702

- East Timor, covering approximately the eastern half of the island of Timor, is declared a Portuguese colony after almost 150 years of steadily increasing Portuguese settlement and influence.

1744–1818

- The First Saudi State, created by Prince Muhammad ibn Saud, takes control of much of the Arabian Peninsula, including the holy Muslim cities of Mecca and Medina. The state is invaded and dissolved by the Ottomans who restore their authority over the area.

1800–1942

- Period of direct Dutch rule over the Dutch East Indies, which consisted of much of the territory of present-day Indonesia. The Dutch East Indies are established as a Dutch colony under direct Dutch government rule with the nationalization of possessions of the Dutch East India Company in 1800. Effective Dutch rule over the territory ends with the Japanese invasion of 1942, during World War II, but Indonesian independence is not recognized by the Dutch government until 1949.

1821–29

- Greek war of independence against the Ottoman Empire. After many years of bitter conflict and the destruction of a large Ottoman fleet by combined Western naval forces at the Battle of Navarino (1827), Ottoman forces are driven out, and Greece achieves full independence from Ottoman rule in 1832.

1824–91

- The Second Saudi State grows to prominence on the Arabian Peninsula. It is defeated and destroyed by the House of Al Rashid, a rival Arab Muslim clan.

1830–48

- France captures the city of Algiers and gradually establishes colonial control over the whole of present-day Algeria.

1839–42

- First Anglo-Afghan War. A British invasion of Afghanistan intended to secure the northern borders of British-ruled India from Russian influence is defeated.

1878–80

- Second Anglo-Afghan War. A second British invasion of Afghanistan results in much of the country becoming a British protectorate.

1892

- The Trucial States, a series of small independent sheikdoms along the Arabian Peninsula coast of the Persian Gulf that will later form the United Arab Emirates, become protectorates of the British Empire.

1902

- The Third Saudi State is founded by Abd al-Aziz al-Saud after recapturing the Al Saud's ancestral capital city Riyadh from the Al Rashid.

1907

- In Iran a new constitution limits the power of the monarchy for the first time.

Chronology

1914–18

- World War I has a major impact on the Muslim world. The Ottoman Empire, the leading power in the Muslim Middle East, allies itself with the Central Powers at the beginning of the war and is defeated by the alliance led by the Allied powers: Britain and France. Ottoman territories in the Middle East outside of Anatolia are subsequently partitioned under British and French mandates, radically altering the political map of the region and laying the foundations for the emergence of the modern states of Syria, Jordan, Lebanon, Iraq, and Israel. In Persia invading British, Russian, and, later, Armenian forces are also victorious, greatly increasing Western influence in what will become the modern state of Iran. In the Arabian Peninsula and elsewhere in the Middle East irregular Arab forces stage an uprising against Ottoman rule.

1919–23

- Turkish war of independence. The remainder of the defeated Ottoman Empire in Anatolia is invaded by Greece, Armenia, and France. A Turkish nationalist movement led by Mustafa Kemal Atatürk drives these forces back and establishes the modern Republic of Turkey in 1923.

1919

- Third Anglo-Afghan War. Britain wins a military victory, but Afghanistan ceases to be a British protectorate and becomes a fully independent state.

1920

- The territory of present-day Iraq is placed under a British mandate by the League of Nations.

1925

- Abd al-Aziz al-Saud captures the holy Muslim cities of Mecca and Medina for the Third Saudi State.
- In Iran parliament elects Reza Shah (also known as Reza Pahlavi) to the throne.

1932

- The Third Saudi State becomes the modern Kingdom of Saudi Arabia with Abd al-Aziz al-Saud as monarch.
- Iraq becomes an independent state ruled by Faisal I, but Britain retains military bases in the country.

THE MUSLIM WORLD

1933–73

- Reign of Mohammed Zahir Shah, the last king of Afghanistan. He is deposed in a coup led by Mohammed Daoud Khan that makes Afghanistan a republic.

1939–45

- World War II. Major campaigns are fought in parts of the Muslim world between the Allied and Axis powers. In North Africa British, Free French, and U.S. forces prevent Italian and German armies from seizing Egypt and the Suez Canal. In Iraq British forces seize control of the country from a pro-Axis government and restore a pro-British government under King Faisal II. Syria and Lebanon, under the control of the Vichy French government since the Axis occupation of France is successfully invaded by British and Free French forces. In Southeast Asia the Japanese invade and conquer the Dutch East Indies, holding the territory until their surrender in 1945 when Indonesia is established as an independent state.

1941

- During World War II British and Russian forces invade Iran and depose the monarch, Reza Shah. Reza Shah's son, Muhammad Reza Pahlavi, is installed on the throne by the British.

1945

- Indonesia declares independence from the Dutch following the withdrawal of Japanese forces at the end of World War II. Sukarno is appointed as the country's first president. Guerrilla warfare with Dutch forces continues until the Netherlands recognizes Indonesian independence in 1949.

1948

- Israel declares its independence, sparking an immediate war with neighboring Arab-Muslim nations who are fundamentally opposed to the creation of an Israeli state in territory they regard as the rightful home of Palestinian Arabs. Forces from Egypt, Lebanon, Syria, Jordan, and Iraq fail to defeat Israel in the First Arab-Israeli War (1948–49).

1953

- In Iran British and U.S. intelligence services orchestrate a coup that overthrows the democratically elected government of Prime Minister Mohammed Mosaddeq and restores the authority of the shah, essentially creating a dictatorship friendly to the Western powers and opposed to the Soviet Union.

Chronology

1954–62

- Algerian war of independence against France. The Algerian National Liberation Front (FLN) leads a long and bitter conflict against French rule that ends with Algerian independence but at the cost of widespread devastation in the country and more than a million dead. Hundreds of thousands of French settlers flee Algeria, further damaging the country's economy. The FLN becomes the governing party and is to remain in sole power for the next 40 years.

1956–57

- Suez Crises. President Gamal Abdel Nasser of Egypt nationalizes the Suez Canal, taking it out of the control of the Anglo-French company that had owned it. Britain and France conclude a secret deal with Israel in which Israel agrees to invade Egypt, giving Britain and France an excuse to intervene militarily and retake control of the canal zone. Although militarily successful the plan fails when the United States puts political pressure on all three countries to withdraw. The Suez Crisis marks the ascendancy of the United States over the nations of western Europe as the leading foreign power in the Middle East. The part of the crisis that involved conflict between Israel and Egypt is sometimes referred to as the Second Arab-Israeli War.

1958–61

- Syria and Egypt unite to form the United Arab Republic (UAR) in what is hoped to be the first step in the creation of a pan-Arab state encompassing all the Arab nations of the Middle East. The UAR is dissolved when Syria withdraws following a coup in Damascus. Egypt continues to be known officially as the United Arab Republic until 1971.
- Egypt, Syria, and Yemen form the United Arab State (UAS). For most of this period Egypt and Syria are also officially conjoined as the United Arab Republic (UAR) but Yemen retains a greater degree of independence as a member of the UAS. The union is dissolved in 1961 following the collapse of the UAR.

1958

- Iraq and Jordan form the Arab Federation, a short-lived attempt to unite the two countries in response to the formation of the United Arab Republic and the United Arab State by Egypt, Syria, and Yemen. The federation is dissolved after only six months when King Faisal II of Iraq is deposed in a military coup.
- Iraq becomes a republic with Abdel-Karim Qassim as its first president.

1960

- The Organization of Petroleum Exporting Countries (OPEC) is founded in Baghdad, Iraq, by Iran, Iraq, Kuwait, Saudi Arabia, and Venezuela as a means of increasing revenues from the sale of oil by coordinating pricing and production among its members. Qatar, Indonesia, Libya, the United Arab Emirates, Algeria, and Nigeria also joined OPEC by 1971.

1963

- In Iraq members of the Baath Party stage a coup that removes Abdel-Karim Qasim from power. Abd-al-Salam becomes prime minister.

1964

- Palestine Liberation Organization (PLO) founded in the West Bank by Palestinian Arabs with the aim of liberating Palestine from what it referred to as Israeli occupation through armed struggle. PLO fighters begin attacking Israel from bases in Jordan, Lebanon, and Syria, as well as from within the Gaza Strip and West Bank.

1966

- In Indonesia a period of political upheaval leads to President Sukarno handing emergency powers to Suharto, who becomes president the following year.

1967

- Third Arab-Israeli War (also known as the Six-Day War). Israel launches air attacks against Egypt claiming that Egypt is planning to invade. In just six days Israel defeats the militaries of Egypt, Jordan, and Syria and conquers the Sinai Peninsula, the Gaza Strip, the West Bank, East Jerusalem, and the Golan Heights. Israel's occupation of its conquests in this war are to become one of the leading sources of tension between Israel and the Arab world for the rest of the century and beyond.

1968

- In Iraq a second Baathist coup installs Ahmad Hasan al-Bakr as president.
- Britain announces its intention to withdraw from its protection agreements with Bahrain, Qatar, and the seven Trucial States. These territories begin negotiations to form a union of Arab Emirates.

1971

- Bahrain and Qatar withdraw from the proposed union of Arab Emirates to be formed with the formal Trucial States leaving the emirates of Abu Dhabi, Dubai, Sharjah, Ajman, Umm al-Qaiwain, and Fujairah to form the United

Arab Emirates (UAE). The emirate of Ras al-Khaimah joins the UAE the following year.

1973

- Fourth Arab-Israeli War (also known as the Yom Kippur War). Israel is just able to halt an attack by Syrian and Egyptian forces into the Sinai Peninsula and the Golan Heights (captured from Egypt and Syria, respectively, in the 1967 Arab-Israeli War) and then launches counterattacks that strike deep into Syria and Egypt before the threat of Soviet military intervention forces a ceasefire. The near total defeat of Egypt and Syria leads to a change of foreign policy in both countries toward achieving a lasting peace with Israel.

1975

- East Timor declares independence from Portugal. A few days later the territory is invaded and annexed by neighboring Indonesia although the United Nations refuses to recognize Indonesia's claim.

1978

- The Camp David accords are signed by Israel and Egypt. After negotiations sponsored by U.S. president Jimmy Carter, Israel and Egypt reach an agreement that leads directly to the 1979 Israel-Egypt Peace Treaty in which Israel agrees to withdraw from the Sinai Peninsula in return for a lasting peace.
- In Afghanistan Mohammed Daoud is overthrown in a coup that brings the leftist People's Democratic Party to power. Conservative elements in the countryside begin a series of revolts against the central government.

1979

- Islamic revolution in Iran. Following months of political unrest the shah flees into exile and senior religious leader Ayatollah Ruhollah Khomeini returns to Iran from exile and seizes power. The country is declared an Islamic Republic with Khomeini as Supreme Leader.
- Soviet invasion of Afghanistan. The socialist government of Afghanistan invites Soviet forces to provide protection against increasingly violent rebellions by mujahideen rebels.
- In Iran President Al-Bakr resigns and is succeeded by his vice president, Saddam Hussein.

1979–81

- Iran hostage crisis. During the chaos of Iran's Islamic revolution a group of Islamist radicals occupy the U.S. embassy in Tehran and hold 53 U.S. citizens captive for 444 days. A failed attempt to rescue the hostages by U.S. forces severely damages the administration of President Jimmy Carter. Relations between Iran and the United States reach a new low.

1979–89

- Soviet war in Afghanistan. Soviet forces become involved in a long conflict with mujahideen rebels for control of the country. The mujahideen control much of the rugged and mountainous countryside and are aided by money and weapons provided by the United States, Saudi Arabia, and Pakistan. The war ends with the withdrawal of Soviet forces, but civil war between rival mujahideen factions and the central government continues.

1980–88

- Iran-Iraq War. Iraqi president Saddam Hussein launches an invasion of Iran that leads to a devastating conflict between the two states in which hundreds of thousands are killed on both sides. The United States provides material and intelligence aid to Iraq despite concerns about the Iraqi military's use of chemical and biological weapons.

1988

- Islamist terrorist group al-Qaeda founded by Osama bin Laden, probably in Pakistan.

1989

- In Algeria constitutional reforms carried out by the governing National Liberation Front legalize opposition parties for the first time and promise open and free elections. The Islamic Salvation Party (FIS), one of the newly legal opposition parties, begins to build mass support.

1990–91

- Persian Gulf War. Iraq invades and occupies the neighboring state of Kuwait. The United States leads a coalition made up of Saudi Arabia, the United Kingdom, Egypt, and dozens of other nations in a military campaign that liberates Kuwait and drives into Iraq. Saudi Arabia's decision to allow U.S. and other non-Muslim forces to deploy in its territory is controversial among Saudi Arabians and in the wider Muslim world. The U.S. decision to stop short of a full invasion of Iraq in order to unseat President Saddam Hussein is also criticized.

1992

- In Algeria the Islamic Salvation Party (FIS) is on the verge of winning the country's first national elections and forming a government when the army carries out a coup, suspends the constitution, and bans the FIS.

- In Afghanistan mujahideen elements capture the capital, Kabul, and depose President Mohammad Najibullah, who had been installed by the Soviets in 1986.

1992–2005

- Algerian civil war. Rebels loyal to the banned Islamic Salvation Party (FIS) form the Islamic Salvation Army (AIS) and battle government forces in an attempt to depose the secular political elite and return to democracy. More radical Muslim elements form the Armed Islamic Group (GIA) and fight both the government and the AIS to establish a nondemocratic Islamic republic. Hundreds of thousands of Algerians are killed in fighting that ends with a cease-fire declaration by the AIS in 1997 and the destruction of the GIA by the end of 2005. The Algerian army and the long-established political elite of the country remain firmly in power.

1993

- Signing of the Oslo accords between Israel and the Palestine Liberation Organization. Israel agrees to grant Palestinians self-government in the Gaza Strip and parts of the West Bank through the creation of the Palestinian National Authority.
- Palestine Liberation Organization (PLO) chairman Yasser Arafat recognizes the state of Israel as part of ongoing negotiations to achieve a Palestinian-Israeli peace settlement. Israel recognizes the PLO as the representative of the Palestinian people.

1994

- In Afghanistan the Pashtun-dominated Taliban organization begins a military campaign to wrest control from the coalition government formed by mujahideen elements.
- Palestinian Liberation Organization (PLO) chairman Yasser Arafat, Israeli prime minister Yitzhak Rabin, and Israeli foreign minister Shimon Peres are awarded the Nobel Peace Prize for their roles in the negotiations that led to the 1993 Oslo Accords. Yitzhak Rabin is assassinated the following year by a right-wing Israeli radical opposed to the Oslo Accords.

1996

- In Afghanistan the Taliban captures Kabul and establishes a highly conservative Islamist regime. Forces opposed to the Taliban form a loose federation known as the Northern Alliance.
- In Qatar the Arab Al Jazeera satellite television news station is launched following the abolition of censorship laws.

1997–2005

- In Iran Mohammad Khatami serves two terms as president advocating freedom of expression, civil society, better international relations, and other policies that contrast with the regimes of Khomeini and former president Akbar Hashemi Rafsanjani.

1997

- In Egypt 59 foreign tourists are murdered by Islamist terrorists. The Egyptian government bans Islamist groups.

1998

- Al-Qaeda operatives bomb the U.S. embassies in Nairobi, Kenya, and Dar es Salaam, Tanzania, killing more than 200 people and injuring more than 5,000.
- The United States launches missile attacks against suspected al-Qaeda bases in Afghanistan in retaliation for the embassy bombings in Africa.
- In Indonesia Suharto's regime is toppled by widespread public unrest. B J Habibie becomes president, promising national elections.

1999

- Indonesia ends its 24-year occupation of East Timor, and the territory is placed under the control of a United Nations interim administration pending a referendum on autonomy.
- Violence breaks out between Muslim and Christian communities on the Indonesian Moluccan Islands.
- In the Indonesian province of Aceh militant Islamist rebels try to win independence from the central government.

2000

- The U.S. naval vessel USS *Cole* is damaged in a suicide attack carried out by al-Qaeda operatives while it is docked in Aden, Yemen. The British embassy in Aden is also bombed.
- In Indonesia a radical Muslim militia calling itself Laskar Jihad becomes involved in the ongoing violence between Christians and Muslims on the Moluccan Islands.

2001

- *September:* Nineteen terrorists associated with the Islamist extremist group al-Qaeda hijack four commercial airliners deliberately flying two of them into the towers of the World Trade Center in New York City and a third into the Pentagon in Washington, D.C. The fourth airliner crashes in rural Pennsylvania. The attacks kills 2,973 people as well as the 19 hijackers. The U.S. government quickly identifies al-Qaeda leader Osama bin Laden as responsible for the attacks and calls on the Taliban regime in Afghanistan to surrender bin Laden and close all al-Qaeda bases.

- *October:* Invasion of Afghanistan by the United States. U.S. special forces form an alliance with an umbrella organization of Afghan militias known as the Northern Alliance and overthrow the Taliban regime.

2001–10

- War in Afghanistan. Following the U.S.-led invasion of the country that brings about the swift overthrow of the Taliban regime U.S. and other coalition forces become involved in a protracted conflict with surviving and resurgent Taliban guerrillas who are attempting to overthrow the coalition-backed government.

2002

- On the Indonesian island of Bali Islamist terrorists believed to belong to Jemaah Islamiyah carry out bomb attacks that kill 202 people and injure 240 others. Many of the victims are Western tourists.
- East Timor becomes independent in keeping with the results of the 1999 autonomy referendum.
- Iran begins construction of its first nuclear reactor leading to objections from the United States and other nations over fears that Iran is intending to acquire the technology and material to construct nuclear weapons.

2003

- Invasion of Iraq. U.S., British, and allied forces invade Iraq, depose Saddam Hussein, and dismantle the ruling Baath Party. An interim U.S. administration is established with the aim of establishing a new democratic constitution in the country.
- In Saudi Arabia suicide bombers kill 35 people in attacks on compounds for Western residents. Seventeen others are also killed in a series of terrorist attacks the same year.

2003–10

- War in Iraq. Following the rapid invasion and occupation of Iraq the U.S.-led coalition becomes involved in a long-running conflict with several different guerrilla forces opposed to the occupation.

2004

- In Iraq the U.S. administration devolves power to an interim Iraqi government pending national elections.

- Palestine Liberation Organization (PLO) chairman Yasser Arafat dies. He is succeeded by Mahmoud Abbas.
- In Madrid, Spain, terrorists believed to be associated with al-Qaeda bomb four commuter trains killing 191 people and wounding 1,800.
- In Afghanistan Hamid Karzai is elected to the presidency.
- In Pakistan government troops launch an assault on Taliban and al-Qaeda elements in the Federally Administered Tribal Areas of the Waziristan region. The campaign leads to a long-running conflict between the Taliban and the Pakistani government that escalates over the next six years.
- In Indonesia more than 220,000 people are killed after a powerful earthquake off the island of Sumatra produces devastating tsunami waves.

2005

- An autonomous Kurdish region is declared in northern Iraq with Massoud Barzani as its first elected president.
- The Transnational Iraqi Assembly is elected in Iraq's first democratic elections in 50 years.
- Conservative former mayor of Tehran, Mahmoud Ahmadinejad, is elected president of Iran. Many potential opponents are barred from standing by religious authorities. Ahmadinejad's policies mark a retreat from the reforming ambitions of his predecessor Mohammad Khatami.
- The International Atomic Energy Agency (IAEA) accuses Iran of contravening the Nuclear Non-Proliferation Treaty by restarting its uranium-enrichment program. The Iranian government insists the program is for peaceful nuclear energy production purposes.
- In Indonesia the Aceh insurgency ends with the government conceding limited self-governance to the province.

2006

- In the territory of the Palestinian Authority elections bring the Islamist party Hamas to power for the first time. Western donors who regard Hamas as a terrorist organization cut off aid to the Palestinian Authority.
- In Iraq leading Kurdish politician Jalal Talibani is elected president.
- Former president of Iraq Saddam Hussein is found guilty of crimes against humanity by an Iraqi court and executed.
- The first limited democratic elections take place in the United Arab Emirates.

2007

- In Iraq the Kurdish regional government assumes responsibility for security in the autonomous northern Kurdish region.

- The International Atomic Energy Agency claims that Iran will be capable of producing nuclear weapons within three years. The United States imposes strong economic sanctions against Iran in response.
- In Algeria an Islamist group calling itself al-Qaeda in the Islamic Maghreb carries out a series of bomb attacks against civilian and military targets.

2008

- In Algeria 60 people are killed in attacks carried out by al-Qaeda in the Islamic Maghreb.
- Israel launches air and ground attacks against the Gaza Strip in response to rocket attacks on Israel carried out by Palestinian militants.
- In Pakistan a wave of terrorist attacks carried out by Taliban elements or sympathizers kills hundreds of civilians and security force personnel.

2009

- In Iran the country's 10th presidential elections since the Islamic Revolution of 1979 lead to widespread antigovernment demonstrations when opponents of victorious president Mahmoud Ahmadinejad accuse him of committing electoral fraud to retain office.
- In Dubai, a part of the United Arab Emirates, the global economic downturn causes a major financial crisis as its property development boom stalls and neighboring Abu Dhabi steps in with billions of dollars worth of support to help the emirate meet its debt payments.
- US president Barack Obama announces an increase in US troop numbers in Afghanistan to combat the growing Taliban insurgency and to help train Afghan security forces.
- In Pakistan hundreds are killed by attacks carried out by Taliban sympathizers as the government's war against the Taliban in the Federally Administered Tribal Areas continues.
- In Indonesia terrorist bomb attacks on hotels in Jakarta produce fears that Islamist violence may resurge.

2010

- Unusually heavy monsoon rains cause severe flooding in Pakistan, submerging more than one-fifth of the total land area of the country and severely affecting more than 20 million people (about an eight of the population).
- Burj Khalifa tower, the world's tallest building, opens in Dubai, United Arab Emirates.

Glossary

Allah The Muslim name for God.

Arabization The influence of Arab culture on a non-Arab population that eventually results in that population adopting the Arabic language and Arab customs.

ayatollah An honorific title given to prominent Shia clerics.

B.C.E. An abbreviation for "Before the Common Era," a term used to refer to the time period preceding the first year of the revised Gregorian calendar.

burka (burqa) A loose-fitting garment that covers the entire body and with a veiled opening for the eyes. Traditionally worn by women in some Muslim cultures.

caliph A historical title for the supreme ruler of an Islamic state. Caliph is an English transliteration of the Arabic term khalifa, meaning "successor." In early Islamic history the title of caliph was held by the political and spiritual successors of the prophet Muhammad as heads of the Arab-Muslim polity. Subsequently the title was claimed by or attributed to the leaders of several different Muslim sects.

C.E. An abbreviation for "Common Era," a term used to refer to the time period that began with the first year of the revised Gregorian calendar.

clan A group of people, usually several lineages, who claim descent from a common ancestor or ancestors.

Dar al-Islam An Arabic term used in Islamic scholarship to refer to all the nations where Muslims are able to practice their religion freely. The term means "house of Islam."

emir A title of high nobility used throughout the Arab world and historically in some Turkic states. The precise rank of the title has varied considerably across time periods and geography.

fatwa An opinion or pronouncement on a point of Islamic law made by an Islamic scholar. The term is often used in the West to refer to statements

358

made by Islamic radicals calling for war or executions, but this is a very rare form of a common practice.

hadith A general term for reports about the actions or words of the prophet Muhammad. Originally transmitted orally, hadiths were later evaluated by Muslim scholars and written down in collections. These collections continue to be important references in discussions of Islamic law or history to the present day.

hijab An Arabic term referring to the convention of modest dress for Muslims. The term is commonly used to refer to women's dress only. Precise definitions vary between cultures, but the conventions for women's dress usually require the complete covering of the body, except the face and hands.

Hijra An Arabic word meaning "migration" commonly used to refer to the emigration of the prophet Muhammad to the city of Medina in 622 C.E.

imam In Shia Islam the imams are historical figures believed to have been the rightful successors of the prophet Muhammad. In Sunni Islam imam is used more generally to refer to religious leaders and teachers.

insurgency An armed rebellion against the authority of a local or national government carried out primarily by nonprofessional soldiers.

intifada An Arabic word meaning "shaking off" that is often loosely translated as "rebellion" or "uprising." The term has been used to refer to several rebellions or protracted periods of civil disturbance by Arabic-speaking communities in North Africa and the Middle East in the 20th and 21st centuries, most famously the First Intifada (1987–93) and the Second, or al-Aqsa, Intifada (beginning in 2000) of the Palestinians against Israeli rule.

iqta A form of tax farming that developed during the Abbasid Caliphate period (750–1258). Tax farming is the practice of assigning the responsibility for collecting state taxation for a particular area to a local governor, military official, or other important figure.

Islamism A loose term encompassing a diverse set of ideologies that may be characterized as holding that Islam should be a political as well as a religious framework. Islamists often believe in the enforcement of sharia law and oppose the influence of non-Muslim, particularly Western, influences on Muslim-majority countries.

itjihad A term in Islamic law that describes the process of making a legal decision based on interpretations of the laws in the Quran and in accepted Muslim traditions.

jihad An Arabic term meaning "to struggle" or "to strive." Historically the term has been used to describe the individual Muslim's duty to strive to improve the self and the society in which one lives. One part of the meaning of the term has always referred to a Muslim's duty to engage in warfare when required to do so under the terms of Islamic law. Precise definitions differ among Muslim denominations.

Kaaba   An approximately cube-shaped building in the city of Mecca, Saudi Arabia. It is more than 2 thousand years old and is regarded as the most sacred site in Islam. All Muslims face toward the Kaaba during prayers.

madrassa   An Arabic word meaning "school." A madrassa may be religious (Muslim or non-Muslim) or secular. Historically the role of madrassas was to teach the principles of Islam as well as many other subjects, and in the present day the great majority of madrassas continue this tradition.

Maghreb   The Arabic name for the region comprising Morocco, Algeria, and Tunisia.

Mahdi   In some interpretations of Islamic theology the Mahdi is a prophesized figure who will live on earth in the final years before the day of resurrection bringing truth, peace, and justice. Several Muslim leaders have claimed to be the incarnation of the Mahdi from the seventh to the 20th centuries but none has received wide recognition.

marabout   An Islamic religious leader or teacher in West Africa or, historically, in North Africa. In the Berber language marabout means "saint."

Middle East   A geopolitical term encompassing an area of southwestern Asia and North Africa but without clearly defined borders. Most of the nations of the Middle East are Muslim-majority Arab nations, but the term also usually includes Iran and Israel.

militant   A general term for an individual engaged in armed conflict who does not belong to the military or law enforcement agencies of a sovereign government.

militia   An armed force made up of nonprofessional soldiers not usually funded or supported by a sovereign government.

monotheism   The belief in a single, all-powerful god.

monotheistic   The practice of believing in only one god.

mosque   A Muslim place of worship.

mujahideen   Plural of the Arabic word mujahid, meaning "one who fights for justice." It is related to the Arabic word jihad and is sometimes used to describe Muslims militants.

nomad   Used to describe a particular lifestyle followed by many desert-dwelling peoples. Nomads are "wanderers" (the word derives from *nomas*, Latin for "wandering shepherd"), but they usually travel well-used paths, and their movements are dictated by the demands of trade or the needs of their herds for pasture and water.

oasis   A fertile pocket in an arid region where water from an underground source reaches the surface.

Glossary

pan-Arabism A political ideology that aims to unite all Arab peoples in a single nation. Pan-Arabist ambitions are usually secular and socialist.

polity A general term that refers to a group with some form of cohesive political organization. It may refer to a loosely organized society, such as a tribe, but can also mean any politically organized group, including a state or an empire.

protectorate A state or territory that is controlled by a usually stronger nation. In particular it is used to refer to the colonies established by Europeans in Africa.

Quran The central religious text of Islam.

radical Islam A very general term often used to refer to Islamists who use or threaten violence to achieve their aims.

Ramadan The name of the ninth month of the Islamic calendar and the religious observances that Muslims undertake during this month. Muslims traditionally fast between dawn and sunset during Ramadan, say additional prayers, and are encouraged to read the Quran.

sayyid An honorific Arabic title afforded to males descended from the prophet Muhammad through his grandsons.

sharia The system of Islamic law, which governs all aspects of a Muslim's life. The Arabic term means "the path to the water hole."

Shia or Shii A member of the Shia denomination of Islam.

Shia or Shii Islam The second largest denomination of Islam.

Sufism A mystical tradition in Islam.

sultan An Islamic title that has been used historically for many different offices of state. The title was first used by Mahmud of Ghazni, the founder of the Turkic Ghaznavid dynasty (975–1187), which ruled much of present-day Iran and Iraq, to distinguish his worldly authority from the spiritual authority of the caliph. Rulers of the Seljuk and Ottoman Empires typically held the title sultan, and the title is still in use in the present day by the monarchs of certain Muslim states such as Oman and Brunei.

Sunni A member of the Sunni denomination of Islam.

Sunni Islam The largest denomination of Islam.

ummah An Arabic term for "community" or "nation." In the context of pan-Arabism it is used to refer collectively to all Arabic-speaking peoples or Arab nation-states. In the context of Islam it is used to refer collectively to all Muslims.

Index

Page numbers in **boldface** indicate major treatment of a subject. Page numbers followed by *c* indicate entries in the chronology. Page numbers followed by *f* indicate figures. Page numbers followed by *g* indicate glossary entries. Page numbers followed by *m* indicate maps.

Index

Index

Index

Index

Index

Index

Index

W

Wahhab, Muhammad ibn
  Abd al- 98
Wahhabism (Muwahhidism)
  18, 19, 98
Wahid, Abdurrahman 93,
  305*b*
war, in Quran 17
war on terror. *See*
  Afghanistan War; Iraq War
Waziristan, war in 121
weapons of mass destruction
  in Iran 58
  and Iraq 60, 64, 65–66
Webb, Mohammed
  Alexander Russell, *Islam in
  America* 129–133
Weinberger, Caspar 58, 305*b*
West Bank 287*m*, 350*c*, 353*c*
"What Do the Muslims
  Want?" (Muhammad,
  1965) 141–144
White Revolution 52

women
  in Algeria 103
  in Iran, under shah 52
  Muslim-American **39–40**
  under Taliban 119
  in UAE 114, 115
women's rights 39–40
Works Progress
  Administration (WPA),
  interview with Mike
  Abdallah (1939) 137–141
World Bank, modernization
  theory in 6
World Community of Al-
  Islam in the West 36
World Muslim Congress 318
World Trade Center bombing
  (1993) 43, 354*c*–355*c*
World War I 347*c*
World War II **69–70**, 348*c*

Y

Yasid I 21

Yathrib. *See* Medina
Yemen
  Arab nationalist
    revolution in 71
  Muslim immigrants
    from 33
  al-Qaeda attacks in 73,
    354*c*
  sharia in, women under
    39
  in United Arab State
    349*c*
Yom Kippur War 351*c*
Younsi, Djahid 107
Yudhoyono, Susilo Bambang
  92–93, 305*b*

Z

Zahir Shah, Mohammed
  348*c*
Zarqawi, Abu Musab al- 66,
  305*b*
Zeroual, Liamine 107

379